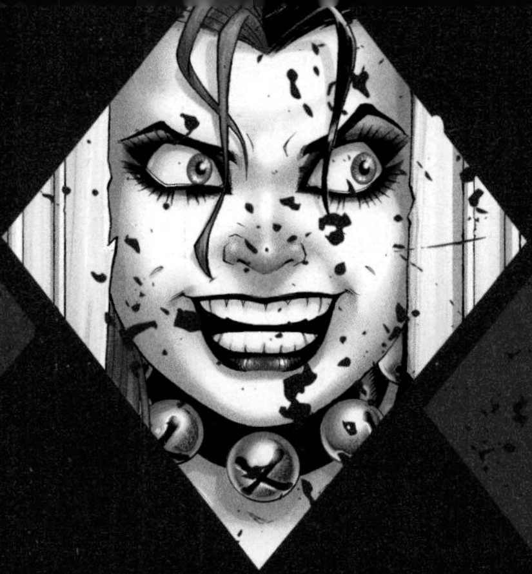

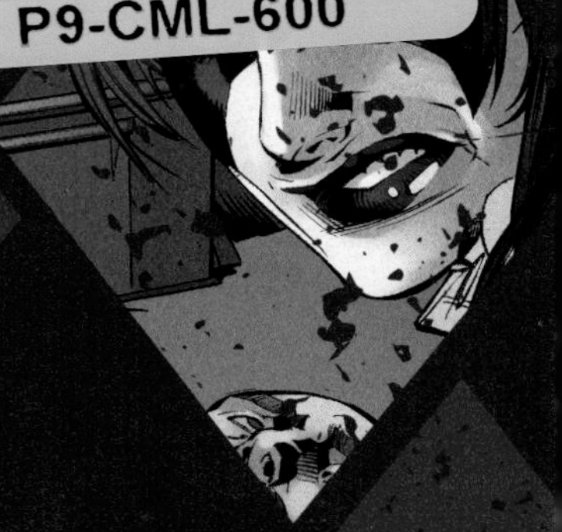

HARLEY QUINN'S GREATEST HITS

HARLEY QUINN
created by
PAUL DINI and **BRUCE TIMM**

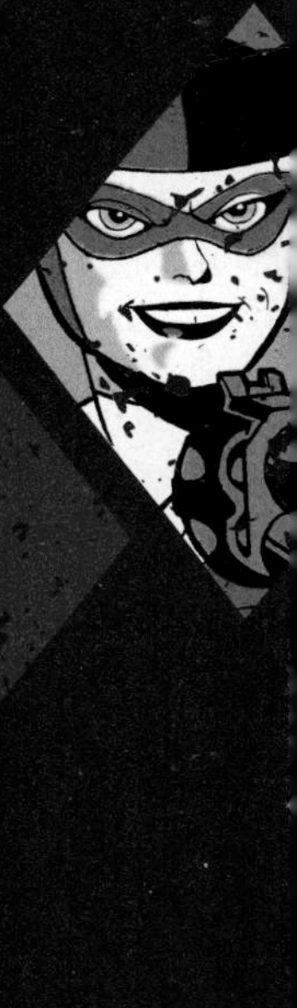

BATMAN
created by
BOB KANE with **BILL FINGER**

SUPERMAN
created by
JERRY SIEGEL and **JOE SHUSTER**
By special arrangement with the Jerry Siegel family

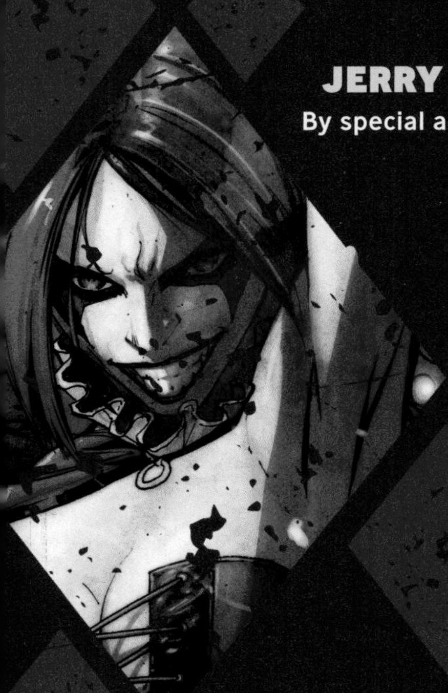

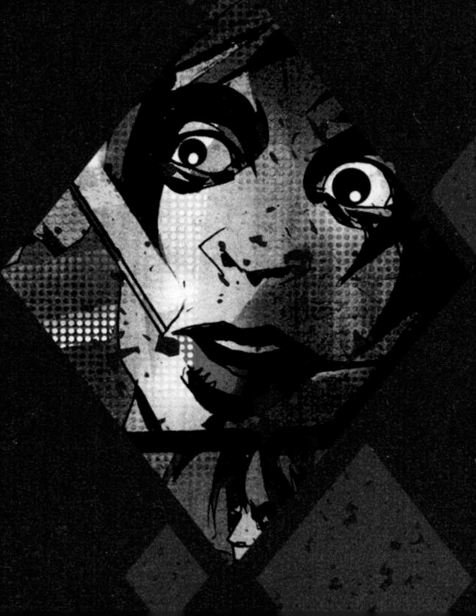

ELISABETH V. GEHRLEIN SCOTT PETERSON BOB SCHRECK
MIKE MARTS PAT MCCALLUM CHRIS CONROY ANDY KHOURI Editors – Original Series
HARVEY RICHARDS Associate Editor – Original Series
DARREN VINCENZO MORGAN DONTAVILLE JANELLE ASSELIN
SEAN MACKIEWICZ KATIE KUBERT DAVE WIELGOSZ Assistant Editors – Original Series
JEB WOODARD Group Editor – Collected Editions
ROBIN WILDMAN Editor – Collected Edition
STEVE COOK Design Director – Books
SARABETH KETT Publication Design

BOB HARRAS Senior VP – Editor-in-Chief, DC Comics

DIANE NELSON President DAN DIDIO and JIM LEE Co-Publishers GEOFF JOHNS Chief Creative Officer
AMIT DESAI Senior VP – Marketing & Global Franchise Management NAIRI GARDINER Senior VP – Finance
SAM ADES VP – Digital Marketing BOBBIE CHASE VP – Talent Development
MARK CHIARELLO Senior VP – Art, Design & Collected Editions JOHN CUNNINGHAM VP – Content Strategy
ANNE DEPIES VP – Strategy Planning & Reporting DON FALLETTI VP – Manufacturing Operations
LAWRENCE GANEM VP – Editorial Administration & Talent Relations
ALISON GILL Senior VP – Manufacturing & Operations HANK KANALZ Senior VP – Editorial Strategy & Administration
JAY KOGAN VP – Legal Affairs DEREK MADDALENA Senior VP – Sales & Business Development
JACK MAHAN VP – Business Affairs DAN MIRON VP – Sales Planning & Trade Development
NICK NAPOLITANO VP – Manufacturing Administration CAROL ROEDER VP – Marketing
EDDIE SCANNELL VP – Mass Account & Digital Sales COURTNEY SIMMONS Senior VP – Publicity & Communications
JIM (SKI) SOKOLOWSKI VP – Comic Book Specialty & Newsstand Sales SANDY YI Senior VP – Global Franchise Management

HARLEY QUINN'S GREATEST HITS

DC Comics, 2900 West Alameda Ave., Burbank, CA 91505
Printed by RR Donnelley, Owensville, MO, USA. 6/24/16. First Printing.
ISBN: 978-1-4012-7008-7

PEFC Certified
Printed on paper from sustainably managed forests and controlled sources
PEFC/29-31-75
www.pefc.org

Collection Cover Art by
AMANDA CONNER with ALEX SINCLAIR

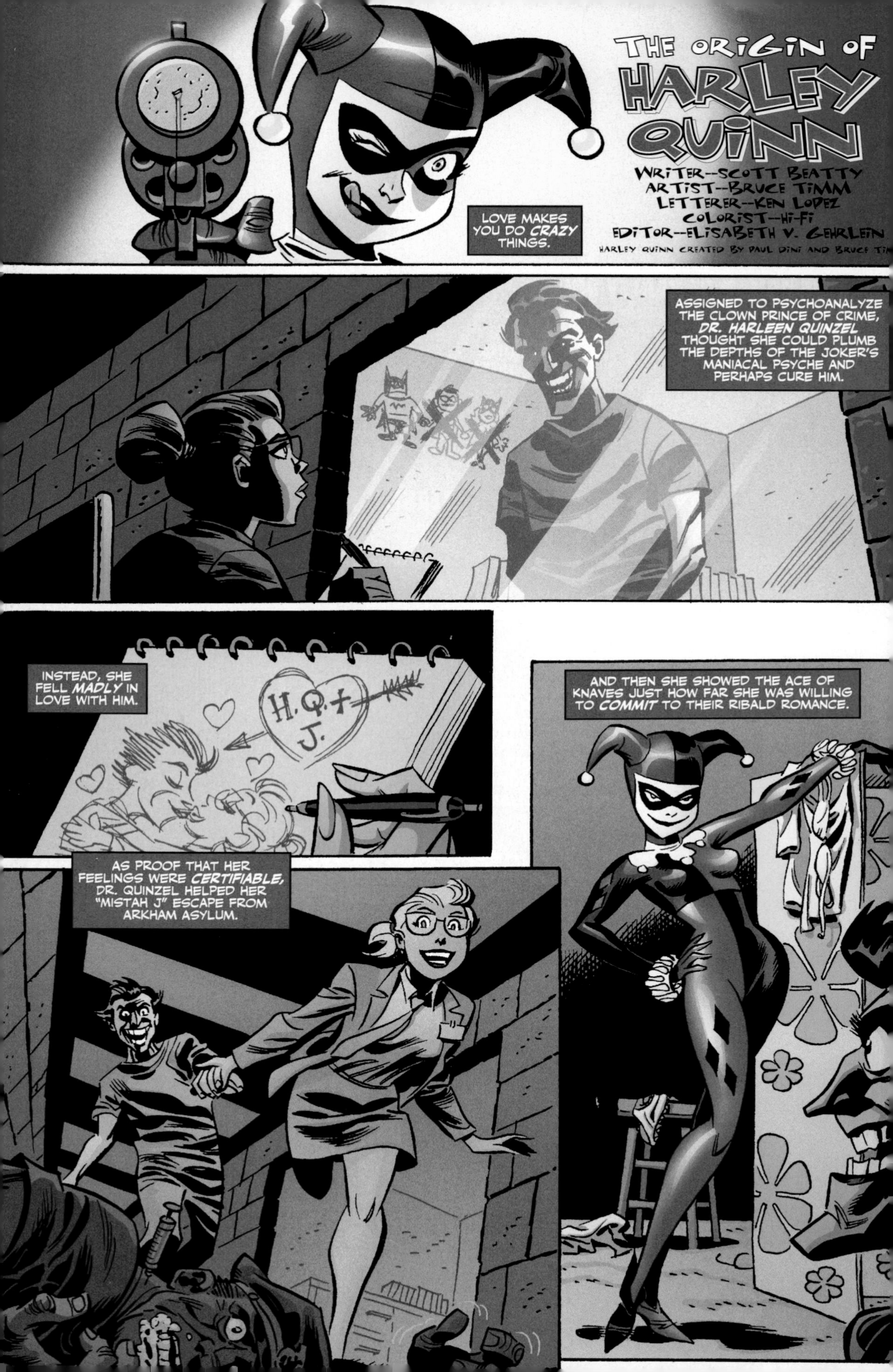
THE ORIGIN OF
HARLEY QUINN
WRITER--SCOTT BEATTY
ARTIST--BRUCE TIMM
LETTERER--KEN LOPEZ
COLORIST--HI-FI
EDITOR--ELISABETH V. GEHRLEIN
HARLEY QUINN CREATED BY PAUL DINI AND BRUCE TIM
LOVE MAKES YOU DO CRAZY THINGS.
ASSIGNED TO PSYCHOANALYZE THE CLOWN PRINCE OF CRIME, DR. HARLEEN QUINZEL THOUGHT SHE COULD PLUMB THE DEPTHS OF THE JOKER'S MANIACAL PSYCHE AND PERHAPS CURE HIM.
INSTEAD, SHE FELL MADLY IN LOVE WITH HIM.
H.Q. + J.
AND THEN SHE SHOWED THE ACE OF KNAVES JUST HOW FAR SHE WAS WILLING TO COMMIT TO THEIR RIBALD ROMANCE.
AS PROOF THAT HER FEELINGS WERE CERTIFIABLE, DR. QUINZEL HELPED HER "MISTAH J" ESCAPE FROM ARKHAM ASYLUM.

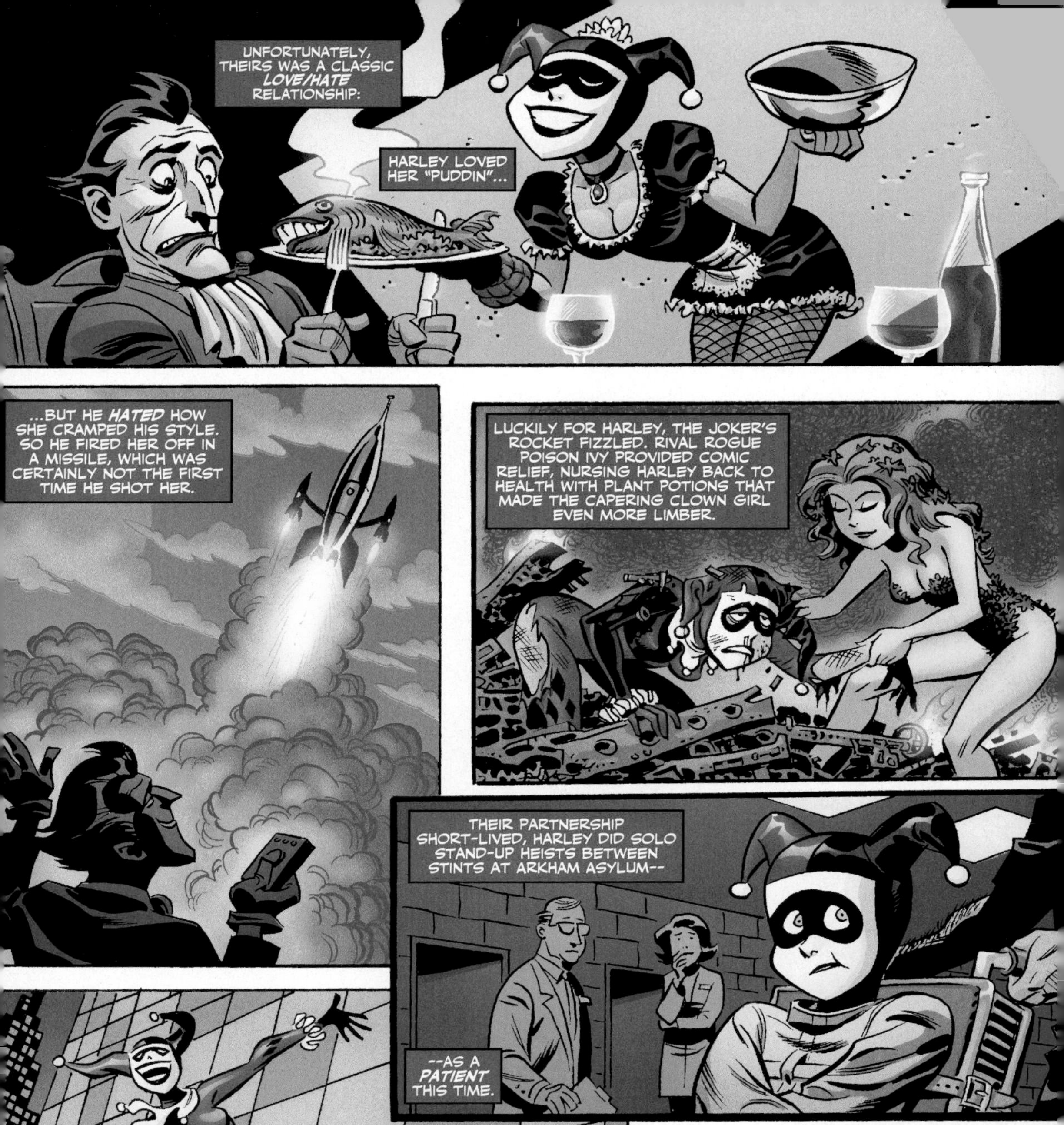
UNFORTUNATELY, THEIRS WAS A CLASSIC LOVE/HATE RELATIONSHIP:
HARLEY LOVED HER "PUDDIN"...
...BUT HE HATED HOW SHE CRAMPED HIS STYLE. SO HE FIRED HER OFF IN A MISSILE, WHICH WAS CERTAINLY NOT THE FIRST TIME HE SHOT HER.
LUCKILY FOR HARLEY, THE JOKER'S ROCKET FIZZLED. RIVAL ROGUE POISON IVY PROVIDED COMIC RELIEF, NURSING HARLEY BACK TO HEALTH WITH PLANT POTIONS THAT MADE THE CAPERING CLOWN GIRL EVEN MORE LIMBER.
THEIR PARTNERSHIP SHORT-LIVED, HARLEY DID SOLO STAND-UP HEISTS BETWEEN STINTS AT ARKHAM ASYLUM--
--AS A PATIENT THIS TIME.

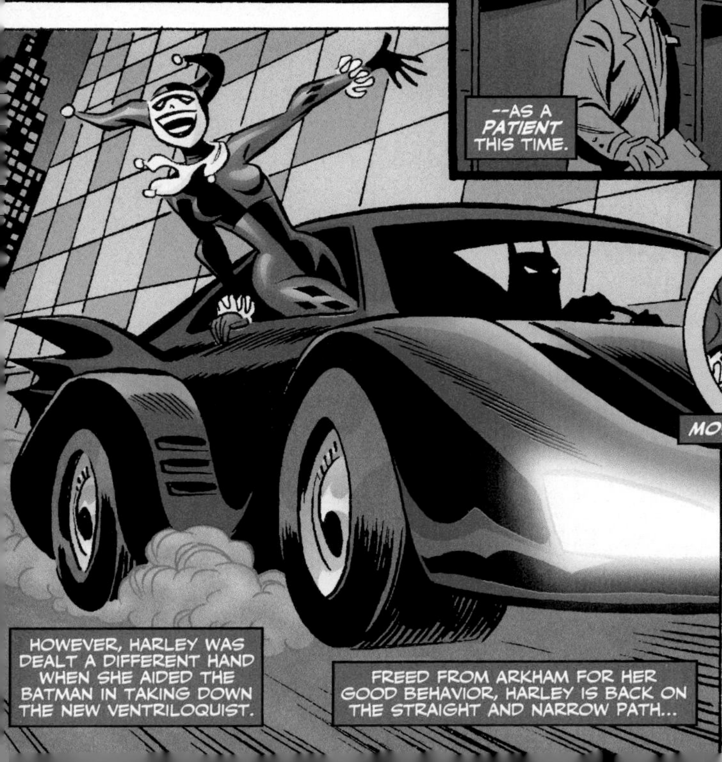
HOWEVER, HARLEY WAS DEALT A DIFFERENT HAND WHEN SHE AIDED THE BATMAN IN TAKING DOWN THE NEW VENTRILOQUIST.
FREED FROM ARKHAM FOR HER GOOD BEHAVIOR, HARLEY IS BACK ON THE STRAIGHT AND NARROW PATH...

POWERS AND WEAPONS:

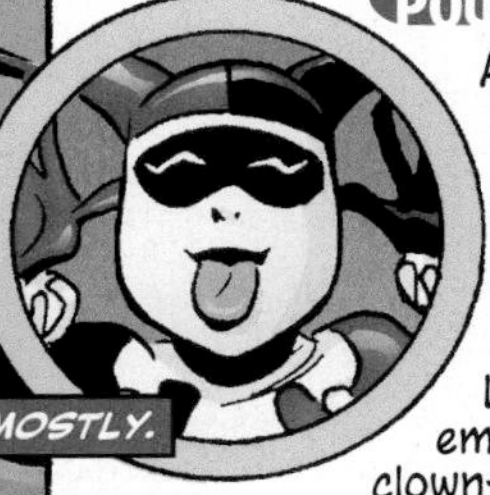
MOSTLY.

As a result of Poison Ivy's "treatment," Harley's strength and agility were increased dramatically, and she became immune to most toxins, including Joker-Venom. Like "Mistah J," Harley employs a variety of clown-themed gag weapons, including oversized pistols and mallets. Hyenas are her favorite pets.

ESSENTIAL STORYLINES:

- BATMAN: HARLEY QUINN
- HARLEY QUINN: PRELUDES AND KNOCK-KNOCK JOKES
- HARLEY AND IVY: LOVE ON THE LAM
- DETECTIVE COMICS 831, 837
- COUNTDOWN TO FINAL CRISIS VOL. 1-4

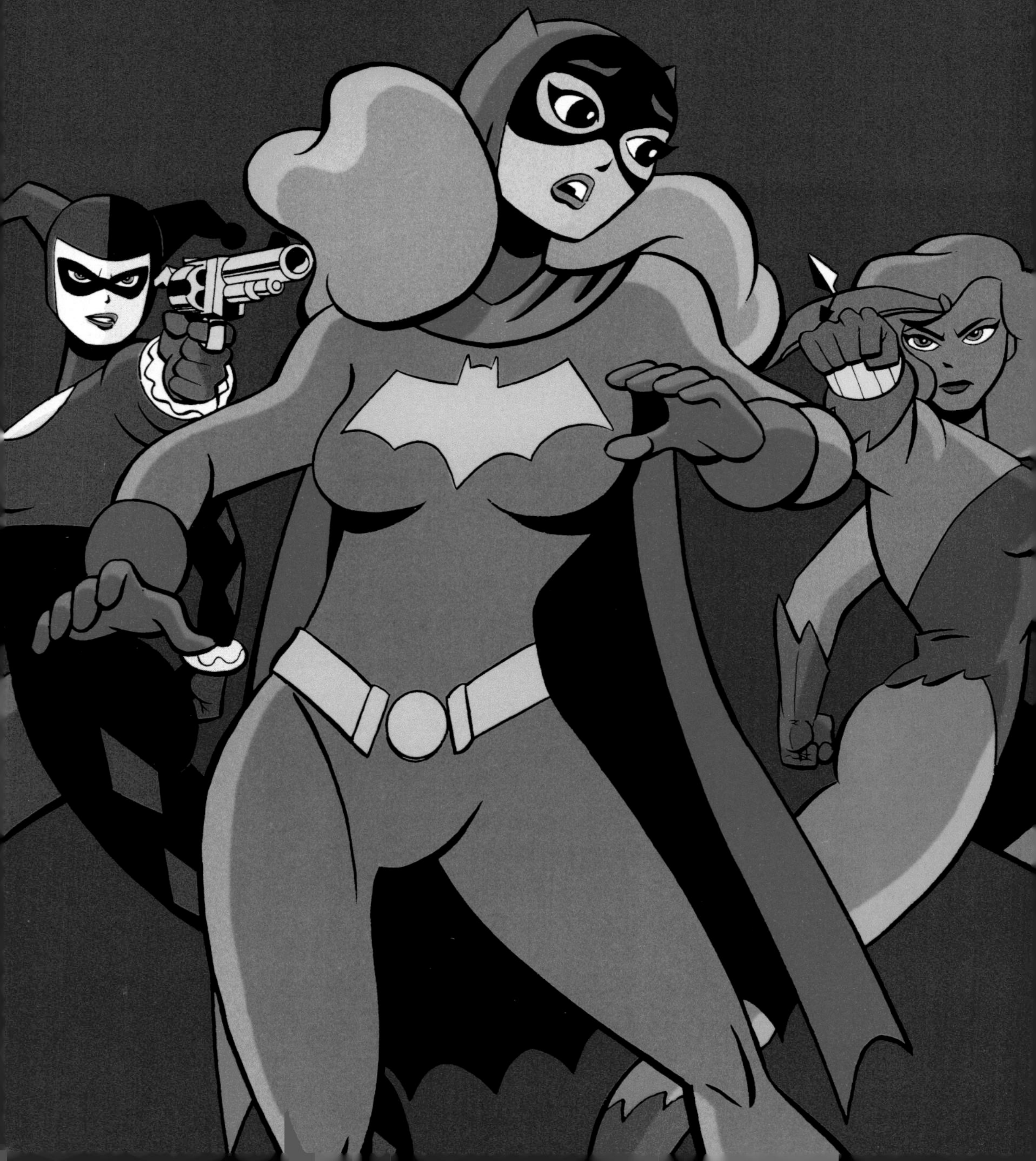

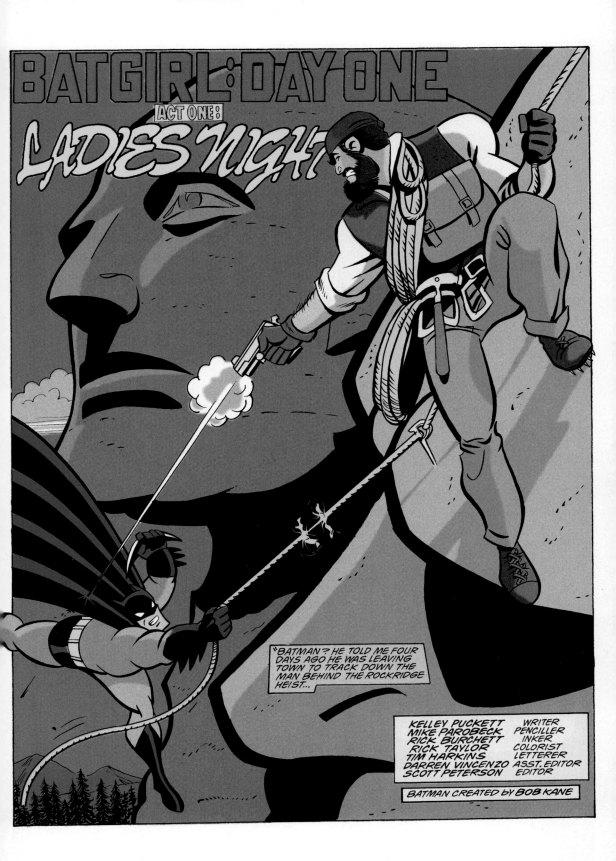

BATGIRL: DAY ONE

ACT ONE: LADIES NIGHT

"BATMAN? HE TOLD ME FOUR DAYS AGO HE WAS LEAVING TOWN TO TRACK DOWN THE MAN BEHIND THE ROCKRIDGE HEIST..."

KELLEY PUCKETT — WRITER
MIKE PAROBECK — PENCILLER
RICK BURCHETT — INKER
RICK TAYLOR — COLORIST
TIM HARKINS — LETTERER
DARREN VINCENZO — ASST. EDITOR
SCOTT PETERSON — EDITOR

BATMAN CREATED BY BOB KANE

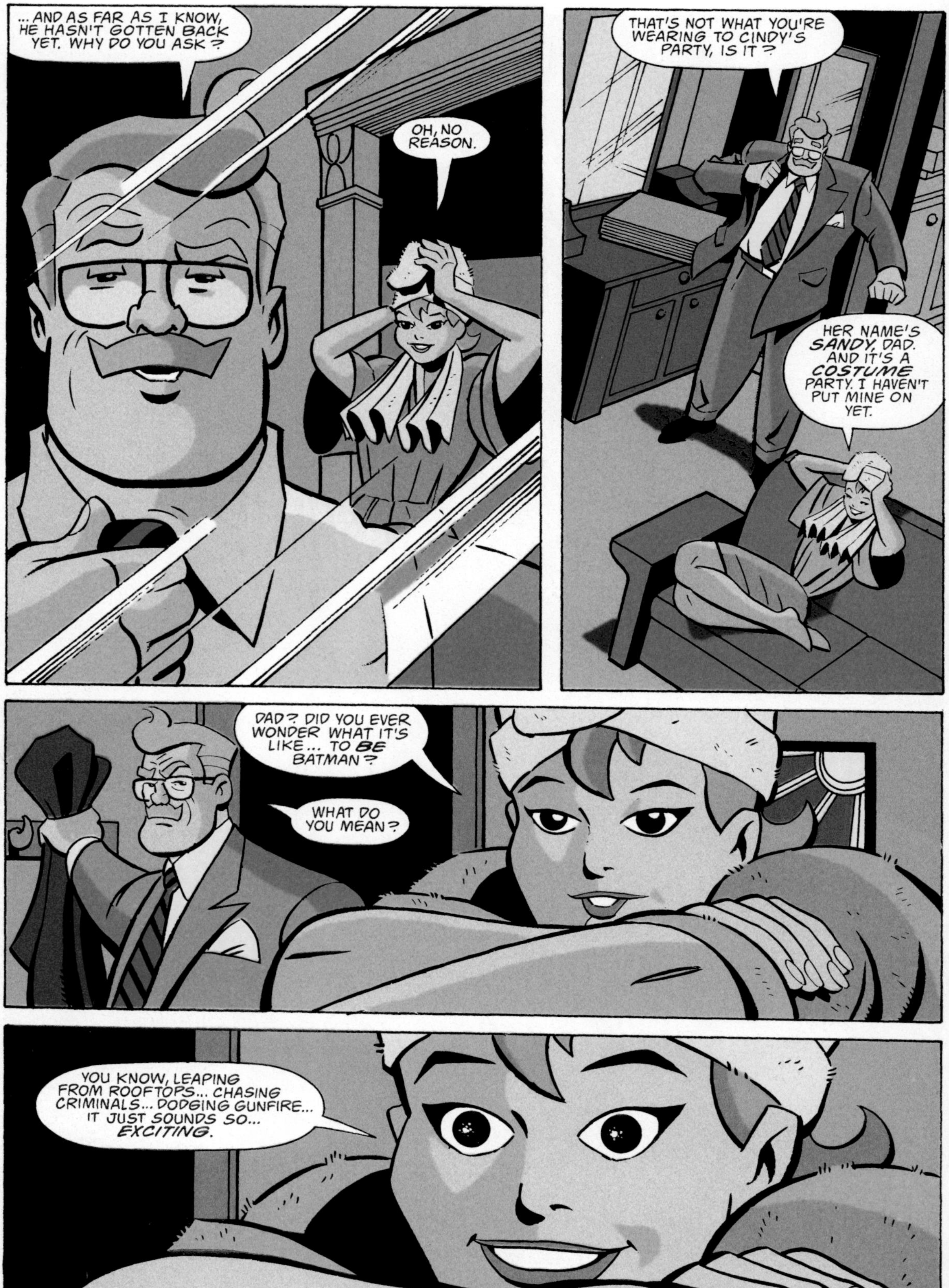
...AND AS FAR AS I KNOW, HE HASN'T GOTTEN BACK YET. WHY DO YOU ASK?
OH, NO REASON.
THAT'S NOT WHAT YOU'RE WEARING TO CINDY'S PARTY, IS IT?
HER NAME'S SANDY, DAD. AND IT'S A COSTUME PARTY. I HAVEN'T PUT MINE ON YET.
DAD? DID YOU EVER WONDER WHAT IT'S LIKE... TO BE BATMAN?
WHAT DO YOU MEAN?
YOU KNOW, LEAPING FROM ROOFTOPS... CHASING CRIMINALS... DODGING GUNFIRE... IT JUST SOUNDS SO... EXCITING.
2

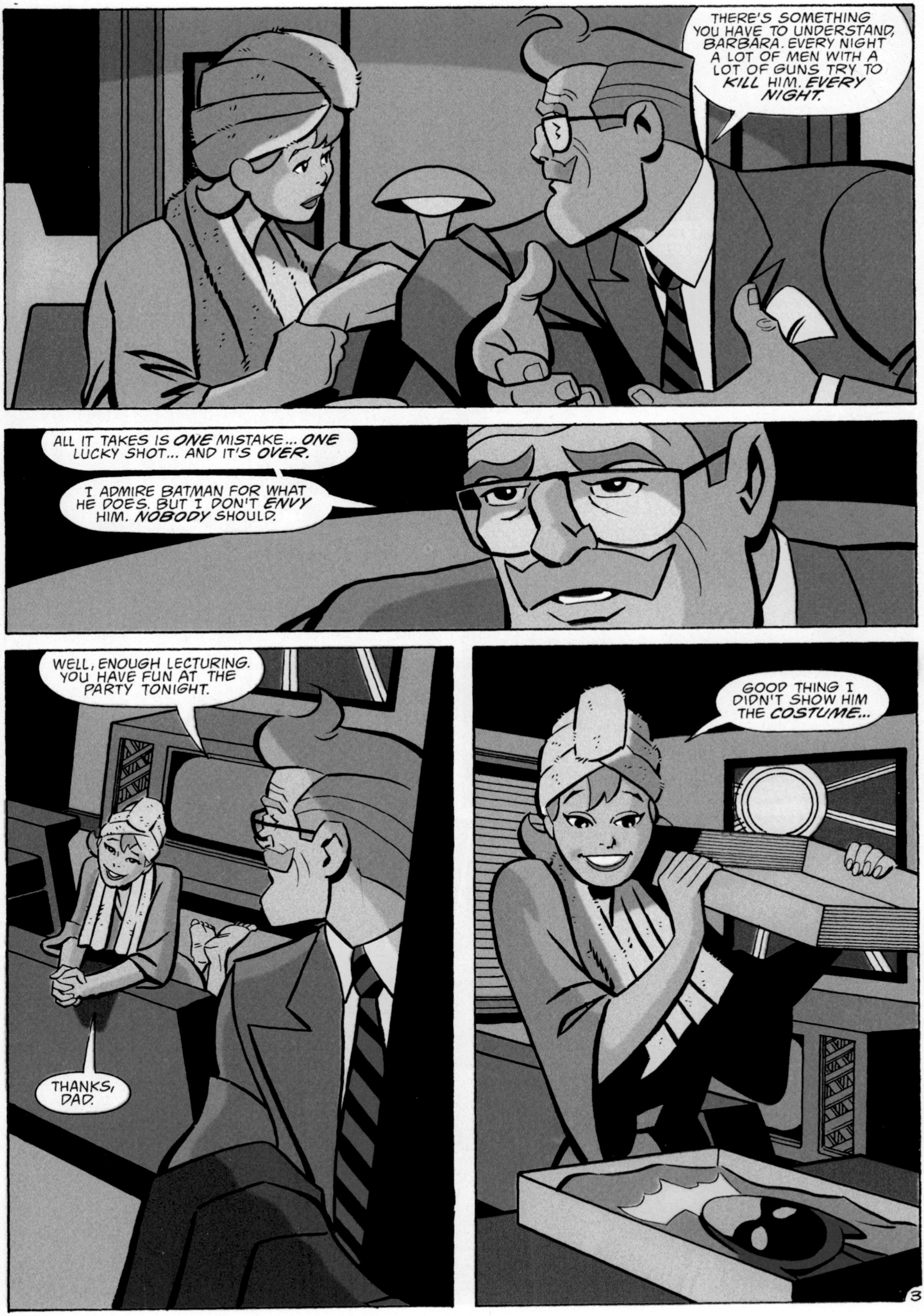
THERE'S SOMETHING YOU HAVE TO UNDERSTAND, BARBARA. EVERY NIGHT A LOT OF MEN WITH A LOT OF GUNS TRY TO KILL HIM. EVERY NIGHT.
ALL IT TAKES IS ONE MISTAKE... ONE LUCKY SHOT... AND IT'S OVER.
I ADMIRE BATMAN FOR WHAT HE DOES. BUT I DON'T ENVY HIM. NOBODY SHOULD.
WELL, ENOUGH LECTURING. YOU HAVE FUN AT THE PARTY TONIGHT.
THANKS, DAD.
GOOD THING I DIDN'T SHOW HIM THE COSTUME...
3

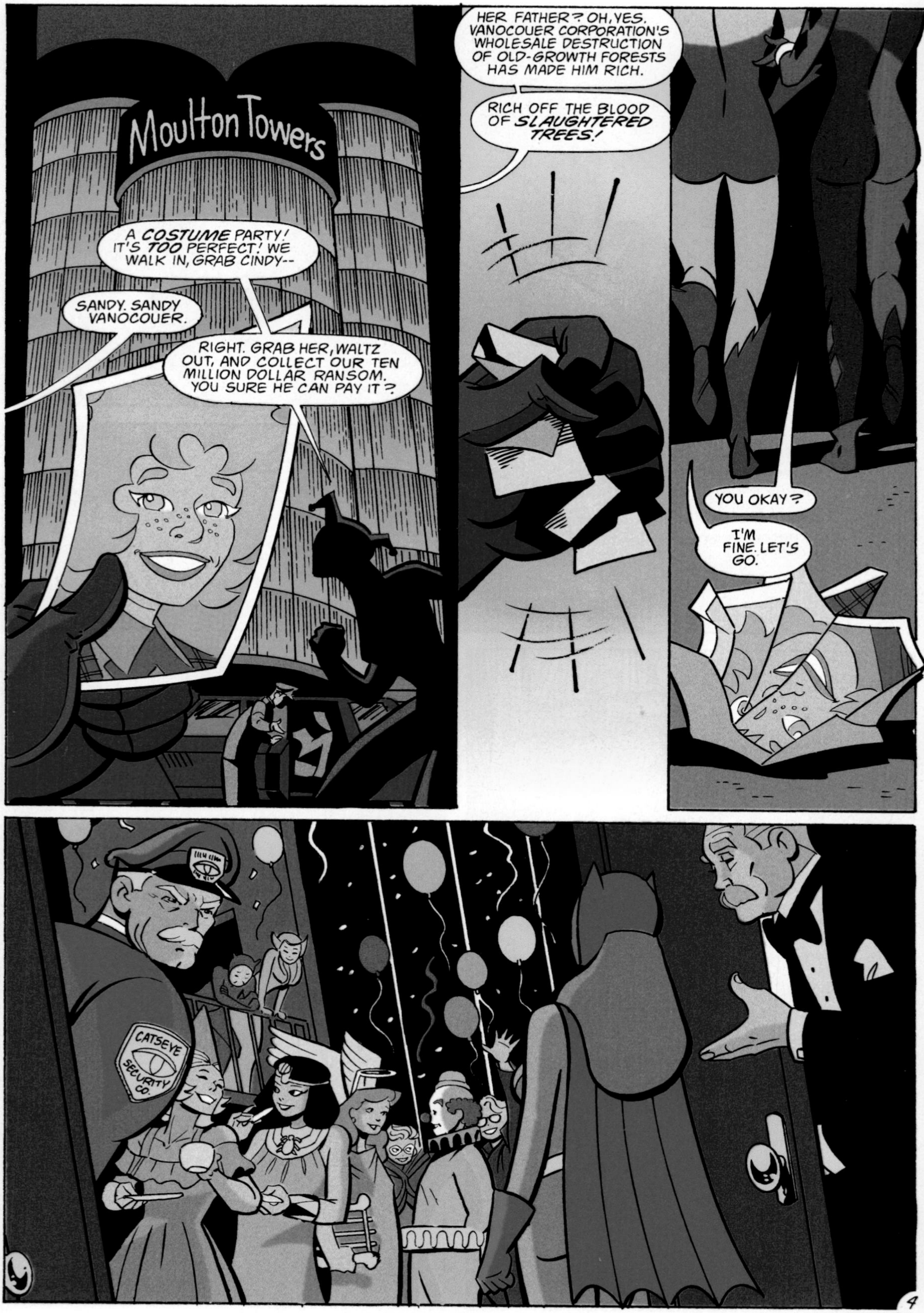
Moulton Towers
A COSTUME PARTY! IT'S TOO PERFECT! WE WALK IN, GRAB CINDY--
SANDY. SANDY VANOCOUER.
RIGHT. GRAB HER, WALTZ OUT, AND COLLECT OUR TEN MILLION DOLLAR RANSOM. YOU SURE HE CAN PAY IT?
HER FATHER? OH, YES. VANOCOUER CORPORATION'S WHOLESALE DESTRUCTION OF OLD-GROWTH FORESTS HAS MADE HIM RICH.
RICH OFF THE BLOOD OF SLAUGHTERED TREES!
YOU OKAY?
I'M FINE. LET'S GO.
CATSEYE SECURITY CO.
4

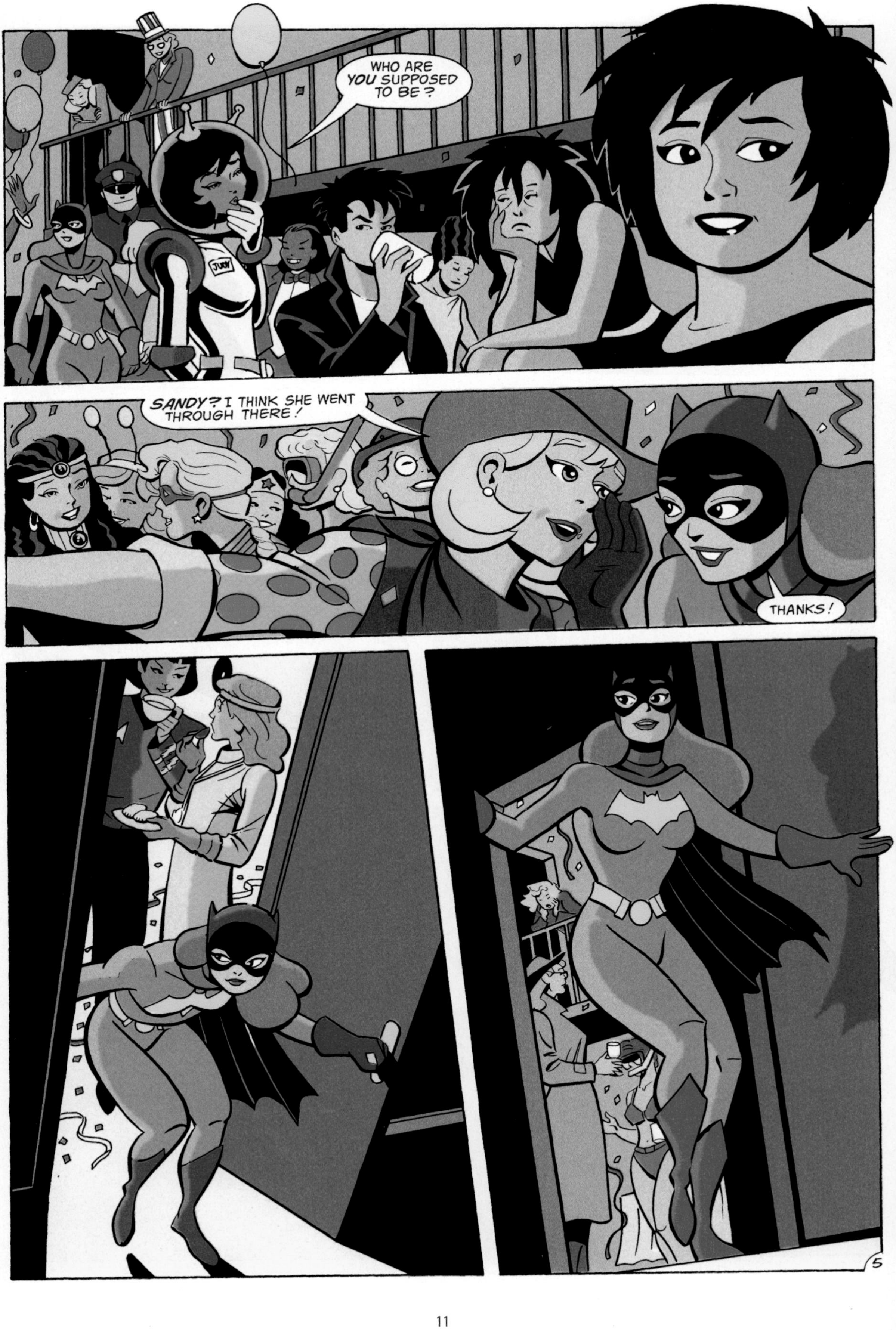
WHO ARE YOU SUPPOSED TO BE?
SANDY? I THINK SHE WENT THROUGH THERE!
THANKS!
5

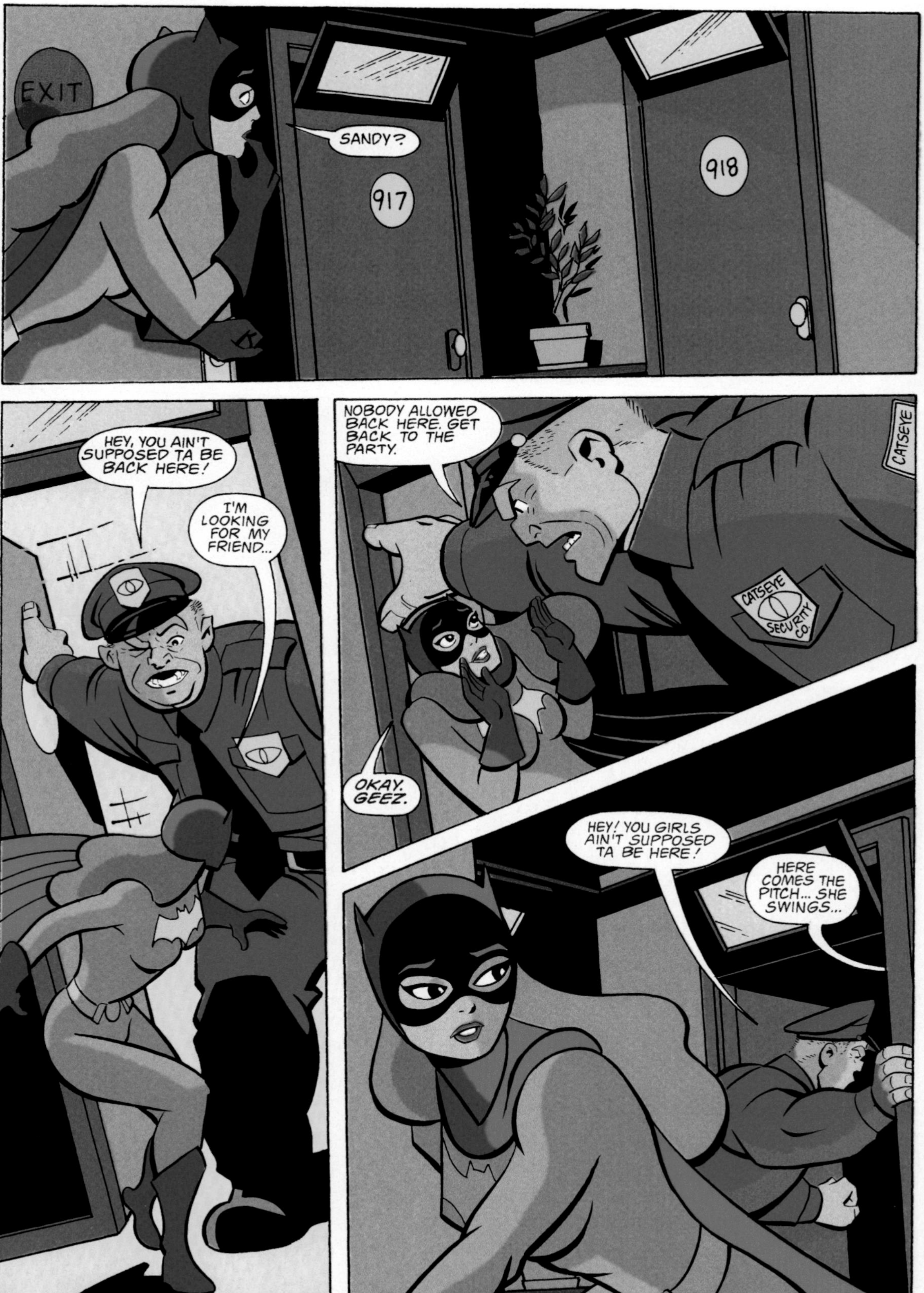
EXIT
SANDY?
917
918
HEY, YOU AIN'T SUPPOSED TA BE BACK HERE!
I'M LOOKING FOR MY FRIEND...
NOBODY ALLOWED BACK HERE. GET BACK TO THE PARTY.
CATSEYE
CATSEYE SECURITY CO.
OKAY. GEEZ.
HEY! YOU GIRLS AIN'T SUPPOSED TA BE HERE!
HERE COMES THE PITCH... SHE SWINGS...
6

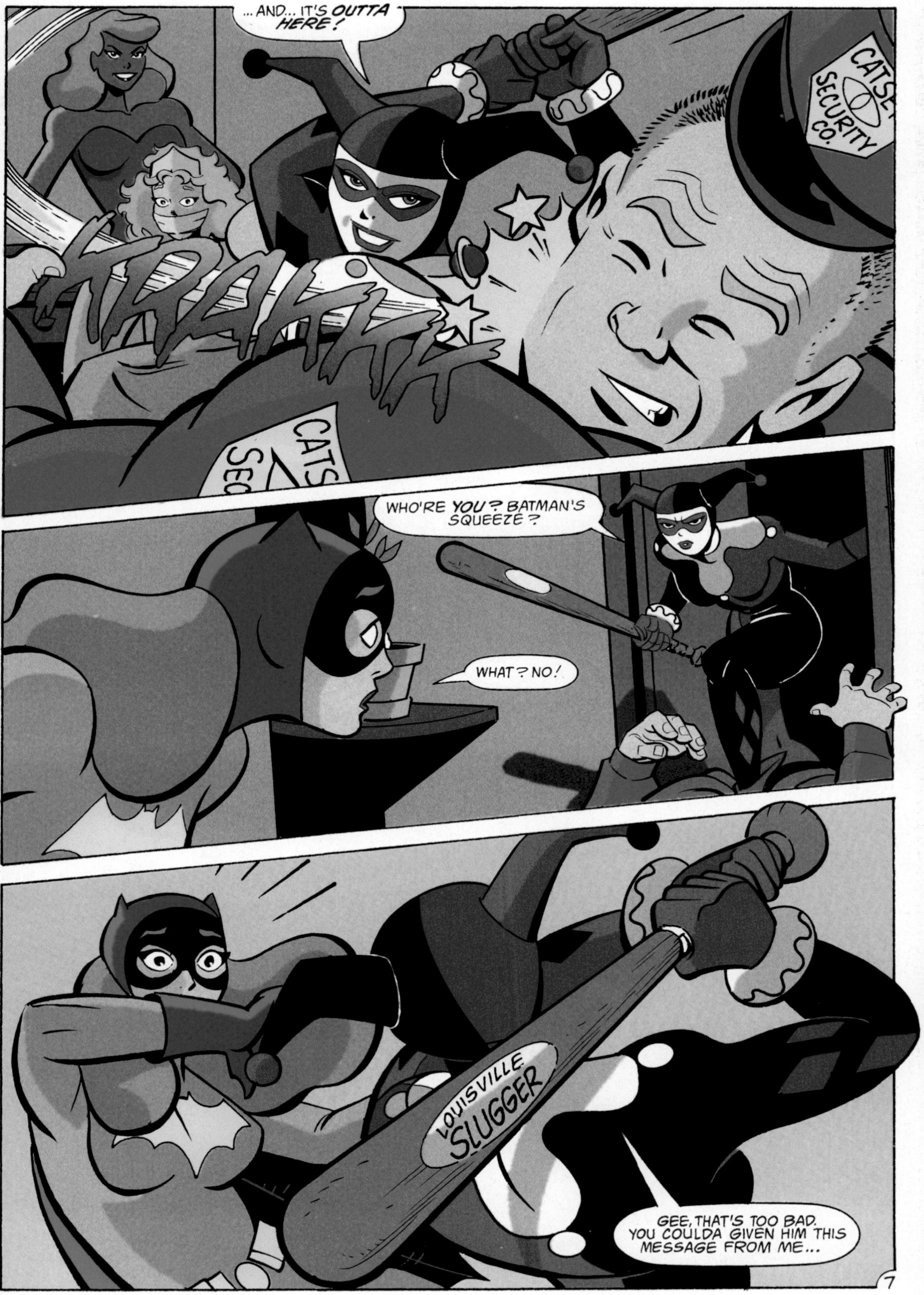
...AND... IT'S OUTTA HERE!
CATSEY SECURITY CO.
CATS SEC
WHO'RE YOU? BATMAN'S SQUEEZE?
WHAT? NO!
LOUISVILLE SLUGGER
GEE, THAT'S TOO BAD. YOU COULDA GIVEN HIM THIS MESSAGE FROM ME...
7

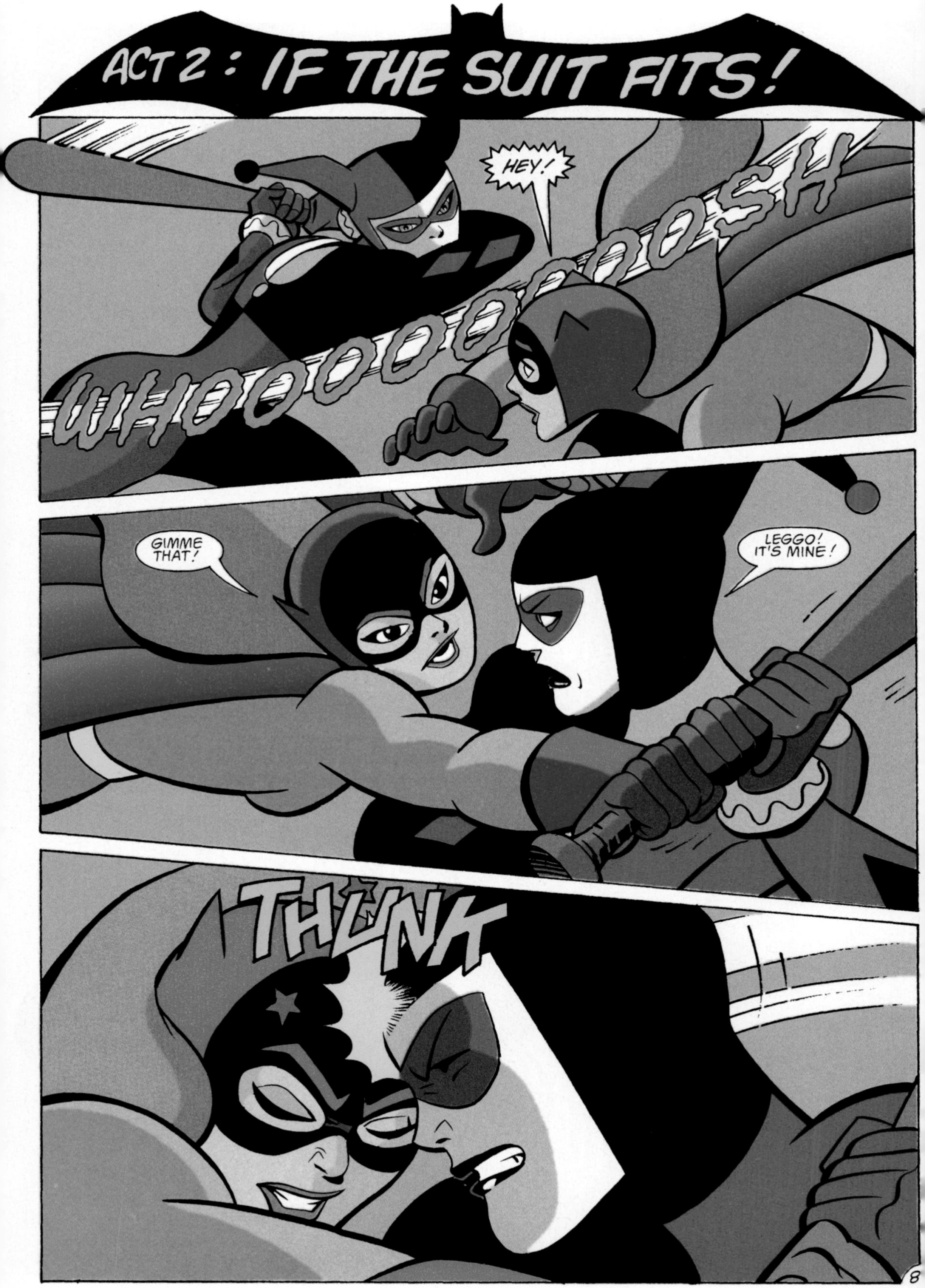
ACT 2 : IF THE SUIT FITS!
HEY!
WHOOOOOOOOOOSH
GIMME THAT!
LEGGO! IT'S MINE!
THUNK
8

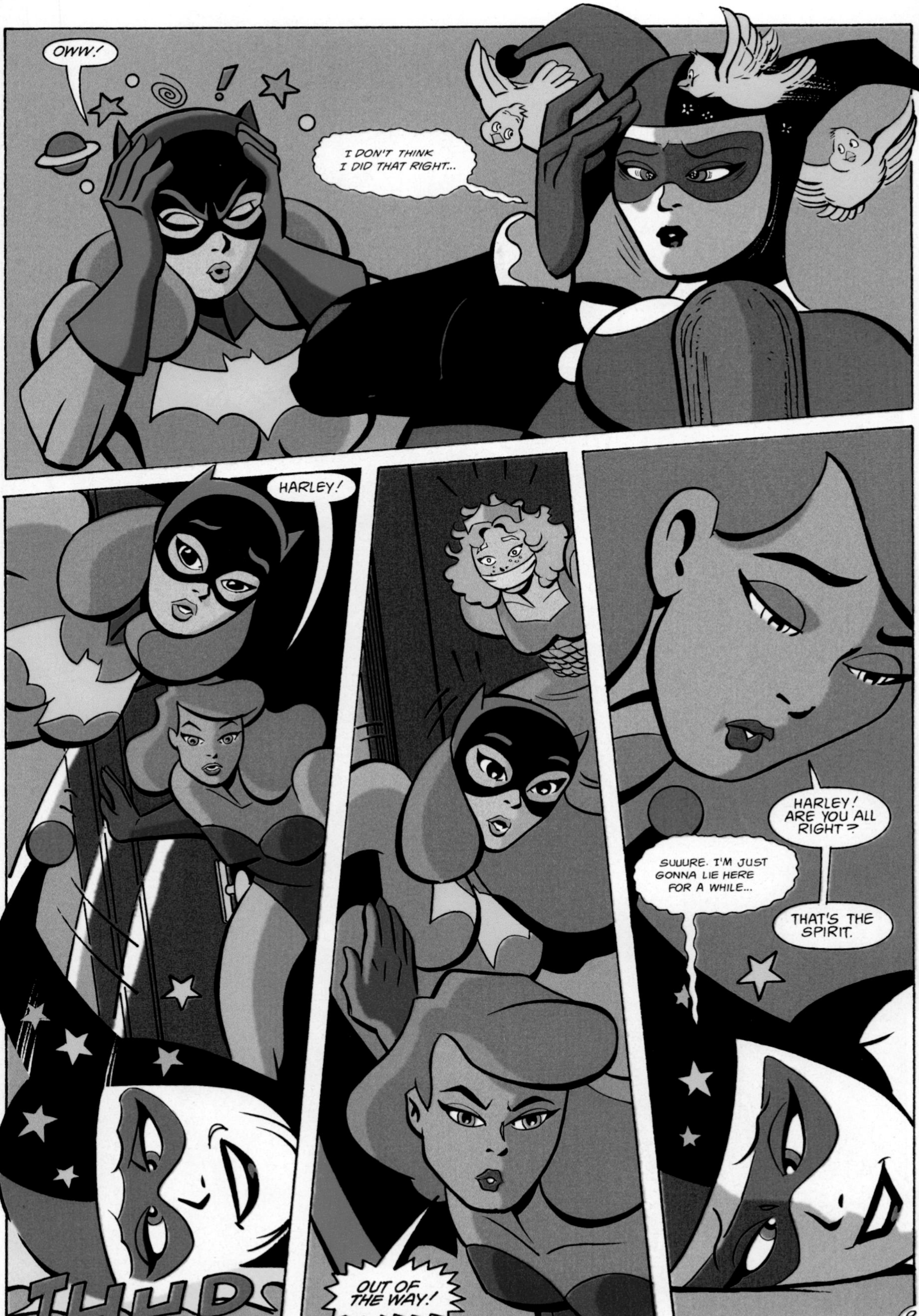
OWW!
I DON'T THINK I DID THAT RIGHT...
HARLEY!
THUD
OUT OF THE WAY!
HARLEY! ARE YOU ALL RIGHT?
SUUURE. I'M JUST GONNA LIE HERE FOR A WHILE...
THAT'S THE SPIRIT.
9

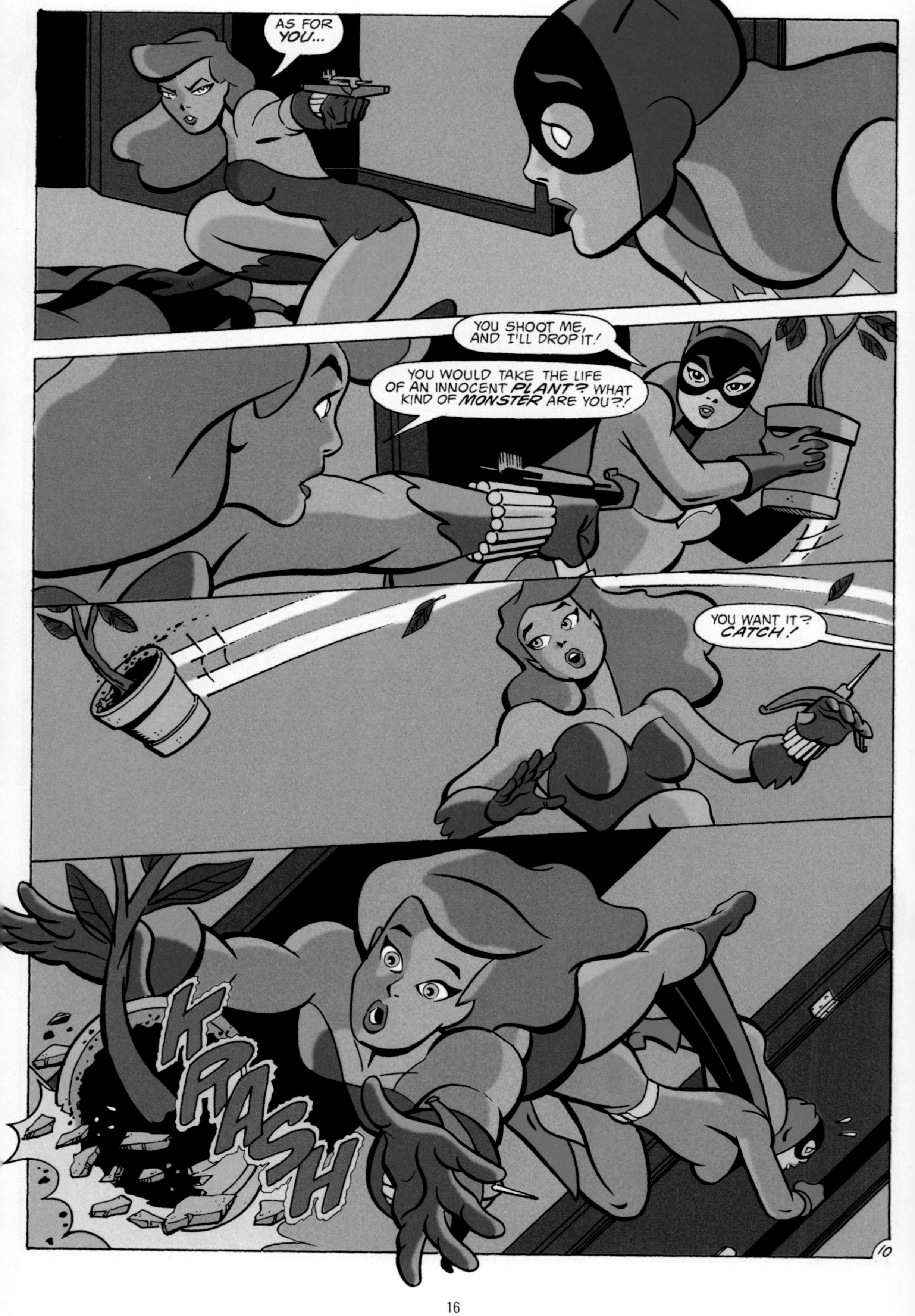
AS FOR *YOU*...
YOU SHOOT ME, AND I'LL DROP IT!
YOU WOULD TAKE THE LIFE OF AN INNOCENT *PLANT?* WHAT KIND OF *MONSTER* ARE YOU?!
YOU WANT IT? *CATCH!*
KRASH
10

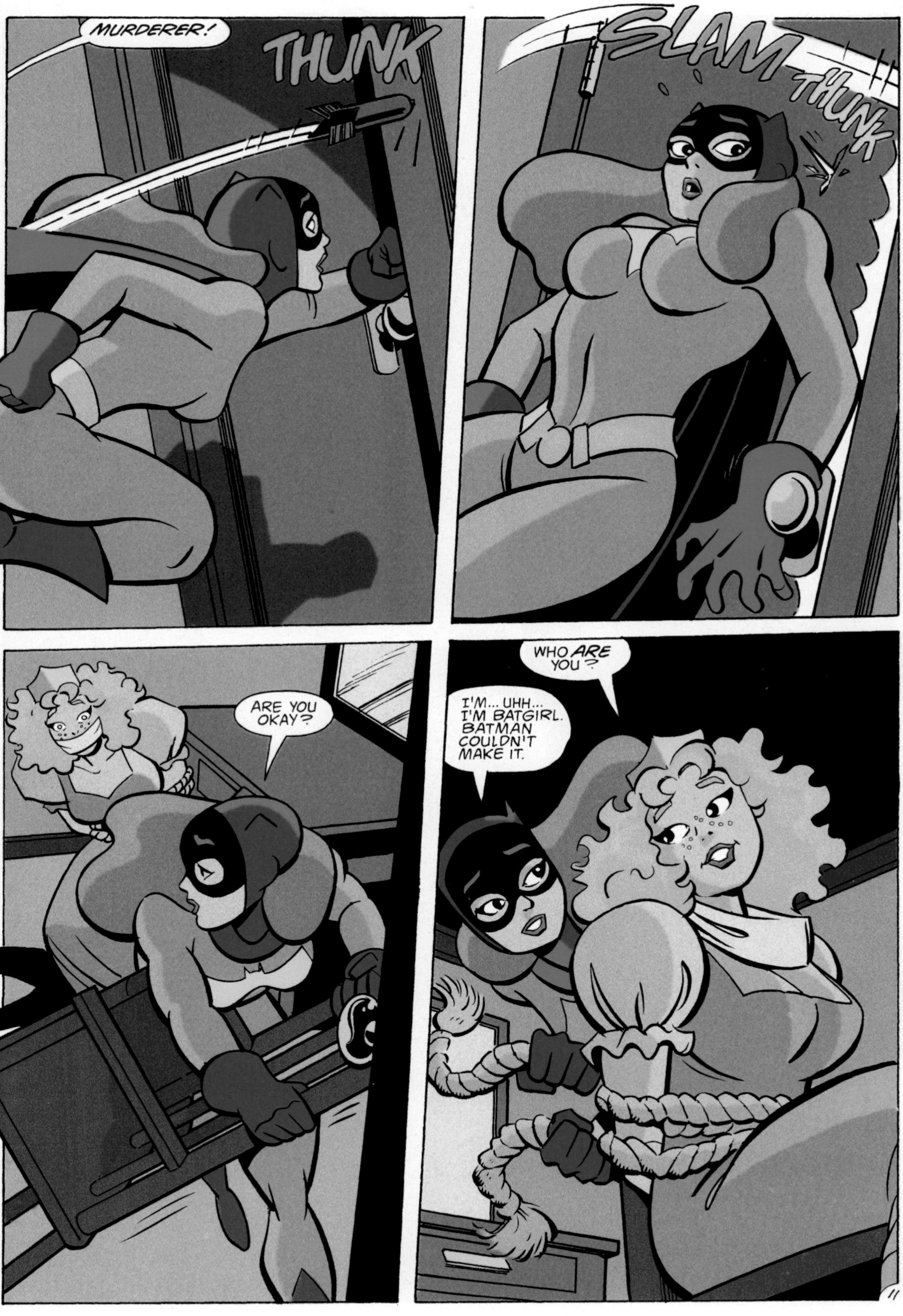
MURDERER!
THUNK
SLAM
THUNK
ARE YOU OKAY?
WHO ARE YOU?
I'M... UHH... I'M BATGIRL. BATMAN COULDN'T MAKE IT.
11

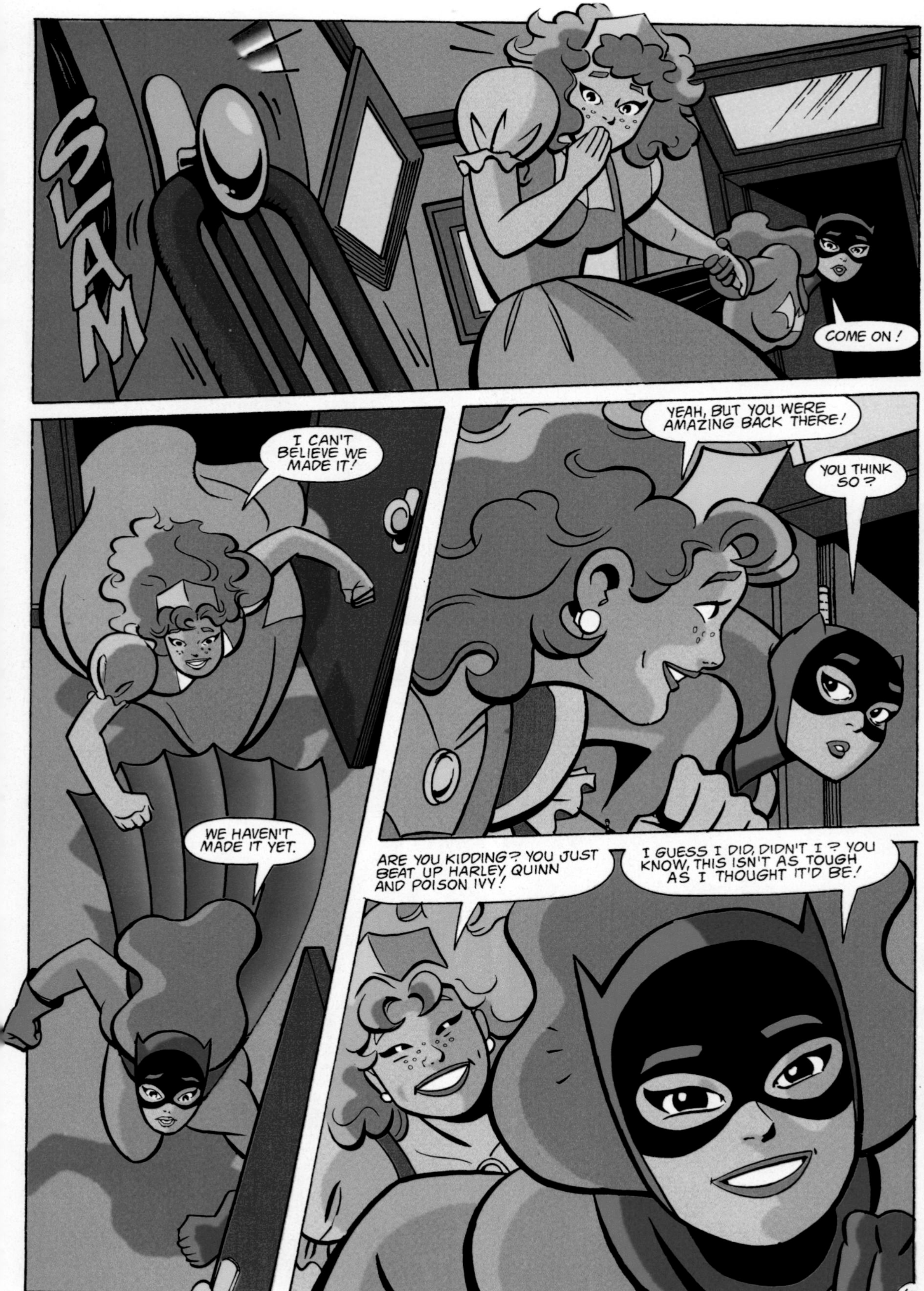
SLAM
COME ON!
I CAN'T BELIEVE WE MADE IT!
WE HAVEN'T MADE IT YET.
YEAH, BUT YOU WERE AMAZING BACK THERE!
YOU THINK SO?
ARE YOU KIDDING? YOU JUST BEAT UP HARLEY QUINN AND POISON IVY!
I GUESS I DID, DIDN'T I? YOU KNOW, THIS ISN'T AS TOUGH AS I THOUGHT IT'D BE!
12

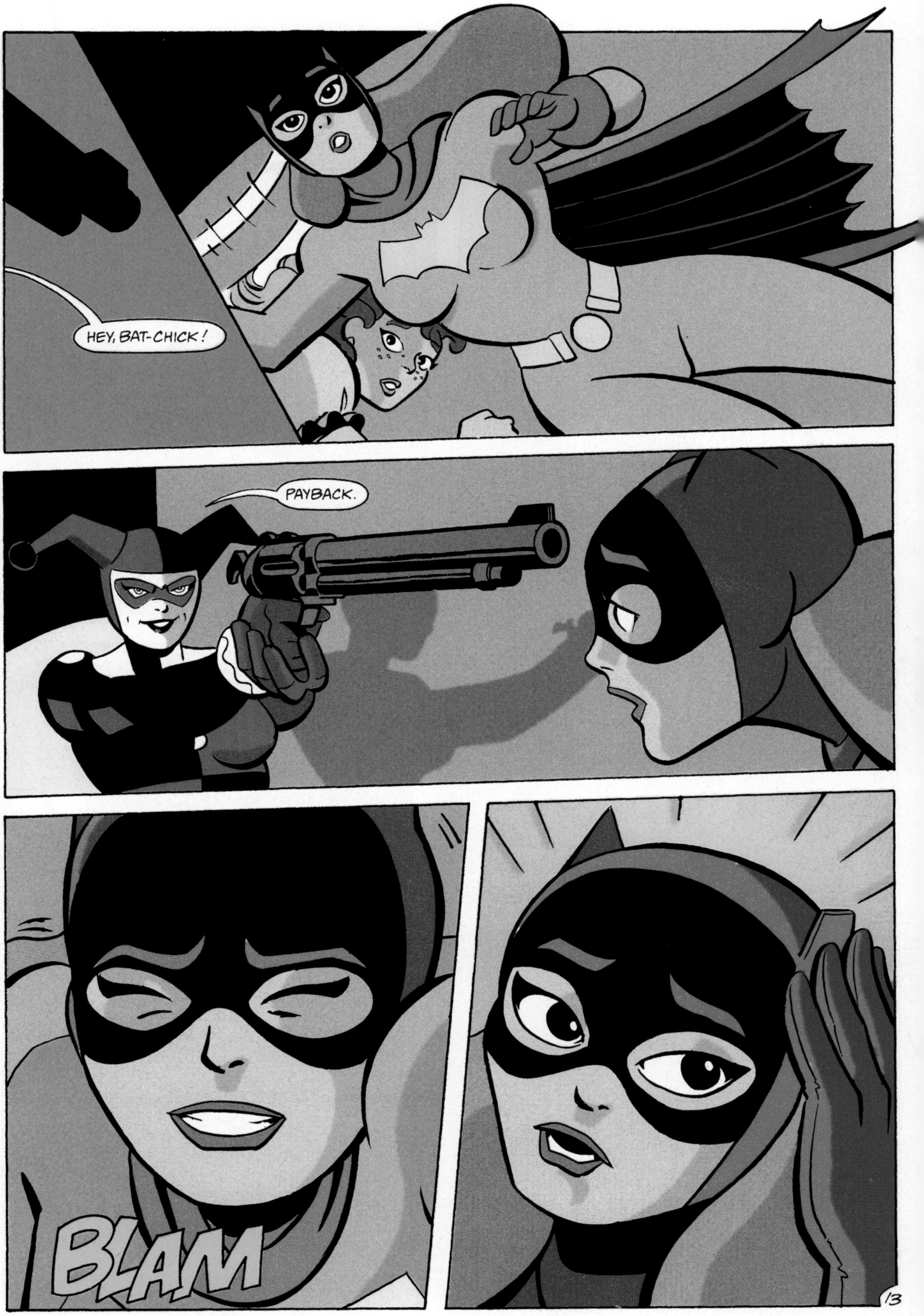
HEY, BAT-CHICK!
PAYBACK.
BLAM
13

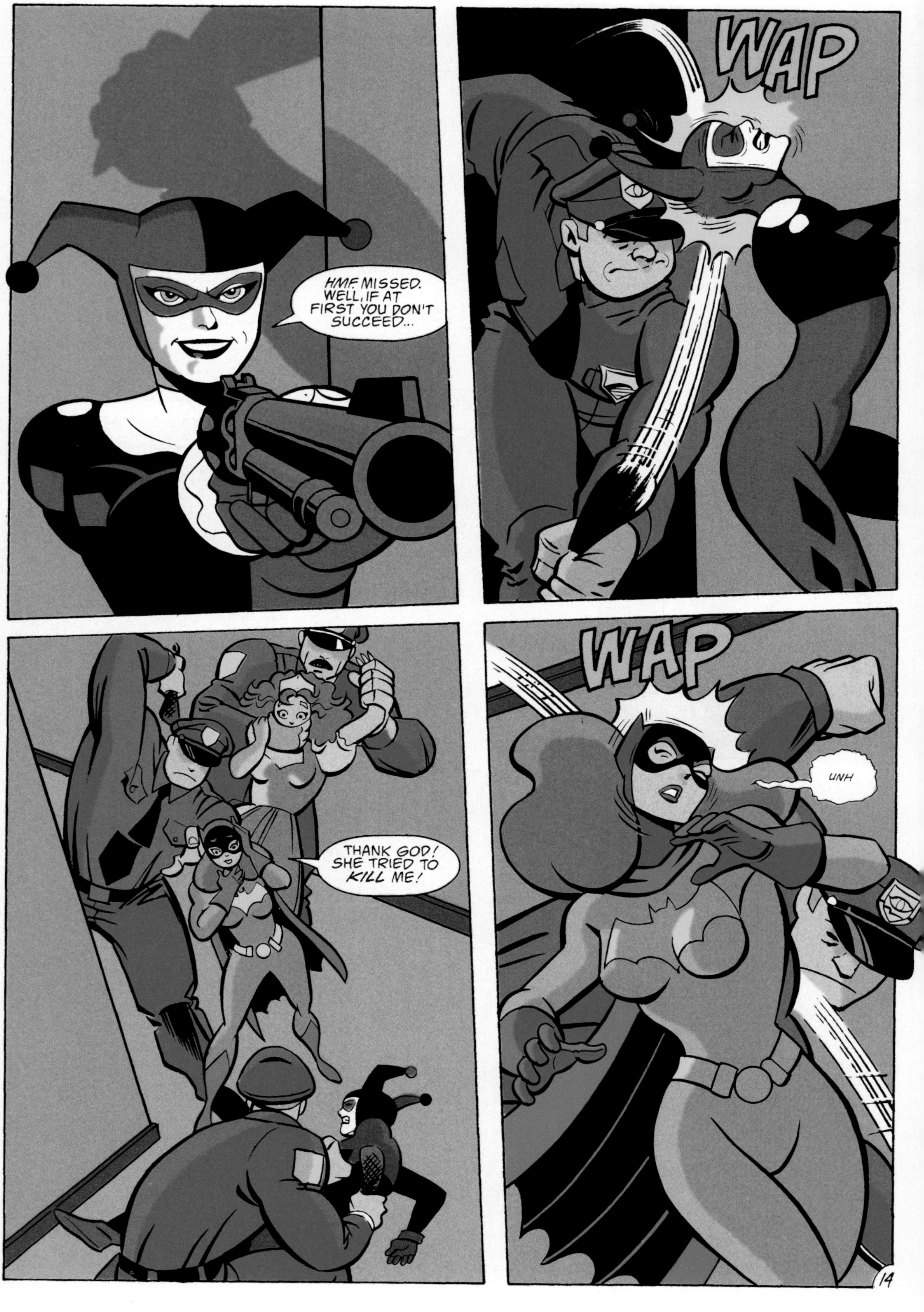
HMF. MISSED. WELL, IF AT FIRST YOU DON'T SUCCEED...
WAP
THANK GOD! SHE TRIED TO KILL ME!
WAP
UNH
14

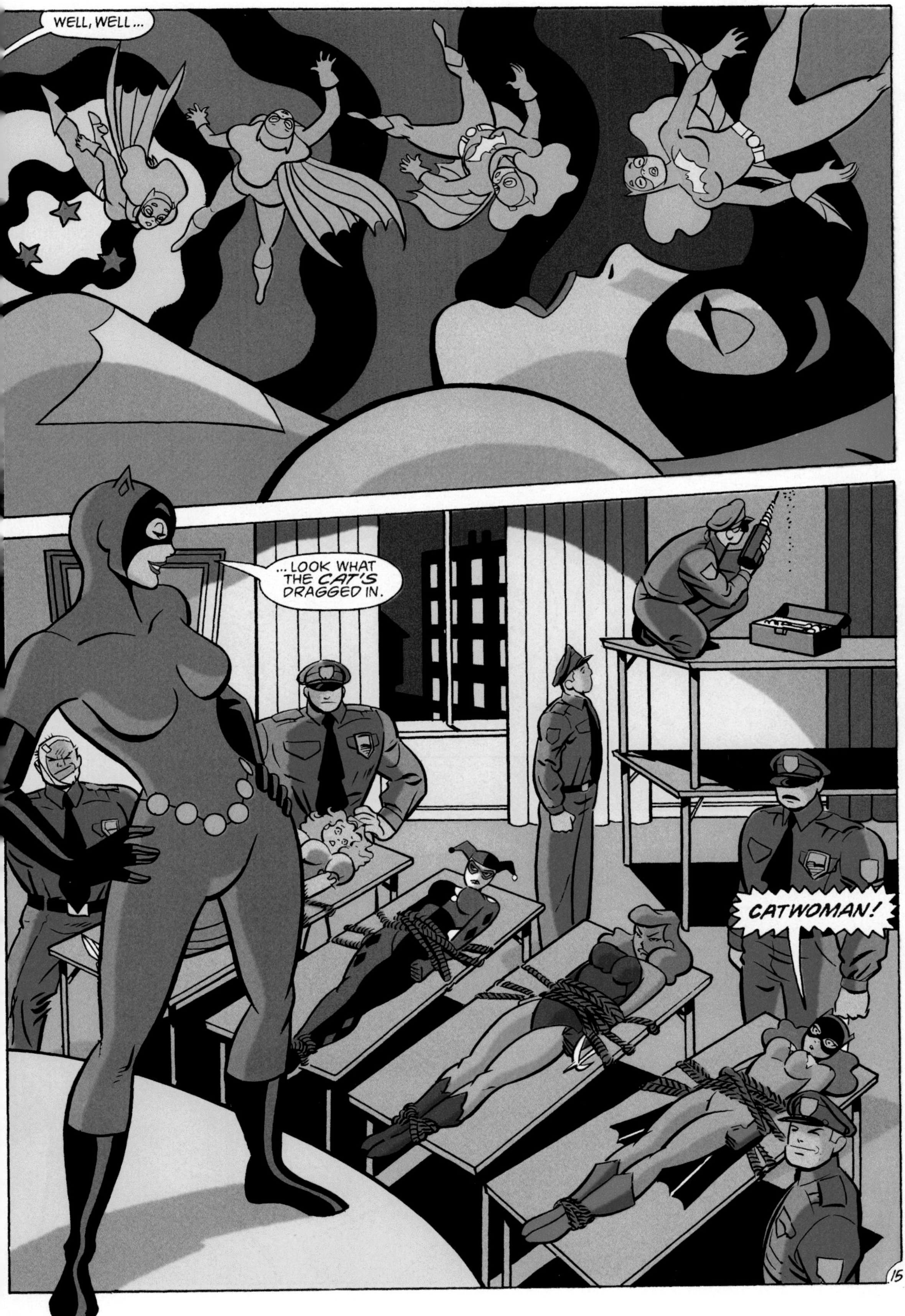
WELL, WELL...
...LOOK WHAT THE CAT'S DRAGGED IN.
CATWOMAN!
15

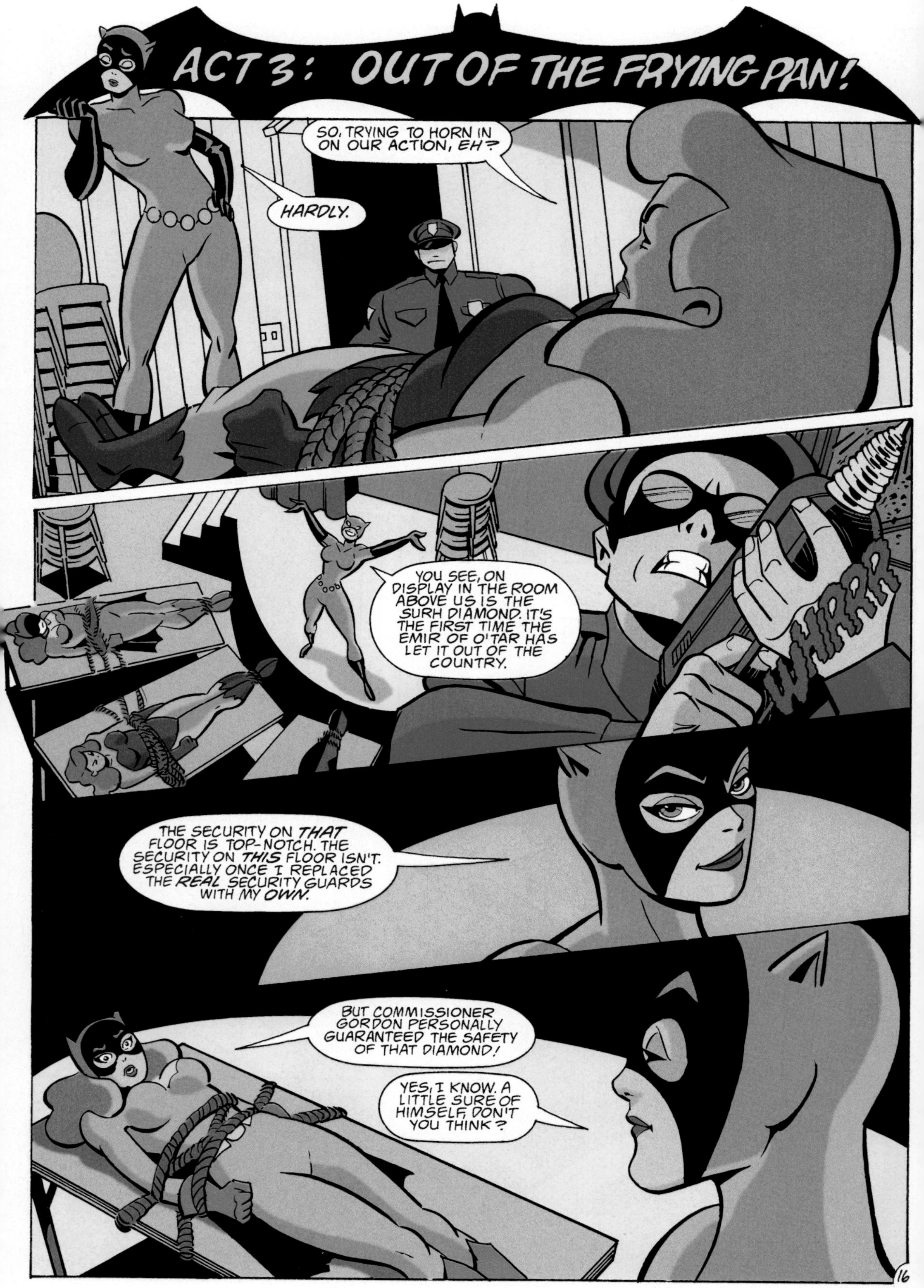
ACT 3: OUT OF THE FRYING PAN!
SO, TRYING TO HORN IN ON OUR ACTION, EH?
HARDLY.
YOU SEE, ON DISPLAY IN THE ROOM ABOVE US IS THE SURH DIAMOND. IT'S THE FIRST TIME THE EMIR OF O'TAR HAS LET IT OUT OF THE COUNTRY.
WHIRRR
THE SECURITY ON THAT FLOOR IS TOP-NOTCH. THE SECURITY ON THIS FLOOR ISN'T. ESPECIALLY ONCE I REPLACED THE REAL SECURITY GUARDS WITH MY OWN.
BUT COMMISSIONER GORDON PERSONALLY GUARANTEED THE SAFETY OF THAT DIAMOND!
YES, I KNOW. A LITTLE SURE OF HIMSELF, DON'T YOU THINK?
16

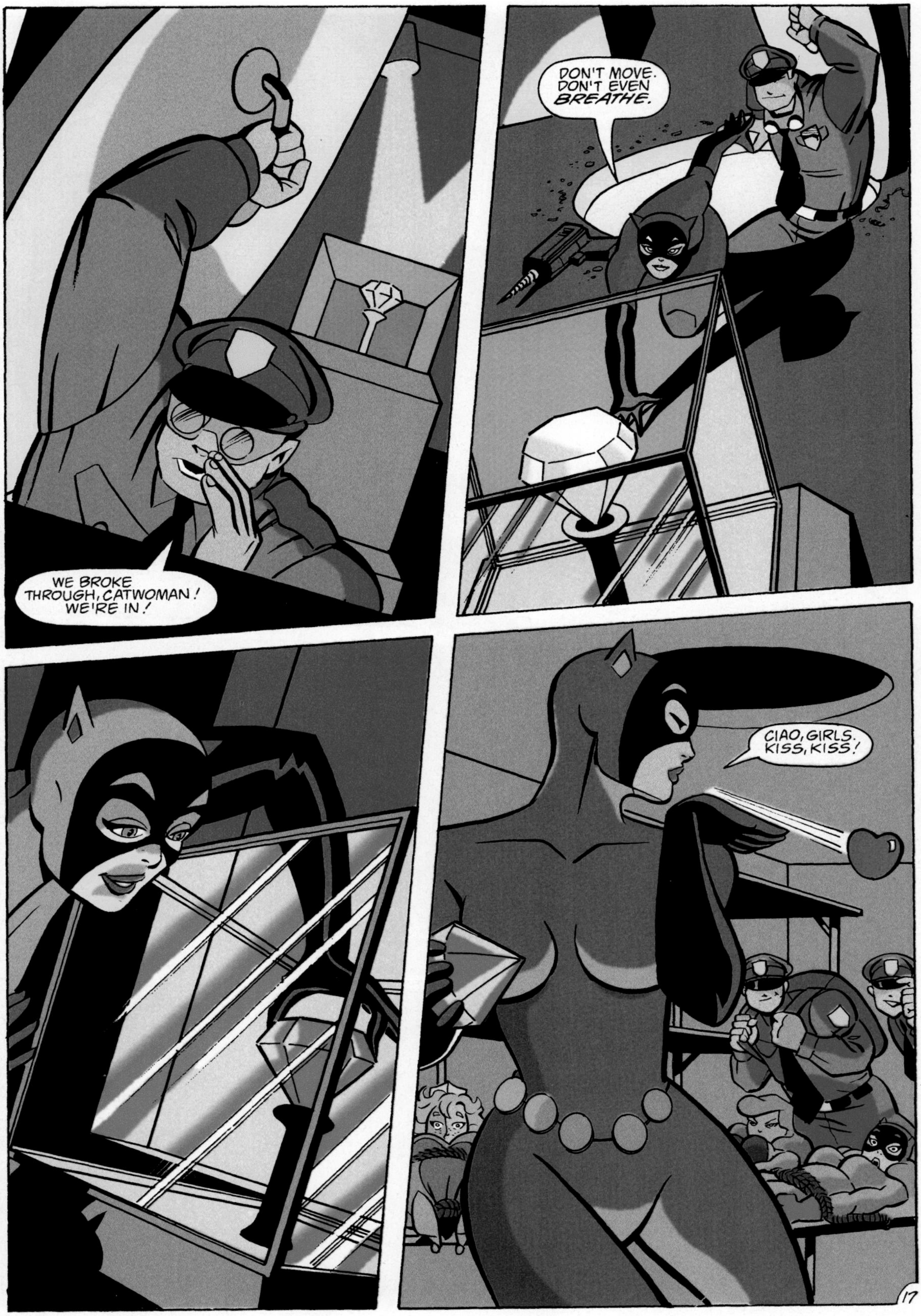
WE BROKE THROUGH, CATWOMAN! WE'RE IN!
DON'T MOVE. DON'T EVEN BREATHE.
CIAO, GIRLS. KISS, KISS!
17

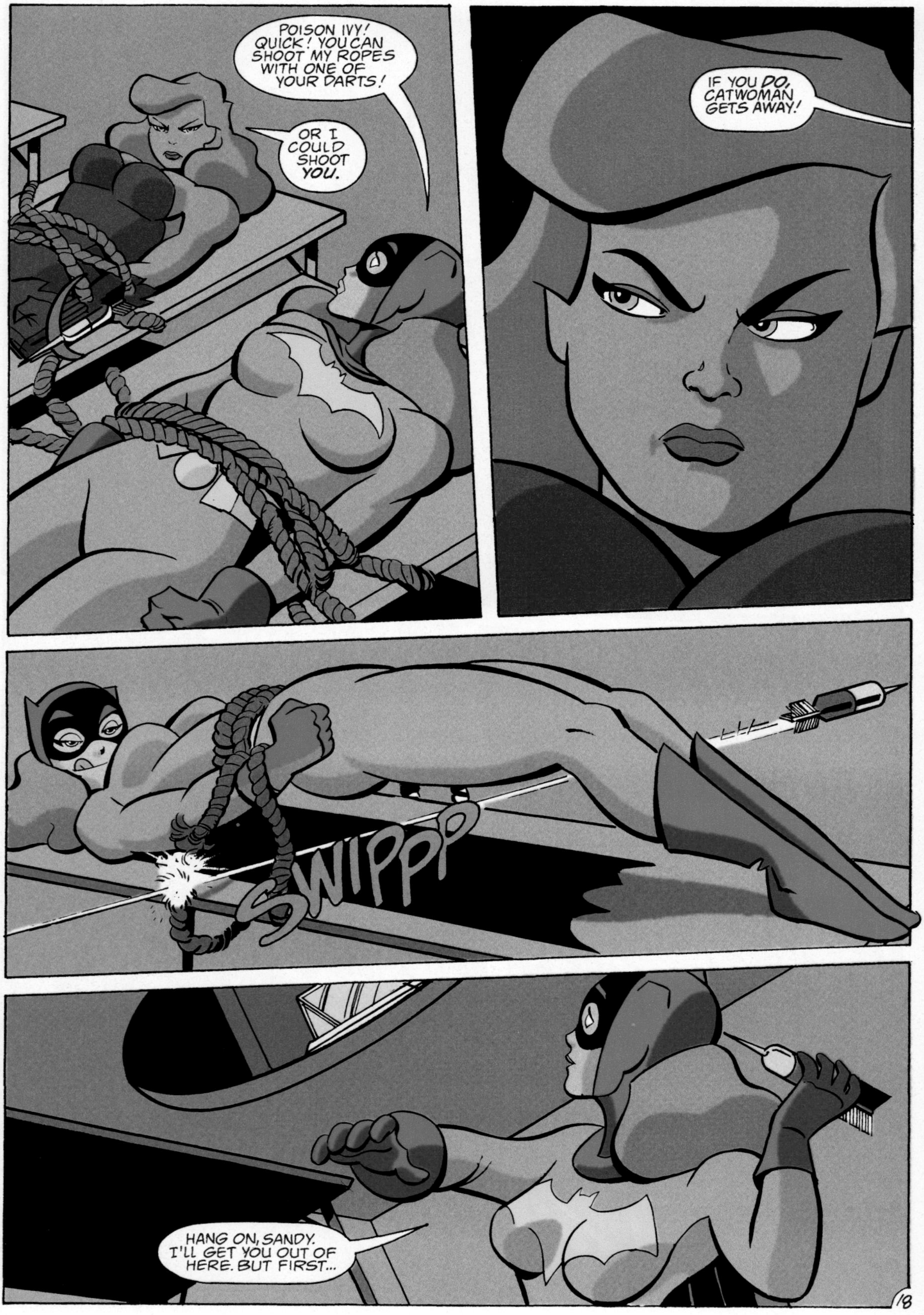
POISON IVY! QUICK! YOU CAN SHOOT MY ROPES WITH ONE OF YOUR DARTS!
OR I COULD SHOOT YOU.
IF YOU DO, CATWOMAN GETS AWAY!
SWIPPP
HANG ON, SANDY. I'LL GET YOU OUT OF HERE. BUT FIRST...
18

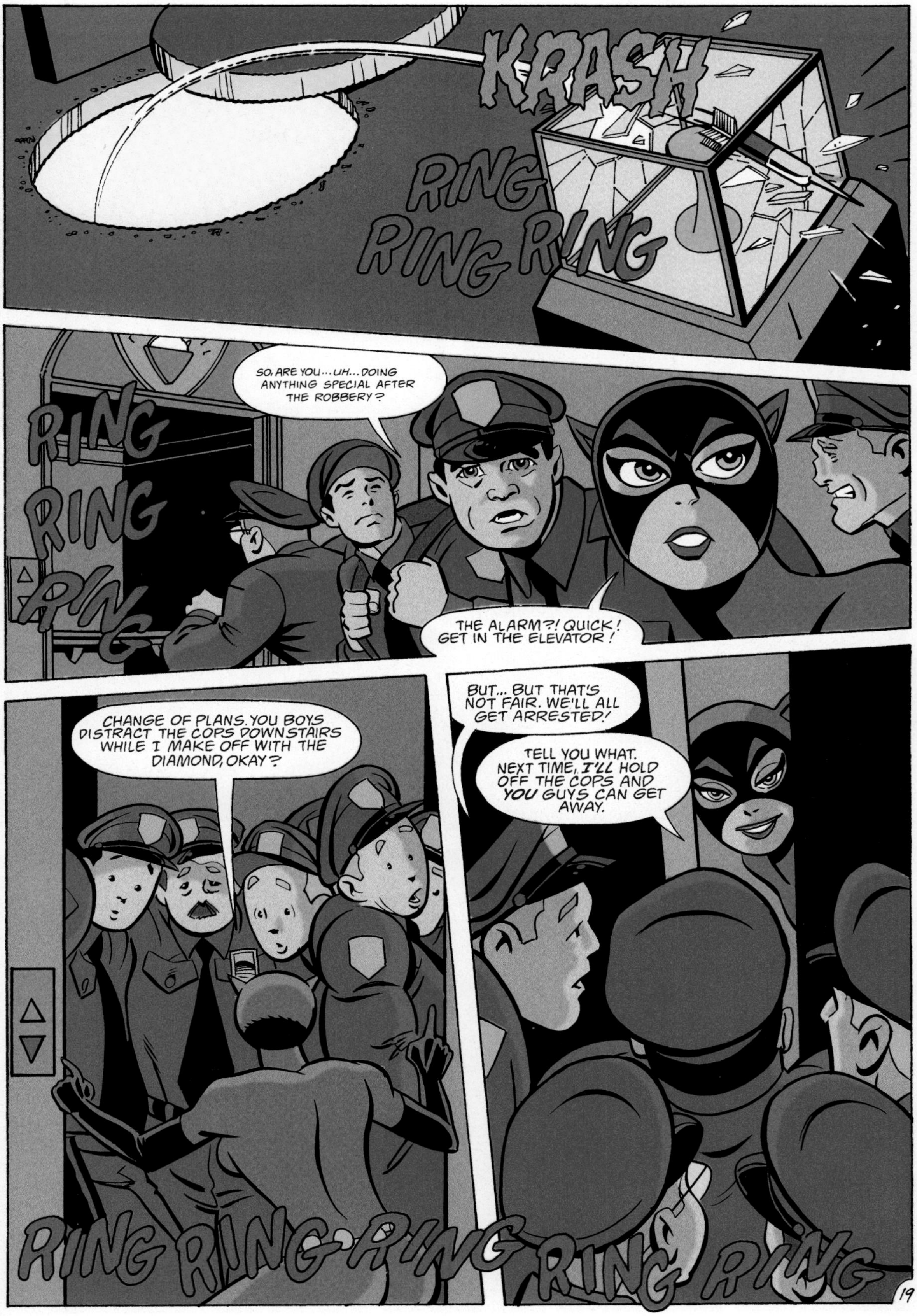
KRASH
RING
RING RING RING
RING
RING
RING
SO, ARE YOU... UH... DOING ANYTHING SPECIAL AFTER THE ROBBERY?
THE ALARM?! QUICK! GET IN THE ELEVATOR!
CHANGE OF PLANS. YOU BOYS DISTRACT THE COPS DOWNSTAIRS WHILE I MAKE OFF WITH THE DIAMOND, OKAY?
BUT... BUT THAT'S NOT FAIR. WE'LL ALL GET ARRESTED!
TELL YOU WHAT. NEXT TIME, *I'LL* HOLD OFF THE COPS AND *YOU* GUYS CAN GET AWAY.
RING RING RING RING RING RING
19

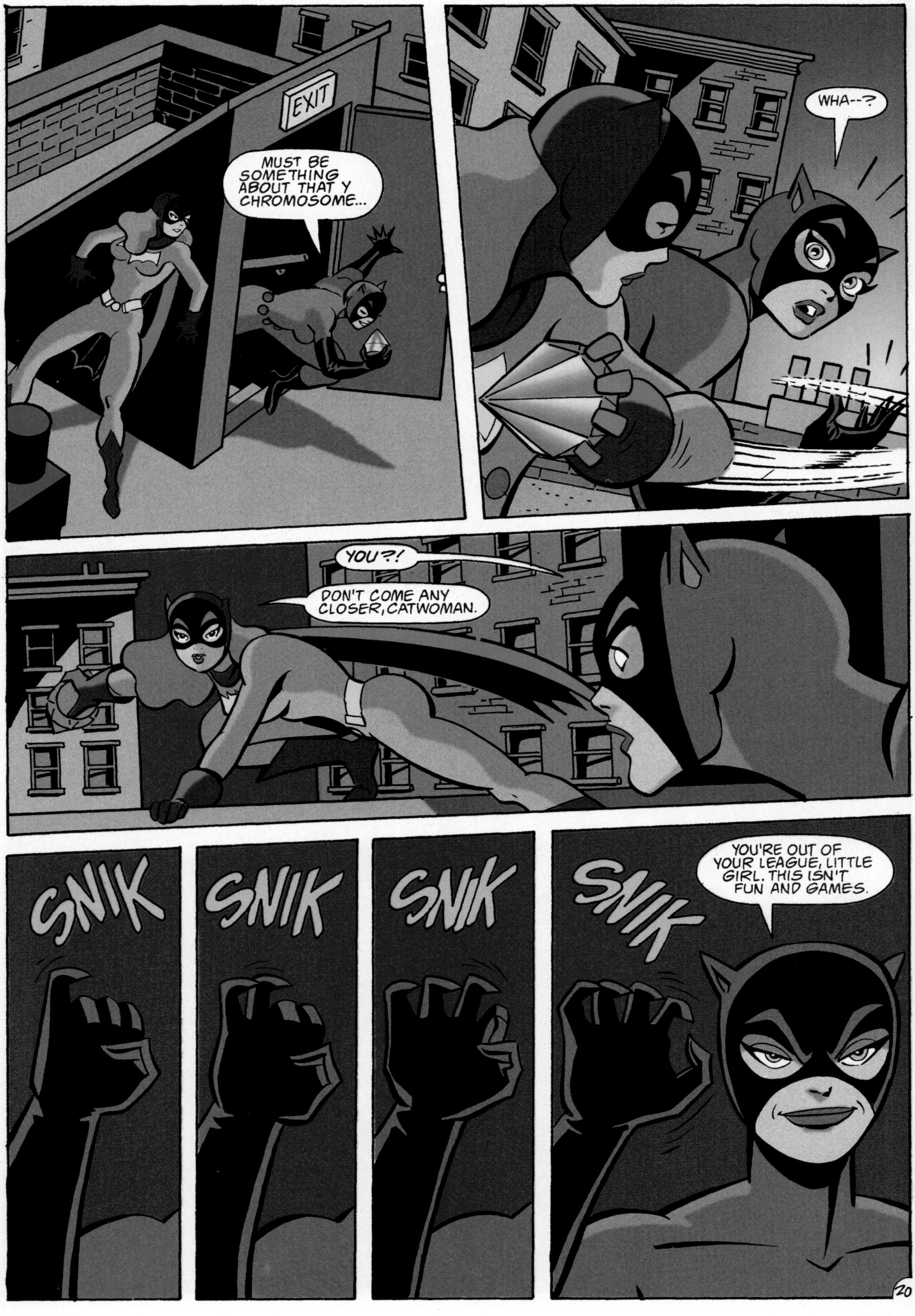
EXIT
MUST BE SOMETHING ABOUT THAT Y CHROMOSOME...
WHA--?
YOU?!
DON'T COME ANY CLOSER, CATWOMAN.
SNIK
SNIK
SNIK
SNIK
YOU'RE OUT OF YOUR LEAGUE, LITTLE GIRL. THIS ISN'T FUN AND GAMES.
20

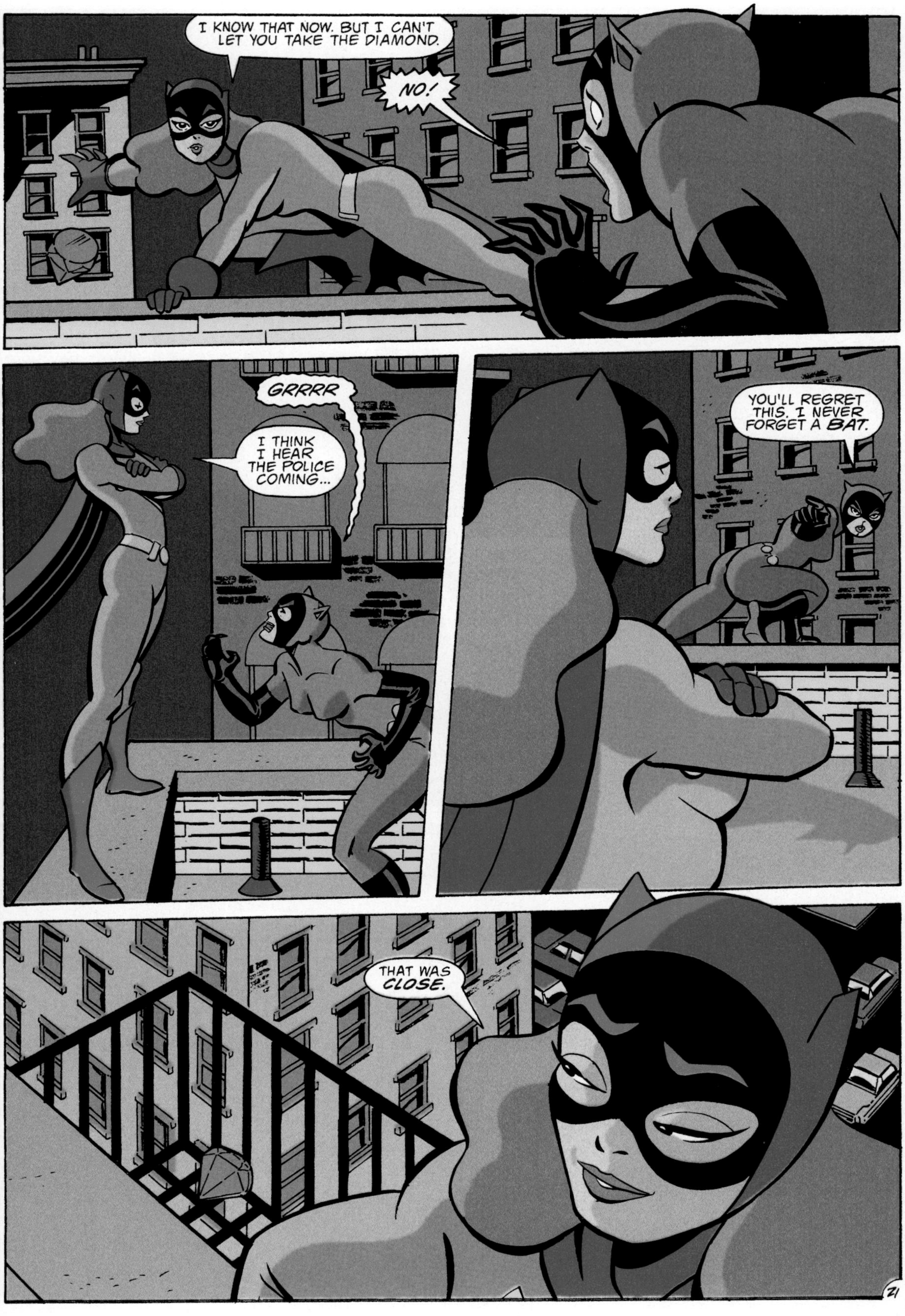

I KNOW THAT NOW. BUT I CAN'T LET YOU TAKE THE DIAMOND.
NO!
GRRRR
I THINK I HEAR THE POLICE COMING...
YOU'LL REGRET THIS. I NEVER FORGET A BAT.
THAT WAS CLOSE.
21

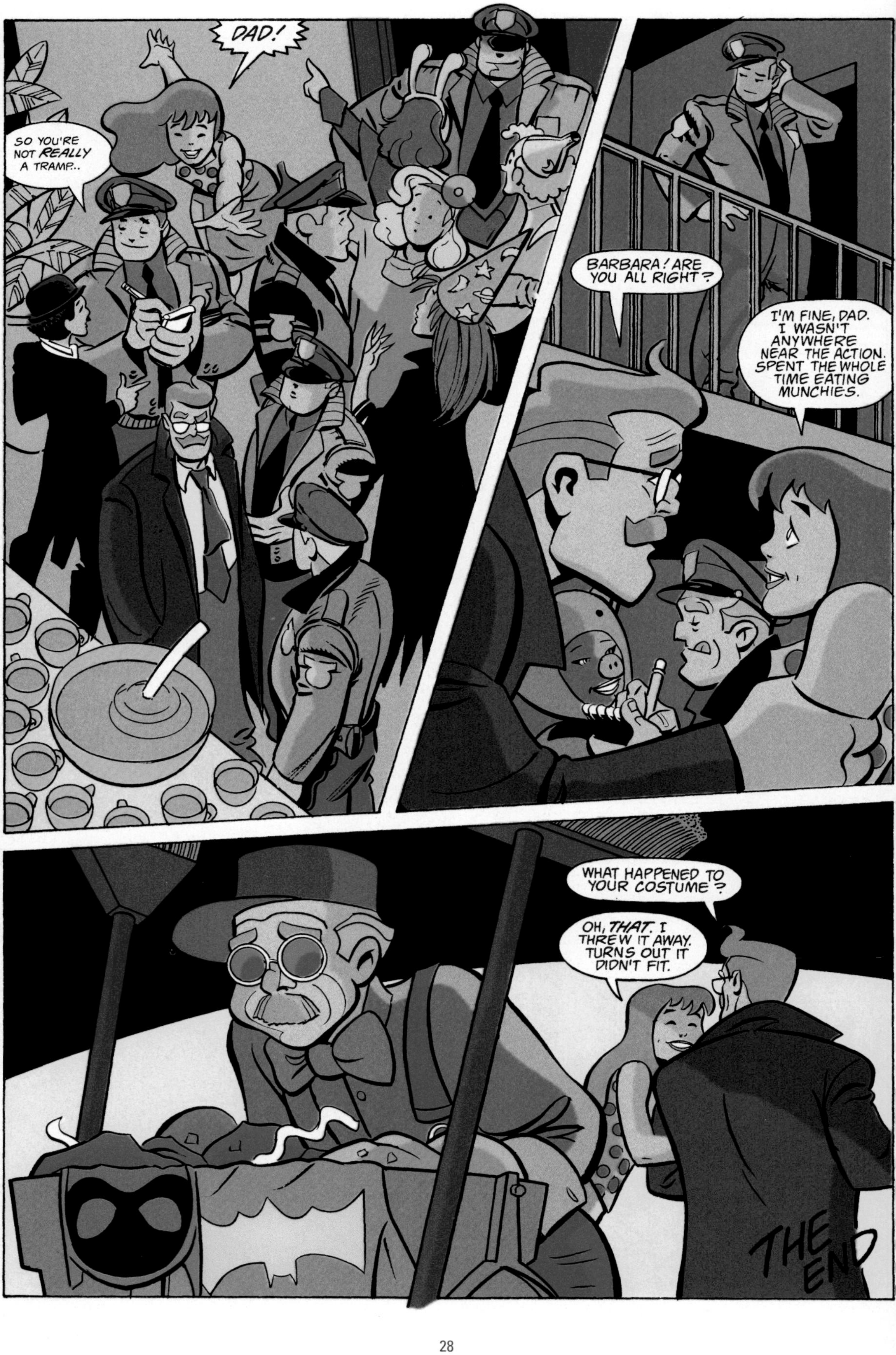
DAD!
SO YOU'RE NOT REALLY A TRAMP..
BARBARA! ARE YOU ALL RIGHT?
I'M FINE, DAD. I WASN'T ANYWHERE NEAR THE ACTION. SPENT THE WHOLE TIME EATING MUNCHIES.
WHAT HAPPENED TO YOUR COSTUME?
OH, THAT. I THREW IT AWAY. TURNS OUT IT DIDN'T FIT.
THE END

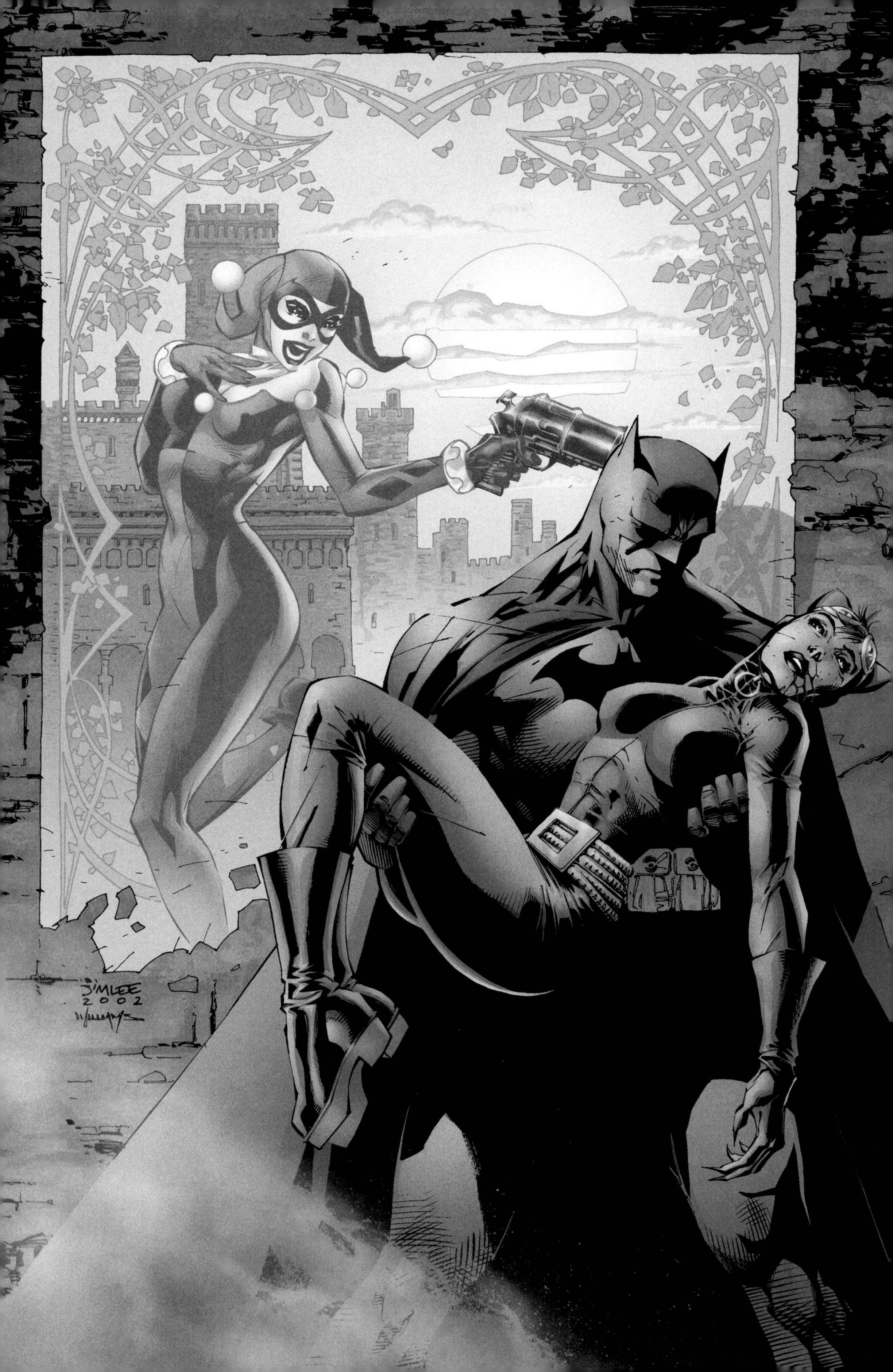
JIMLEE
2002

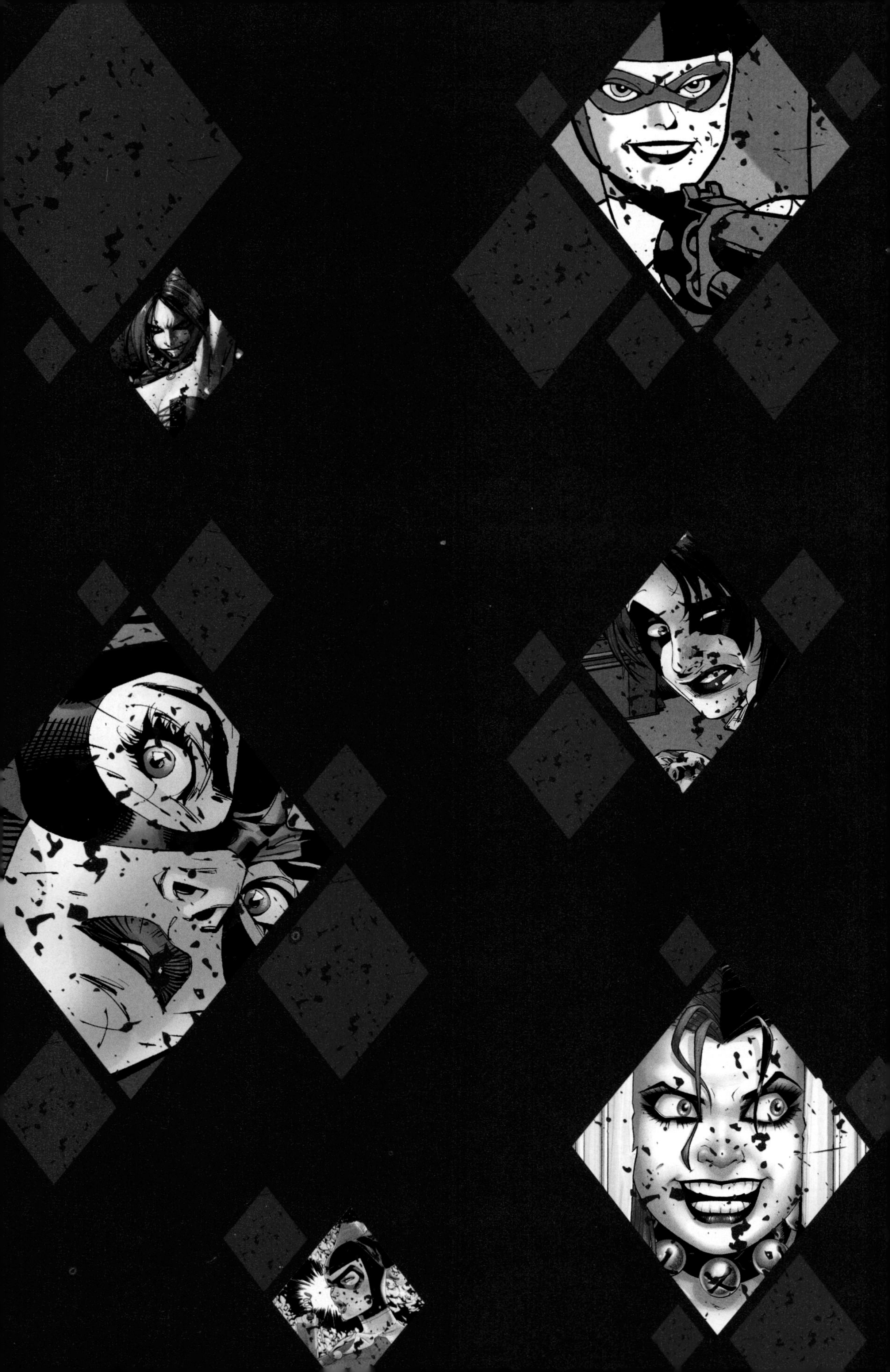

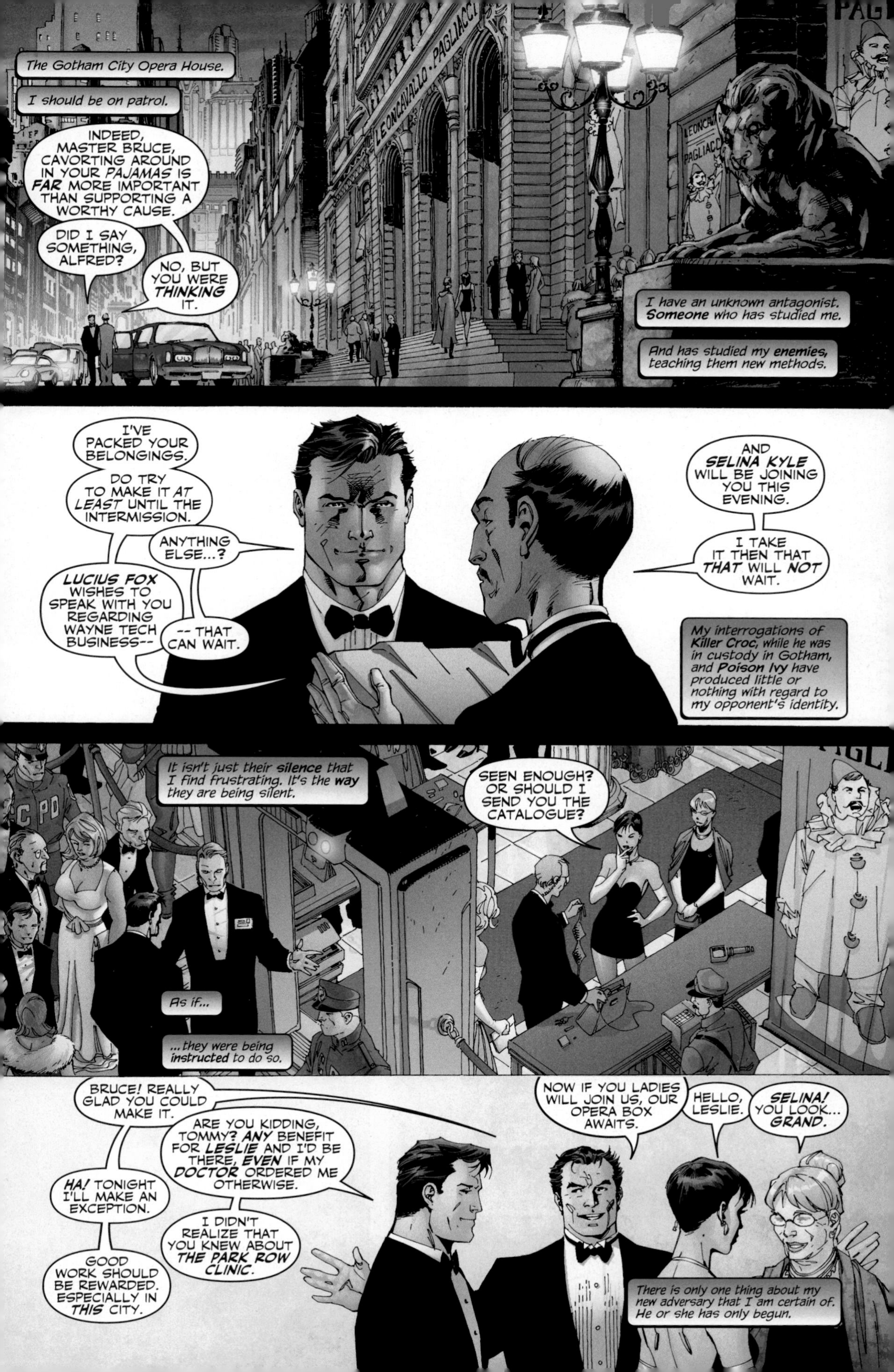

LEONCAVALLO · PAGLIACCI
The Gotham City Opera House.
I should be on patrol.
INDEED, MASTER BRUCE, CAVORTING AROUND IN YOUR PAJAMAS IS FAR MORE IMPORTANT THAN SUPPORTING A WORTHY CAUSE.
DID I SAY SOMETHING, ALFRED?
NO, BUT YOU WERE THINKING IT.
I have an unknown antagonist. Someone who has studied me.
And has studied my enemies, teaching them new methods.
I'VE PACKED YOUR BELONGINGS.
DO TRY TO MAKE IT AT LEAST UNTIL THE INTERMISSION.
ANYTHING ELSE...?
LUCIUS FOX WISHES TO SPEAK WITH YOU REGARDING WAYNE TECH BUSINESS--
-- THAT CAN WAIT.
AND SELINA KYLE WILL BE JOINING YOU THIS EVENING.
I TAKE IT THEN THAT THAT WILL NOT WAIT.
My interrogations of Killer Croc, while he was in custody in Gotham, and Poison Ivy have produced little or nothing with regard to my opponent's identity.
It isn't just their silence that I find frustrating. It's the way they are being silent.
SEEN ENOUGH? OR SHOULD I SEND YOU THE CATALOGUE?
GCPD
As if...
...they were being instructed to do so.
BRUCE! REALLY GLAD YOU COULD MAKE IT.
ARE YOU KIDDING, TOMMY? ANY BENEFIT FOR LESLIE AND I'D BE THERE, EVEN IF MY DOCTOR ORDERED ME OTHERWISE.
HA! TONIGHT I'LL MAKE AN EXCEPTION.
I DIDN'T REALIZE THAT YOU KNEW ABOUT THE PARK ROW CLINIC.
GOOD WORK SHOULD BE REWARDED. ESPECIALLY IN THIS CITY.
NOW IF YOU LADIES WILL JOIN US, OUR OPERA BOX AWAITS.
HELLO, LESLIE.
SELINA! YOU LOOK... GRAND.
There is only one thing about my new adversary that I am certain of. He or she has only begun.

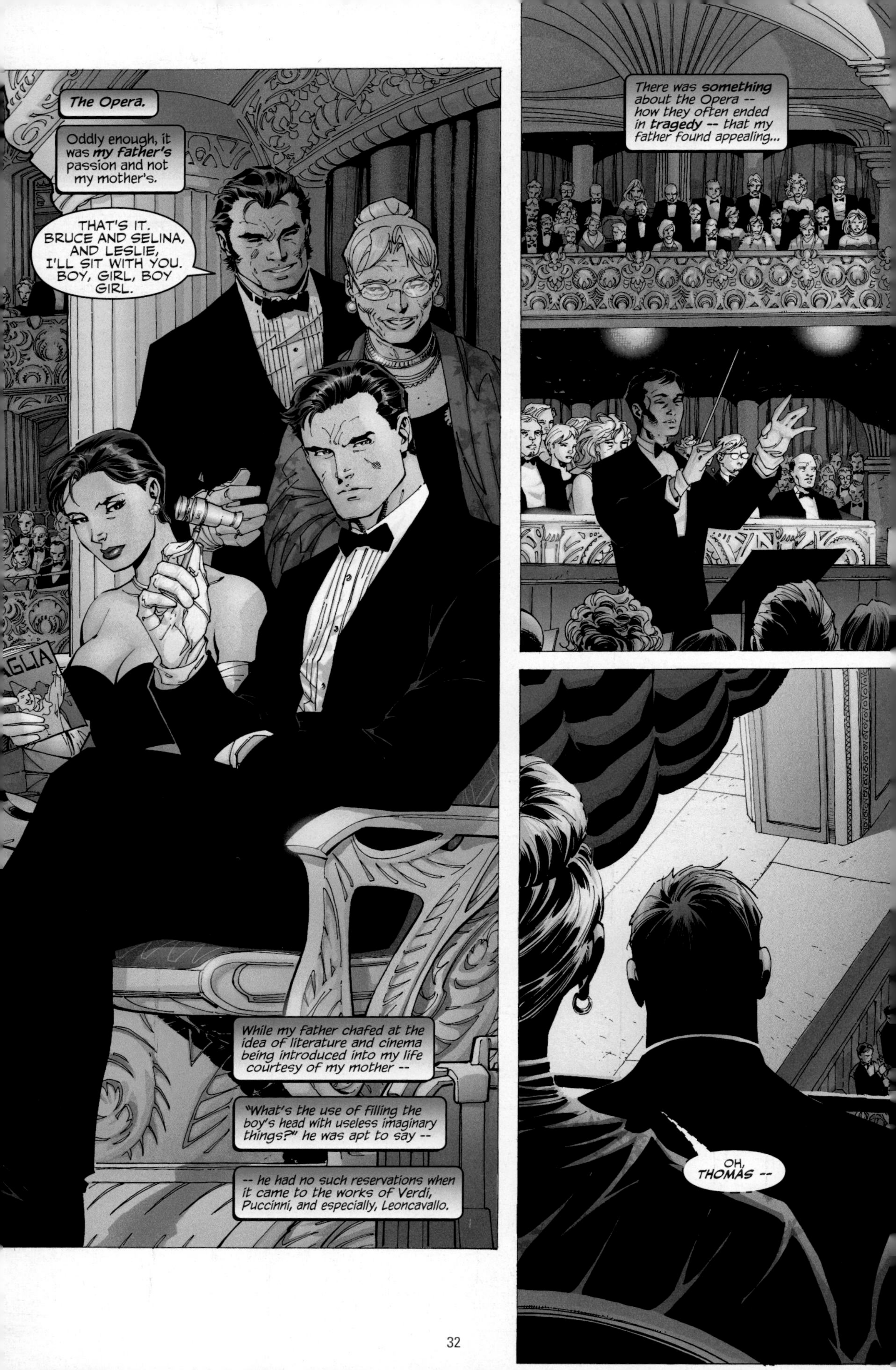
The Opera.
Oddly enough, it was *my father's* passion and not my mother's.
THAT'S IT. BRUCE AND SELINA, AND LESLIE, I'LL SIT WITH YOU. BOY, GIRL, BOY GIRL.
While my father chafed at the idea of literature and cinema being introduced into my life courtesy of my mother --
"What's the use of filling the boy's head with useless imaginary things?" he was apt to say --
-- he had no such reservations when it came to the works of Verdi, Puccini, and especially, Leoncavallo.
There was **something** about the Opera -- how they often ended in **tragedy** -- that my father found appealing...
OH, **THOMAS** --

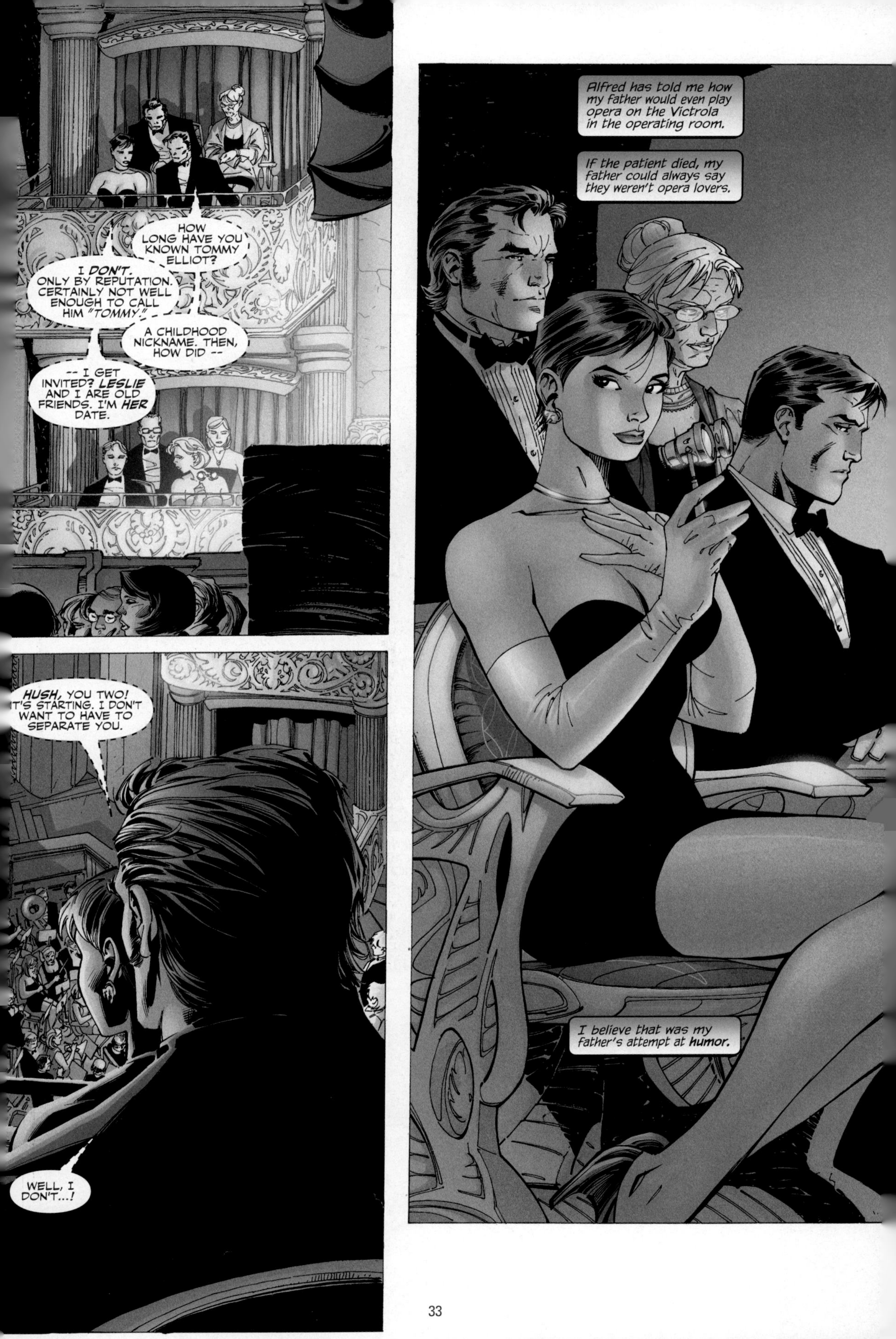
HOW LONG HAVE YOU KNOWN TOMMY ELLIOT?
I DON'T. ONLY BY REPUTATION. CERTAINLY NOT WELL ENOUGH TO CALL HIM "TOMMY."
A CHILDHOOD NICKNAME. THEN, HOW DID --
-- I GET INVITED? LESLIE AND I ARE OLD FRIENDS. I'M HER DATE.
HUSH, YOU TWO! IT'S STARTING. I DON'T WANT TO HAVE TO SEPARATE YOU.
WELL, I DON'T...!
Alfred has told me how my father would even play opera on the Victrola in the operating room.
If the patient died, my father could always say they weren't opera lovers.
I believe that was my father's attempt at humor.

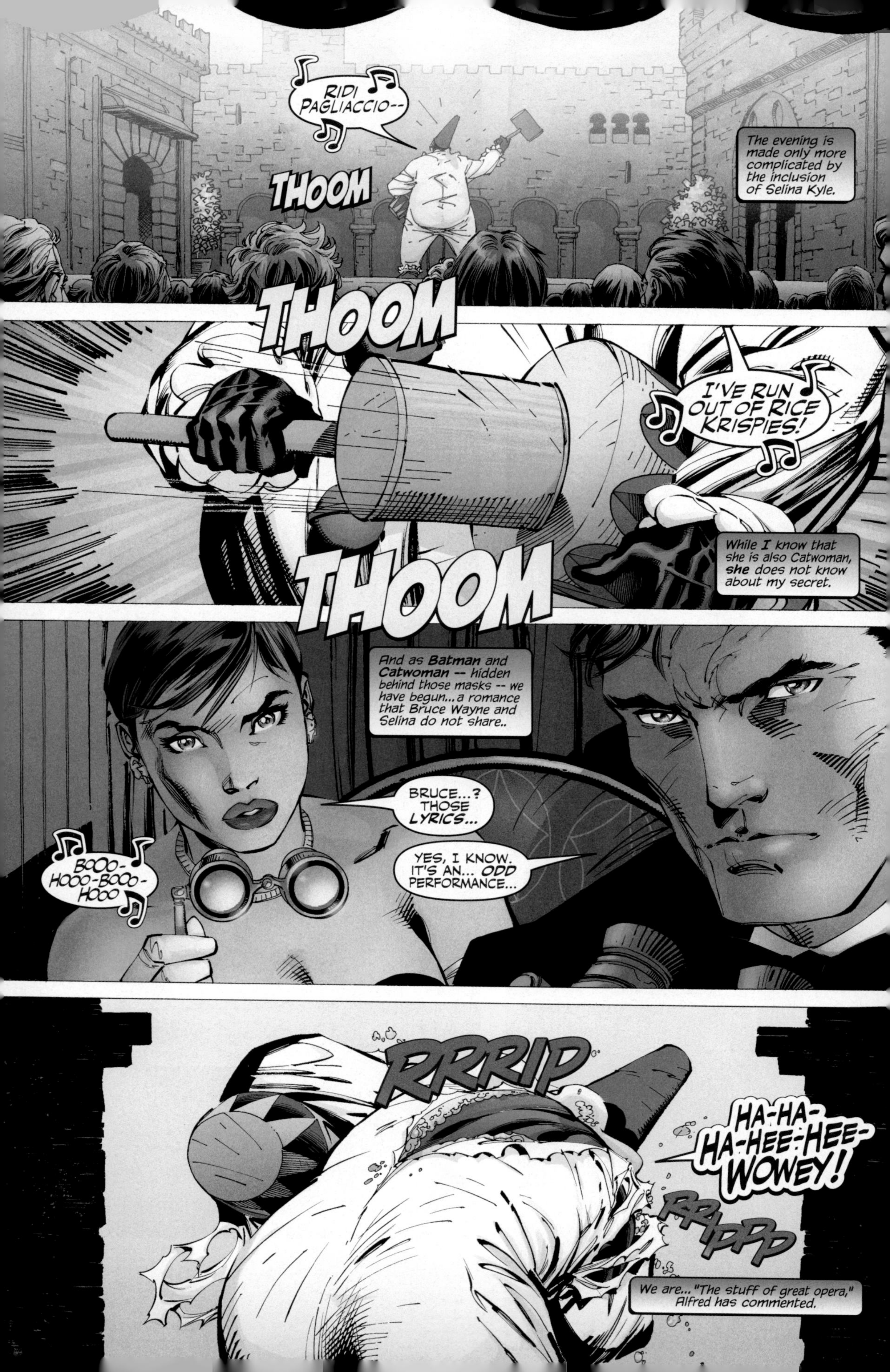
RIDI PAGLIACCIO--
THOOM
The evening is made only more complicated by the inclusion of Selina Kyle.
THOOM
I'VE RUN OUT OF RICE KRISPIES!
THOOM
While I know that she is also Catwoman, she does not know about my secret.
And as Batman and Catwoman -- hidden behind those masks -- we have begun...a romance that Bruce Wayne and Selina do not share..
BRUCE...? THOSE LYRICS...
YES, I KNOW. IT'S AN... ODD PERFORMANCE...
BOOO-HOOO-BOOO-HOOO
RRRIP
HA-HA-HA-HEE-HEE-WOWEY!
RRRIPPP
We are... "The stuff of great opera," Alfred has commented.

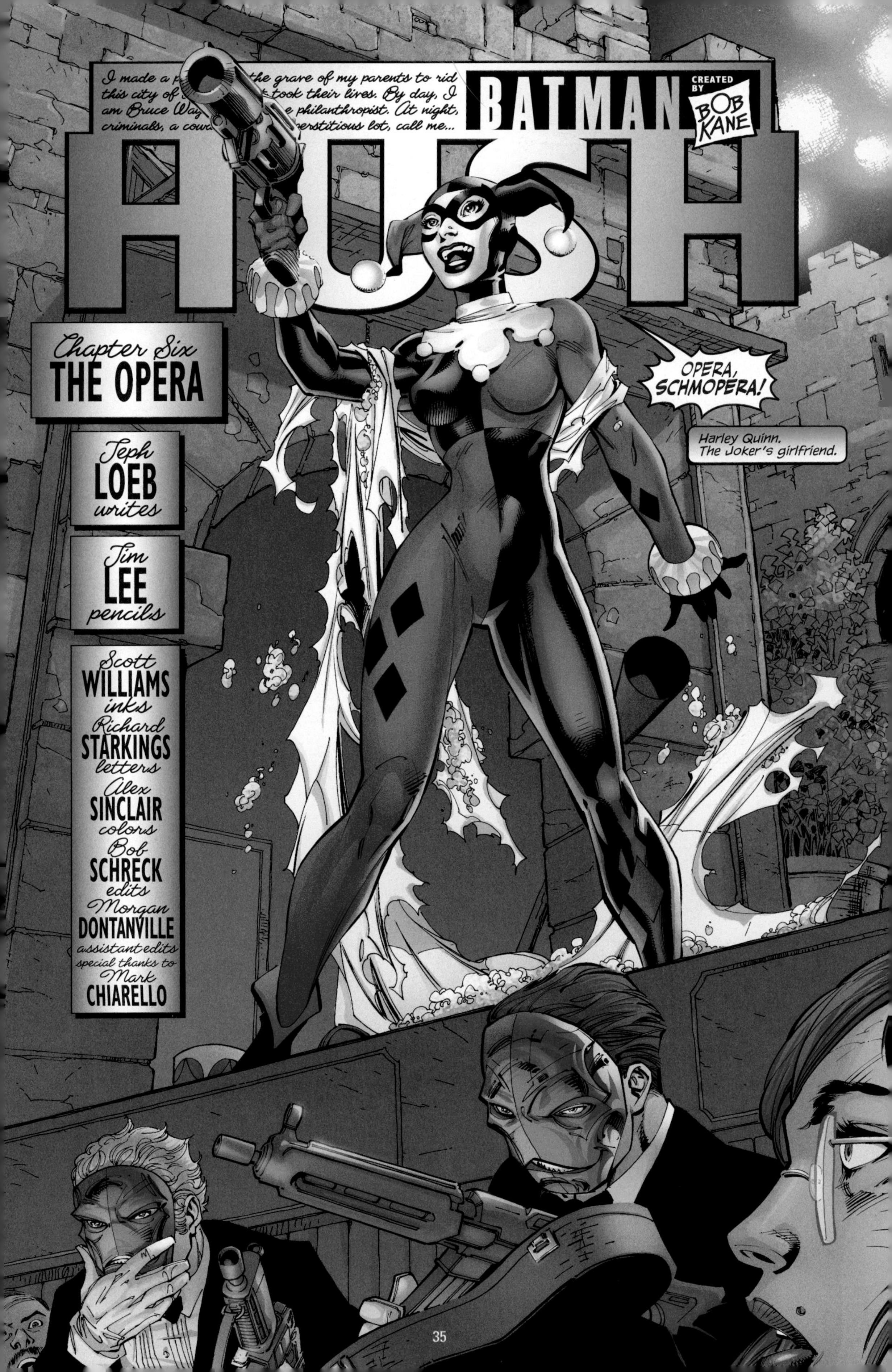
I made a p the grave of my parents to rid
this city of took their lives. By day, I
am Bruce Way e philanthropist. At night,
criminals, a cowa erstitious lot, call me...
BATMAN
CREATED BY BOB KANE
HUSH
Chapter Six
THE OPERA
Jeph LOEB writes
Jim LEE pencils
Scott WILLIAMS inks
Richard STARKINGS letters
Alex SINCLAIR colors
Bob SCHRECK edits
Morgan DONTANVILLE assistant edits
special thanks to Mark CHIARELLO
OPERA, SCHMOPERA!
Harley Quinn.
The Joker's girlfriend.

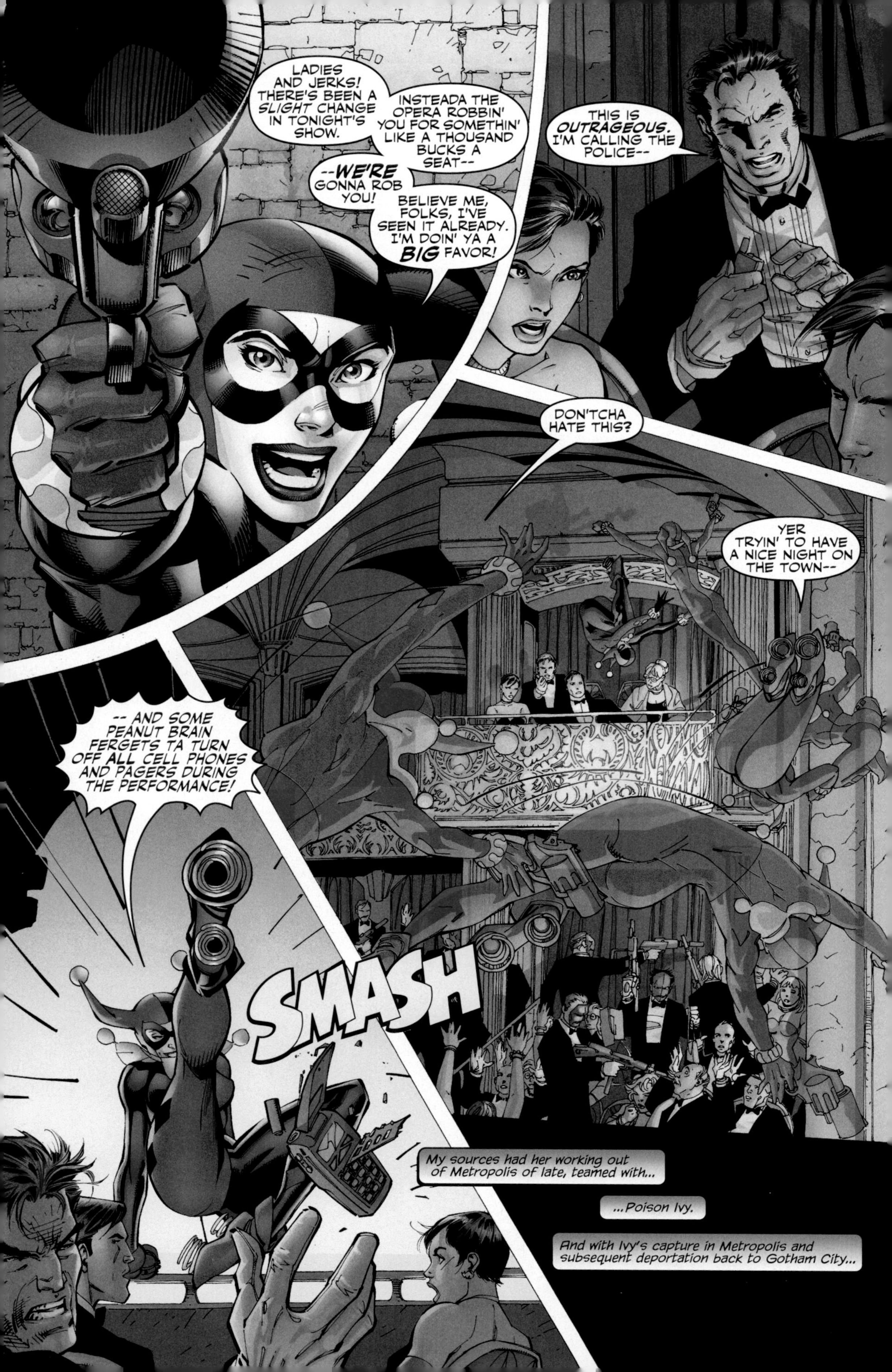

LADIES AND JERKS! THERE'S BEEN A SLIGHT CHANGE IN TONIGHT'S SHOW.
INSTEADA THE OPERA ROBBIN' YOU FOR SOMETHIN' LIKE A THOUSAND BUCKS A SEAT--
--WE'RE GONNA ROB YOU!
BELIEVE ME, FOLKS, I'VE SEEN IT ALREADY. I'M DOIN' YA A BIG FAVOR!
THIS IS OUTRAGEOUS. I'M CALLING THE POLICE--
DON'TCHA HATE THIS?
YER TRYIN' TO HAVE A NICE NIGHT ON THE TOWN--
-- AND SOME PEANUT BRAIN FERGETS TA TURN OFF ALL CELL PHONES AND PAGERS DURING THE PERFORMANCE!
SMASH
My sources had her working out of Metropolis of late, teamed with...
...Poison Ivy.
And with Ivy's capture in Metropolis and subsequent deportation back to Gotham City...

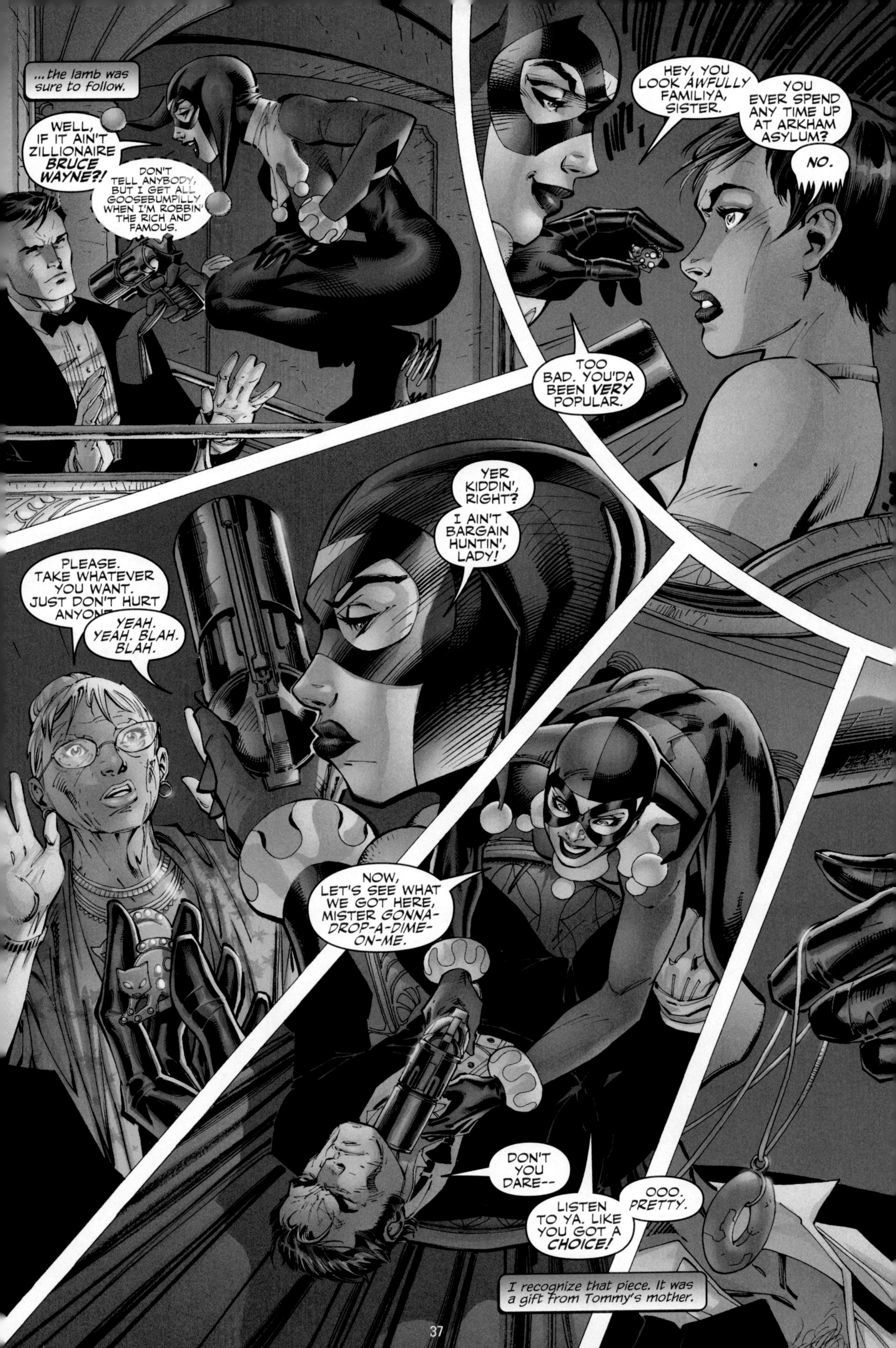
...the lamb was sure to follow.
WELL, IF IT AIN'T ZILLIONAIRE BRUCE WAYNE?!
DON'T TELL ANYBODY, BUT I GET ALL GOOSEBUMPILLY WHEN I'M ROBBIN' THE RICH AND FAMOUS.
HEY, YOU LOOK AWFULLY FAMILIYA, SISTER.
YOU EVER SPEND ANY TIME UP AT ARKHAM ASYLUM?
NO.
TOO BAD. YOU'DA BEEN VERY POPULAR.
YER KIDDIN', RIGHT? I AIN'T BARGAIN HUNTIN', LADY!
PLEASE. TAKE WHATEVER YOU WANT. JUST DON'T HURT ANYON
YEAH. YEAH. BLAH. BLAH.
NOW, LET'S SEE WHAT WE GOT HERE, MISTER GONNA-DROP-A-DIME-ON-ME.
DON'T YOU DARE--
LISTEN TO YA. LIKE YOU GOT A CHOICE!
OOO. PRETTY.
I recognize that piece. It was a gift from Tommy's mother.

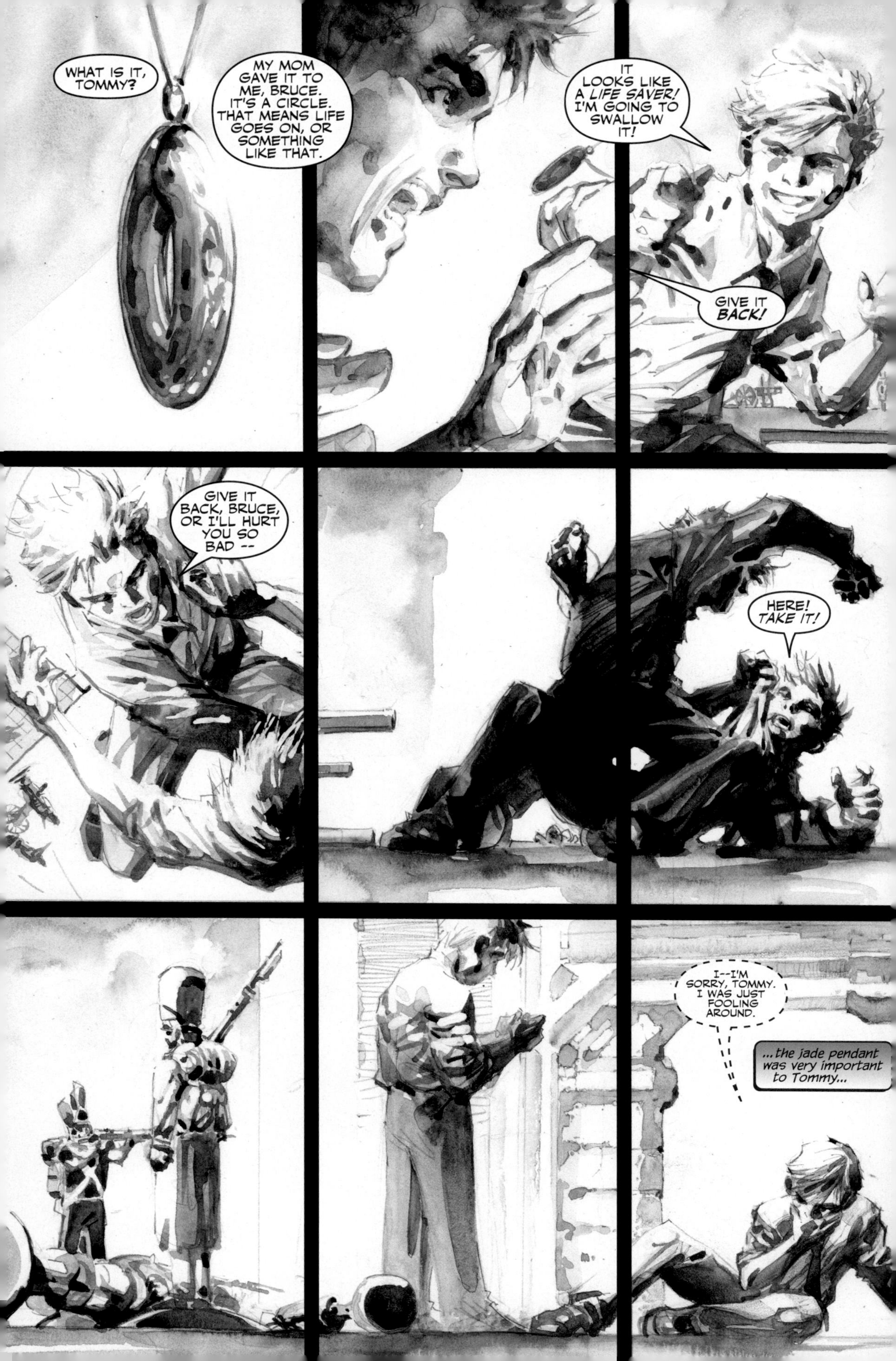
WHAT IS IT, TOMMY?
MY MOM GAVE IT TO ME, BRUCE. IT'S A CIRCLE. THAT MEANS LIFE GOES ON, OR SOMETHING LIKE THAT.
IT LOOKS LIKE A *LIFE SAVER!* I'M GOING TO SWALLOW IT!
GIVE IT *BACK!*
GIVE IT BACK, BRUCE, OR I'LL HURT YOU SO BAD --
HERE! *TAKE IT!*
I--I'M SORRY, TOMMY. I WAS JUST FOOLING AROUND.
...the jade pendant was very important to Tommy...

NO!

I know something of a Mother's things --

FINDERS KEEPERS --

LOSERS --

EEP.

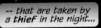

-- that are taken by a thief in the night...

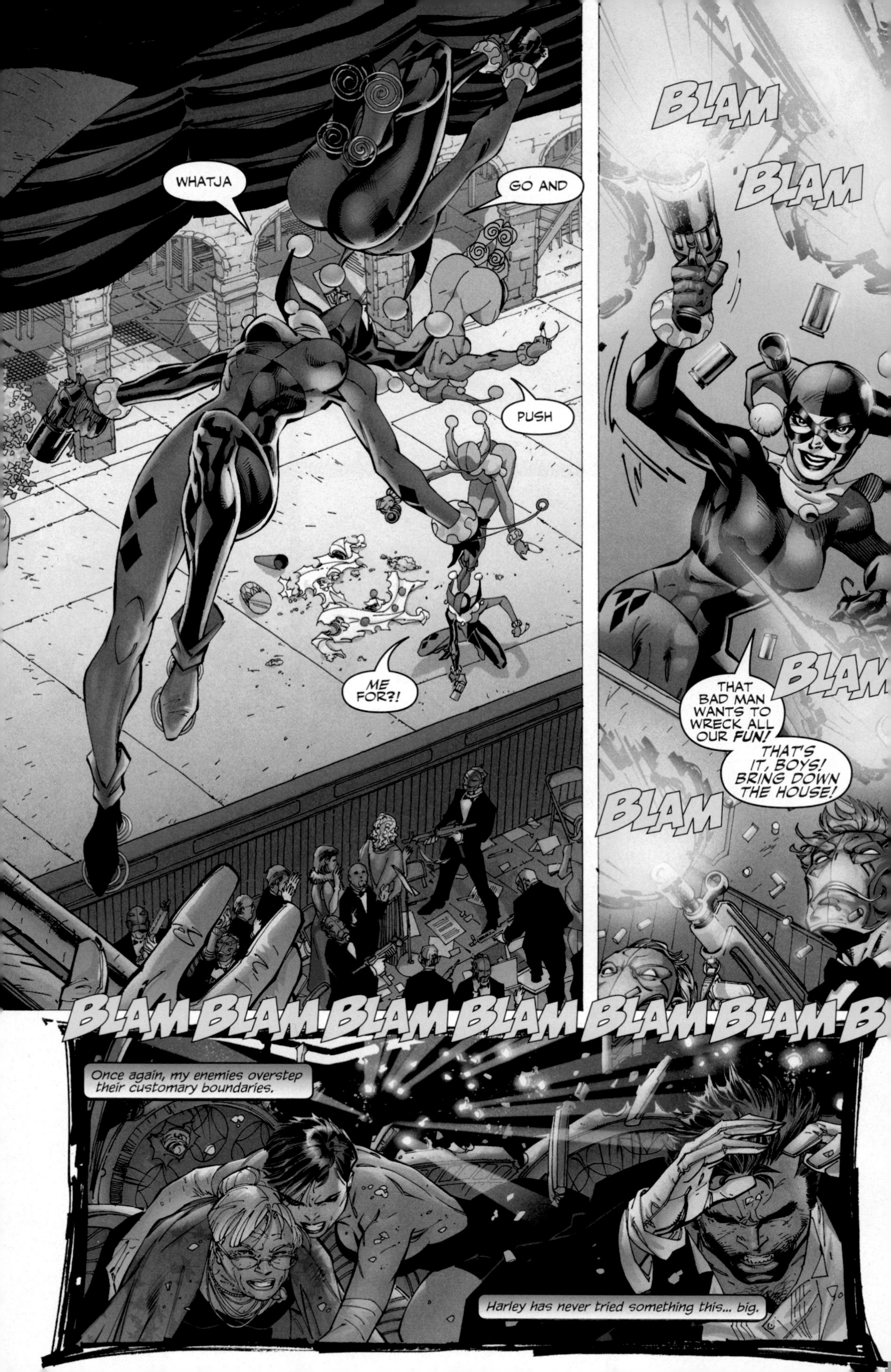
WHATJA
GO AND
PUSH
ME FOR?!
BLAM
BLAM
THAT BAD MAN WANTS TO WRECK ALL OUR FUN!
THAT'S IT, BOYS! BRING DOWN THE HOUSE!
BLAM
BLAM
BLAM BLAM BLAM BLAM BLAM BLAM B
Once again, my enemies overstep their customary boundaries.
Harley has never tried something this... big.

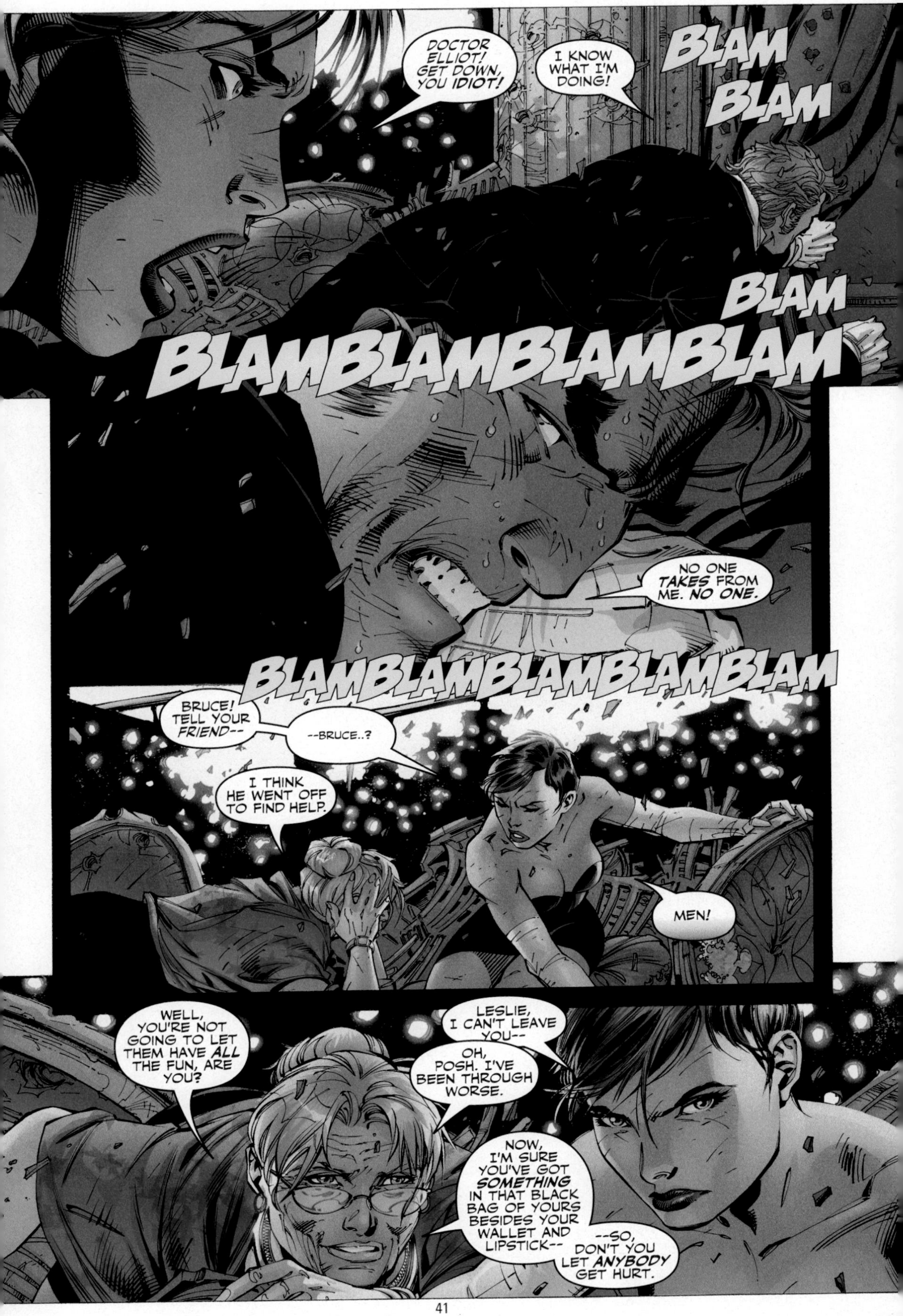
DOCTOR ELLIOT! GET DOWN, YOU IDIOT!
I KNOW WHAT I'M DOING!
BLAM
BLAM
BLAM
BLAMBLAMBLAMBLAM
NO ONE TAKES FROM ME. NO ONE.
BLAMBLAMBLAMBLAMBLAM
BRUCE! TELL YOUR FRIEND--
--BRUCE..?
I THINK HE WENT OFF TO FIND HELP.
MEN!
WELL, YOU'RE NOT GOING TO LET THEM HAVE ALL THE FUN, ARE YOU?
LESLIE, I CAN'T LEAVE YOU--
OH, POSH. I'VE BEEN THROUGH WORSE.
NOW, I'M SURE YOU'VE GOT SOMETHING IN THAT BLACK BAG OF YOURS BESIDES YOUR WALLET AND LIPSTICK--
--SO, DON'T YOU LET ANYBODY GET HURT.

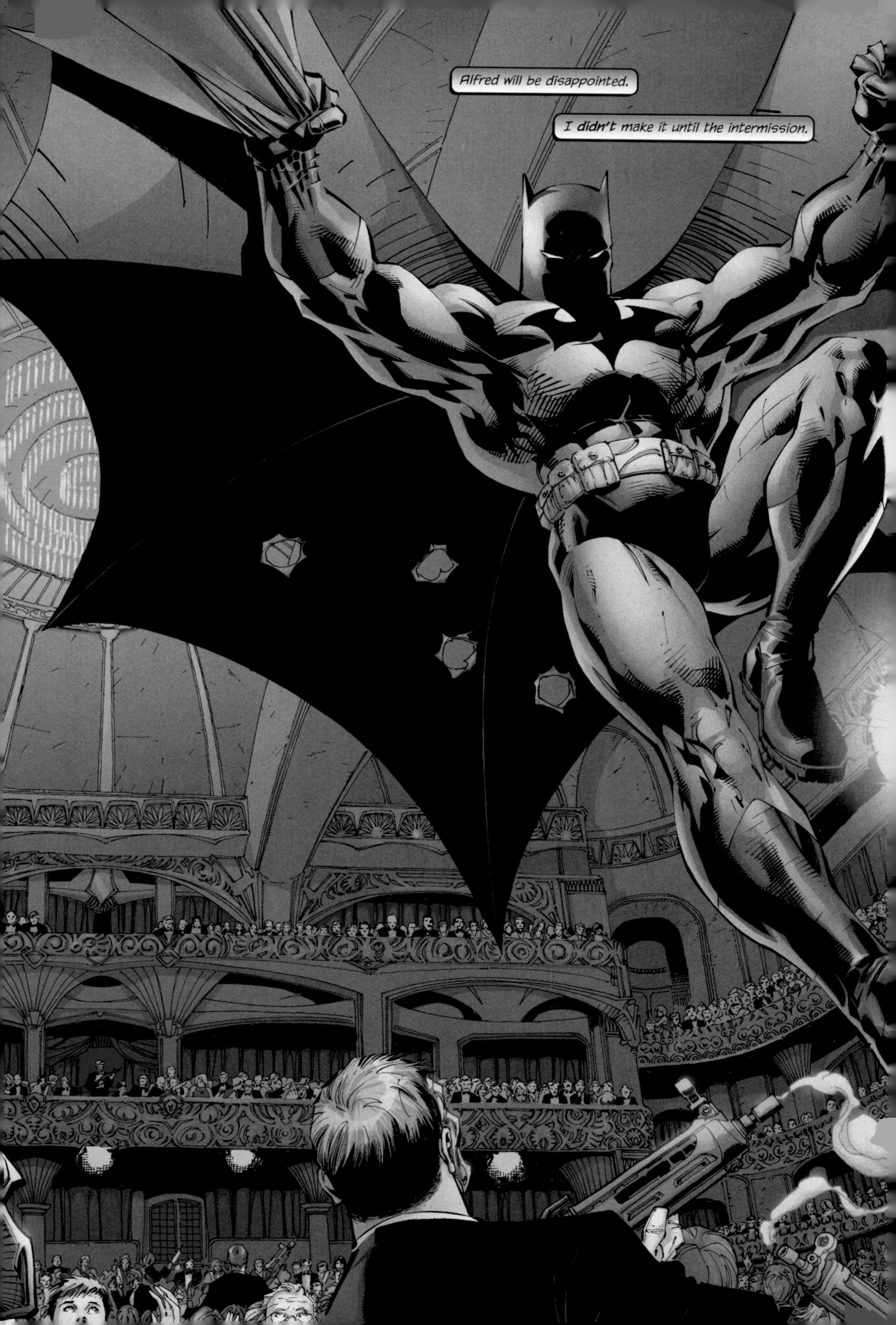
Alfred will be disappointed.
I didn't make it until the intermission.

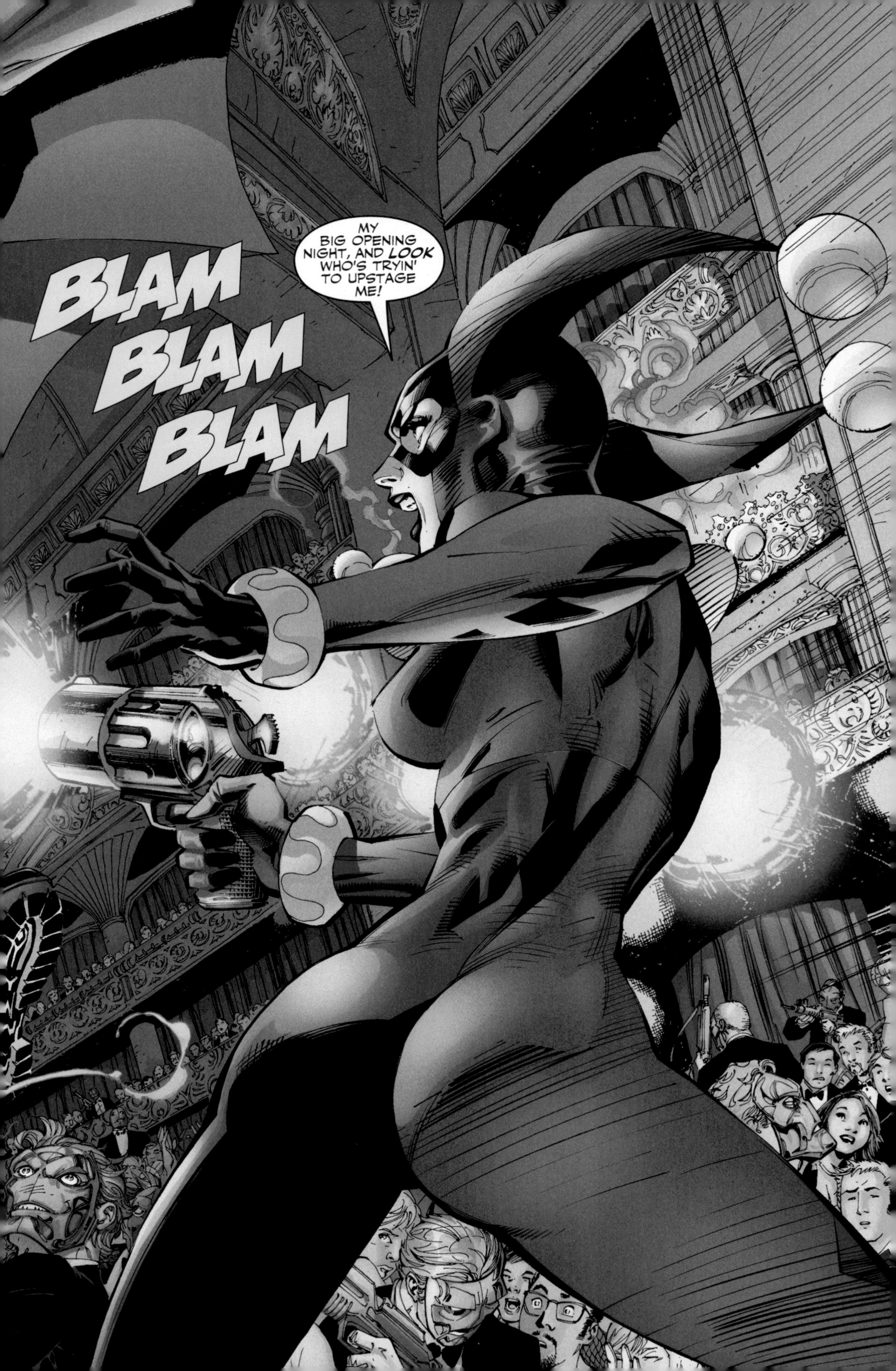
MY BIG OPENING NIGHT, AND LOOK WHO'S TRYIN' TO UPSTAGE ME!
BLAM BLAM BLAM

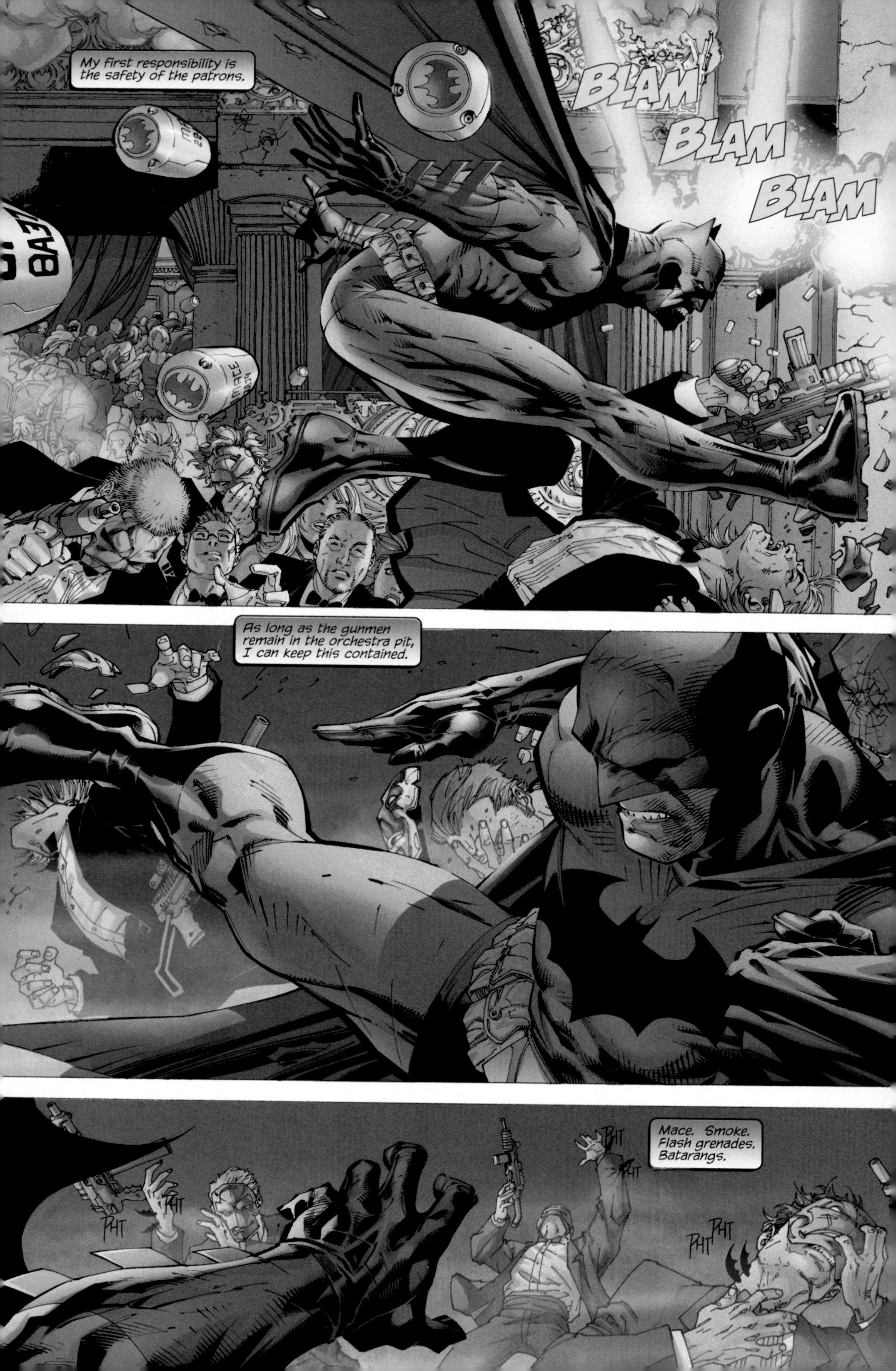
My first responsibility is the safety of the patrons.
BLAM
BLAM
BLAM
As long as the gunmen remain in the orchestra pit, I can keep this contained.
Mace. Smoke. Flash grenades. Batarangs.
PHT
PHT
PHT
PHT
PHT
PHT

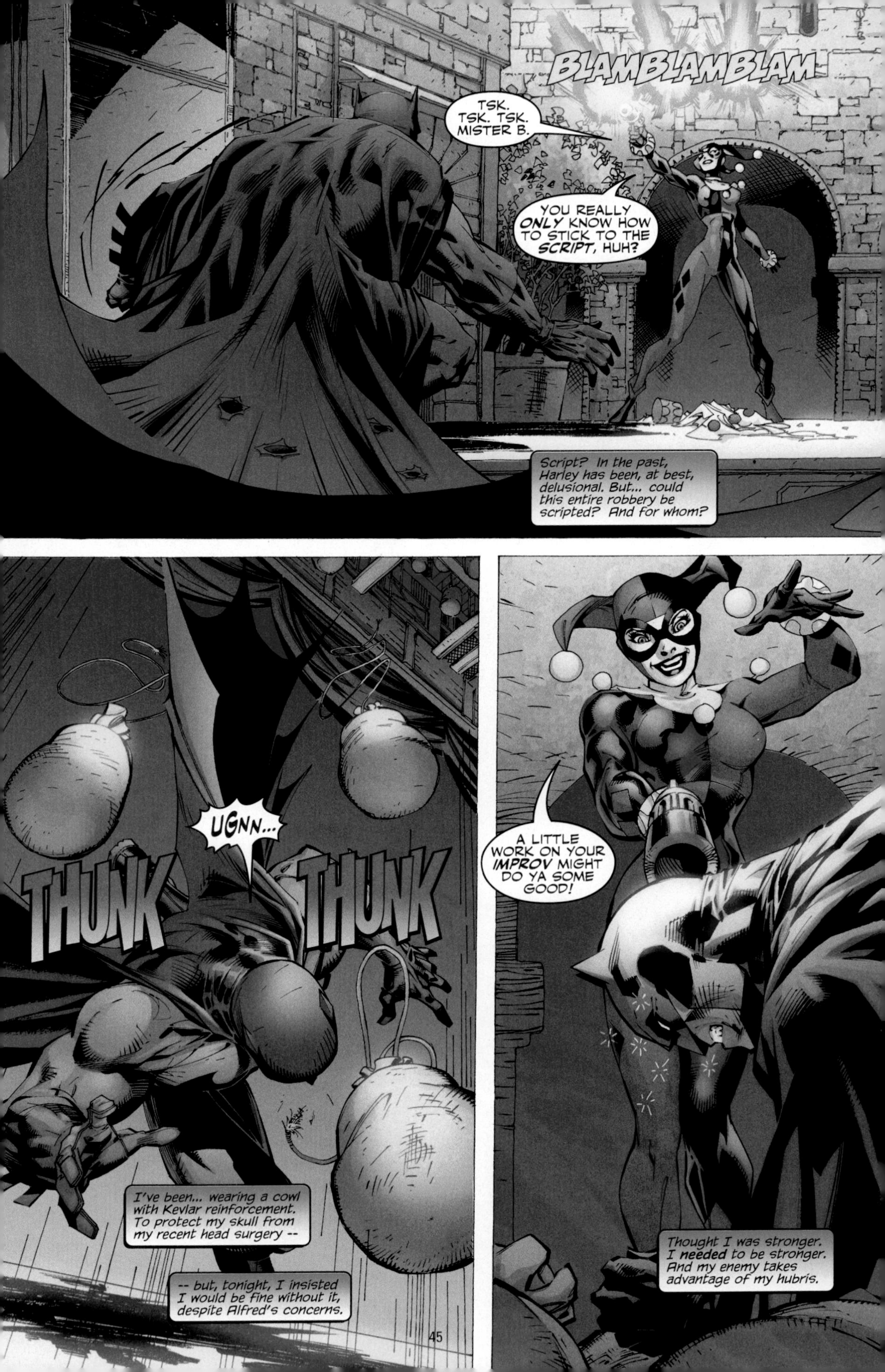
BLAMBLAMBLAM
TSK. TSK. TSK. MISTER B.
YOU REALLY ONLY KNOW HOW TO STICK TO THE SCRIPT, HUH?
Script? In the past, Harley has been, at best, delusional. But... could this entire robbery be scripted? And for whom?
UGNN...
THUNK
THUNK
I've been... wearing a cowl with Kevlar reinforcement. To protect my skull from my recent head surgery --
-- but, tonight, I insisted I would be fine without it, despite Alfred's concerns.
A LITTLE WORK ON YOUR IMPROV MIGHT DO YA SOME GOOD!
Thought I was stronger. I needed to be stronger. And my enemy takes advantage of my hubris.

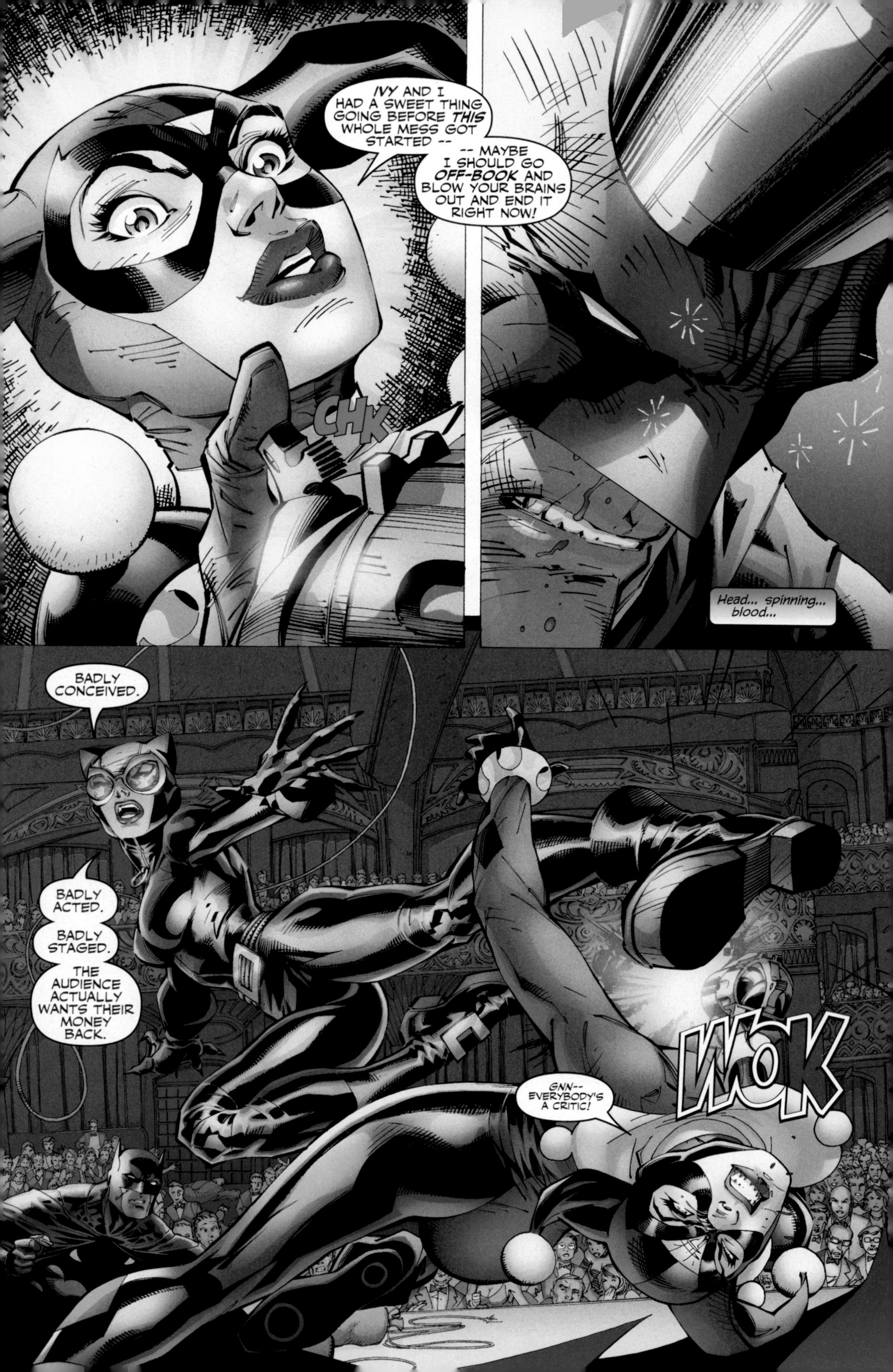
IVY AND I HAD A SWEET THING GOING BEFORE THIS WHOLE MESS GOT STARTED --
-- MAYBE I SHOULD GO OFF-BOOK AND BLOW YOUR BRAINS OUT AND END IT RIGHT NOW!
CHK
Head... spinning... blood...
BADLY CONCEIVED.
BADLY ACTED.
BADLY STAGED.
THE AUDIENCE ACTUALLY WANTS THEIR MONEY BACK.
WOK
GNN-- EVERYBODY'S A CRITIC!

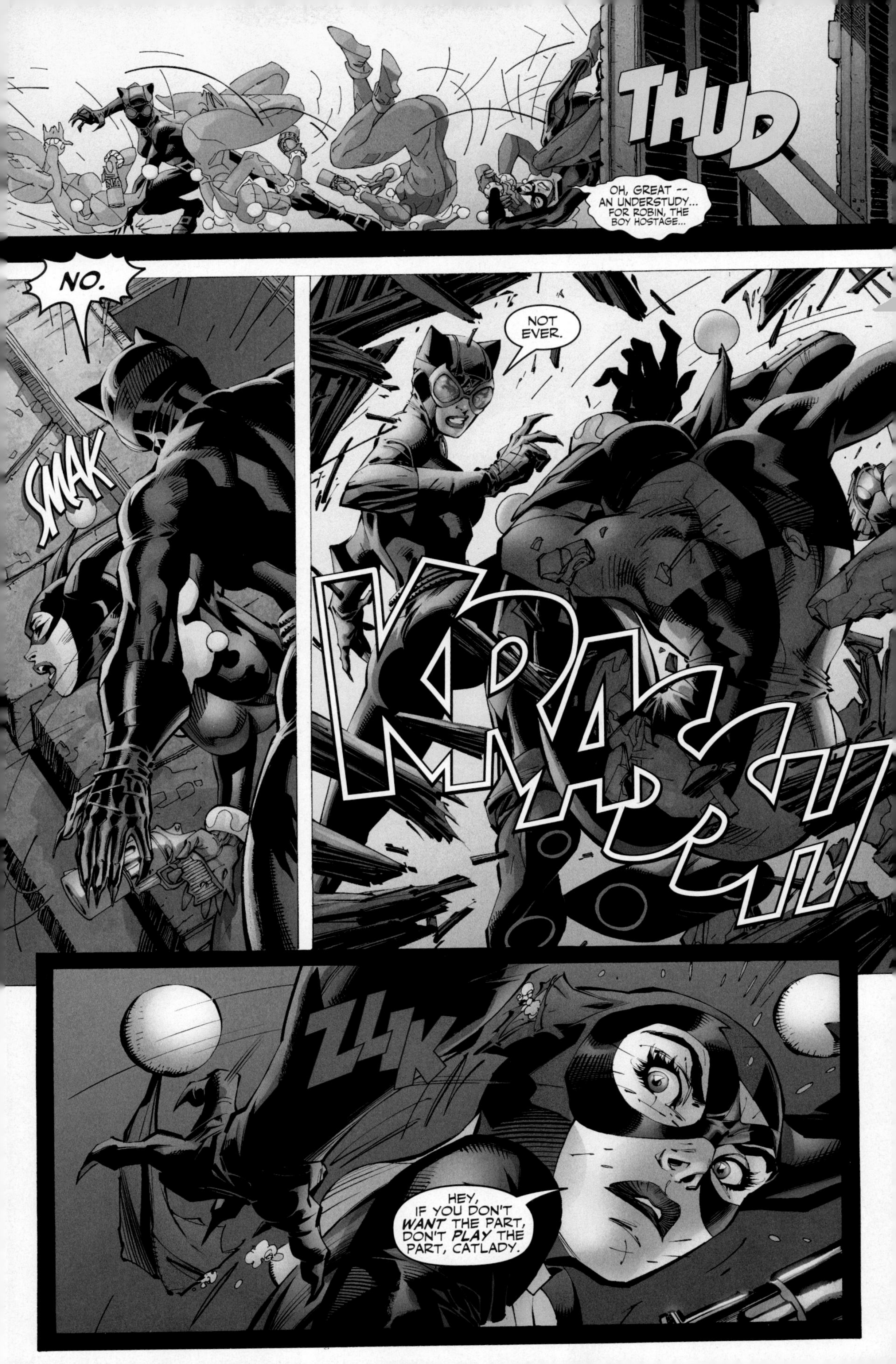
THUD
OH, GREAT -- AN UNDERSTUDY... FOR ROBIN, THE BOY HOSTAGE...
NO.
SMAK
NOT EVER.
KRAKCH
ZZK
HEY, IF YOU DON'T *WANT* THE PART, DON'T *PLAY* THE PART, CATLADY.

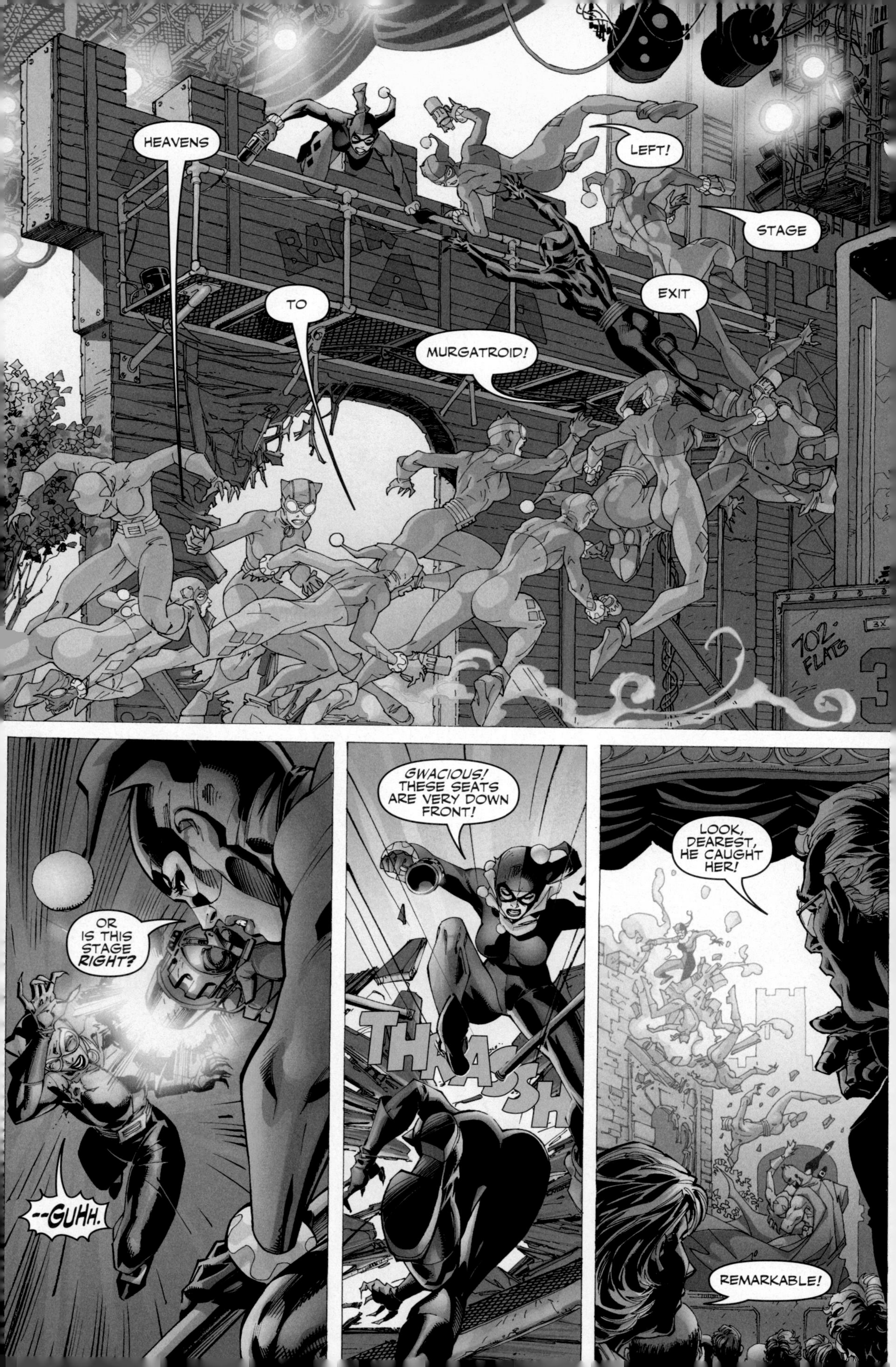
HEAVENS
TO
MURGATROID!
LEFT!
STAGE
EXIT
702 FLATS
OR IS THIS STAGE RIGHT?
--GUHH.
GWACIOUS! THESE SEATS ARE VERY DOWN FRONT!
THRASH
LOOK, DEAREST, HE CAUGHT HER!
REMARKABLE!

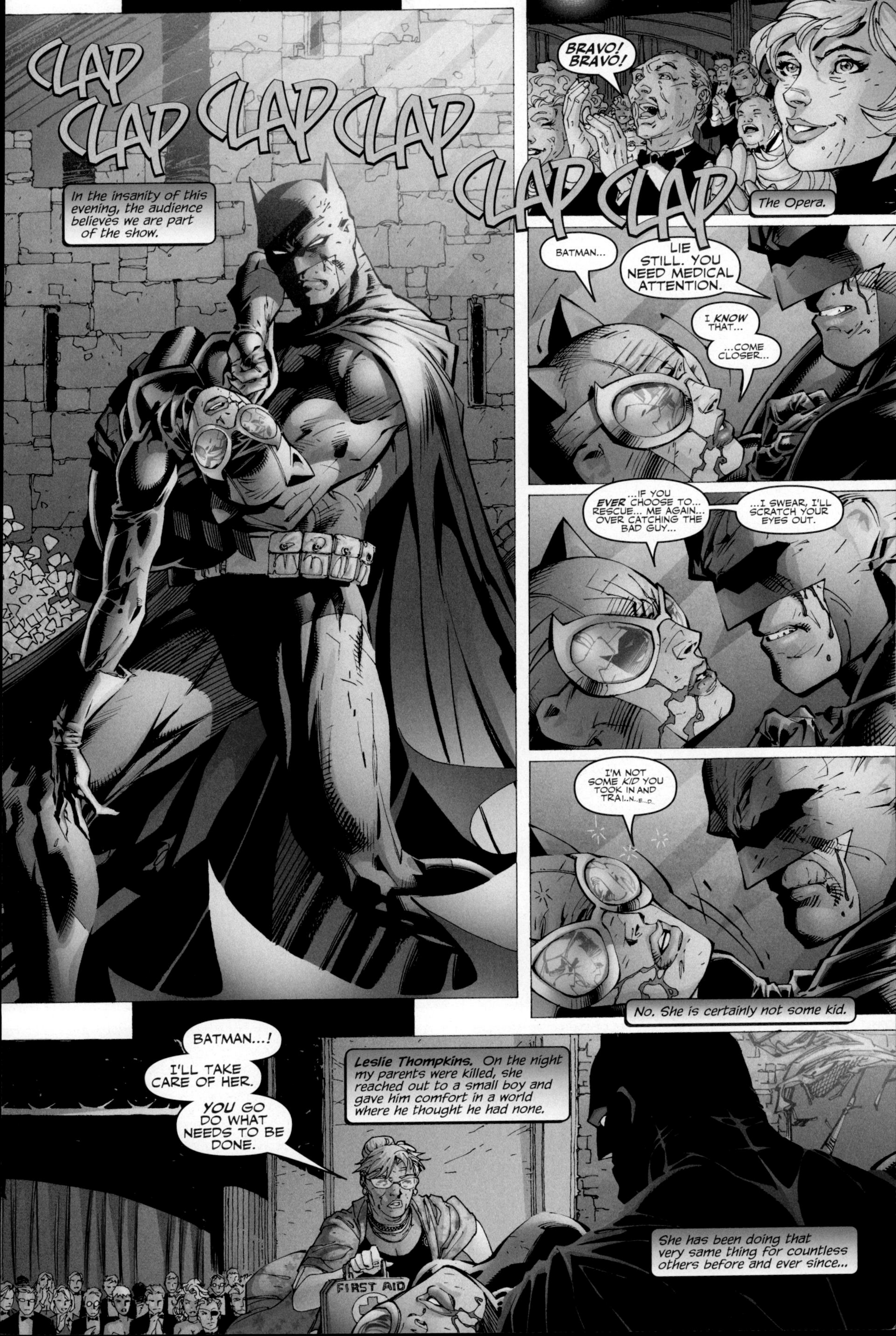
CLAP CLAP CLAP CLAP CLAP CLAP
In the insanity of this evening, the audience believes we are part of the show.
BRAVO! BRAVO!
The Opera.
BATMAN...
LIE STILL. YOU NEED MEDICAL ATTENTION.
I KNOW THAT...
...COME CLOSER...
...IF YOU EVER CHOOSE TO... RESCUE... ME AGAIN... OVER CATCHING THE BAD GUY...
...I SWEAR, I'LL SCRATCH YOUR EYES OUT.
I'M NOT SOME KID YOU TOOK IN AND TRAI..N..E..D.
No. She is certainly not some kid.
BATMAN...!
I'LL TAKE CARE OF HER.
YOU GO DO WHAT NEEDS TO BE DONE.
Leslie Thompkins. On the night my parents were killed, she reached out to a small boy and gave him comfort in a world where he thought he had none.
She has been doing that very same thing for countless others before and ever since...
FIRST AID

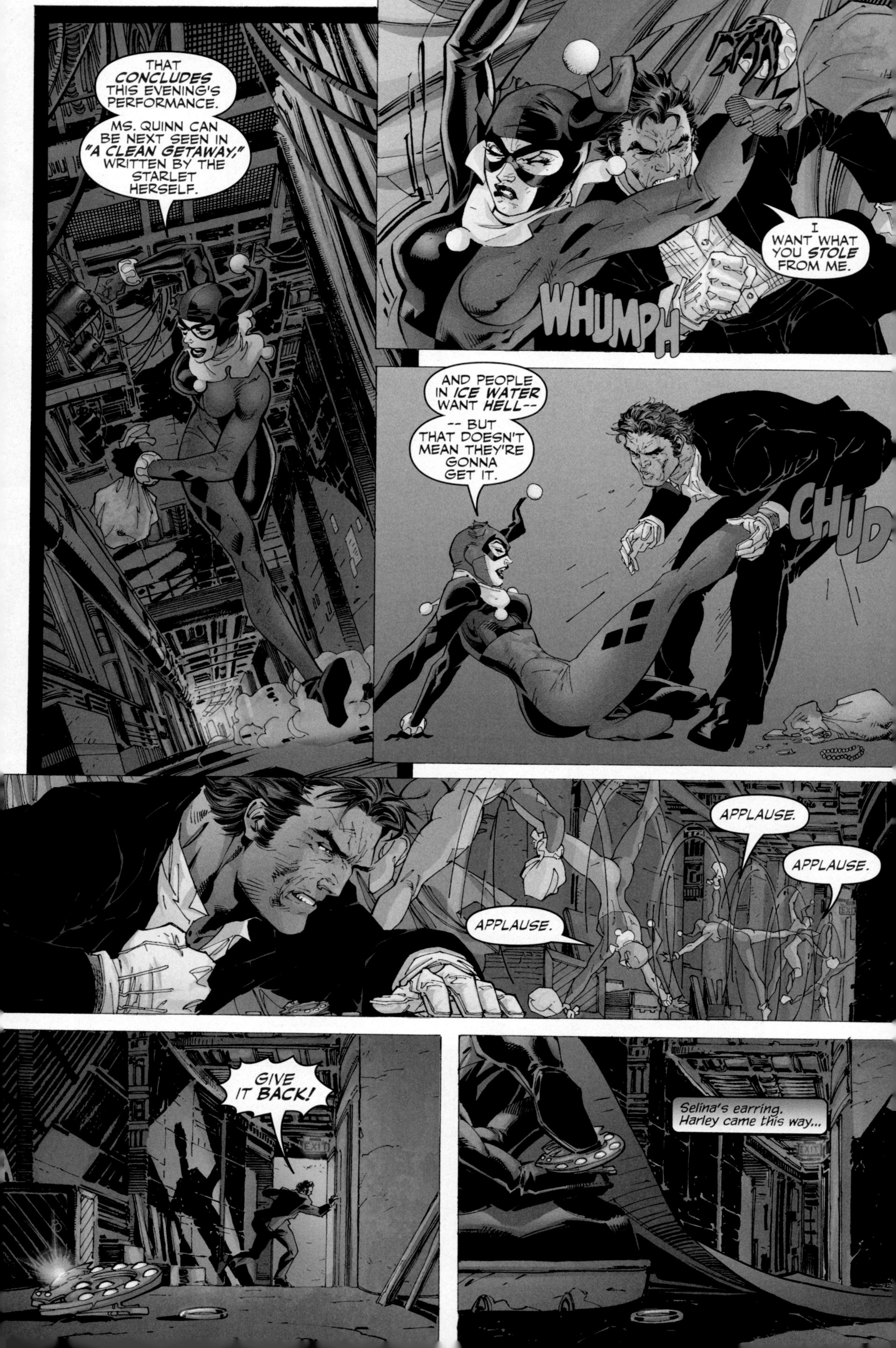
THAT CONCLUDES THIS EVENING'S PERFORMANCE.
MS. QUINN CAN BE NEXT SEEN IN "A CLEAN GETAWAY," WRITTEN BY THE STARLET HERSELF.
I WANT WHAT YOU STOLE FROM ME.
WHUMPH
AND PEOPLE IN ICE WATER WANT HELL--
-- BUT THAT DOESN'T MEAN THEY'RE GONNA GET IT.
CHUD
APPLAUSE.
APPLAUSE.
APPLAUSE.
GIVE IT BACK!
EXIT
Selina's earring. Harley came this way...
EXIT

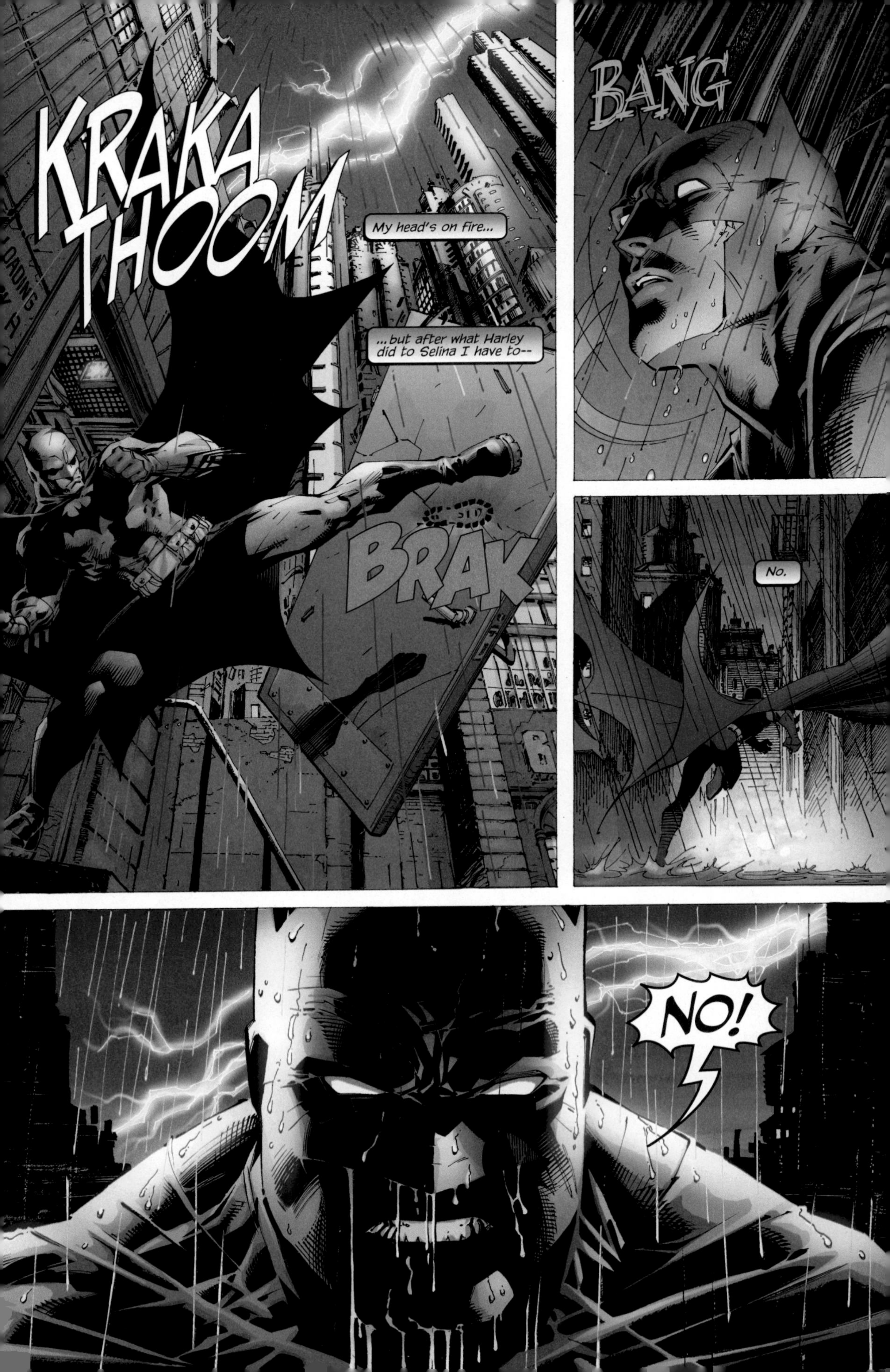
KRAKA THOOM
My head's on fire...
...but after what Harley did to Selina I have to--
BRAK
BANG
No.
NO!

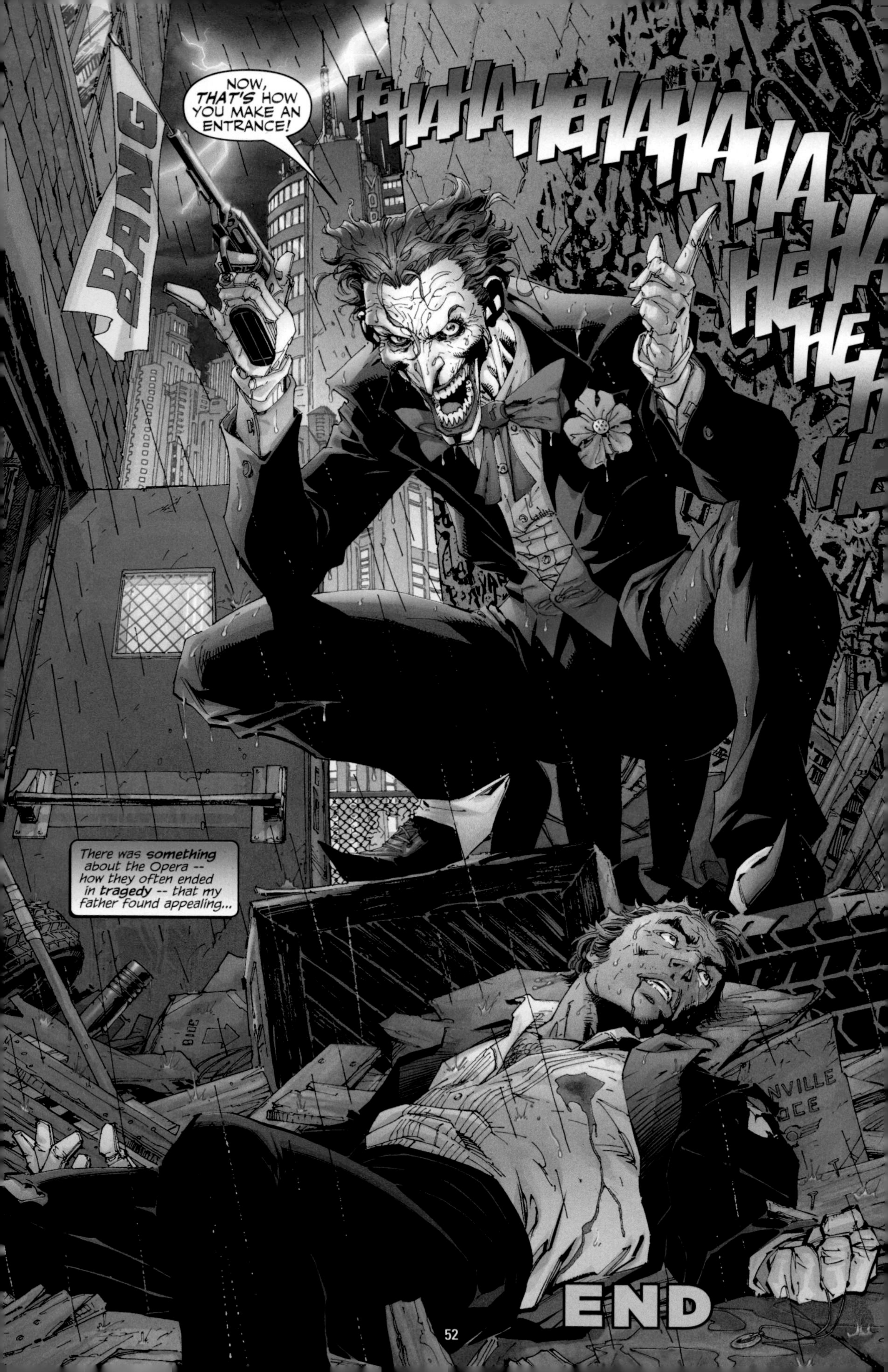

NOW, THAT'S HOW YOU MAKE AN ENTRANCE!
BANG
HEHAHAHEHAHAHAHAHAHEHAHEHEHE
There was something about the Opera -- how they often ended in tragedy -- that my father found appealing...
END

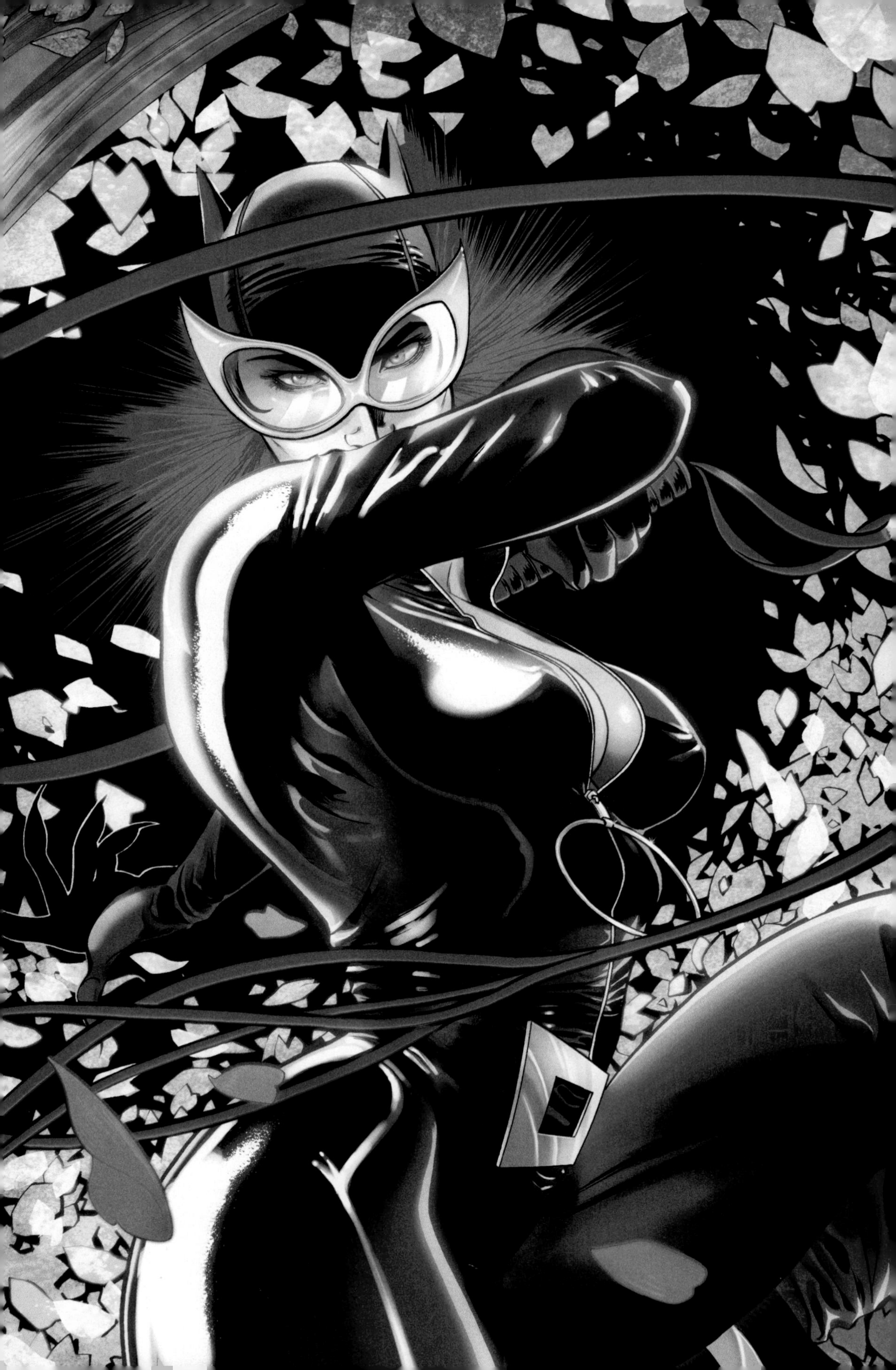

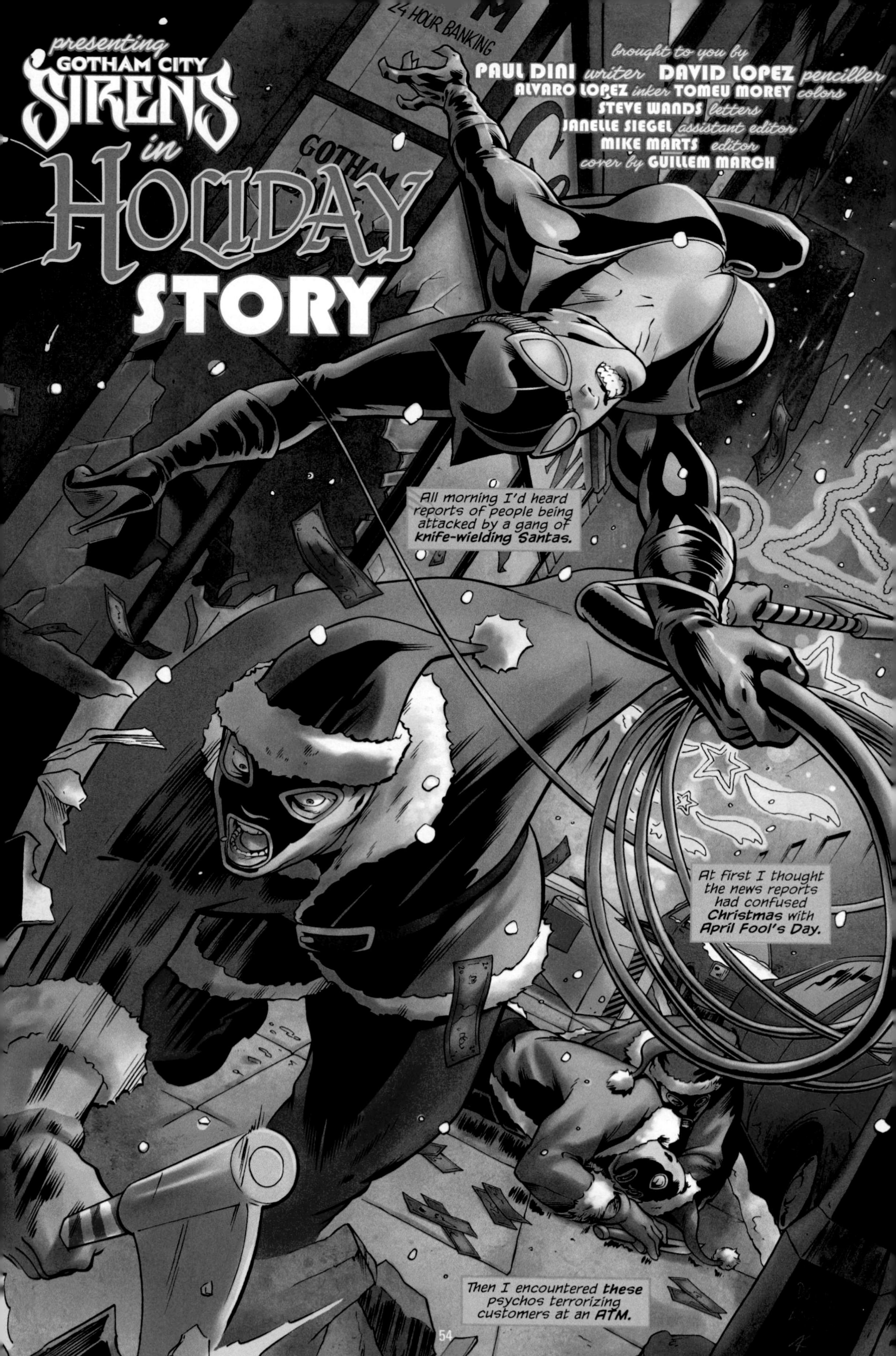
presenting
GOTHAM CITY
SIRENS
in
HOLIDAY
STORY
brought to you by
PAUL DINI writer DAVID LOPEZ penciller
ALVARO LOPEZ inker TOMEU MOREY colors
STEVE WANDS letters
JANELLE SIEGEL assistant editor
MIKE MARTS editor
cover by GUILLEM MARCH
24 HOUR BANKING
GOTHAM
All morning I'd heard reports of people being attacked by a gang of knife-wielding Santas.
At first I thought the news reports had confused Christmas with April Fool's Day.
Then I encountered these psychos terrorizing customers at an ATM.

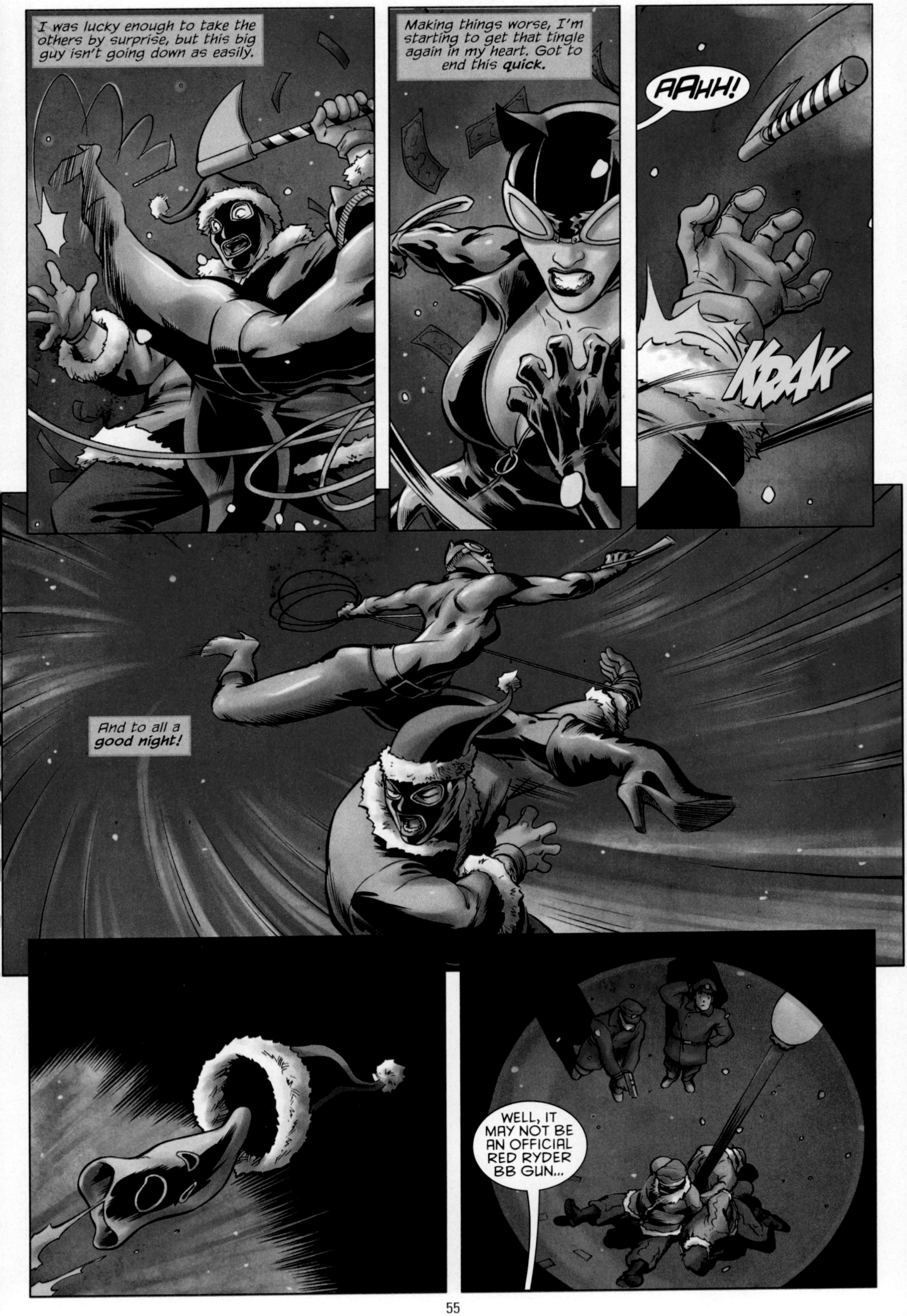
I was lucky enough to take the others by surprise, but this big guy isn't going down as easily.
Making things worse, I'm starting to get that tingle again in my heart. Got to end this **quick.**
AAHH!
KRAK
And to all a **good night!**
WELL, IT MAY NOT BE AN OFFICIAL RED RYDER BB GUN...

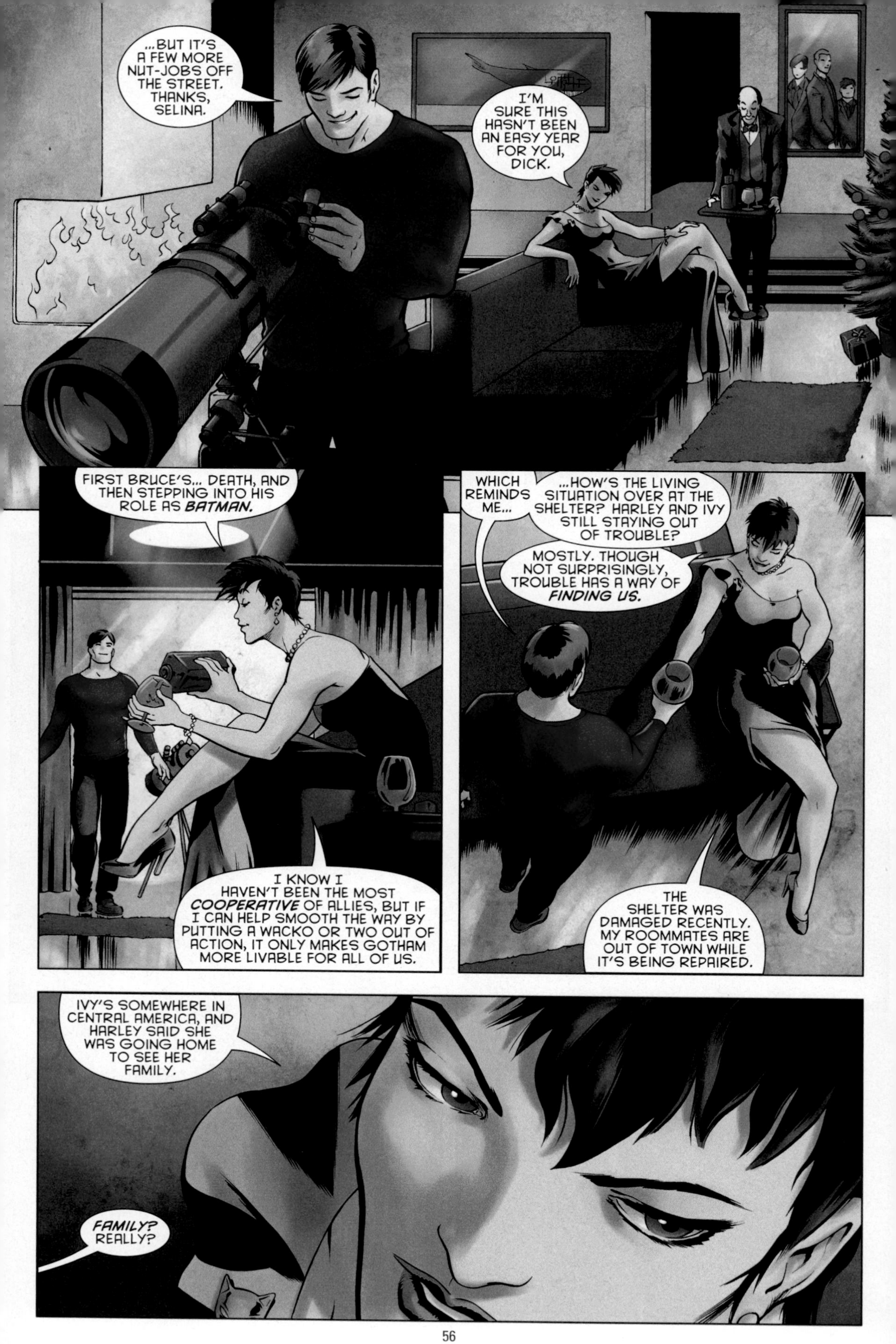
...BUT IT'S A FEW MORE NUT-JOBS OFF THE STREET. THANKS, SELINA.
I'M SURE THIS HASN'T BEEN AN EASY YEAR FOR YOU, DICK.
FIRST BRUCE'S... DEATH, AND THEN STEPPING INTO HIS ROLE AS *BATMAN.*
I KNOW I HAVEN'T BEEN THE MOST *COOPERATIVE* OF ALLIES, BUT IF I CAN HELP SMOOTH THE WAY BY PUTTING A WACKO OR TWO OUT OF ACTION, IT ONLY MAKES GOTHAM MORE LIVABLE FOR ALL OF US.
WHICH REMINDS ME...
...HOW'S THE LIVING SITUATION OVER AT THE SHELTER? HARLEY AND IVY STILL STAYING OUT OF TROUBLE?
MOSTLY. THOUGH NOT SURPRISINGLY, TROUBLE HAS A WAY OF *FINDING US.*
THE SHELTER WAS DAMAGED RECENTLY. MY ROOMMATES ARE OUT OF TOWN WHILE IT'S BEING REPAIRED.
IVY'S SOMEWHERE IN CENTRAL AMERICA, AND HARLEY SAID SHE WAS GOING HOME TO SEE HER FAMILY.
FAMILY? REALLY?

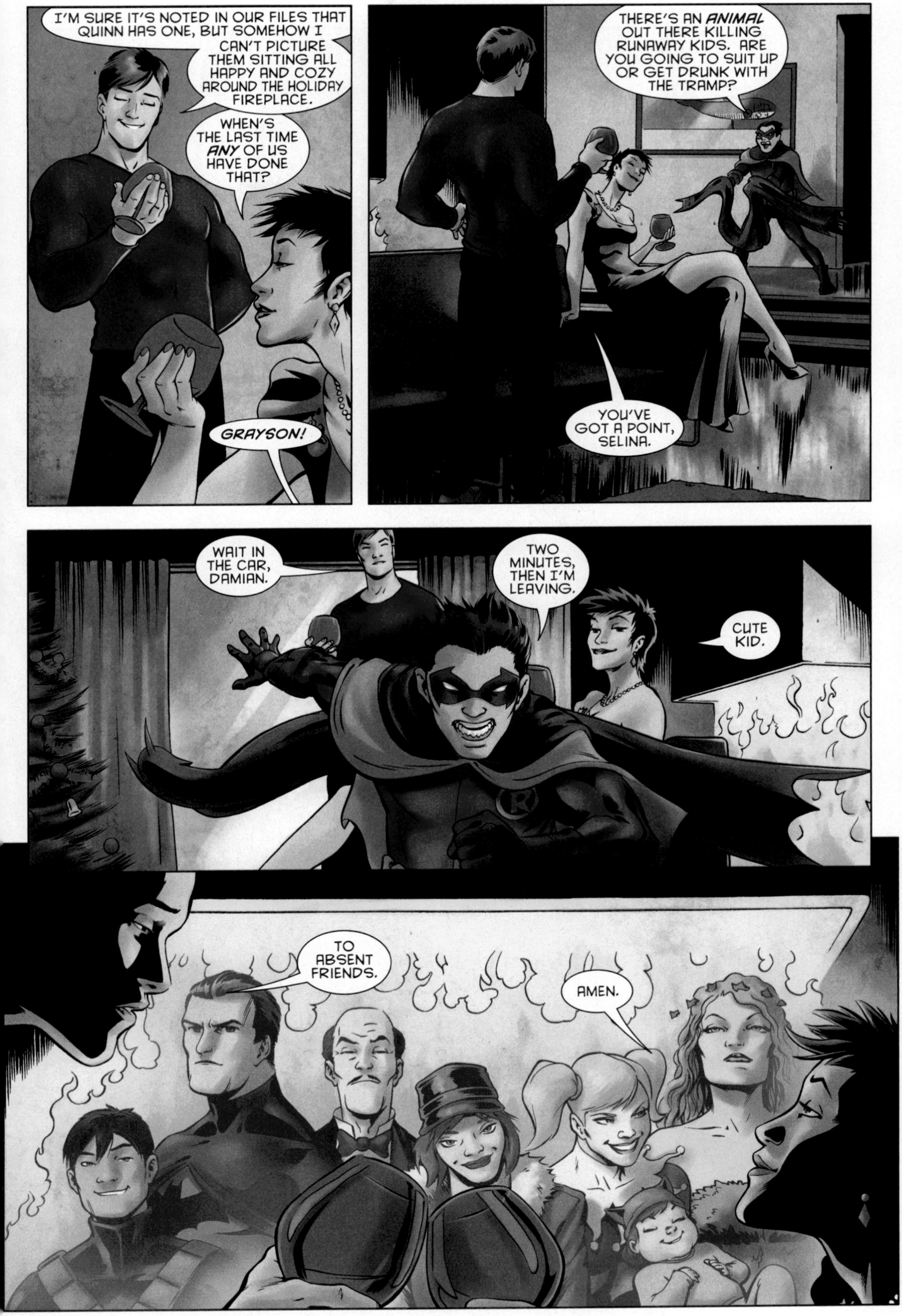
I'M SURE IT'S NOTED IN OUR FILES THAT QUINN HAS ONE, BUT SOMEHOW I CAN'T PICTURE THEM SITTING ALL HAPPY AND COZY AROUND THE HOLIDAY FIREPLACE.
WHEN'S THE LAST TIME ANY OF US HAVE DONE THAT?
GRAYSON!
THERE'S AN ANIMAL OUT THERE KILLING RUNAWAY KIDS. ARE YOU GOING TO SUIT UP OR GET DRUNK WITH THE TRAMP?
YOU'VE GOT A POINT, SELINA.
WAIT IN THE CAR, DAMIAN.
TWO MINUTES, THEN I'M LEAVING.
CUTE KID.
TO ABSENT FRIENDS.
AMEN.

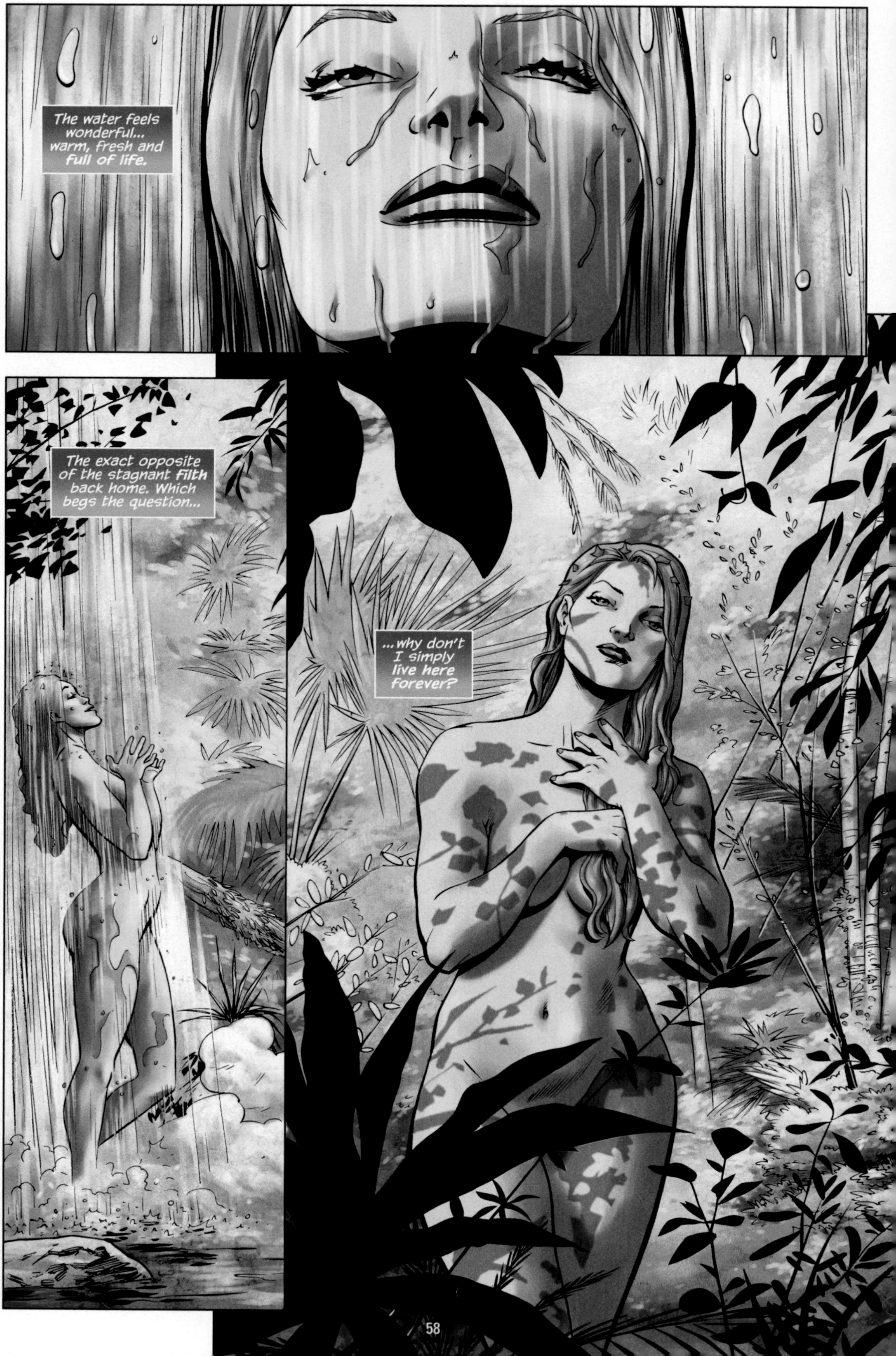
The water feels wonderful... warm, fresh and full of life.
The exact opposite of the stagnant filth back home. Which begs the question...
...why don't I simply live here forever?

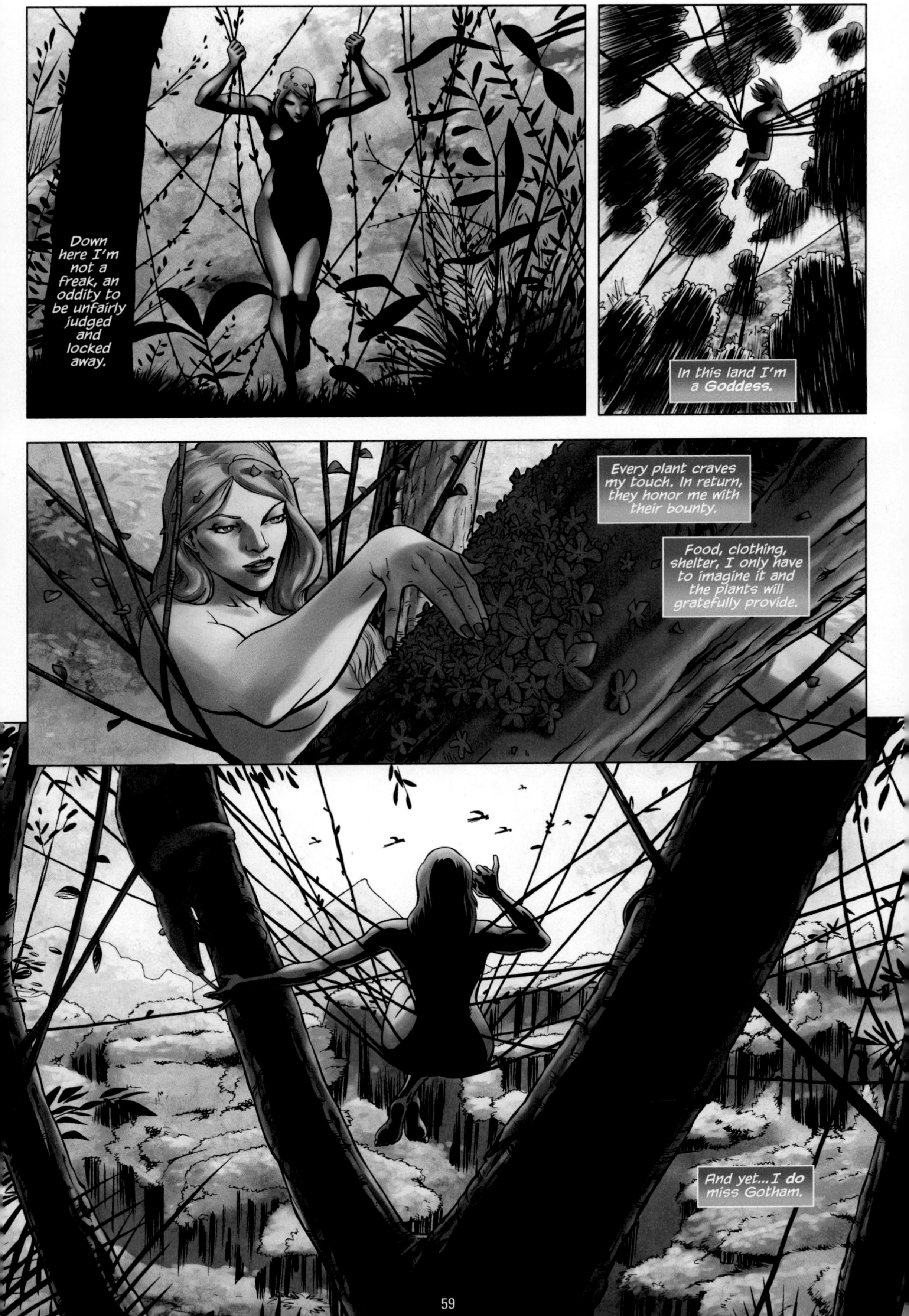
Down here I'm not a freak, an oddity to be unfairly judged and locked away.
In this land I'm a Goddess.
Every plant craves my touch. In return, they honor me with their bounty.
Food, clothing, shelter, I only have to imagine it and the plants will gratefully provide.
And yet...I do miss Gotham.

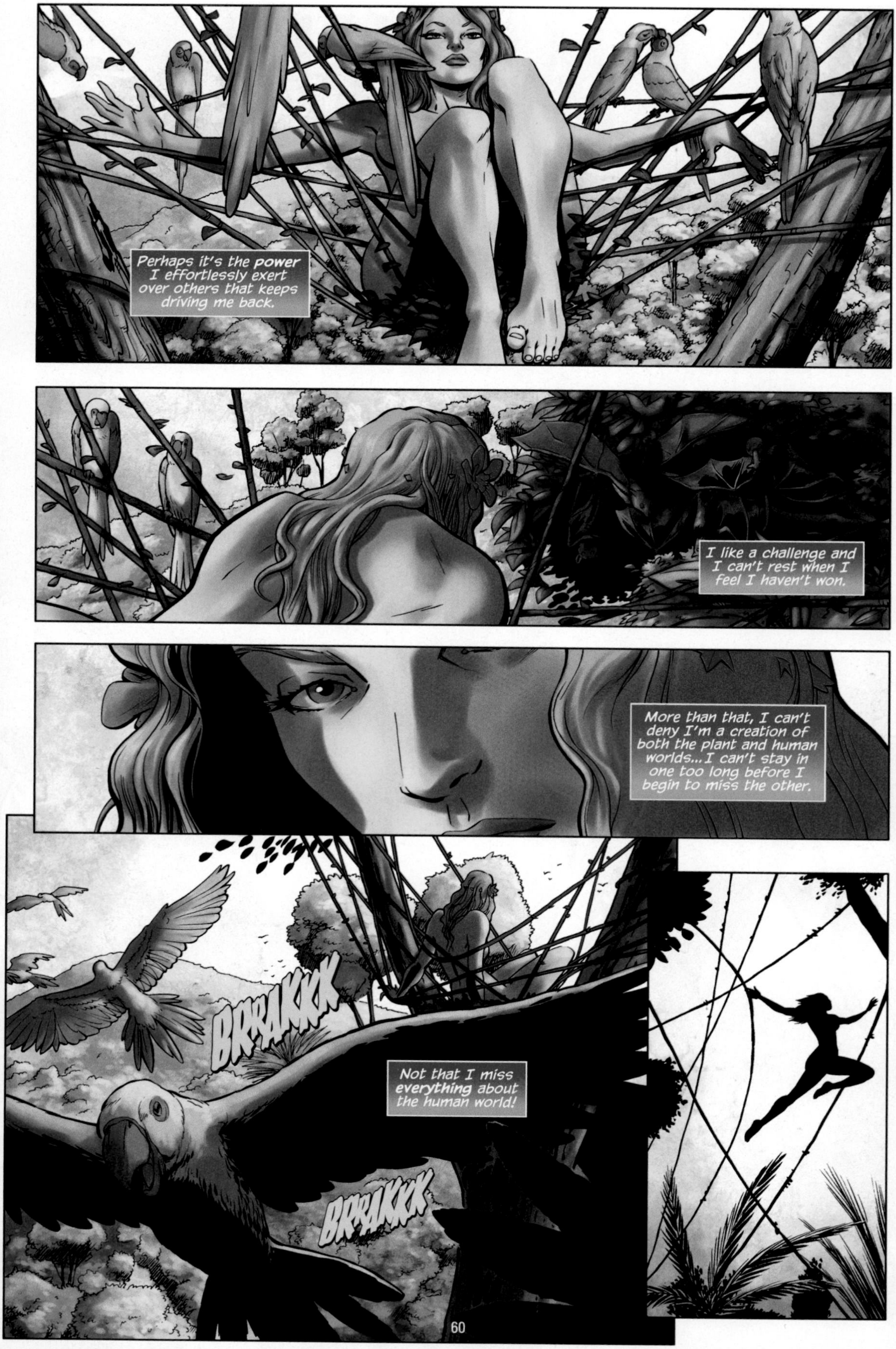

Perhaps it's the **power** I effortlessly exert over others that keeps driving me back.
I like a challenge and I can't rest when I feel I haven't won.
More than that, I can't deny I'm a creation of both the plant and human worlds...I can't stay in one too long before I begin to miss the other.
BRRAKKK
Not that I miss **everything** about the human world!
BRRAKKK

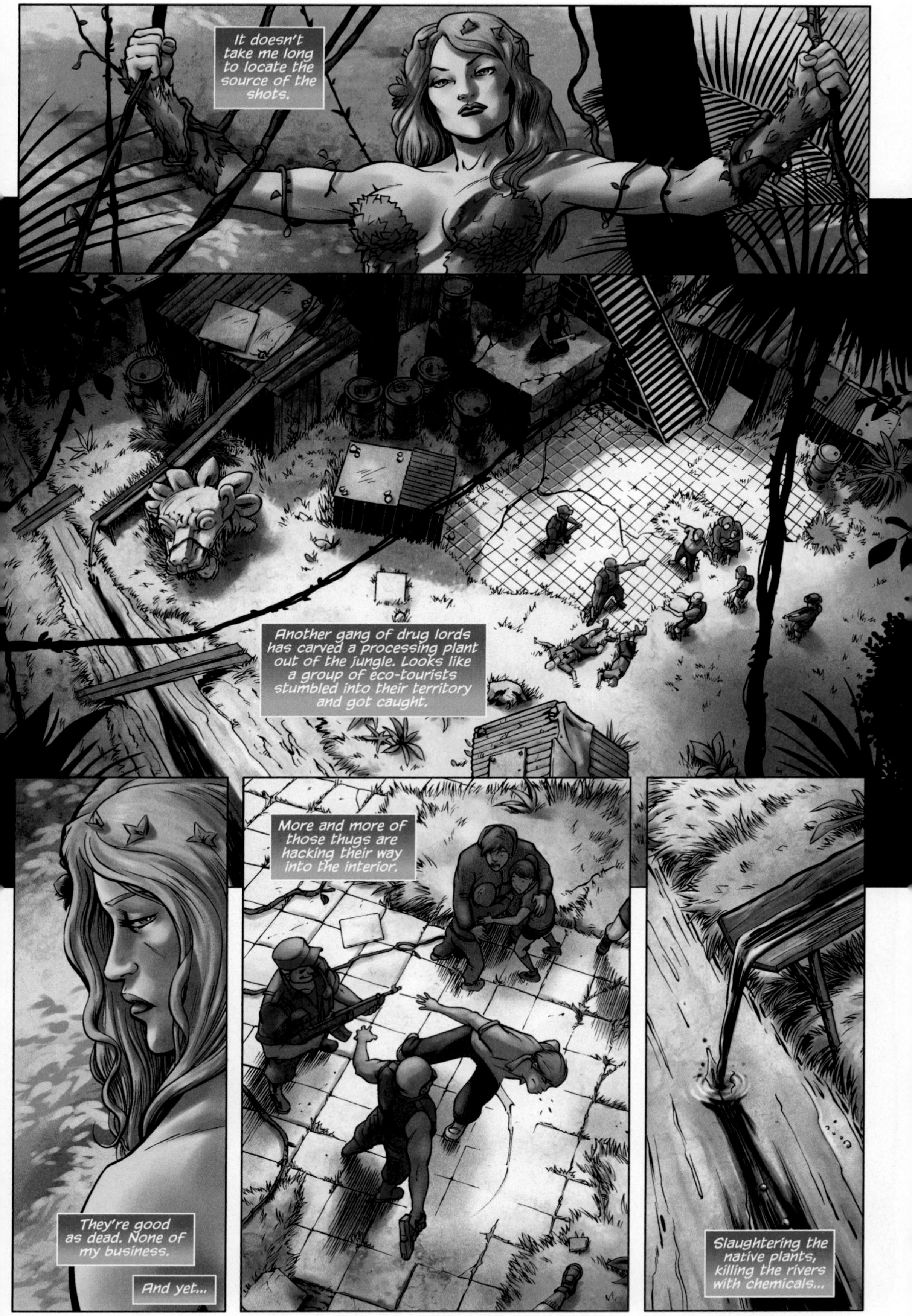

It doesn't take me long to locate the source of the shots.
Another gang of drug lords has carved a processing plant out of the jungle. Looks like a group of eco-tourists stumbled into their territory and got caught.
They're good as dead. None of my business.
And yet...
More and more of those thugs are hacking their way into the interior.
Slaughtering the native plants, killing the rivers with chemicals...

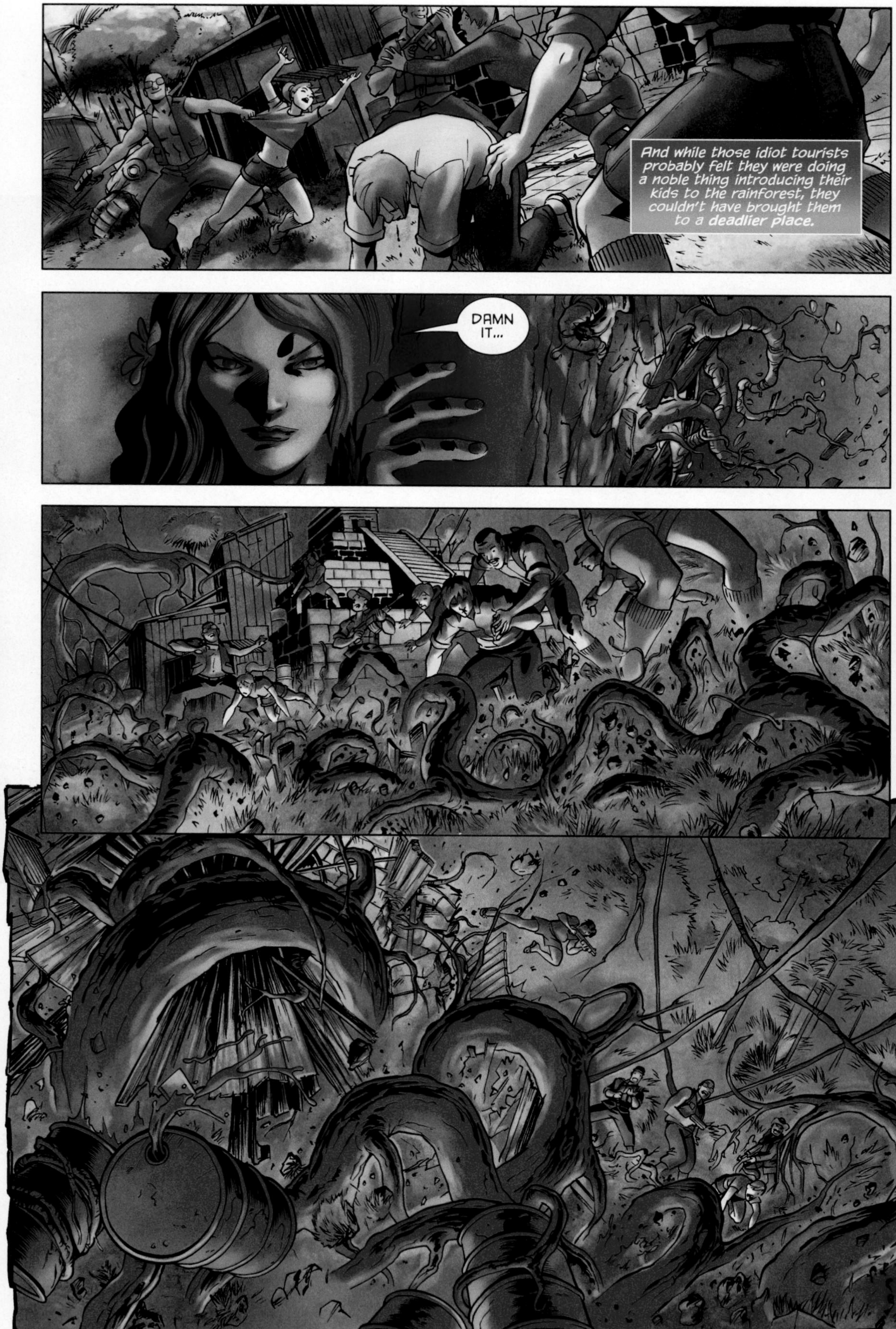
And while those idiot tourists probably felt they were doing a noble thing introducing their kids to the rainforest, they couldn't have brought them to a deadlier place.
DAMN IT...

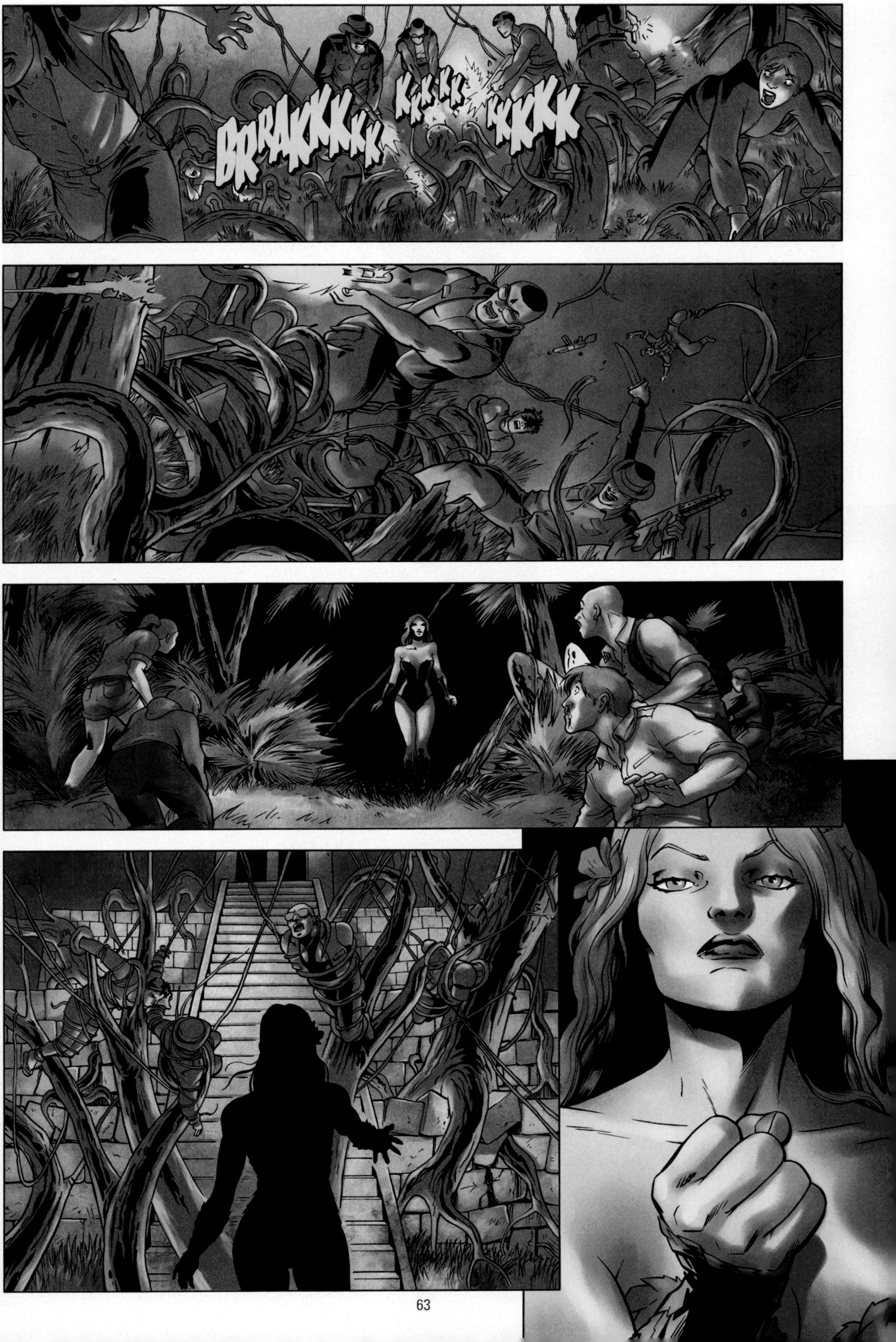
BRRAKKKKK
KKKKKK
KKKKK

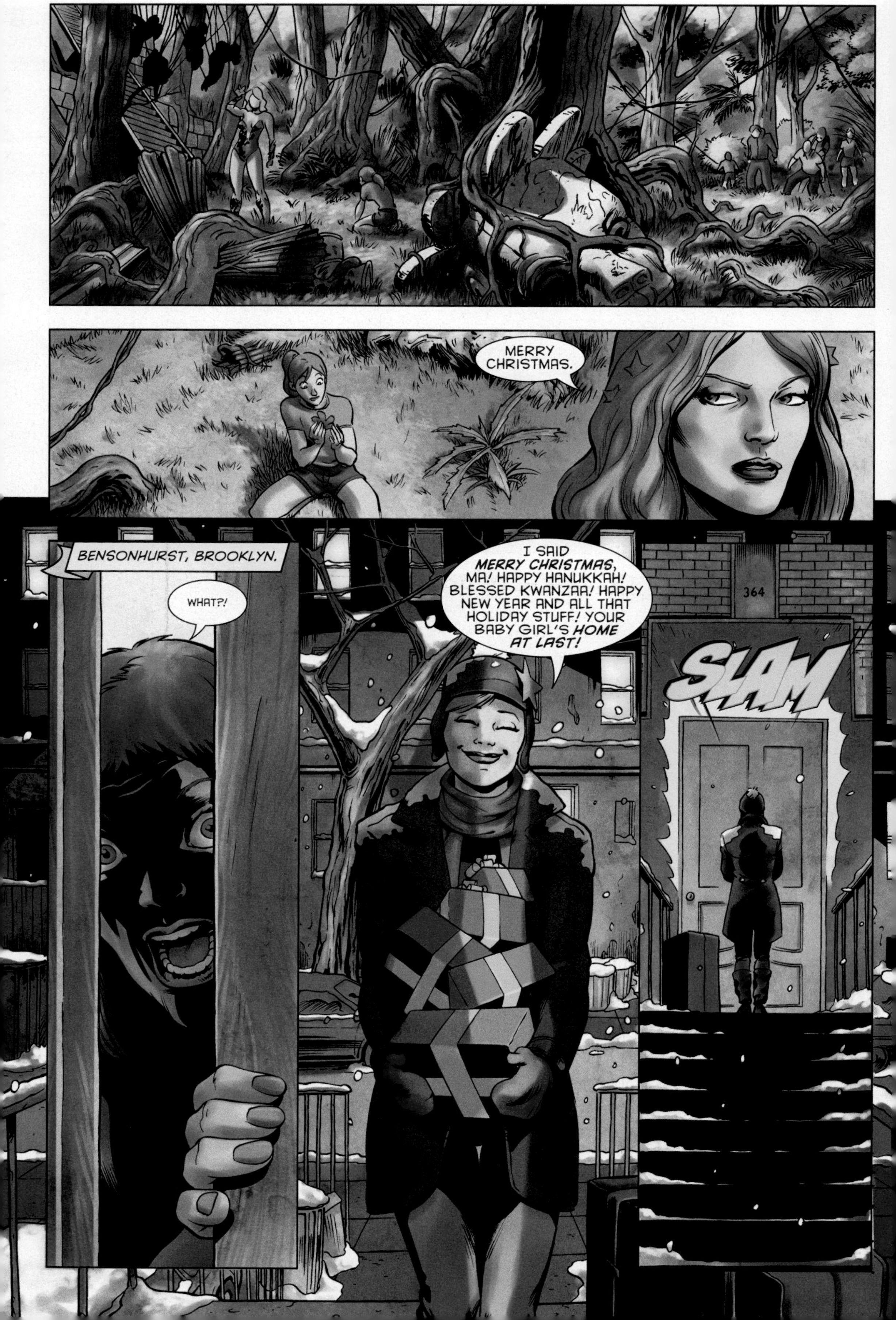
MERRY CHRISTMAS.
BENSONHURST, BROOKLYN.
WHAT?!
I SAID MERRY CHRISTMAS, MA! HAPPY HANUKKAH! BLESSED KWANZAA! HAPPY NEW YEAR AND ALL THAT HOLIDAY STUFF! YOUR BABY GIRL'S HOME AT LAST!
364
SLAM

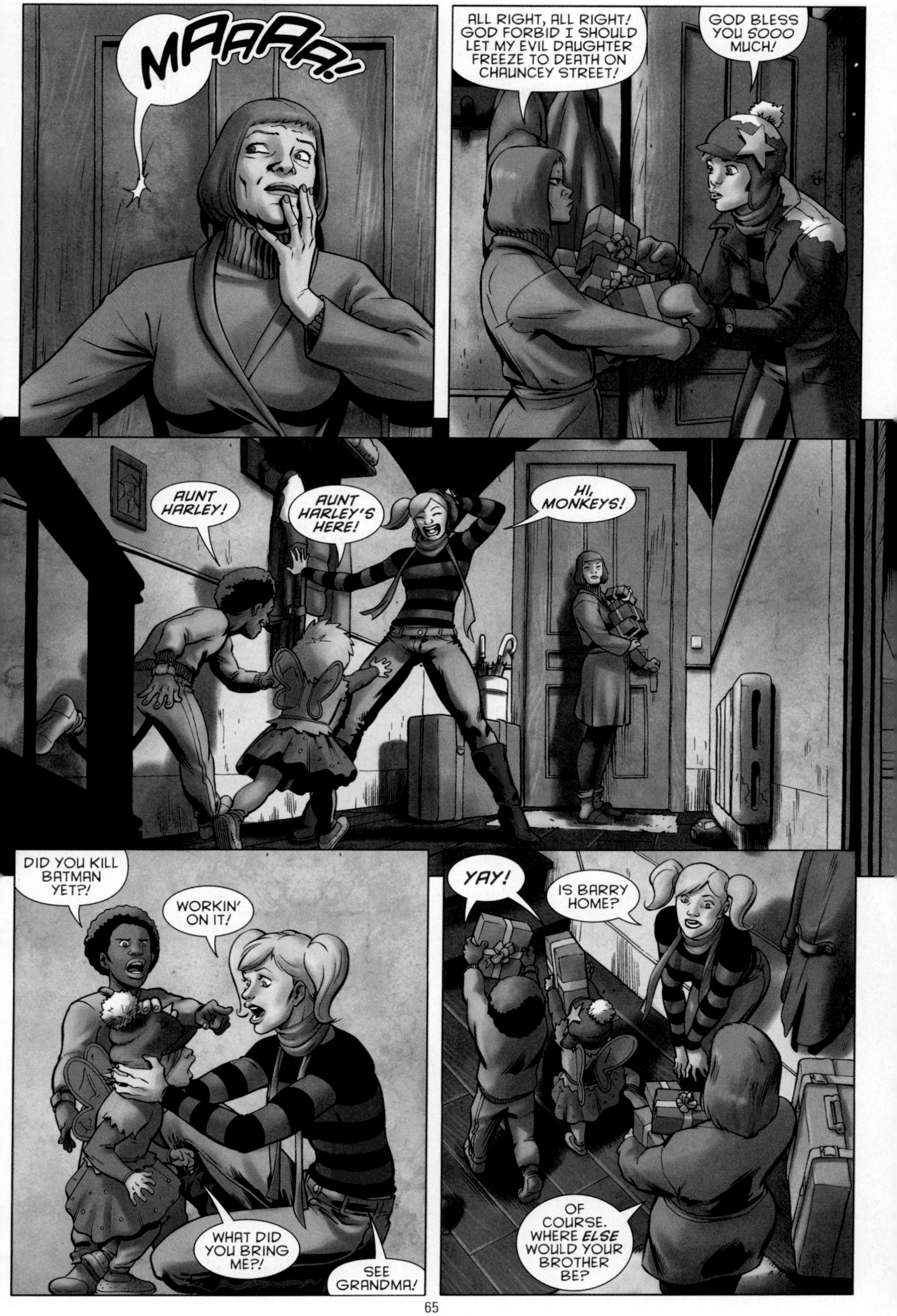
MAAAA!
ALL RIGHT, ALL RIGHT! GOD FORBID I SHOULD LET MY EVIL DAUGHTER FREEZE TO DEATH ON CHAUNCEY STREET!
GOD BLESS YOU SOOO MUCH!
AUNT HARLEY!
AUNT HARLEY'S HERE!
HI, MONKEYS!
DID YOU KILL BATMAN YET?!
WORKIN' ON IT!
WHAT DID YOU BRING ME?!
SEE GRANDMA!
YAY!
IS BARRY HOME?
OF COURSE. WHERE ELSE WOULD YOUR BROTHER BE?

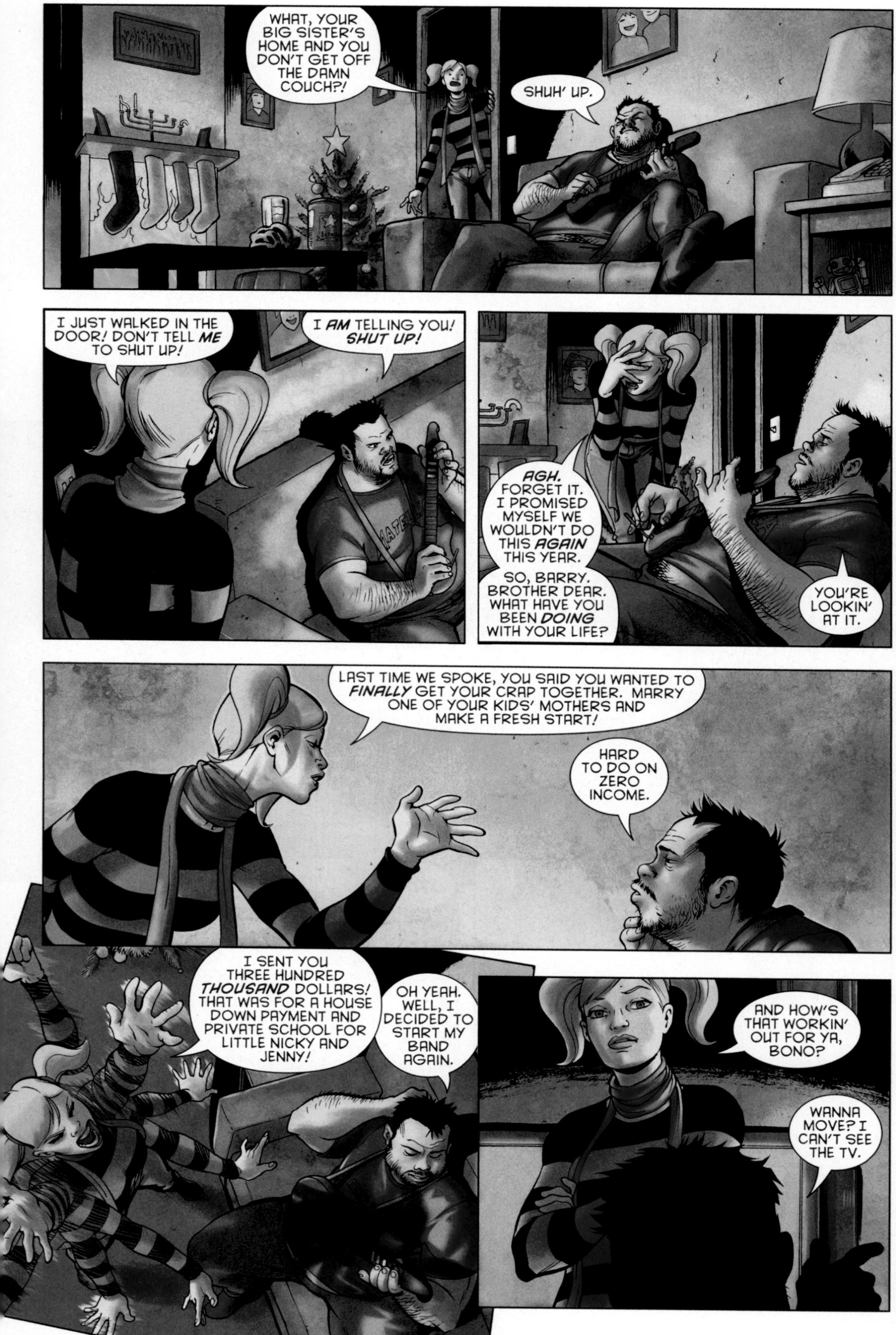
WHAT, YOUR BIG SISTER'S HOME AND YOU DON'T GET OFF THE DAMN COUCH?!
SHUH' UP.
I JUST WALKED IN THE DOOR! DON'T TELL *ME* TO SHUT UP!
I *AM* TELLING YOU! ***SHUT UP!***
AGH. FORGET IT. I PROMISED MYSELF WE WOULDN'T DO THIS *AGAIN* THIS YEAR.
SO, BARRY. BROTHER DEAR. WHAT HAVE YOU BEEN *DOING* WITH YOUR LIFE?
YOU'RE LOOKIN' AT IT.
LAST TIME WE SPOKE, YOU SAID YOU WANTED TO *FINALLY* GET YOUR CRAP TOGETHER. MARRY ONE OF YOUR KIDS' MOTHERS AND MAKE A FRESH START!
HARD TO DO ON ZERO INCOME.
I SENT YOU THREE HUNDRED *THOUSAND* DOLLARS! THAT WAS FOR A HOUSE DOWN PAYMENT AND PRIVATE SCHOOL FOR LITTLE NICKY AND JENNY!
OH YEAH. WELL, I DECIDED TO START MY BAND AGAIN.
AND HOW'S THAT WORKIN' OUT FOR YA, BONO?
WANNA MOVE? I CAN'T SEE THE TV.

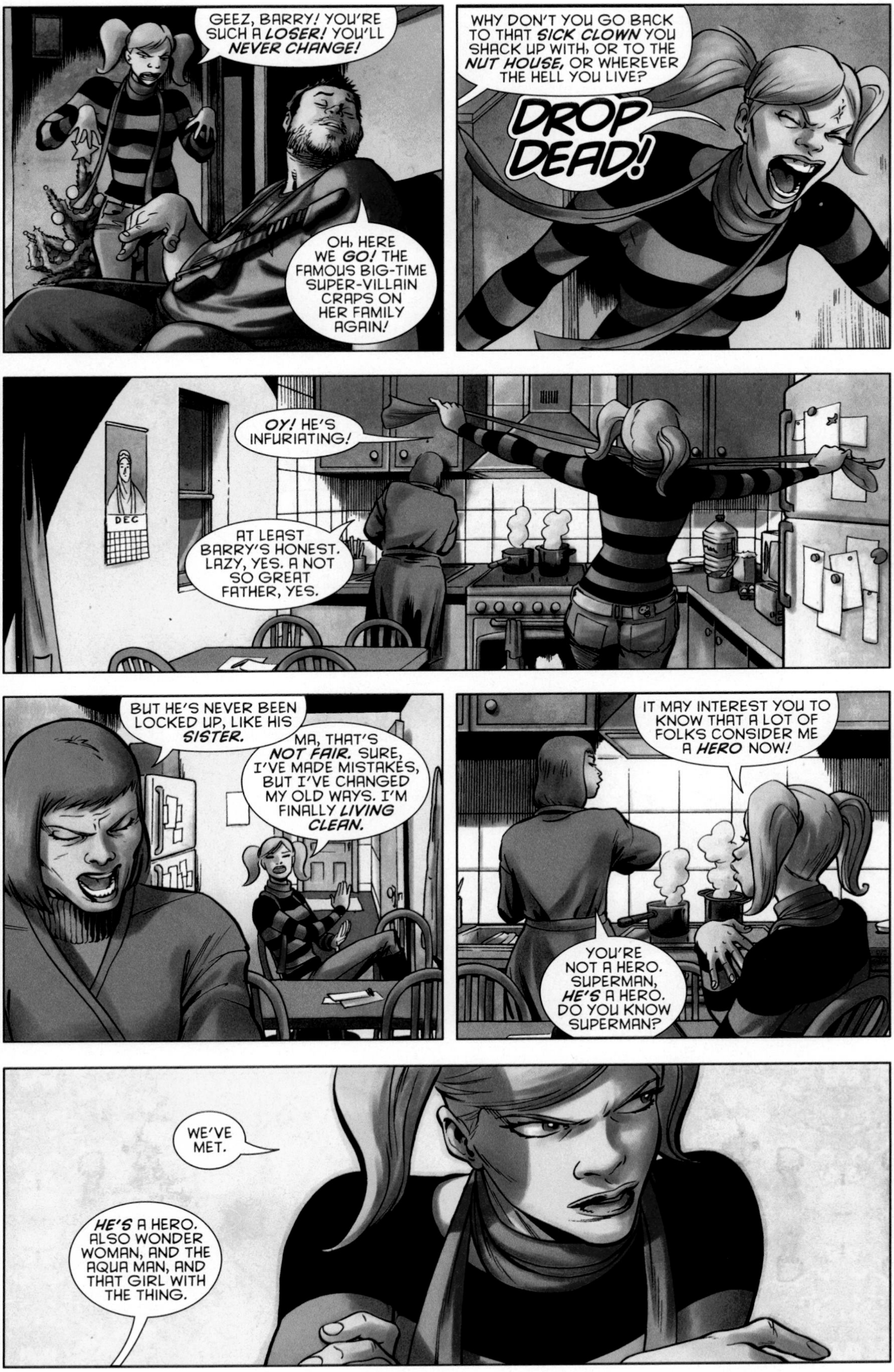
GEEZ, BARRY! YOU'RE SUCH A LOSER! YOU'LL NEVER CHANGE!
OH, HERE WE GO! THE FAMOUS BIG-TIME SUPER-VILLAIN CRAPS ON HER FAMILY AGAIN!
WHY DON'T YOU GO BACK TO THAT SICK CLOWN YOU SHACK UP WITH, OR TO THE NUT HOUSE, OR WHEREVER THE HELL YOU LIVE?
DROP DEAD!
OY! HE'S INFURIATING!
AT LEAST BARRY'S HONEST. LAZY, YES. A NOT SO GREAT FATHER, YES.
DEC
BUT HE'S NEVER BEEN LOCKED UP, LIKE HIS SISTER.
MA, THAT'S NOT FAIR. SURE, I'VE MADE MISTAKES, BUT I'VE CHANGED MY OLD WAYS. I'M FINALLY LIVING CLEAN.
IT MAY INTEREST YOU TO KNOW THAT A LOT OF FOLKS CONSIDER ME A HERO NOW!
YOU'RE NOT A HERO. SUPERMAN, HE'S A HERO. DO YOU KNOW SUPERMAN?
WE'VE MET.
HE'S A HERO. ALSO WONDER WOMAN, AND THE AQUA MAN, AND THAT GIRL WITH THE THING.

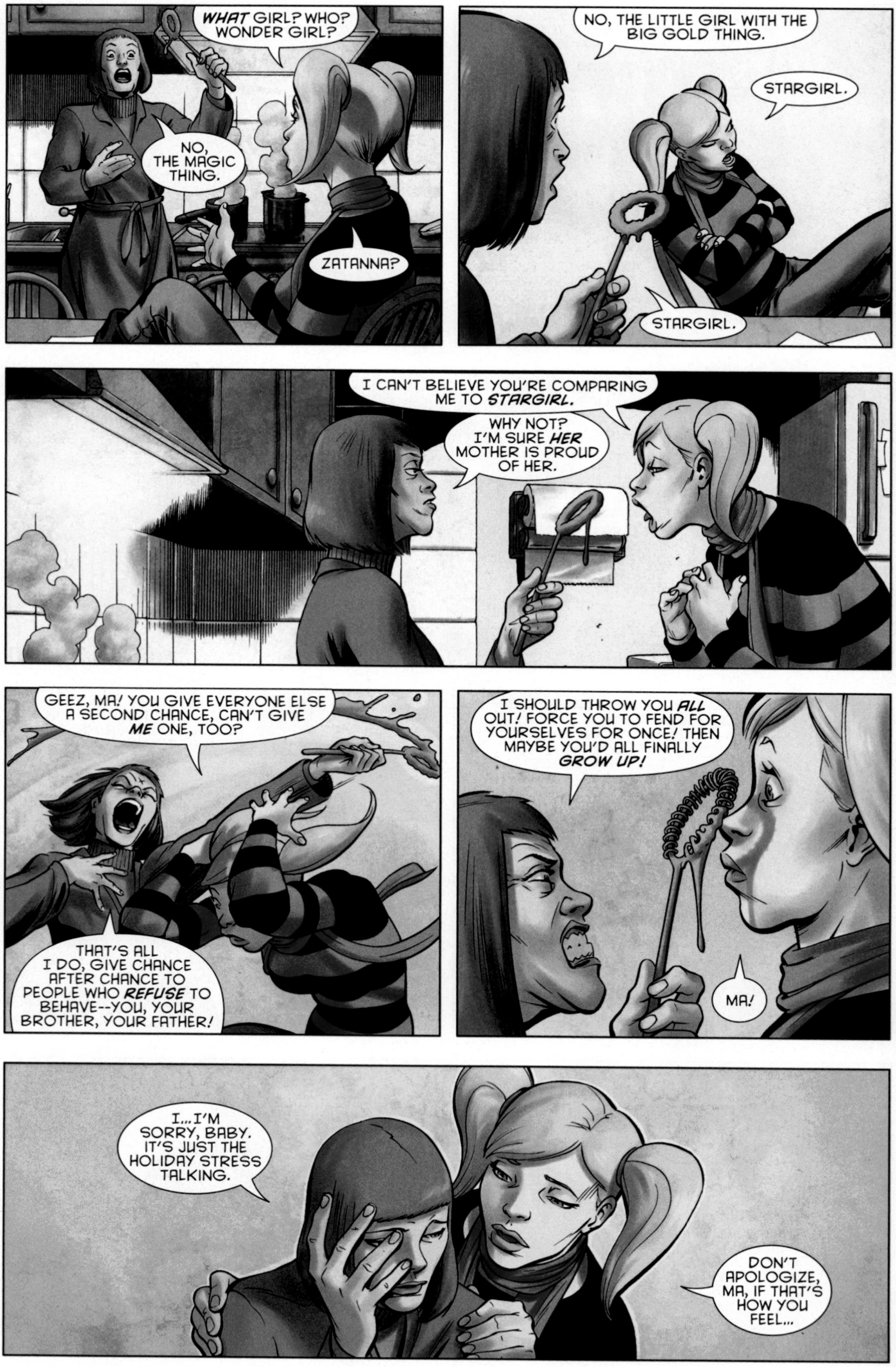
WHAT GIRL? WHO? WONDER GIRL?
NO, THE MAGIC THING.
ZATANNA?
NO, THE LITTLE GIRL WITH THE BIG GOLD THING.
STARGIRL.
STARGIRL.
I CAN'T BELIEVE YOU'RE COMPARING ME TO STARGIRL.
WHY NOT? I'M SURE HER MOTHER IS PROUD OF HER.
GEEZ, MA! YOU GIVE EVERYONE ELSE A SECOND CHANCE, CAN'T GIVE ME ONE, TOO?
THAT'S ALL I DO, GIVE CHANCE AFTER CHANCE TO PEOPLE WHO REFUSE TO BEHAVE--YOU, YOUR BROTHER, YOUR FATHER!
I SHOULD THROW YOU ALL OUT! FORCE YOU TO FEND FOR YOURSELVES FOR ONCE! THEN MAYBE YOU'D ALL FINALLY GROW UP!
MA!
I...I'M SORRY, BABY. IT'S JUST THE HOLIDAY STRESS TALKING.
DON'T APOLOGIZE, MA, IF THAT'S HOW YOU FEEL...

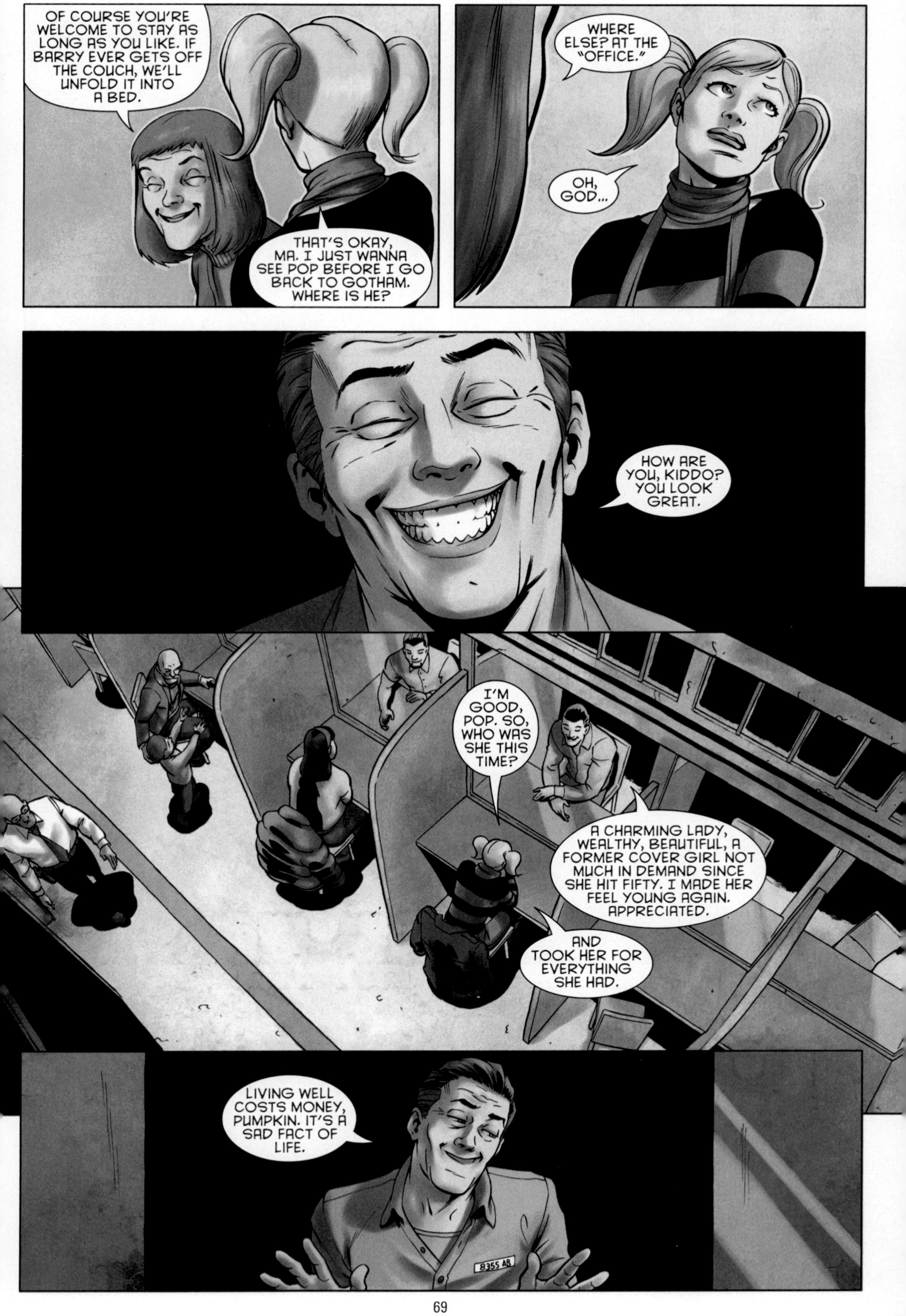
OF COURSE YOU'RE WELCOME TO STAY AS LONG AS YOU LIKE. IF BARRY EVER GETS OFF THE COUCH, WE'LL UNFOLD IT INTO A BED.
THAT'S OKAY, MA. I JUST WANNA SEE POP BEFORE I GO BACK TO GOTHAM. WHERE IS HE?
WHERE ELSE? AT THE "OFFICE."
OH, GOD...
HOW ARE YOU, KIDDO? YOU LOOK GREAT.
I'M GOOD, POP. SO, WHO WAS SHE THIS TIME?
A CHARMING LADY, WEALTHY, BEAUTIFUL, A FORMER COVER GIRL NOT MUCH IN DEMAND SINCE SHE HIT FIFTY. I MADE HER FEEL YOUNG AGAIN. APPRECIATED.
AND TOOK HER FOR EVERYTHING SHE HAD.
LIVING WELL COSTS MONEY, PUMPKIN. IT'S A SAD FACT OF LIFE.
8355 AB

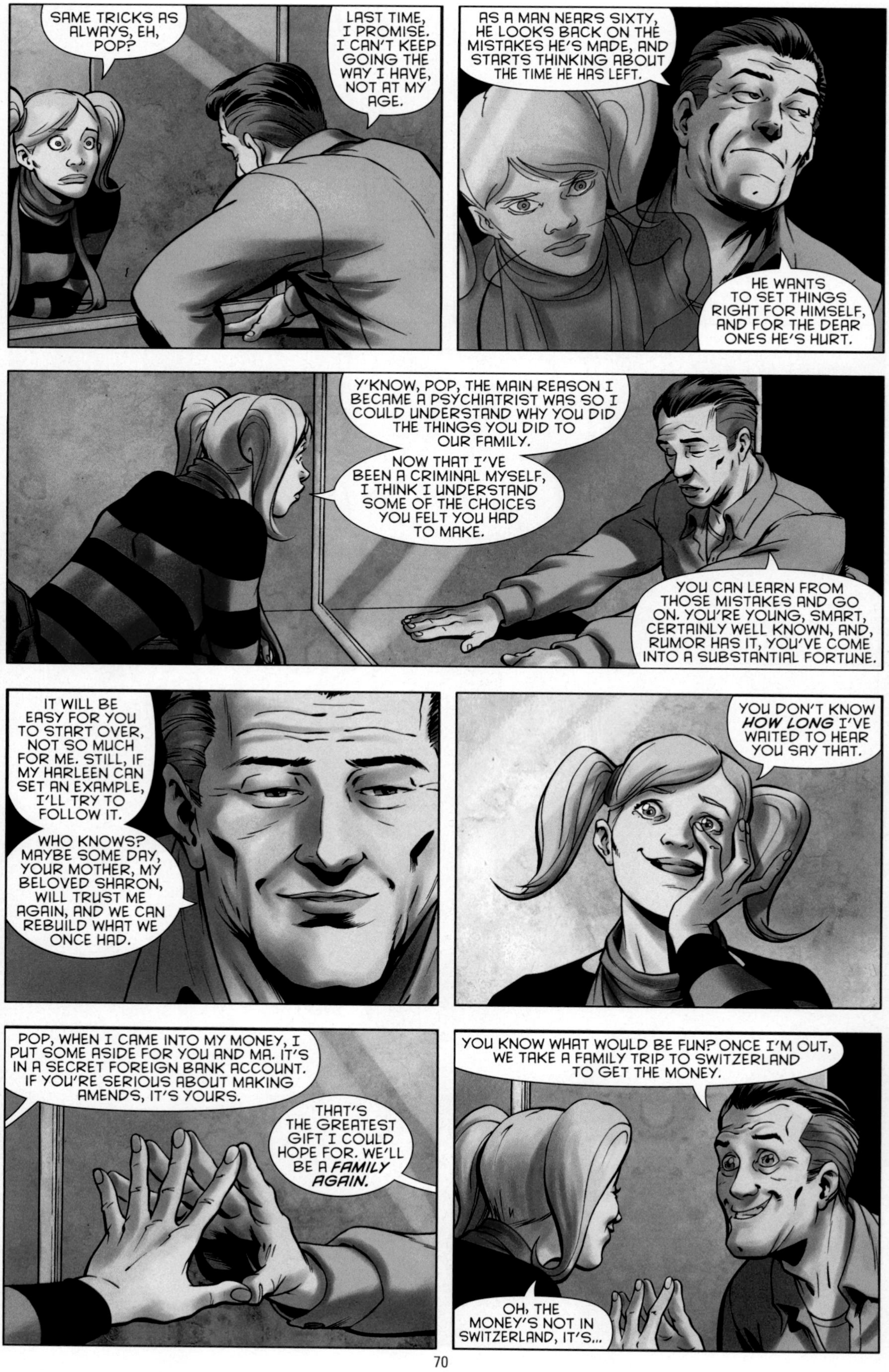

SAME TRICKS AS ALWAYS, EH, POP?
LAST TIME, I PROMISE. I CAN'T KEEP GOING THE WAY I HAVE, NOT AT MY AGE.
AS A MAN NEARS SIXTY, HE LOOKS BACK ON THE MISTAKES HE'S MADE, AND STARTS THINKING ABOUT THE TIME HE HAS LEFT.
HE WANTS TO SET THINGS RIGHT FOR HIMSELF, AND FOR THE DEAR ONES HE'S HURT.
Y'KNOW, POP, THE MAIN REASON I BECAME A PSYCHIATRIST WAS SO I COULD UNDERSTAND WHY YOU DID THE THINGS YOU DID TO OUR FAMILY.
NOW THAT I'VE BEEN A CRIMINAL MYSELF, I THINK I UNDERSTAND SOME OF THE CHOICES YOU FELT YOU HAD TO MAKE.
YOU CAN LEARN FROM THOSE MISTAKES AND GO ON. YOU'RE YOUNG, SMART, CERTAINLY WELL KNOWN, AND, RUMOR HAS IT, YOU'VE COME INTO A SUBSTANTIAL FORTUNE.
IT WILL BE EASY FOR YOU TO START OVER, NOT SO MUCH FOR ME. STILL, IF MY HARLEEN CAN SET AN EXAMPLE, I'LL TRY TO FOLLOW IT.
WHO KNOWS? MAYBE SOME DAY, YOUR MOTHER, MY BELOVED SHARON, WILL TRUST ME AGAIN, AND WE CAN REBUILD WHAT WE ONCE HAD.
YOU DON'T KNOW *HOW LONG* I'VE WAITED TO HEAR YOU SAY THAT.
POP, WHEN I CAME INTO MY MONEY, I PUT SOME ASIDE FOR YOU AND MA. IT'S IN A SECRET FOREIGN BANK ACCOUNT. IF YOU'RE SERIOUS ABOUT MAKING AMENDS, IT'S YOURS.
THAT'S THE GREATEST GIFT I COULD HOPE FOR. WE'LL BE A *FAMILY AGAIN.*
YOU KNOW WHAT WOULD BE FUN? ONCE I'M OUT, WE TAKE A FAMILY TRIP TO SWITZERLAND TO GET THE MONEY.
OH, THE MONEY'S NOT IN SWITZERLAND, IT'S...

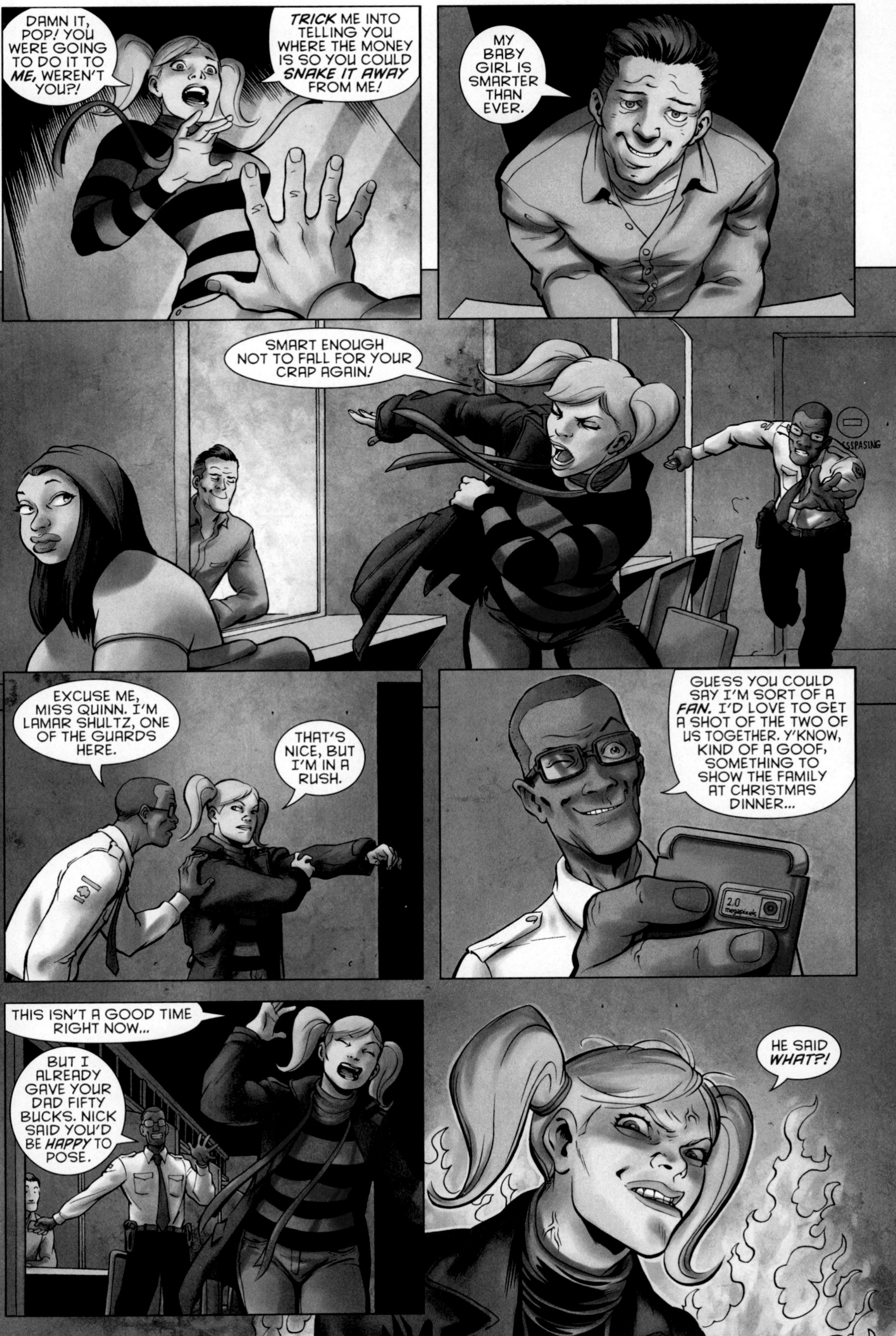
DAMN IT, POP! YOU WERE GOING TO DO IT TO *ME,* WEREN'T YOU?!
TRICK ME INTO TELLING YOU WHERE THE MONEY IS SO YOU COULD ***SNAKE IT AWAY*** FROM ME!
MY BABY GIRL IS SMARTER THAN EVER.
SMART ENOUGH NOT TO FALL FOR YOUR CRAP AGAIN!
SSPASING
EXCUSE ME, MISS QUINN. I'M LAMAR SHULTZ, ONE OF THE GUARDS HERE.
THAT'S NICE, BUT I'M IN A RUSH.
GUESS YOU COULD SAY I'M SORT OF A ***FAN.*** I'D LOVE TO GET A SHOT OF THE TWO OF US TOGETHER. Y'KNOW, KIND OF A GOOF, SOMETHING TO SHOW THE FAMILY AT CHRISTMAS DINNER...
2.0 megapixels
THIS ISN'T A GOOD TIME RIGHT NOW...
BUT I ALREADY GAVE YOUR DAD FIFTY BUCKS. NICK SAID YOU'D BE ***HAPPY*** TO POSE.
HE SAID ***WHAT?!***

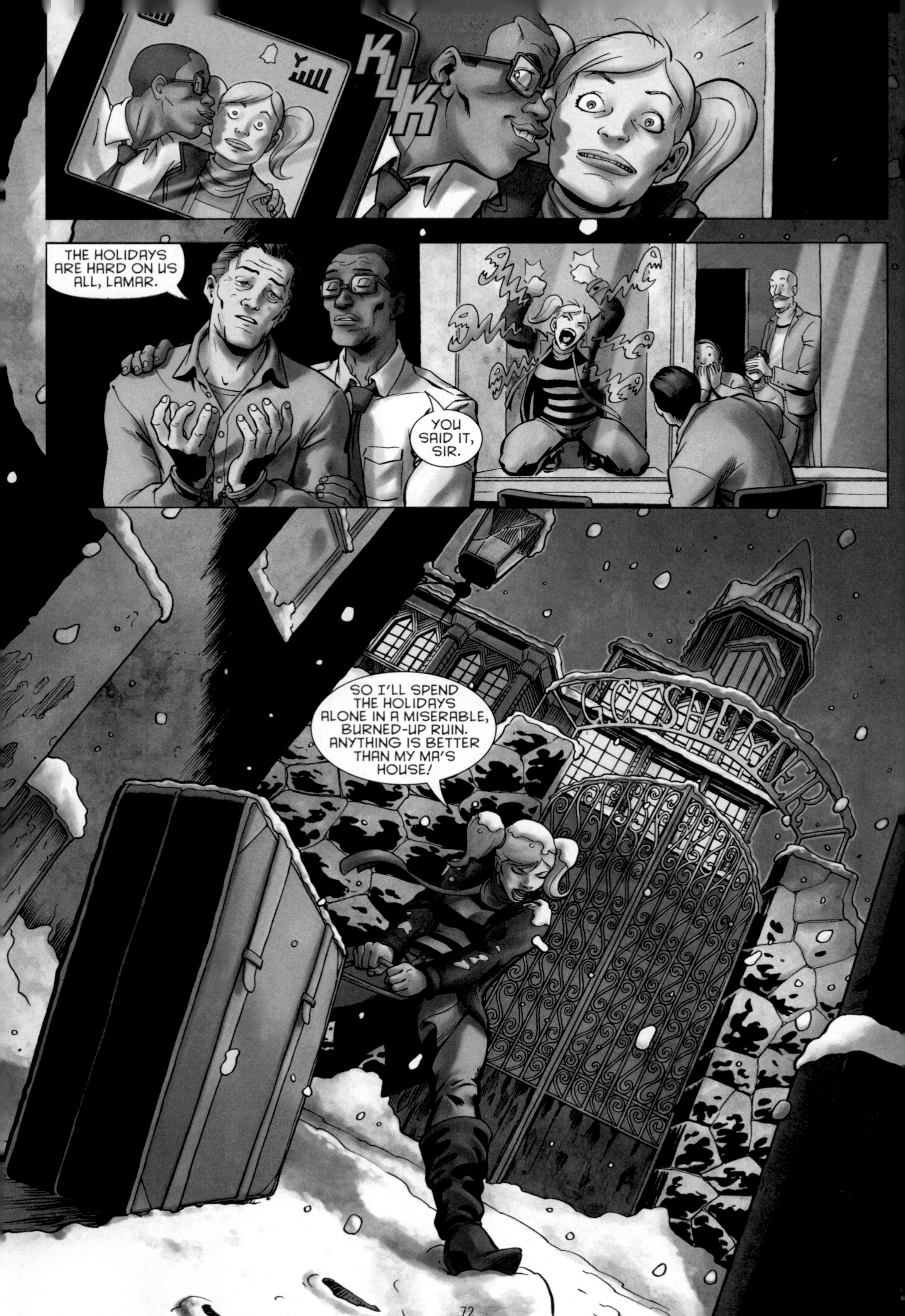
KLIK
THE HOLIDAYS ARE HARD ON US ALL, LAMAR.
YOU SAID IT, SIR.
SO I'LL SPEND THE HOLIDAYS ALONE IN A MISERABLE, BURNED-UP RUIN. ANYTHING IS BETTER THAN MY MA'S HOUSE!

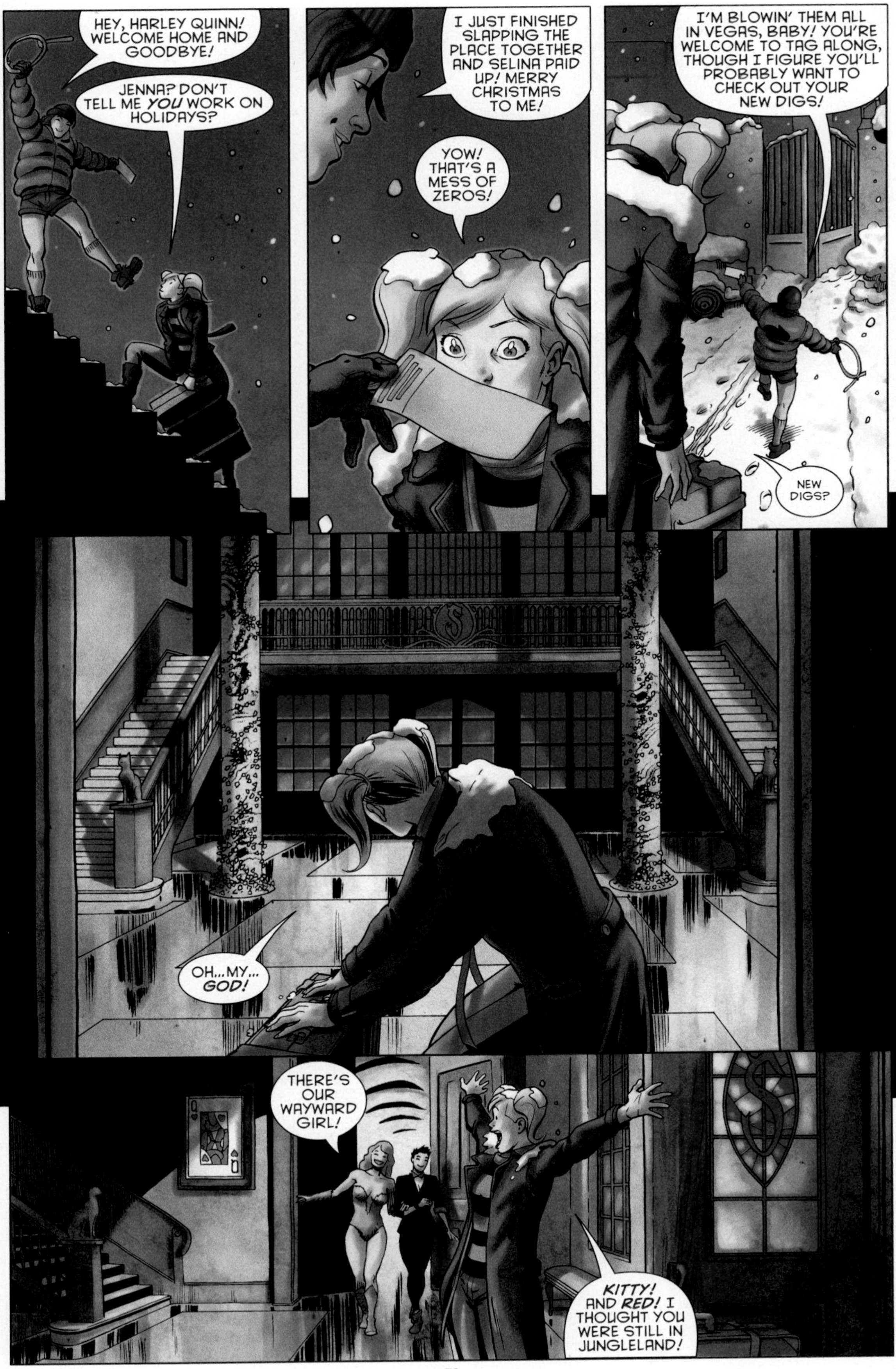
HEY, HARLEY QUINN! WELCOME HOME AND GOODBYE!
JENNA? DON'T TELL ME *YOU* WORK ON HOLIDAYS?
I JUST FINISHED SLAPPING THE PLACE TOGETHER AND SELINA PAID UP! MERRY CHRISTMAS TO ME!
YOW! THAT'S A MESS OF ZEROS!
I'M BLOWIN' THEM ALL IN VEGAS, BABY! YOU'RE WELCOME TO TAG ALONG, THOUGH I FIGURE YOU'LL PROBABLY WANT TO CHECK OUT YOUR NEW DIGS!
NEW DIGS?
OH... MY... *GOD!*
THERE'S OUR WAYWARD GIRL!
KITTY! AND *RED!* I THOUGHT YOU WERE STILL IN JUNGLELAND!

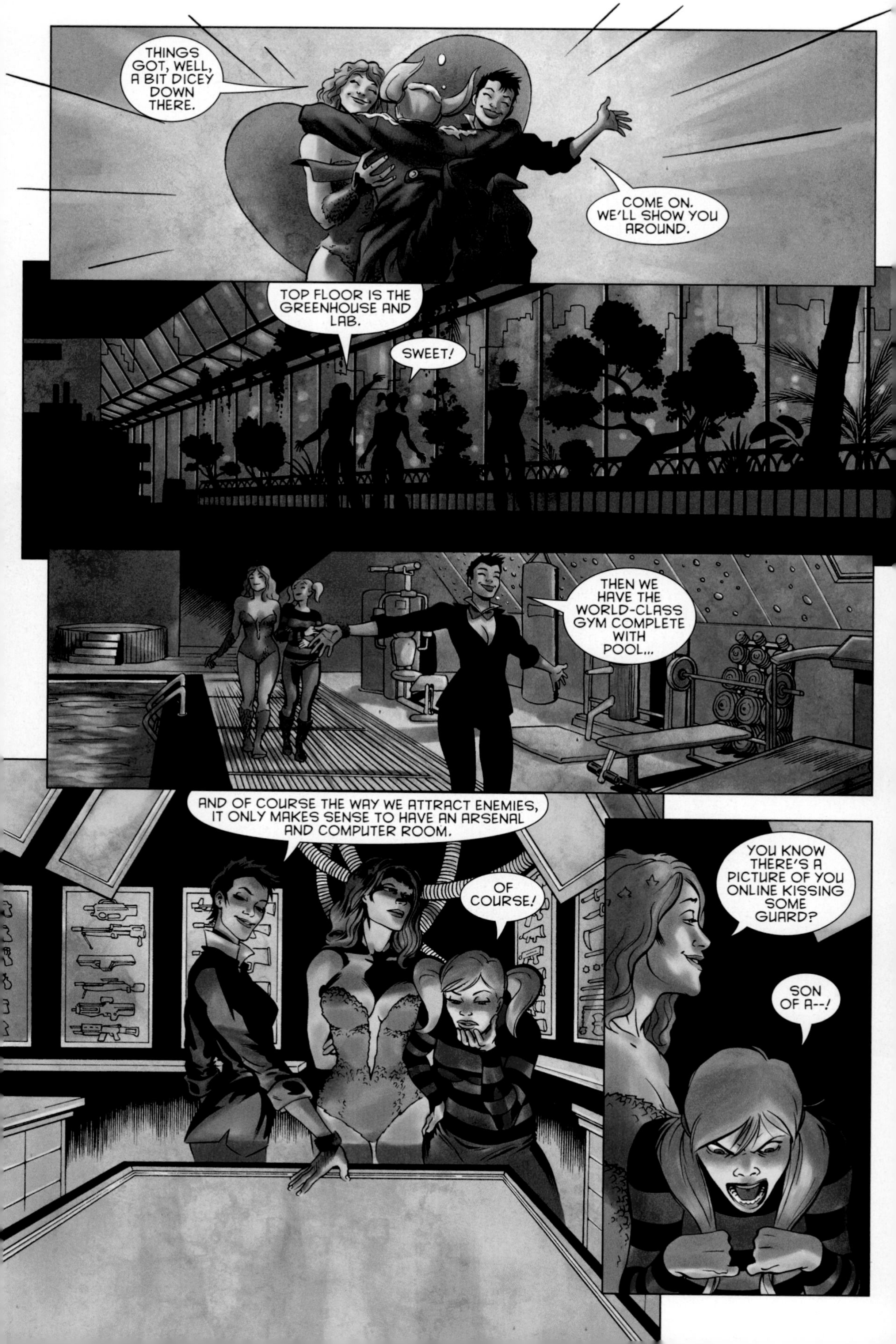
THINGS GOT, WELL, A BIT DICEY DOWN THERE.
COME ON. WE'LL SHOW YOU AROUND.
TOP FLOOR IS THE GREENHOUSE AND LAB.
SWEET!
THEN WE HAVE THE WORLD-CLASS GYM COMPLETE WITH POOL...
AND OF COURSE THE WAY WE ATTRACT ENEMIES, IT ONLY MAKES SENSE TO HAVE AN ARSENAL AND COMPUTER ROOM.
OF COURSE!
YOU KNOW THERE'S A PICTURE OF YOU ONLINE KISSING SOME GUARD?
SON OF A--!

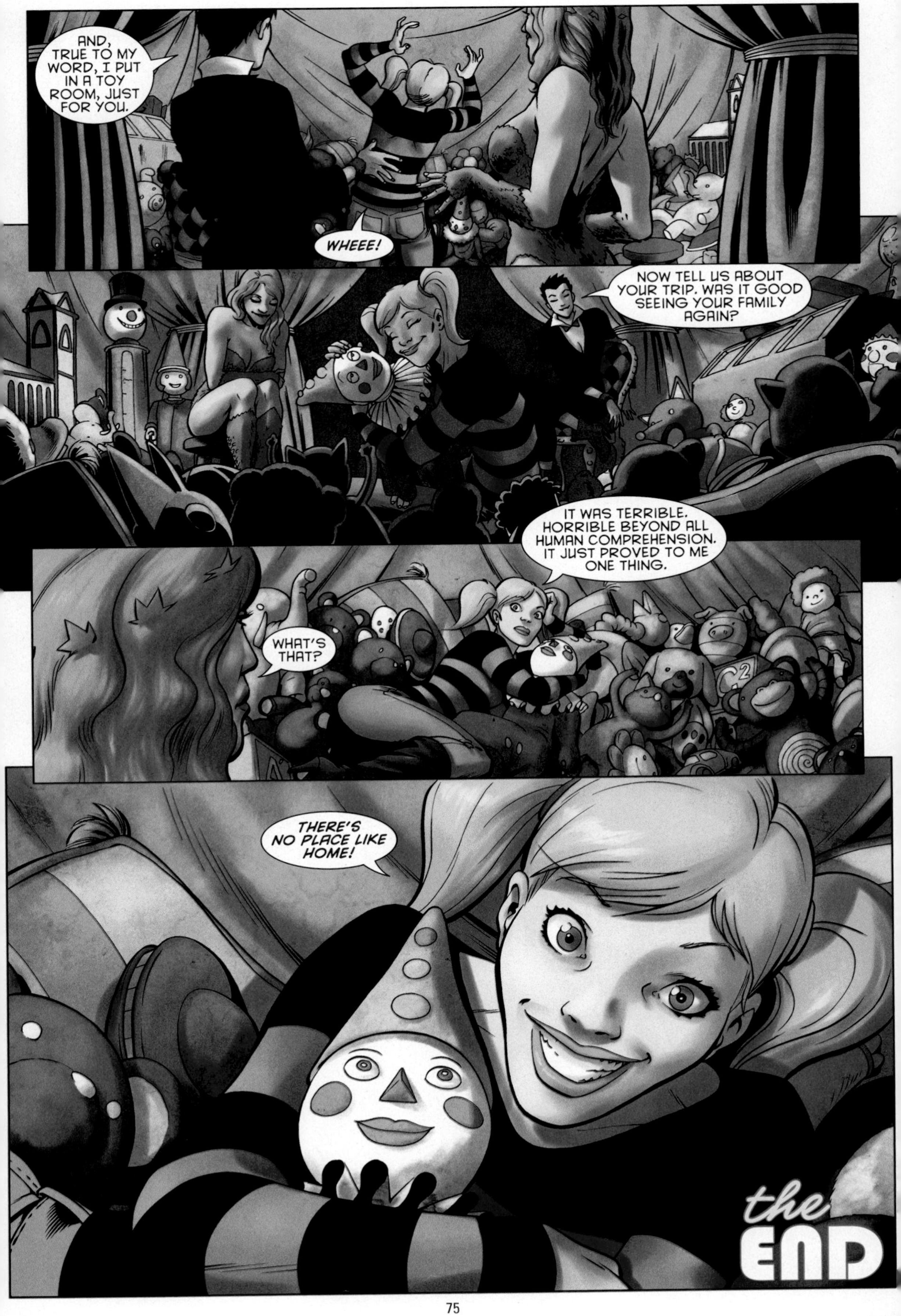
AND, TRUE TO MY WORD, I PUT IN A TOY ROOM, JUST FOR YOU.
WHEEE!
NOW TELL US ABOUT YOUR TRIP. WAS IT GOOD SEEING YOUR FAMILY AGAIN?
IT WAS TERRIBLE. HORRIBLE BEYOND ALL HUMAN COMPREHENSION. IT JUST PROVED TO ME ONE THING.
WHAT'S THAT?
THERE'S NO PLACE LIKE HOME!
the END

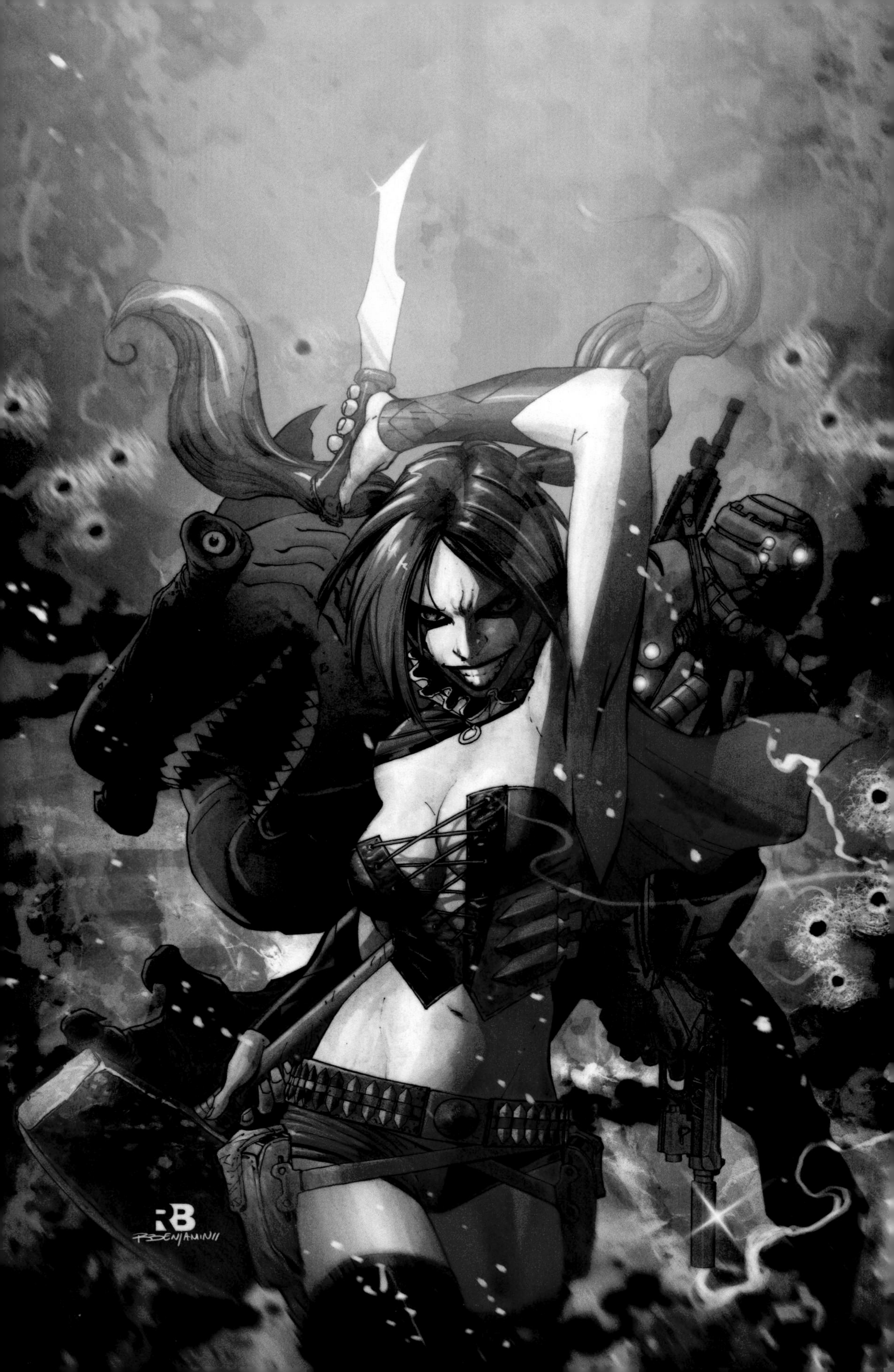
RB

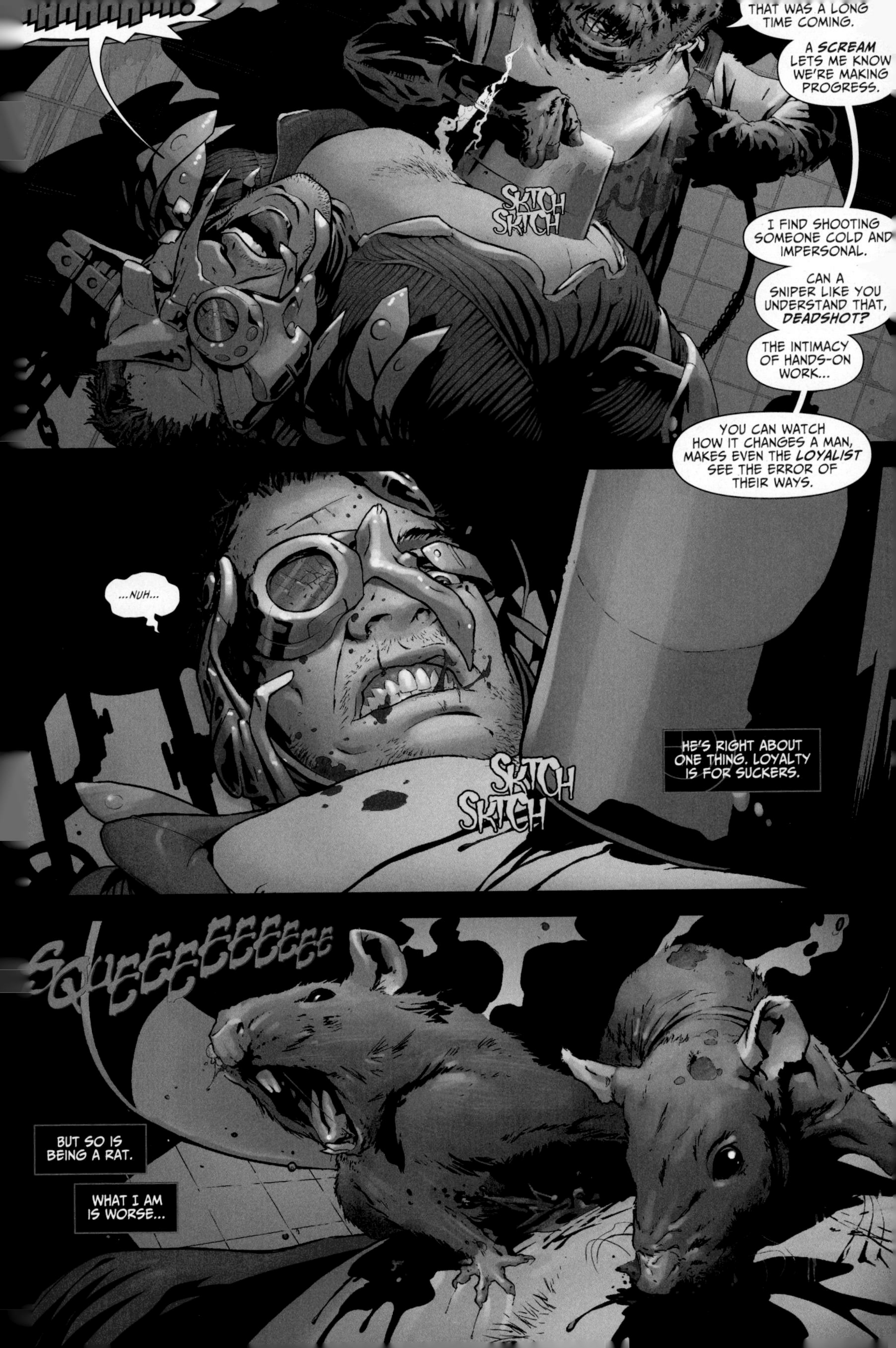
AHHHHH!!!
THAT WAS A LONG TIME COMING.
A SCREAM LETS ME KNOW WE'RE MAKING PROGRESS.
SKTCH SKTCH
I FIND SHOOTING SOMEONE COLD AND IMPERSONAL.
CAN A SNIPER LIKE YOU UNDERSTAND THAT, DEADSHOT?
THE INTIMACY OF HANDS-ON WORK...
YOU CAN WATCH HOW IT CHANGES A MAN, MAKES EVEN THE LOYALIST SEE THE ERROR OF THEIR WAYS.
...NUH...
HE'S RIGHT ABOUT ONE THING. LOYALTY IS FOR SUCKERS.
SKTCH SKTCH
SQUEEEEEEEEEE
BUT SO IS BEING A RAT.
WHAT I AM IS WORSE...

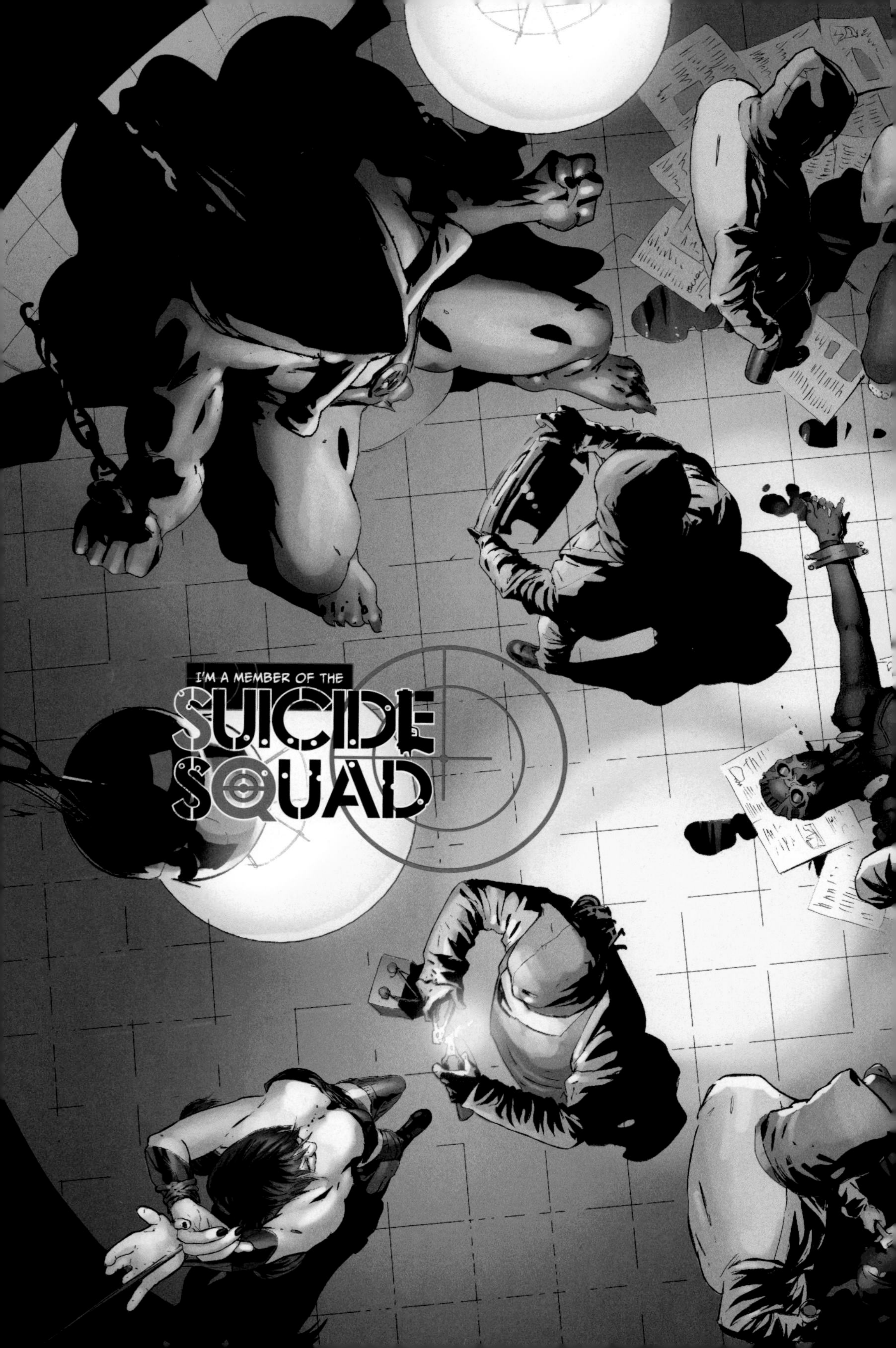
I'M A MEMBER OF THE
SUICIDE SQUAD

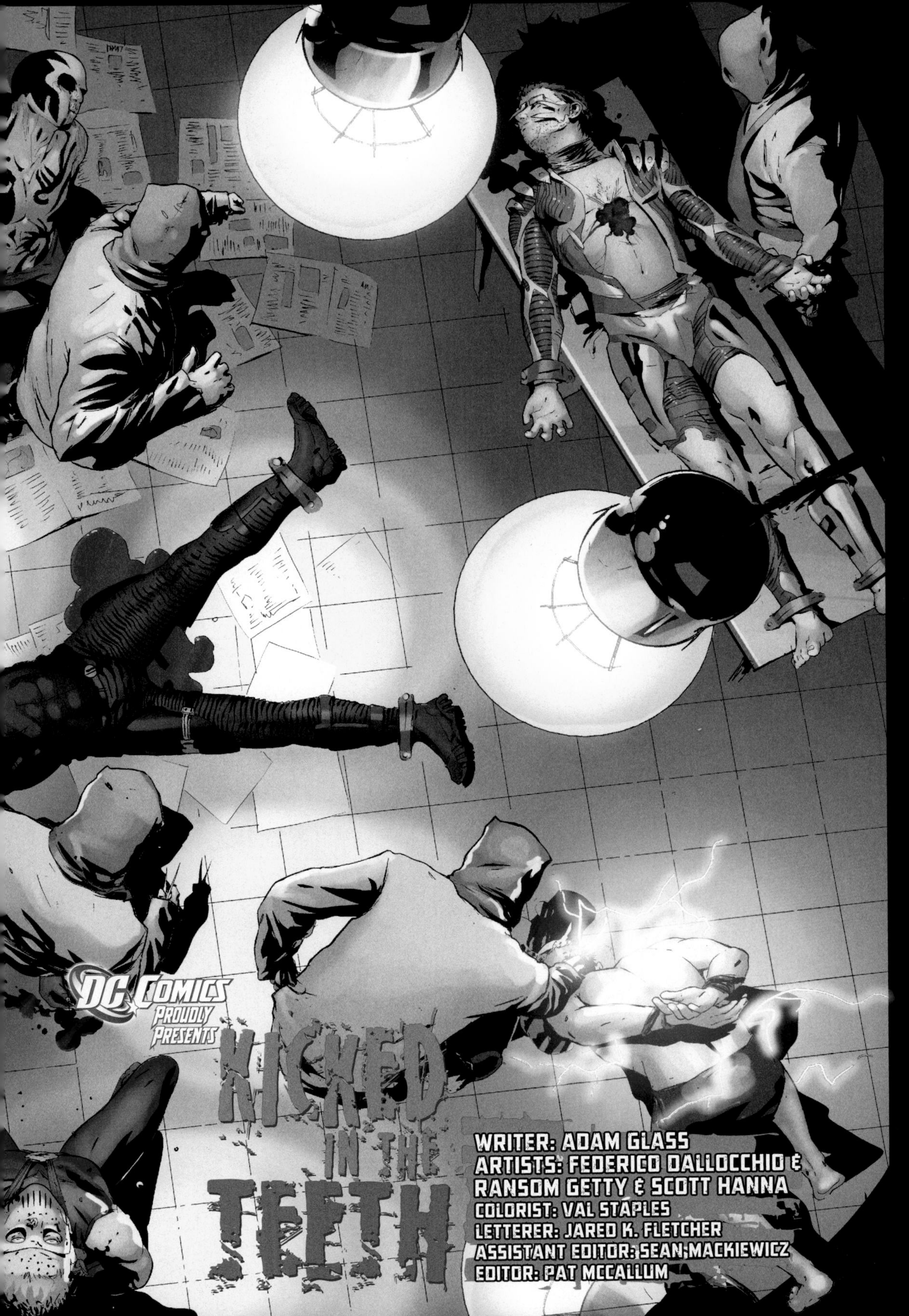
DC COMICS PROUDLY PRESENTS
KICKED IN THE TEETH
WRITER: ADAM GLASS
ARTISTS: FEDERICO DALLOCCHIO & RANSOM GETTY & SCOTT HANNA
COLORIST: VAL STAPLES
LETTERER: JARED K. FLETCHER
ASSISTANT EDITOR: SEAN MACKIEWICZ
EDITOR: PAT MCCALLUM

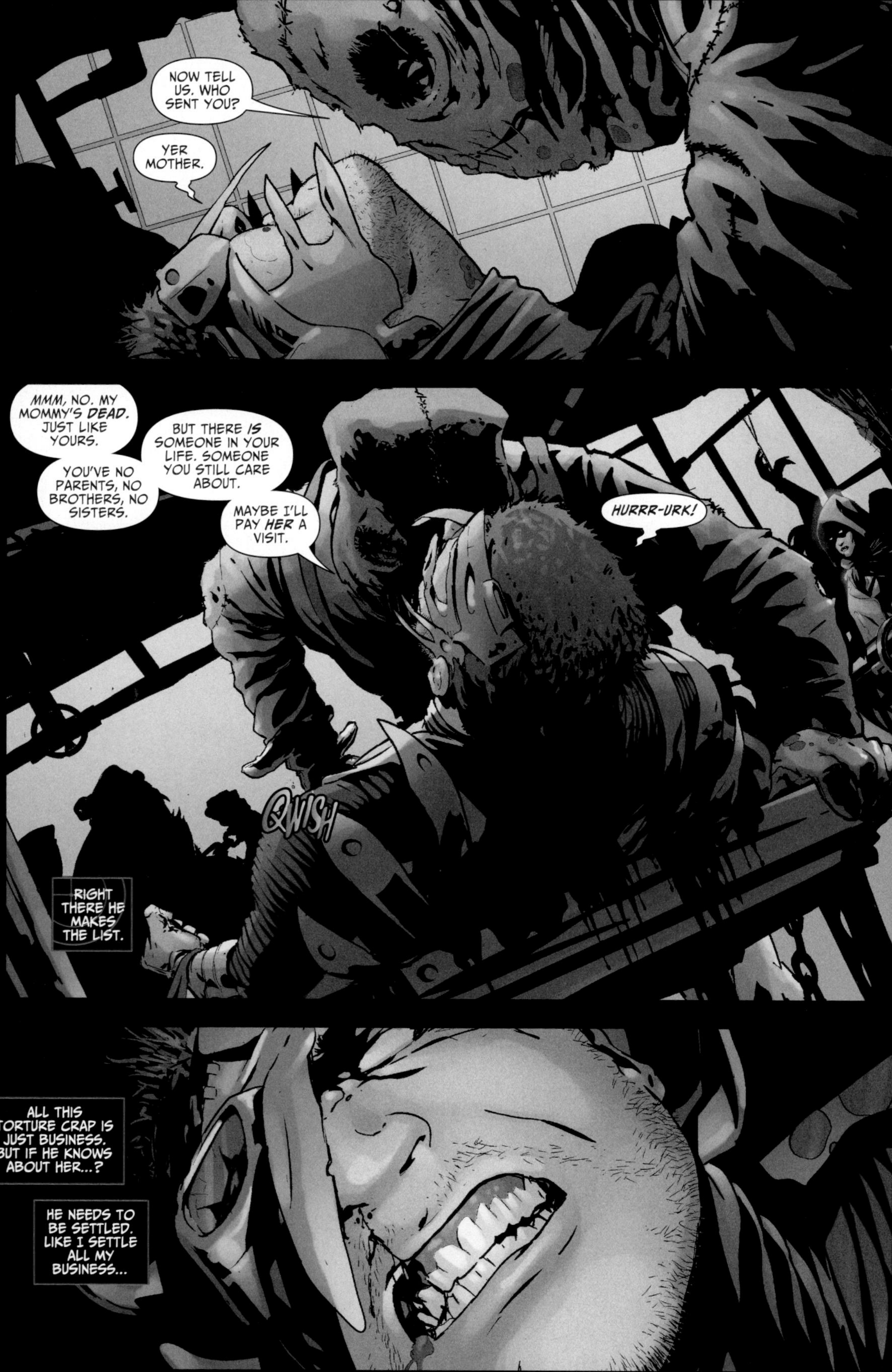

NOW TELL US. WHO SENT YOU?
YER MOTHER.
MMM, NO. MY MOMMY'S DEAD. JUST LIKE YOURS.
YOU'VE NO PARENTS, NO BROTHERS, NO SISTERS.
BUT THERE IS SOMEONE IN YOUR LIFE. SOMEONE YOU STILL CARE ABOUT.
MAYBE I'LL PAY HER A VISIT.
HURRR-URK!
QWISH
RIGHT THERE HE MAKES THE LIST.
ALL THIS TORTURE CRAP IS JUST BUSINESS. BUT IF HE KNOWS ABOUT HER...?
HE NEEDS TO BE SETTLED. LIKE I SETTLE ALL MY BUSINESS...

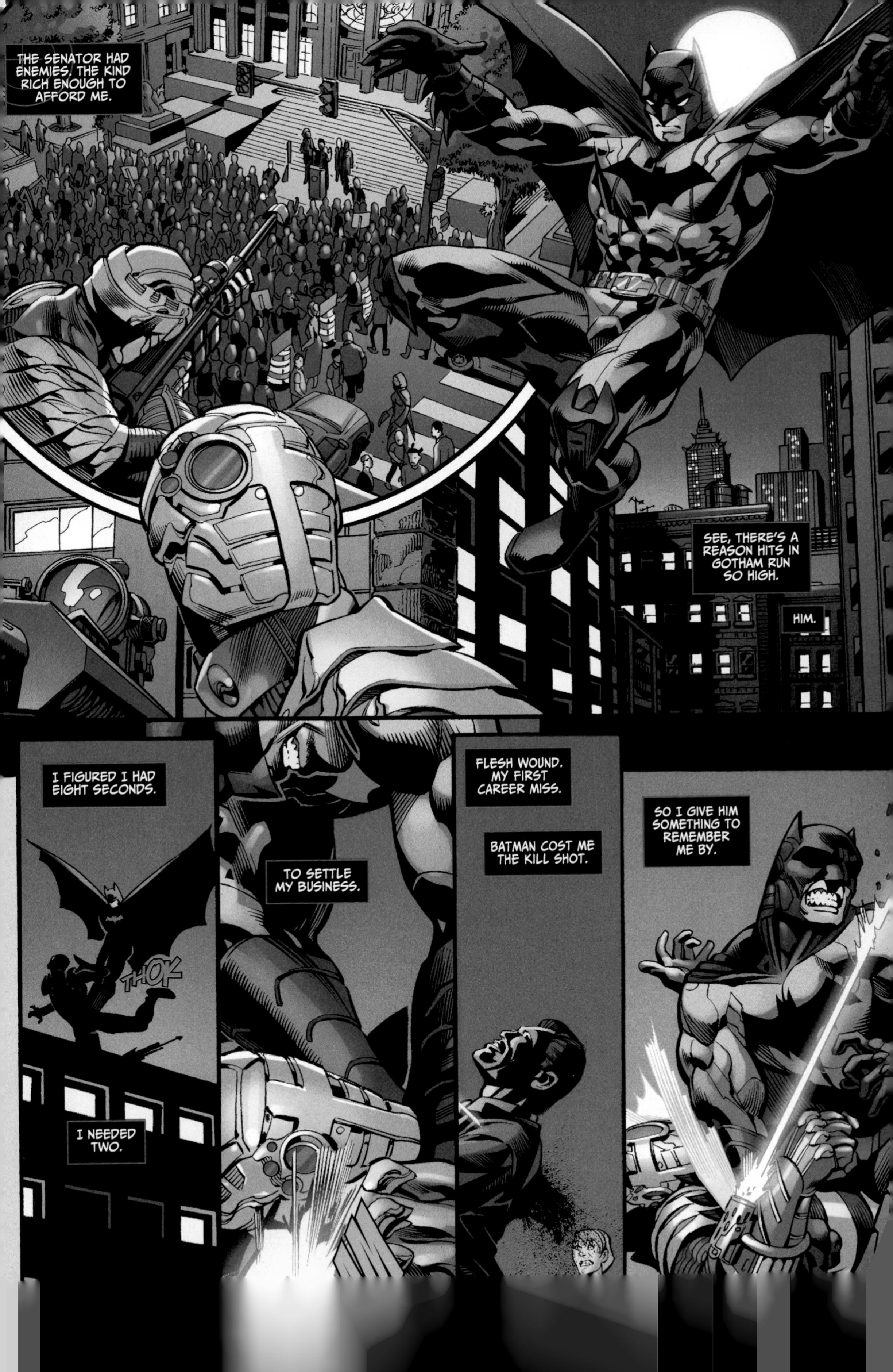
THE SENATOR HAD ENEMIES. THE KIND RICH ENOUGH TO AFFORD ME.
SEE, THERE'S A REASON HITS IN GOTHAM RUN SO HIGH.
HIM.
I FIGURED I HAD EIGHT SECONDS.
THOK
I NEEDED TWO.
TO SETTLE MY BUSINESS.
FLESH WOUND. MY FIRST CAREER MISS.
BATMAN COST ME THE KILL SHOT.
SO I GIVE HIM SOMETHING TO REMEMBER ME BY.

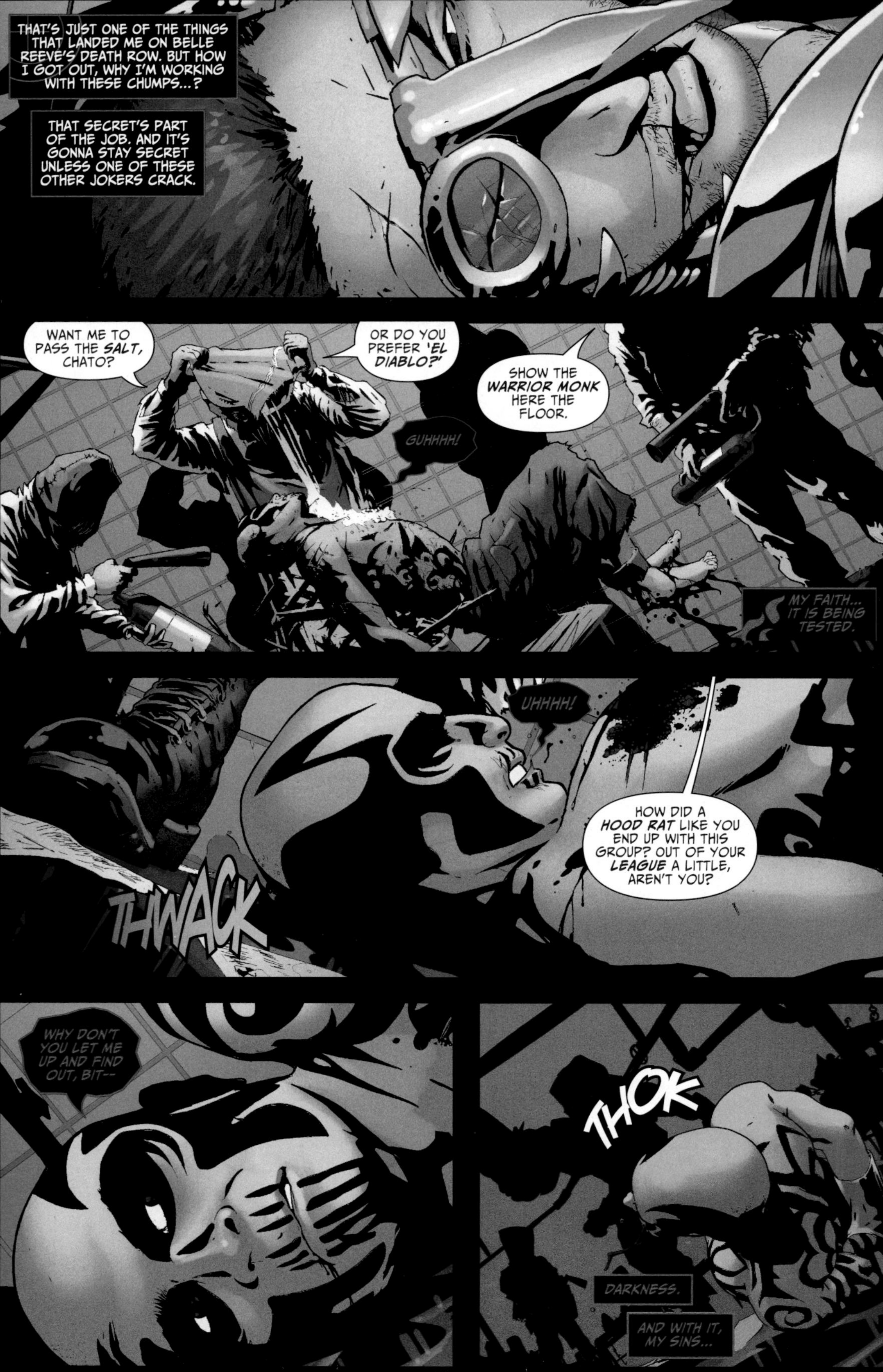
THAT'S JUST ONE OF THE THINGS THAT LANDED ME ON BELLE REEVE'S DEATH ROW. BUT HOW I GOT OUT, WHY I'M WORKING WITH THESE CHUMPS...?
THAT SECRET'S PART OF THE JOB. AND IT'S GONNA STAY SECRET UNLESS ONE OF THESE OTHER JOKERS CRACK.
WANT ME TO PASS THE SALT, CHATO?
OR DO YOU PREFER 'EL DIABLO?'
SHOW THE WARRIOR MONK HERE THE FLOOR.
GUHHHH!
MY FAITH... IT IS BEING TESTED.
UHHHH!
HOW DID A HOOD RAT LIKE YOU END UP WITH THIS GROUP? OUT OF YOUR LEAGUE A LITTLE, AREN'T YOU?
THWACK
WHY DON'T YOU LET ME UP AND FIND OUT, BIT--
THOK
DARKNESS.
AND WITH IT, MY SINS...

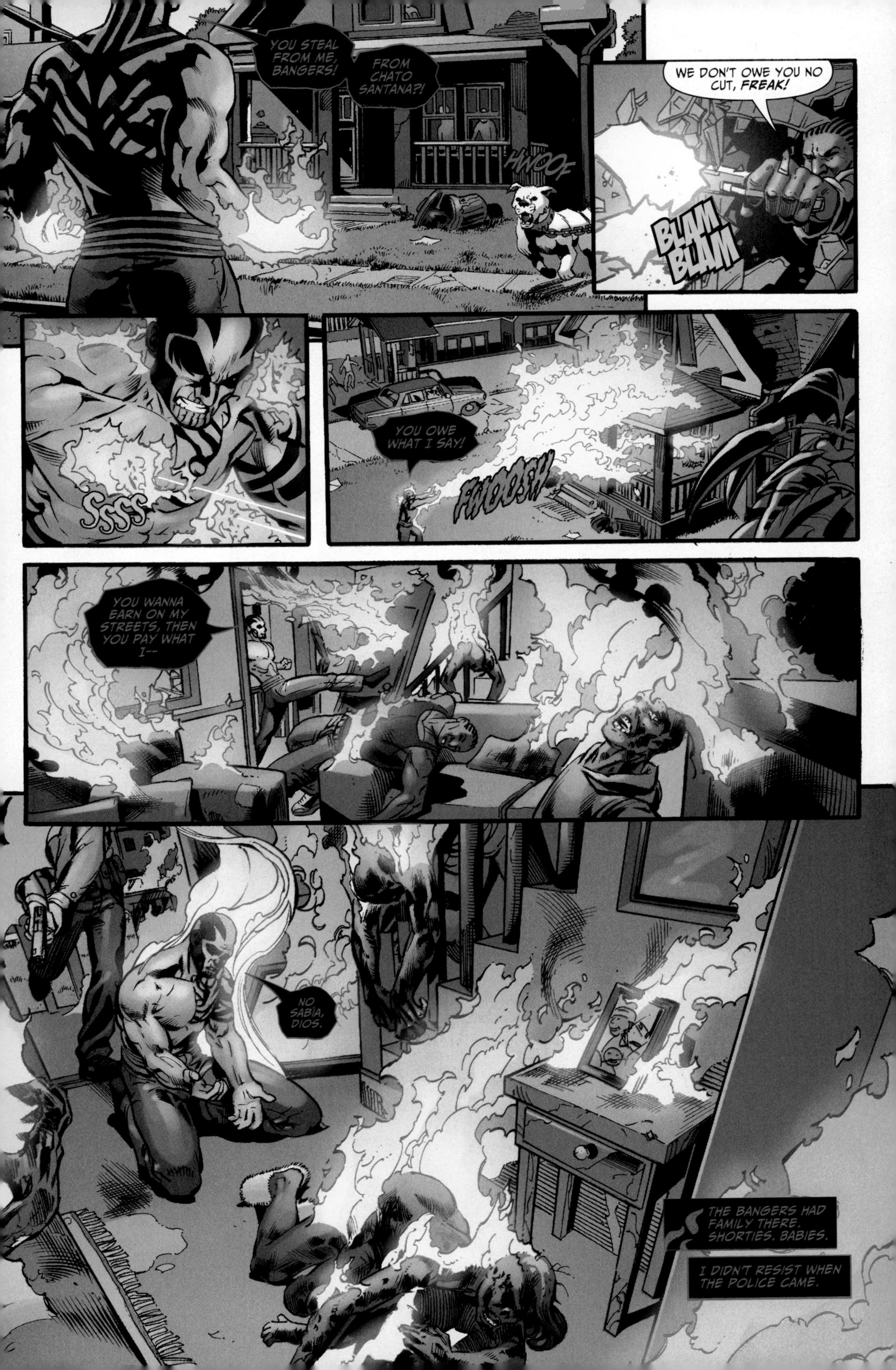

YOU STEAL FROM ME, BANGERS!
FROM CHATO SANTANA?!
HWOOF
WE DON'T OWE YOU NO CUT, FREAK!
BLAM BLAM
SSSS
YOU OWE WHAT I SAY!
FWOOSH
YOU WANNA EARN ON MY STREETS, THEN YOU PAY WHAT I--
NO SABIA, DIOS.
THE BANGERS HAD FAMILY THERE. SHORTIES. BABIES.
I DIDN'T RESIST WHEN THE POLICE CAME.

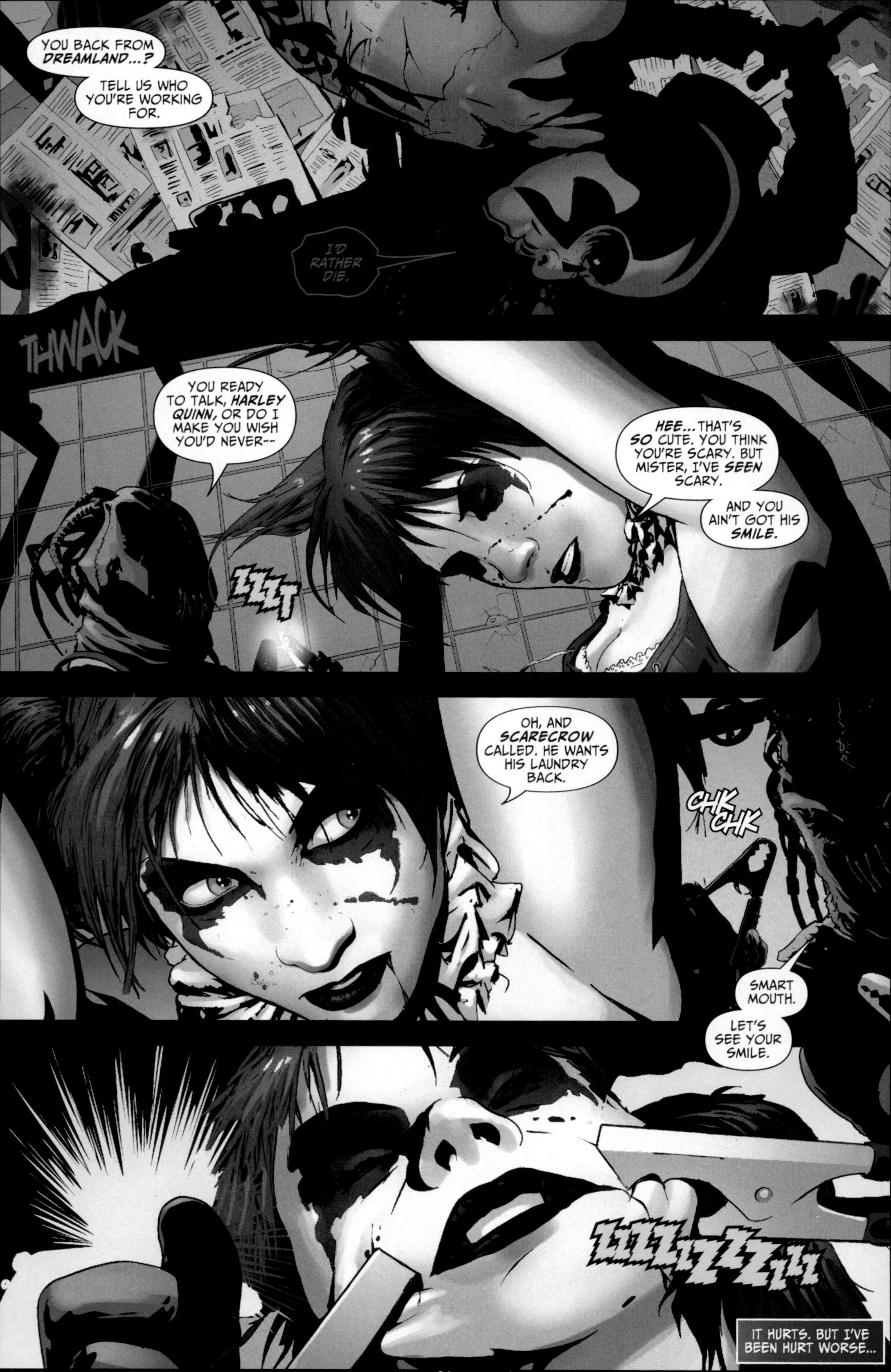
YOU BACK FROM DREAMLAND...?
TELL US WHO YOU'RE WORKING FOR.
I'D RATHER DIE.
THWACK
YOU READY TO TALK, HARLEY QUINN, OR DO I MAKE YOU WISH YOU'D NEVER--
HEE... THAT'S SO CUTE. YOU THINK YOU'RE SCARY. BUT MISTER, I'VE SEEN SCARY.
AND YOU AIN'T GOT HIS SMILE.
ZZZT
OH, AND SCARECROW CALLED. HE WANTS HIS LAUNDRY BACK.
CHK CHK
SMART MOUTH.
LET'S SEE YOUR SMILE.
IT HURTS. BUT I'VE BEEN HURT WORSE...

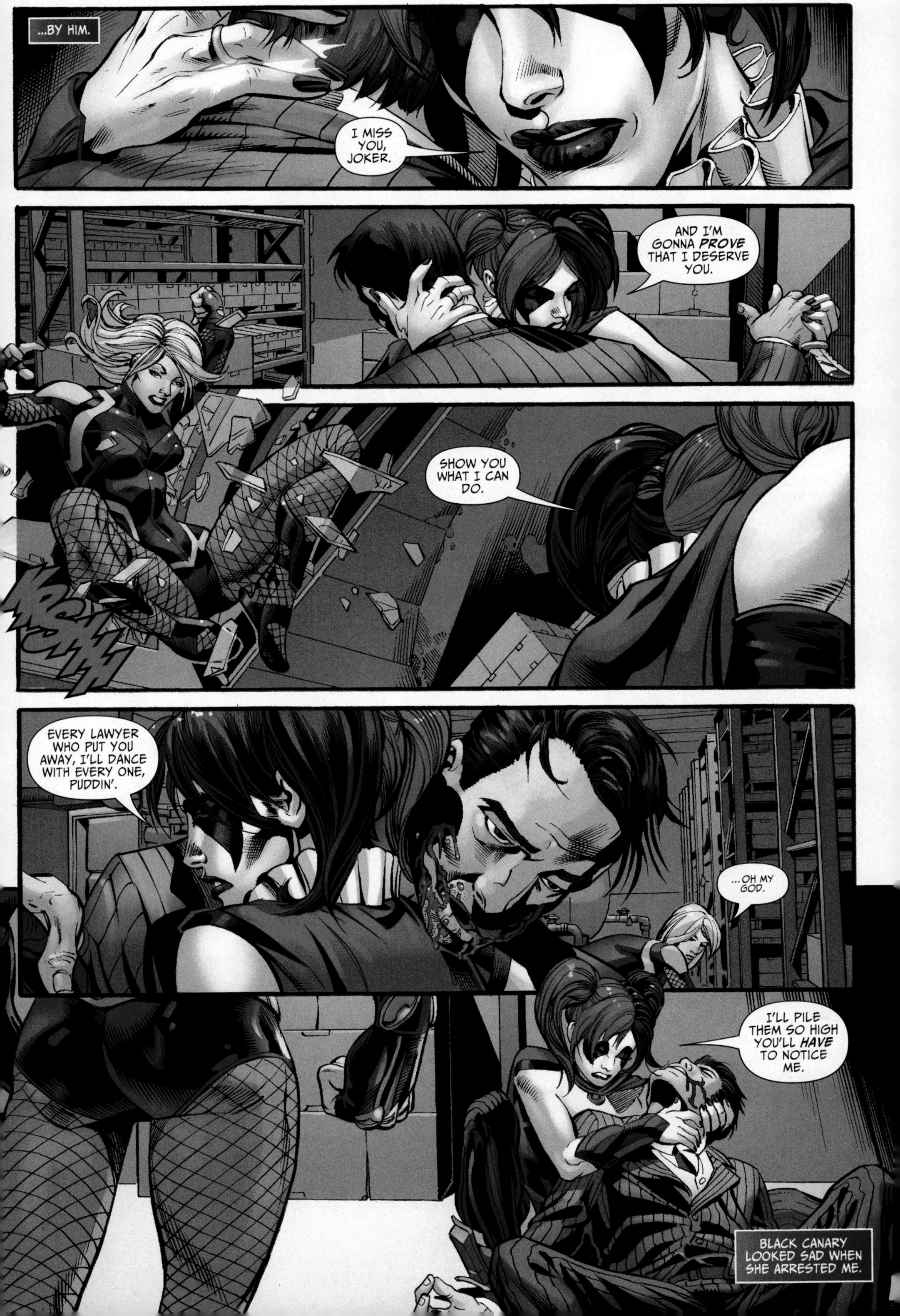
...BY HIM.
I MISS YOU, JOKER.
AND I'M GONNA PROVE THAT I DESERVE YOU.
SHOW YOU WHAT I CAN DO.
EVERY LAWYER WHO PUT YOU AWAY, I'LL DANCE WITH EVERY ONE, PUDDIN'.
...OH MY GOD.
I'LL PILE THEM SO HIGH YOU'LL HAVE TO NOTICE ME.
BLACK CANARY LOOKED SAD WHEN SHE ARRESTED ME.

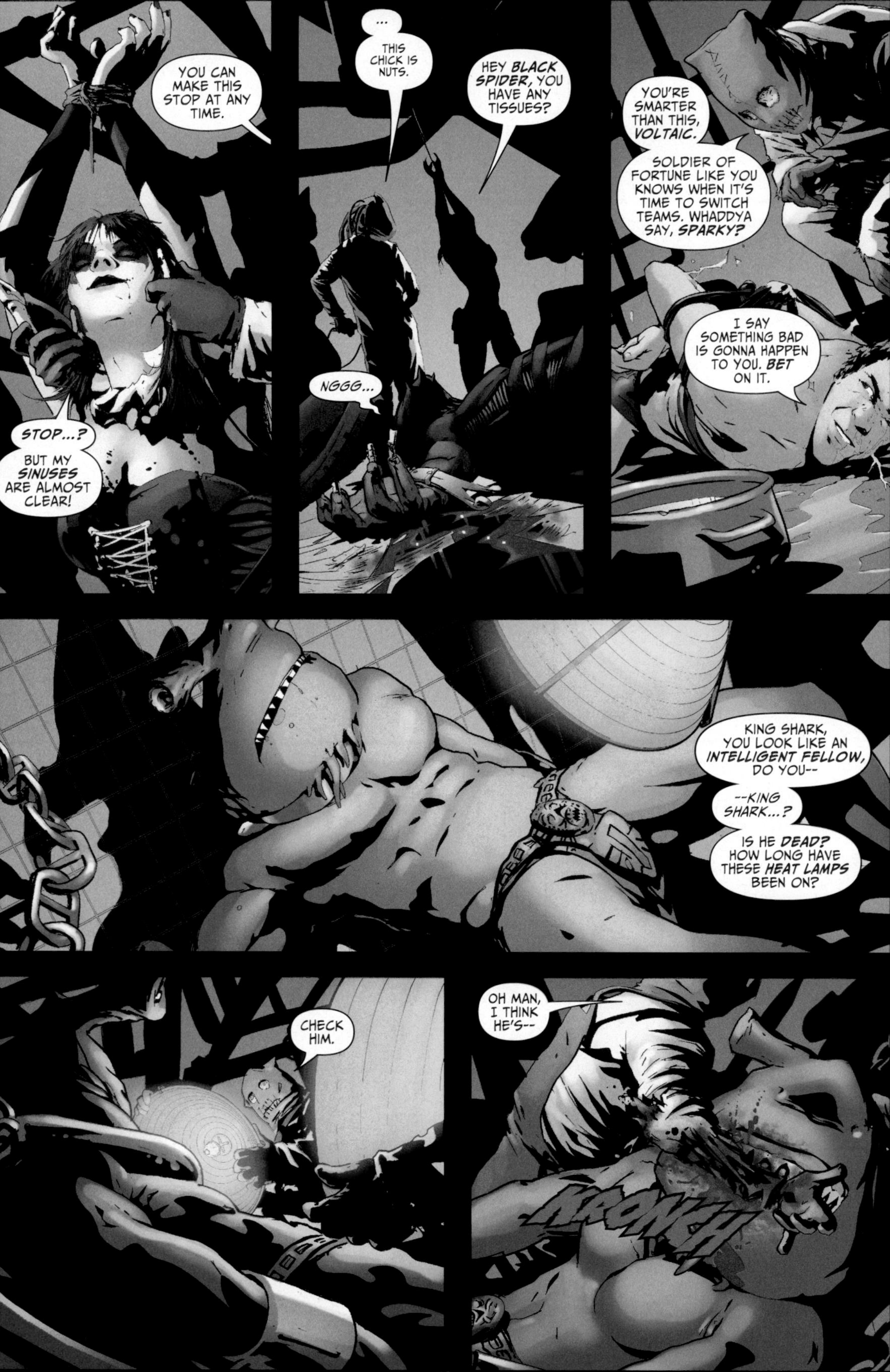
YOU CAN MAKE THIS STOP AT ANY TIME.
STOP...?
BUT MY SINUSES ARE ALMOST CLEAR!
...
THIS CHICK IS NUTS.
HEY BLACK SPIDER, YOU HAVE ANY TISSUES?
NGGG...
YOU'RE SMARTER THAN THIS, VOLTAIC.
SOLDIER OF FORTUNE LIKE YOU KNOWS WHEN IT'S TIME TO SWITCH TEAMS. WHADDYA SAY, SPARKY?
I SAY SOMETHING BAD IS GONNA HAPPEN TO YOU. BET ON IT.
KING SHARK, YOU LOOK LIKE AN INTELLIGENT FELLOW, DO YOU--
--KING SHARK...?
IS HE DEAD? HOW LONG HAVE THESE HEAT LAMPS BEEN ON?
CHECK HIM.
OH MAN, I THINK HE'S--
KRONCH

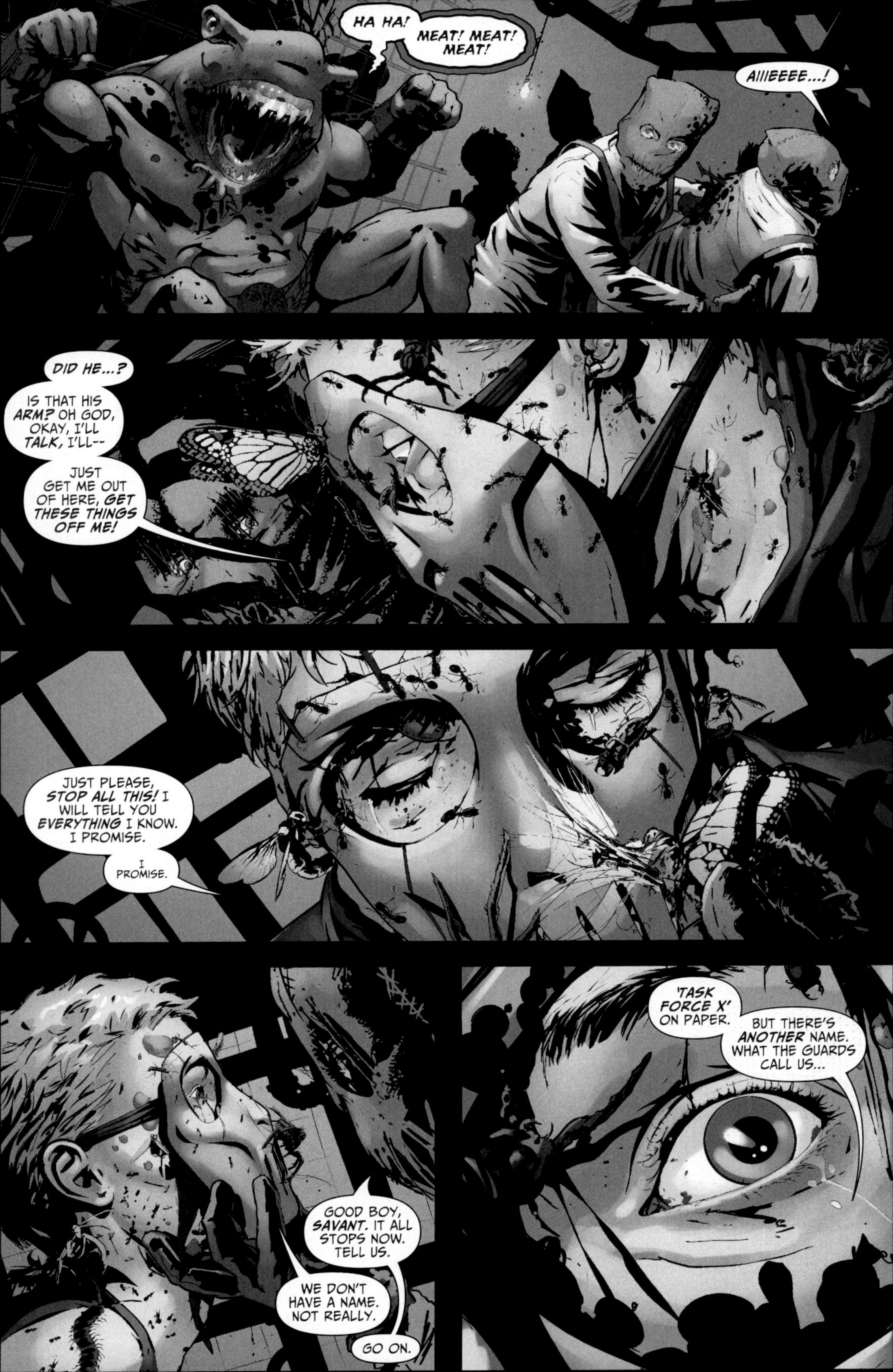
HA HA!
MEAT! MEAT! MEAT!
AIIIEEEE...!
DID HE...?
IS THAT HIS ARM? OH GOD, OKAY, I'LL TALK, I'LL--
JUST GET ME OUT OF HERE, GET THESE THINGS OFF ME!
JUST PLEASE, STOP ALL THIS! I WILL TELL YOU EVERYTHING I KNOW. I PROMISE.
I PROMISE.
GOOD BOY, SAVANT. IT ALL STOPS NOW. TELL US.
WE DON'T HAVE A NAME. NOT REALLY.
GO ON.
'TASK FORCE X' ON PAPER.
BUT THERE'S ANOTHER NAME. WHAT THE GUARDS CALL US...

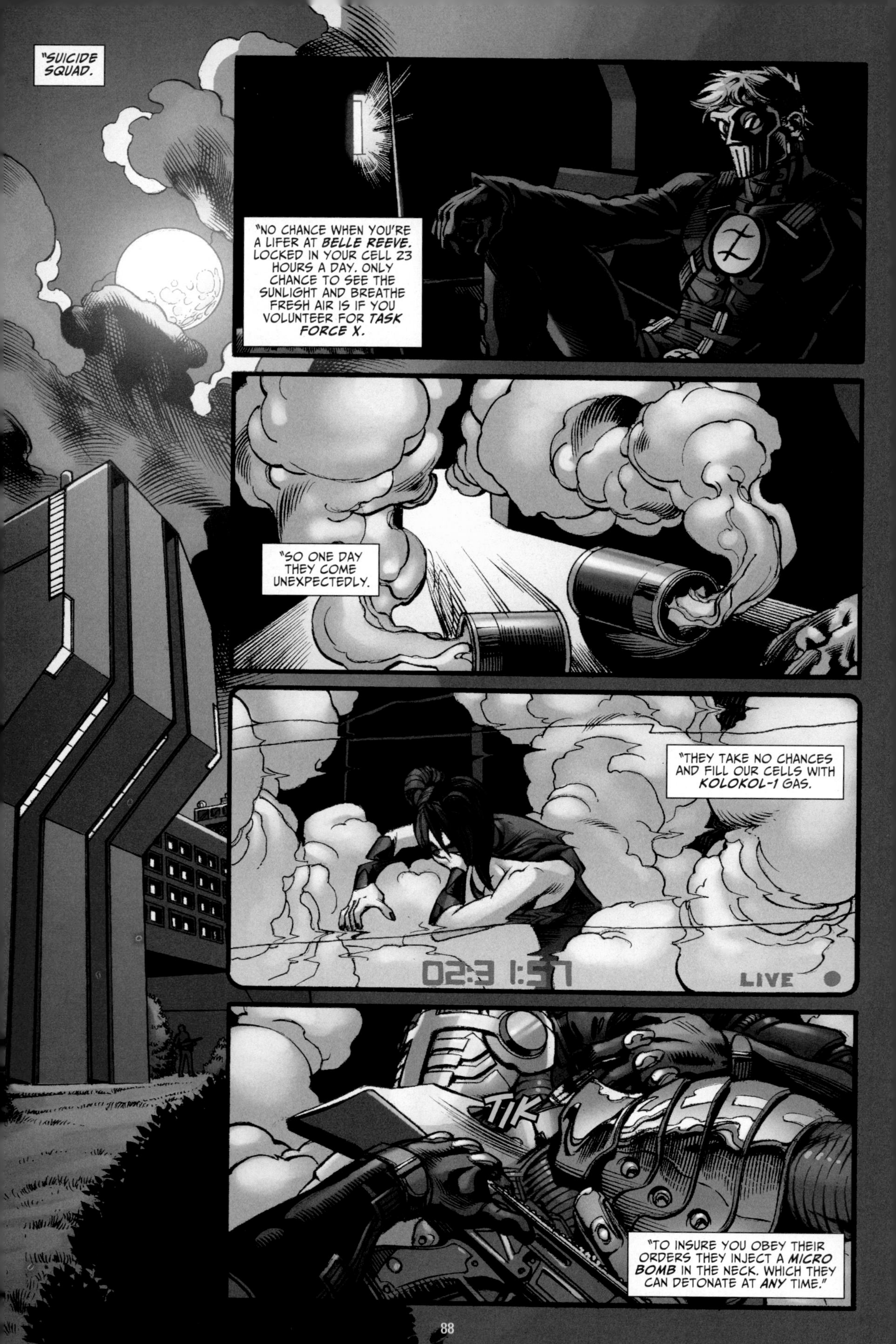
"SUICIDE SQUAD.
"NO CHANCE WHEN YOU'RE A LIFER AT BELLE REEVE. LOCKED IN YOUR CELL 23 HOURS A DAY. ONLY CHANCE TO SEE THE SUNLIGHT AND BREATHE FRESH AIR IS IF YOU VOLUNTEER FOR TASK FORCE X.
"SO ONE DAY THEY COME UNEXPECTEDLY.
"THEY TAKE NO CHANCES AND FILL OUR CELLS WITH KOLOKOL-1 GAS.
02:31:57
LIVE
TIK
"TO INSURE YOU OBEY THEIR ORDERS THEY INJECT A MICRO BOMB IN THE NECK. WHICH THEY CAN DETONATE AT ANY TIME."

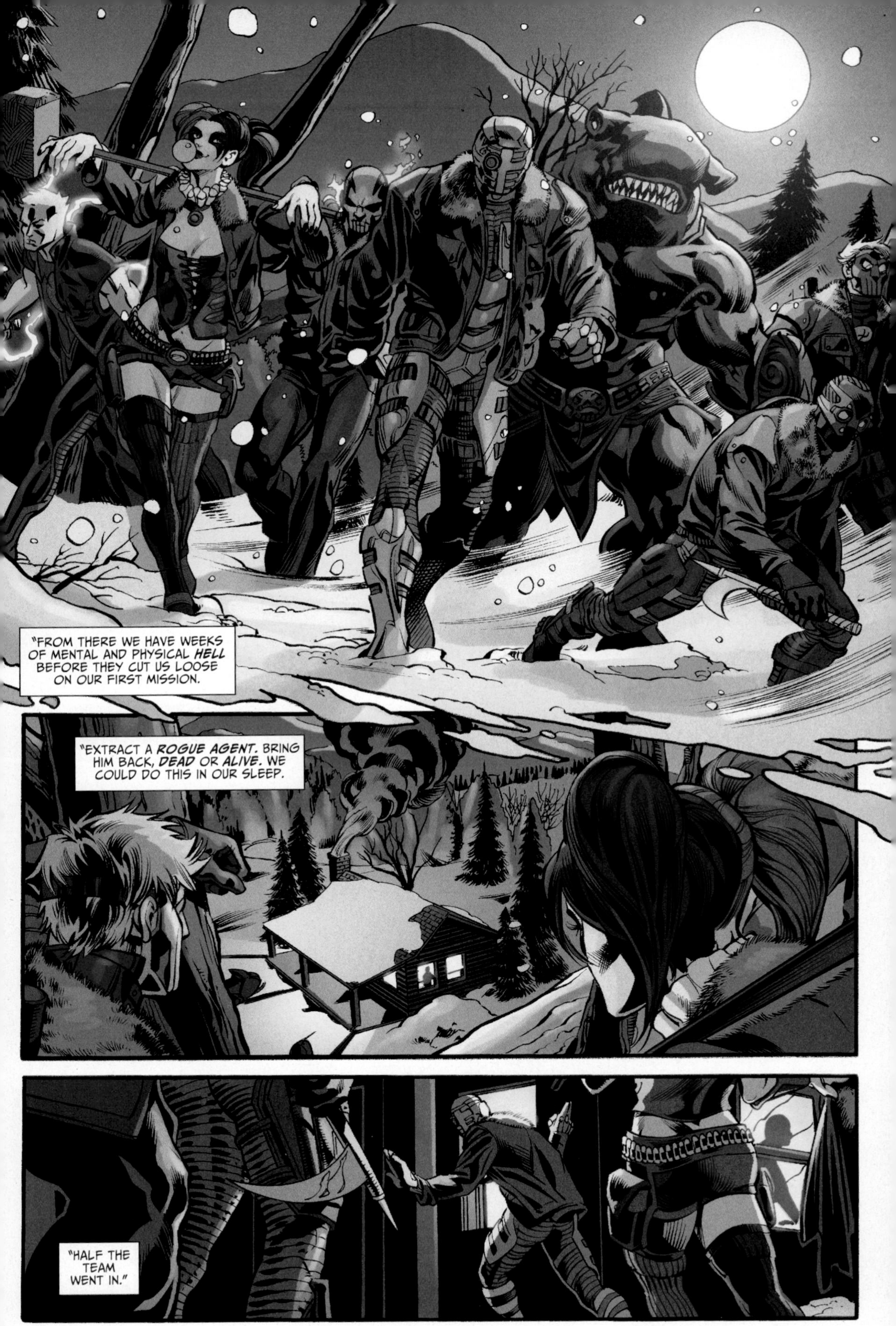
"FROM THERE WE HAVE WEEKS OF MENTAL AND PHYSICAL HELL BEFORE THEY CUT US LOOSE ON OUR FIRST MISSION.
"EXTRACT A ROGUE AGENT. BRING HIM BACK, DEAD OR ALIVE. WE COULD DO THIS IN OUR SLEEP.
"HALF THE TEAM WENT IN."

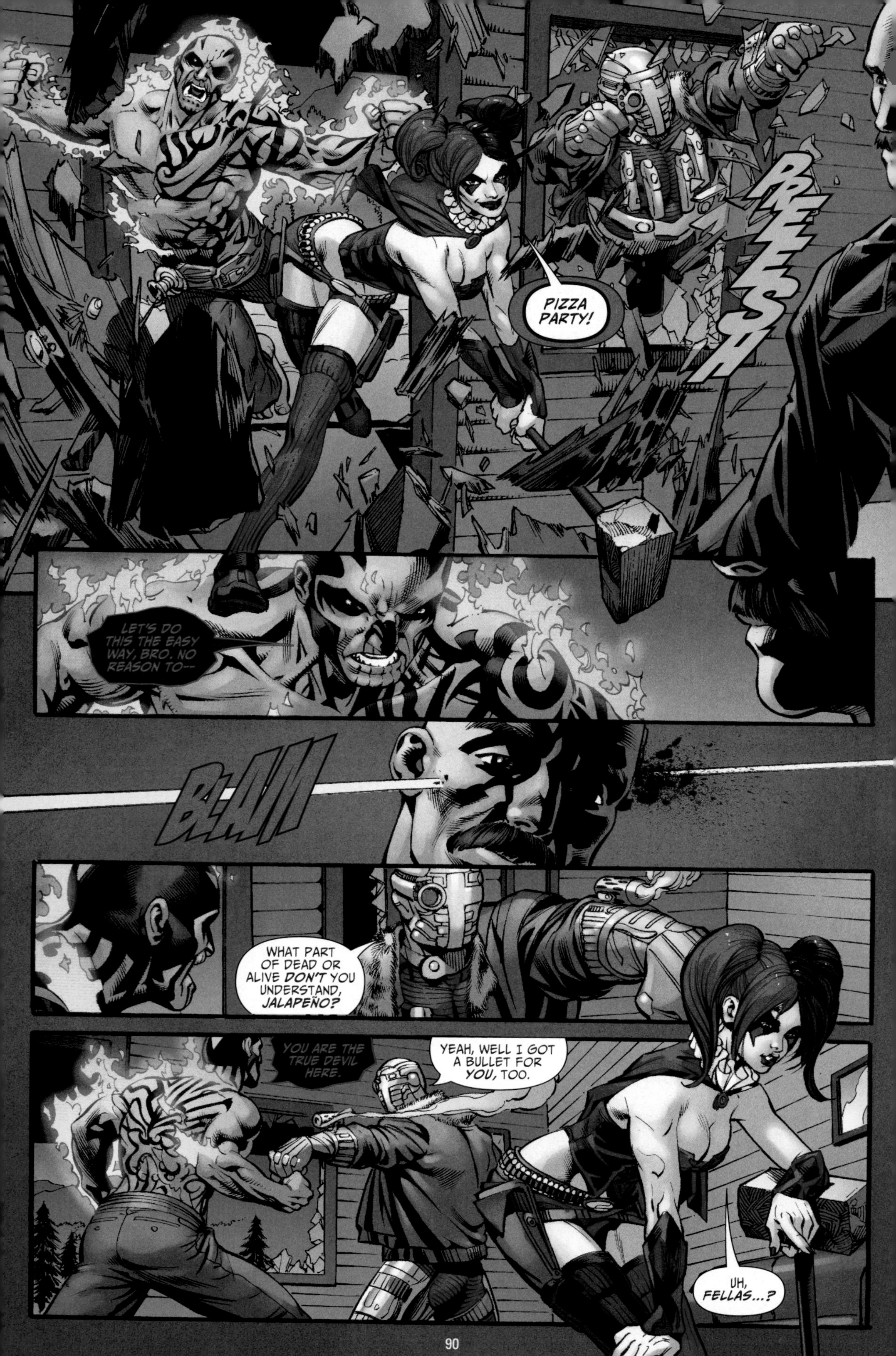

PIZZA PARTY!
FREEESH
LET'S DO THIS THE EASY WAY, BRO. NO REASON TO--
BLAM
WHAT PART OF DEAD OR ALIVE DON'T YOU UNDERSTAND, JALAPEÑO?
YOU ARE THE TRUE DEVIL HERE.
YEAH, WELL I GOT A BULLET FOR YOU, TOO.
UH, FELLAS...?

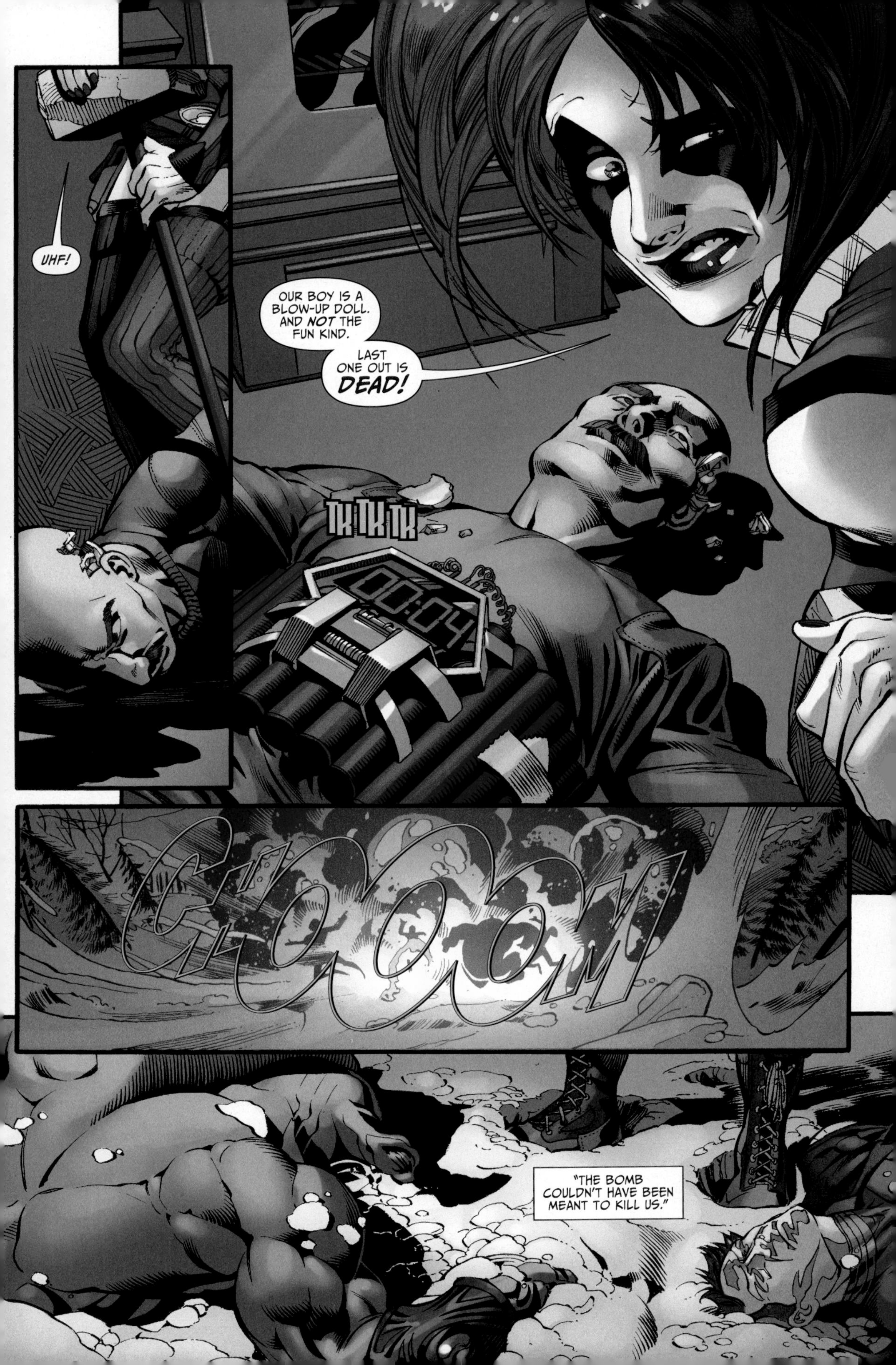
UHF!
OUR BOY IS A BLOW-UP DOLL. AND NOT THE FUN KIND.
LAST ONE OUT IS DEAD!
TK TK TK
00:04
CHOOOM
"THE BOMB COULDN'T HAVE BEEN MEANT TO KILL US."

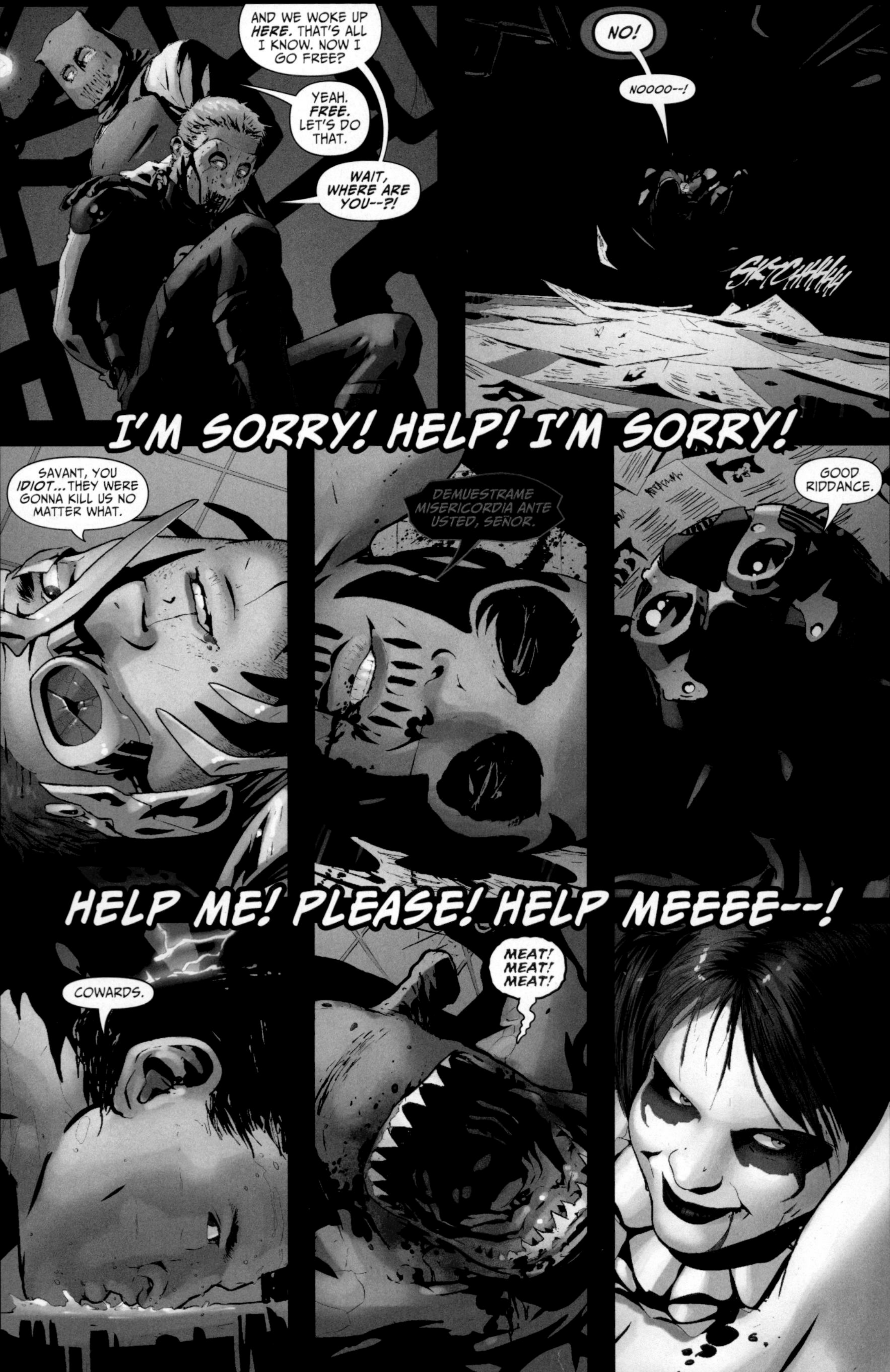

AND WE WOKE UP HERE. THAT'S ALL I KNOW. NOW I GO FREE?
YEAH. FREE. LET'S DO THAT.
WAIT, WHERE ARE YOU--?!
NO!
NOOOO--!
SKRCHHHHH
I'M SORRY! HELP! I'M SORRY!
SAVANT, YOU IDIOT... THEY WERE GONNA KILL US NO MATTER WHAT.
DEMUESTRAME MISERICORDIA ANTE USTED, SEÑOR.
GOOD RIDDANCE.
HELP ME! PLEASE! HELP MEEEE--!
COWARDS.
MEAT! MEAT! MEAT!

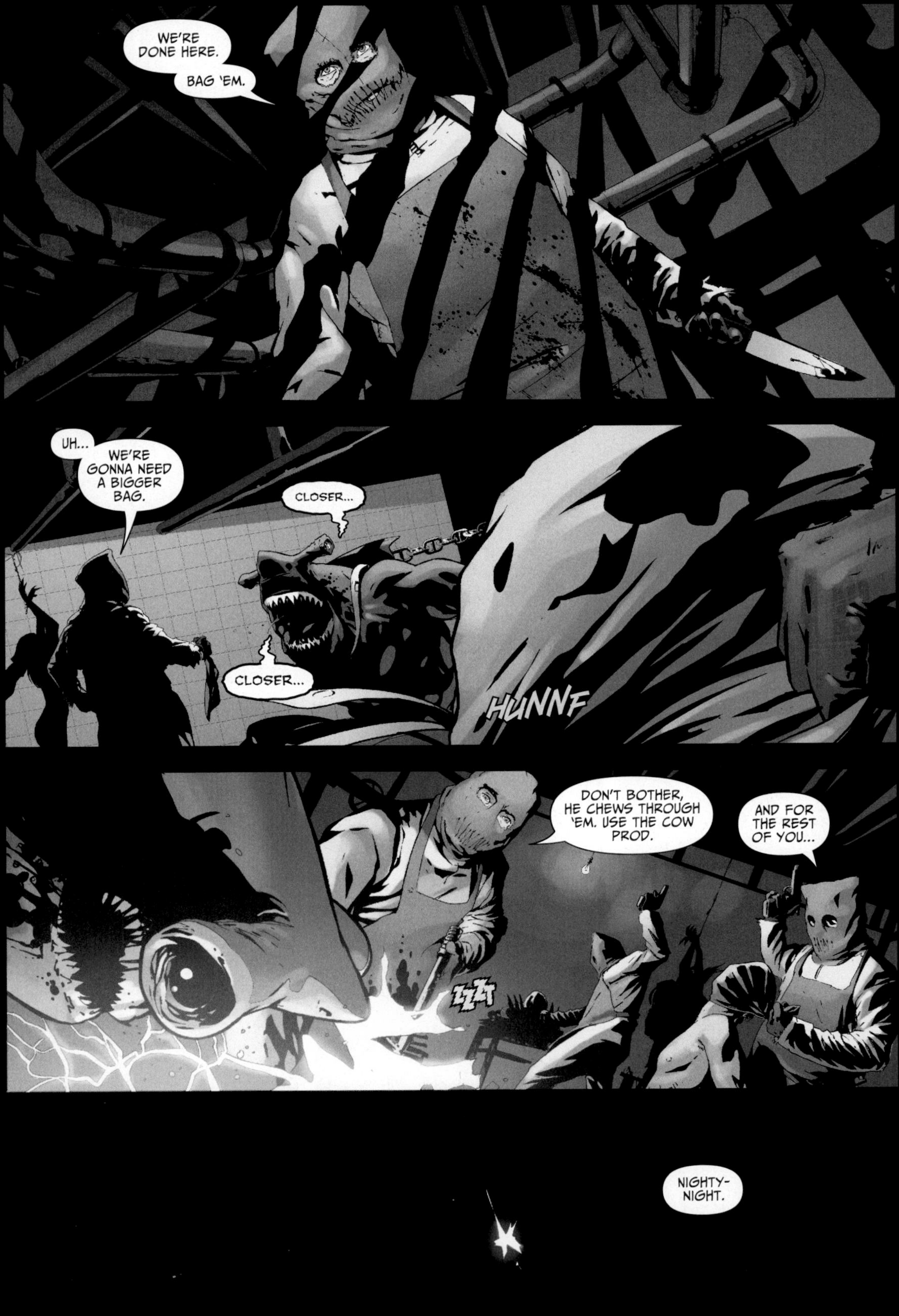
WE'RE DONE HERE.
BAG 'EM.
UH...
WE'RE GONNA NEED A BIGGER BAG.
CLOSER...
CLOSER...
HUNNF
DON'T BOTHER, HE CHEWS THROUGH 'EM. USE THE COW PROD.
AND FOR THE REST OF YOU...
ZZZT
NIGHTY-NIGHT.

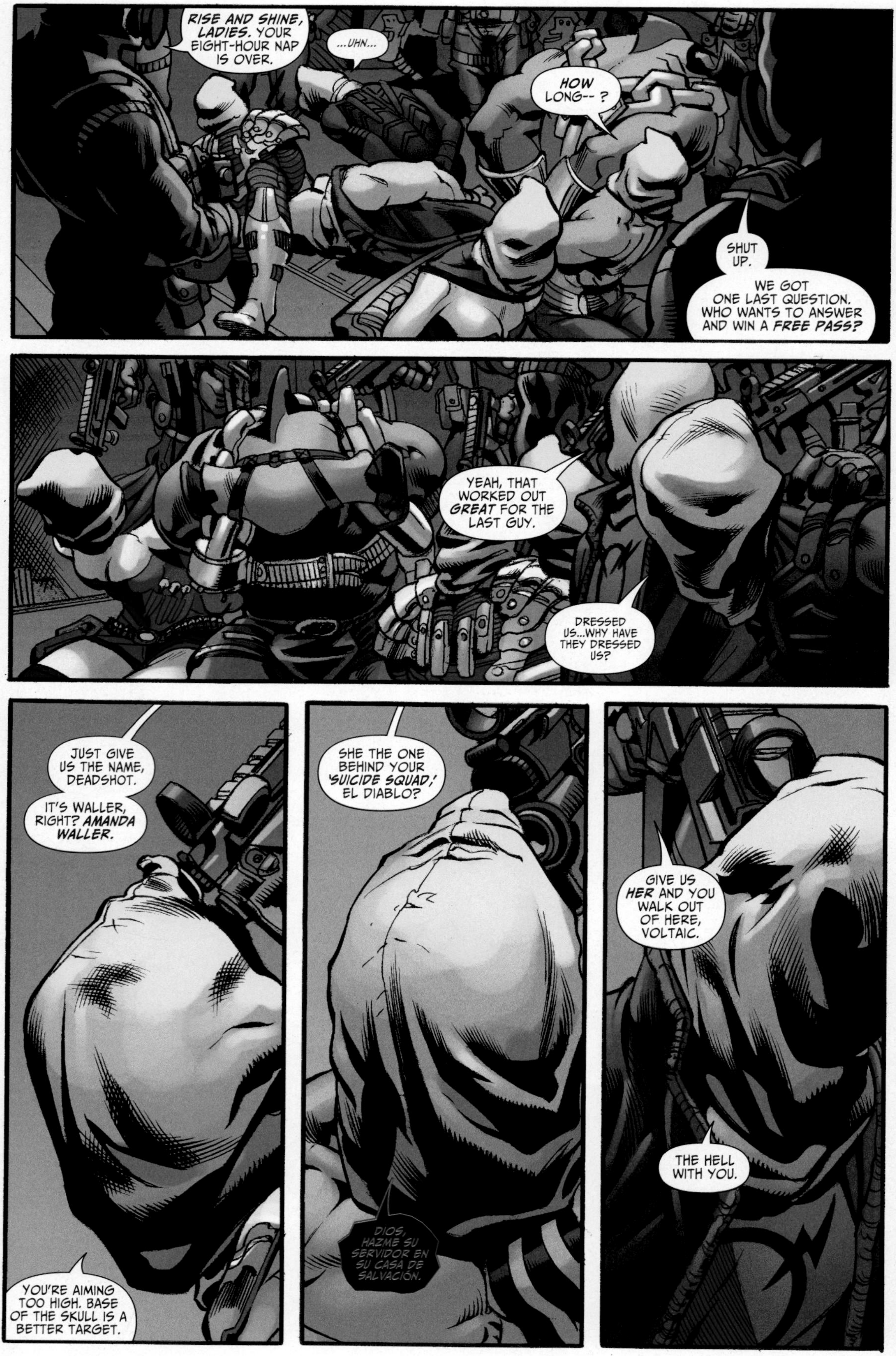
RISE AND SHINE, LADIES. YOUR EIGHT-HOUR NAP IS OVER.
...UHN...
HOW LONG-- ?
SHUT UP.
WE GOT ONE LAST QUESTION. WHO WANTS TO ANSWER AND WIN A FREE PASS?
YEAH, THAT WORKED OUT GREAT FOR THE LAST GUY.
DRESSED US...WHY HAVE THEY DRESSED US?
JUST GIVE US THE NAME, DEADSHOT.
IT'S WALLER, RIGHT? AMANDA WALLER.
YOU'RE AIMING TOO HIGH. BASE OF THE SKULL IS A BETTER TARGET.
SHE THE ONE BEHIND YOUR 'SUICIDE SQUAD,' EL DIABLO?
DIOS, HAZME SU SERVIDOR EN SU CASA DE SALVACIÓN.
GIVE US HER AND YOU WALK OUT OF HERE, VOLTAIC.
THE HELL WITH YOU.

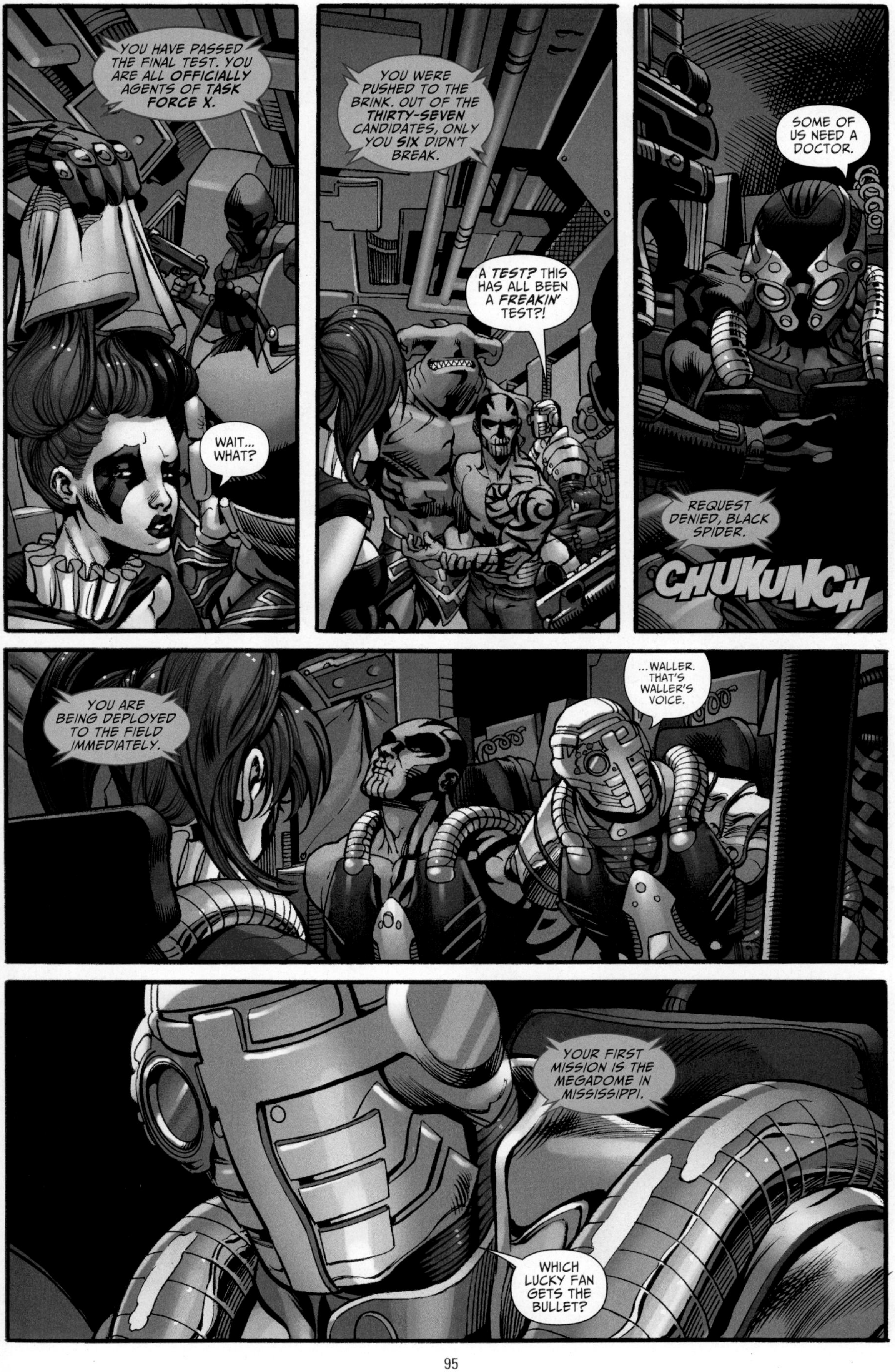
YOU HAVE PASSED THE FINAL TEST. YOU ARE ALL OFFICIALLY AGENTS OF TASK FORCE X.
WAIT... WHAT?
YOU WERE PUSHED TO THE BRINK. OUT OF THE THIRTY-SEVEN CANDIDATES, ONLY YOU SIX DIDN'T BREAK.
A TEST? THIS HAS ALL BEEN A FREAKIN' TEST?!
SOME OF US NEED A DOCTOR.
REQUEST DENIED, BLACK SPIDER.
CHUKUNCH
YOU ARE BEING DEPLOYED TO THE FIELD IMMEDIATELY.
...WALLER. THAT'S WALLER'S VOICE.
YOUR FIRST MISSION IS THE MEGADOME IN MISSISSIPPI.
WHICH LUCKY FAN GETS THE BULLET?

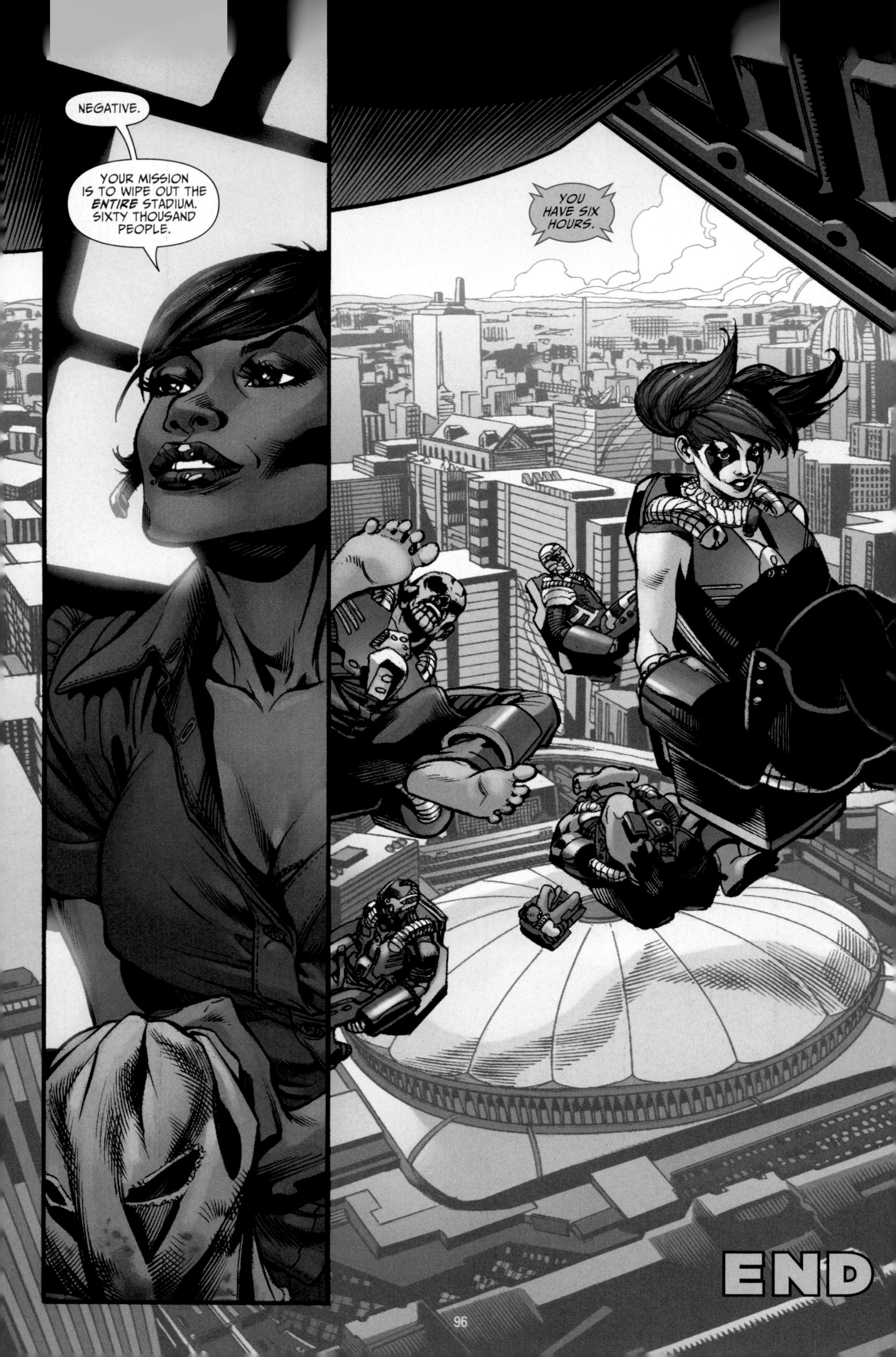
NEGATIVE.
YOUR MISSION IS TO WIPE OUT THE ENTIRE STADIUM. SIXTY THOUSAND PEOPLE.
YOU HAVE SIX HOURS.
END

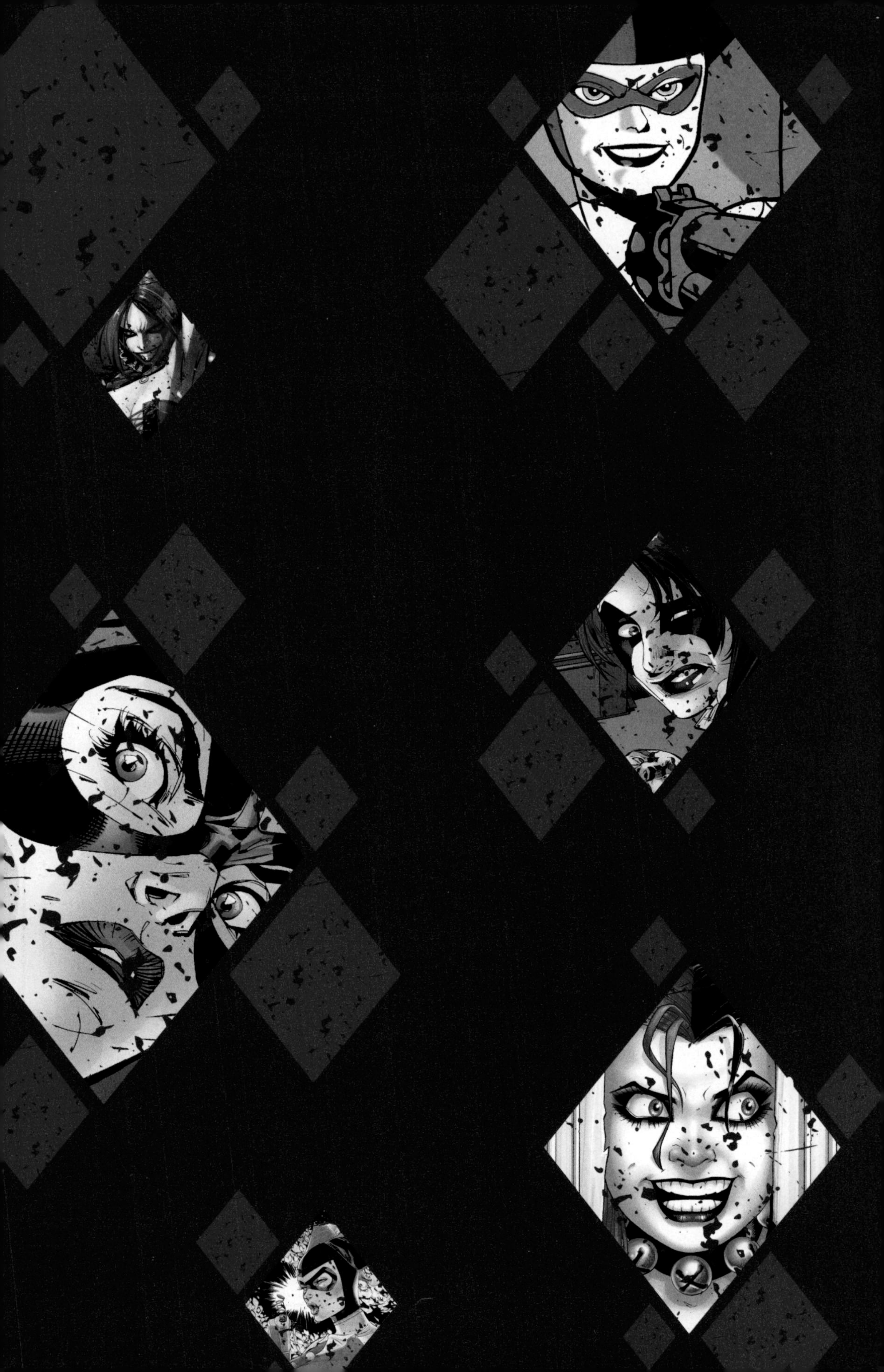

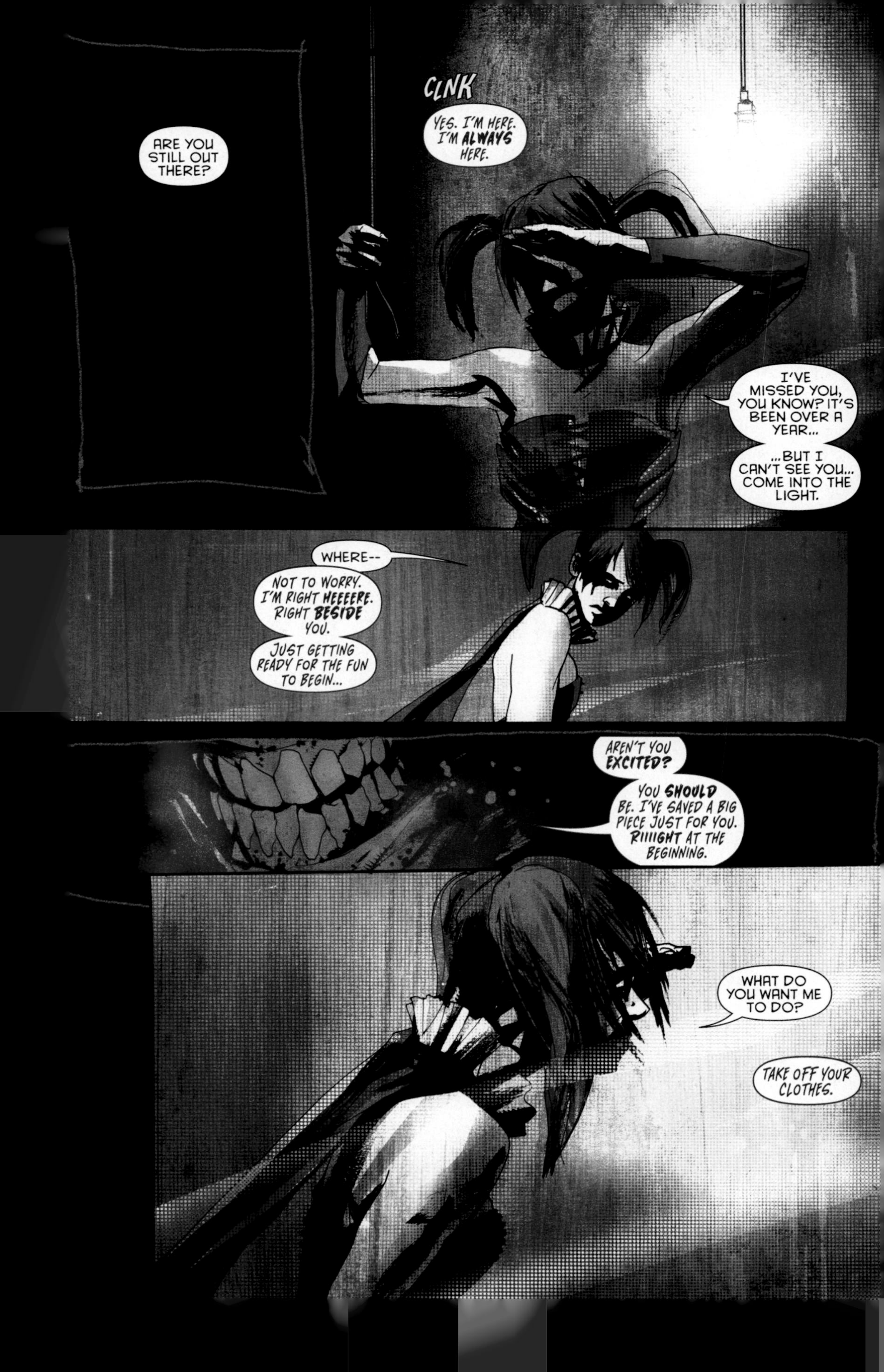

CLNK
ARE YOU STILL OUT THERE?
YES. I'M HERE. I'M ALWAYS HERE.
I'VE MISSED YOU, YOU KNOW? IT'S BEEN OVER A YEAR...
...BUT I CAN'T SEE YOU... COME INTO THE LIGHT.
WHERE--
NOT TO WORRY. I'M RIGHT HEEEERE. RIGHT BESIDE YOU.
JUST GETTING READY FOR THE FUN TO BEGIN...
AREN'T YOU EXCITED?
YOU SHOULD BE. I'VE SAVED A BIG PIECE JUST FOR YOU. RIIIIGHT AT THE BEGINNING.
WHAT DO YOU WANT ME TO DO?
TAKE OFF YOUR CLOTHES.

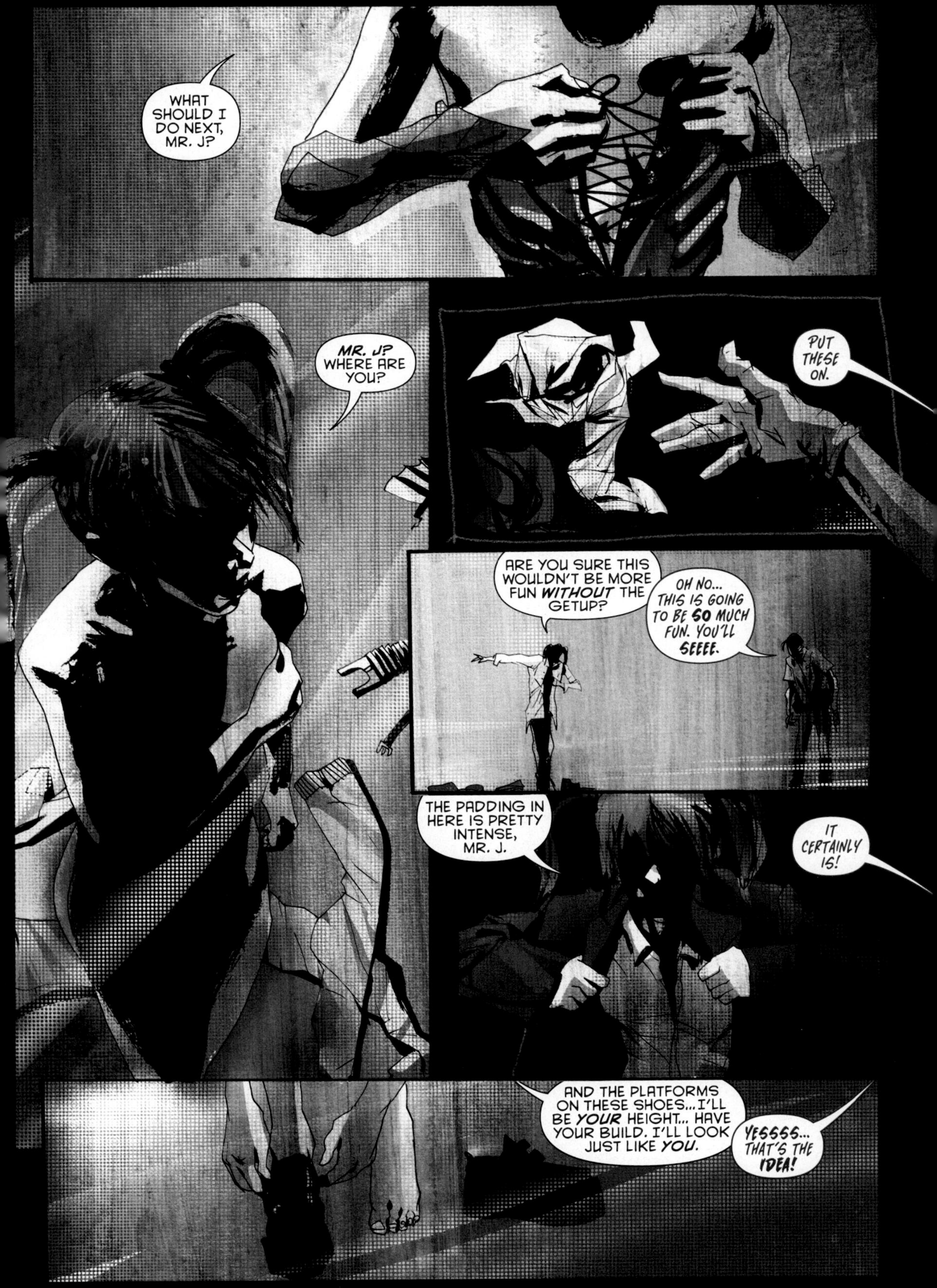
WHAT SHOULD I DO NEXT, MR. J?
MR. J? WHERE ARE YOU?
PUT THESE ON.
ARE YOU SURE THIS WOULDN'T BE MORE FUN WITHOUT THE GETUP?
OH NO... THIS IS GOING TO BE SO MUCH FUN. YOU'LL SEEEE.
THE PADDING IN HERE IS PRETTY INTENSE, MR. J.
IT CERTAINLY IS!
AND THE PLATFORMS ON THESE SHOES... I'LL BE YOUR HEIGHT... HAVE YOUR BUILD. I'LL LOOK JUST LIKE YOU.
YESSSS... THAT'S THE IDEA!

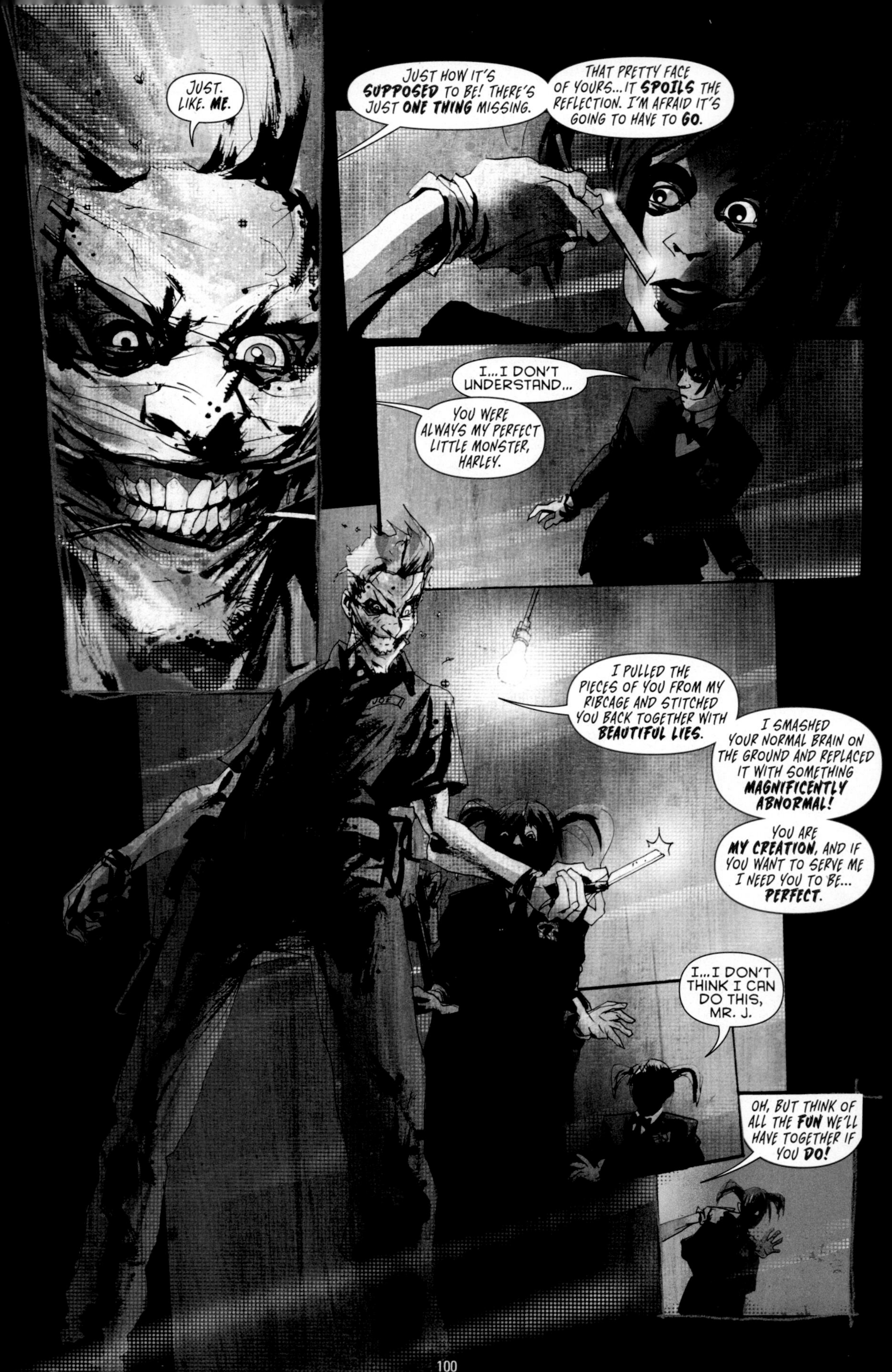
JUST. LIKE. ME.
JUST HOW IT'S SUPPOSED TO BE! THERE'S JUST ONE THING MISSING.
THAT PRETTY FACE OF YOURS... IT SPOILS THE REFLECTION. I'M AFRAID IT'S GOING TO HAVE TO GO.
I... I DON'T UNDERSTAND...
YOU WERE ALWAYS MY PERFECT LITTLE MONSTER, HARLEY.
JOE
I PULLED THE PIECES OF YOU FROM MY RIBCAGE AND STITCHED YOU BACK TOGETHER WITH BEAUTIFUL LIES.
I SMASHED YOUR NORMAL BRAIN ON THE GROUND AND REPLACED IT WITH SOMETHING MAGNIFICENTLY ABNORMAL!
YOU ARE MY CREATION, AND IF YOU WANT TO SERVE ME I NEED YOU TO BE... PERFECT.
I... I DON'T THINK I CAN DO THIS, MR. J.
OH, BUT THINK OF ALL THE FUN WE'LL HAVE TOGETHER IF YOU DO!

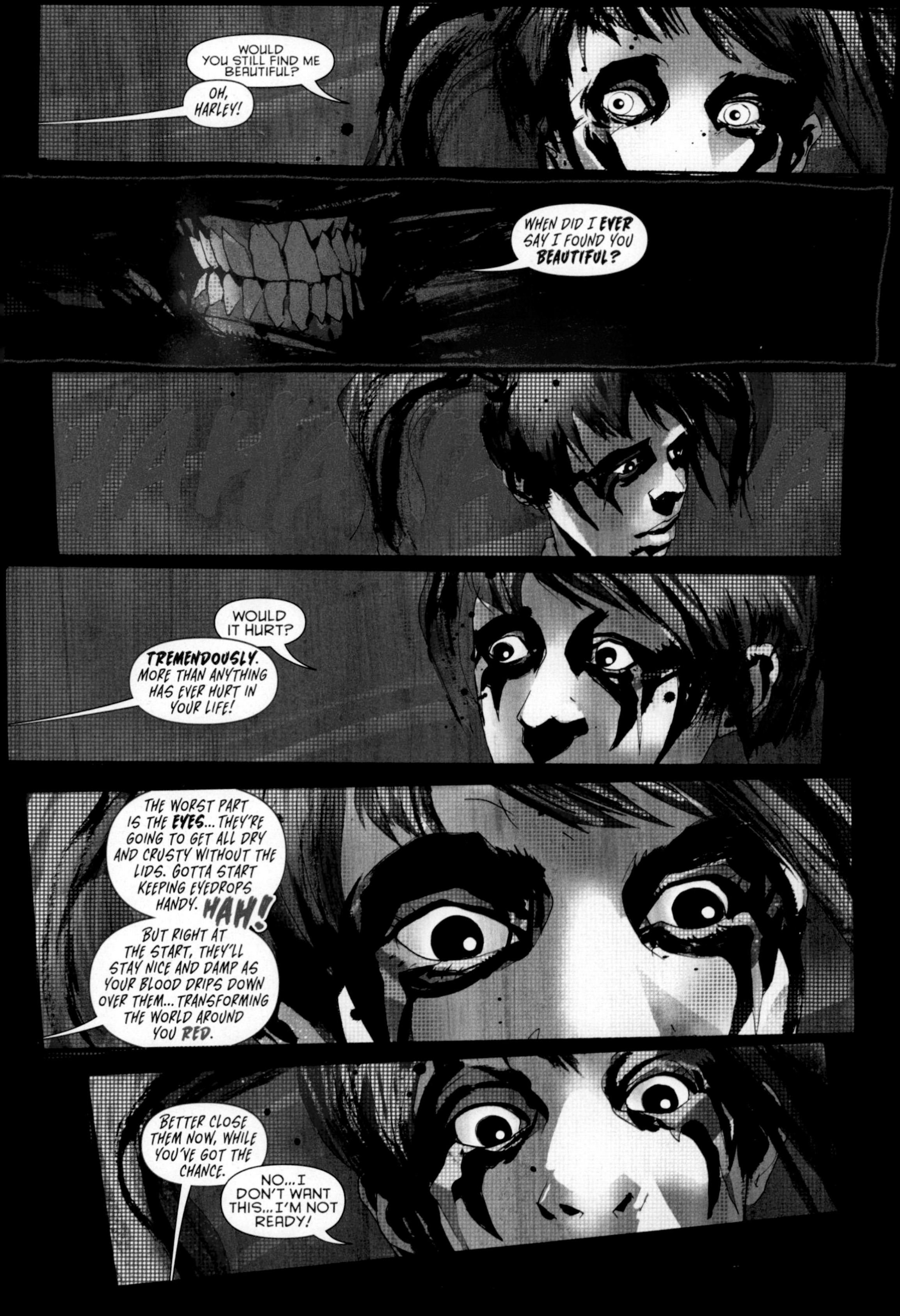
WOULD YOU STILL FIND ME BEAUTIFUL?
OH, HARLEY!
WHEN DID I EVER SAY I FOUND YOU BEAUTIFUL?
WOULD IT HURT?
TREMENDOUSLY. MORE THAN ANYTHING HAS EVER HURT IN YOUR LIFE!
THE WORST PART IS THE EYES... THEY'RE GOING TO GET ALL DRY AND CRUSTY WITHOUT THE LIDS. GOTTA START KEEPING EYEDROPS HANDY. HAH!
BUT RIGHT AT THE START, THEY'LL STAY NICE AND DAMP AS YOUR BLOOD DRIPS DOWN OVER THEM... TRANSFORMING THE WORLD AROUND YOU RED.
BETTER CLOSE THEM NOW, WHILE YOU'VE GOT THE CHANCE.
NO... I DON'T WANT THIS... I'M NOT READY!

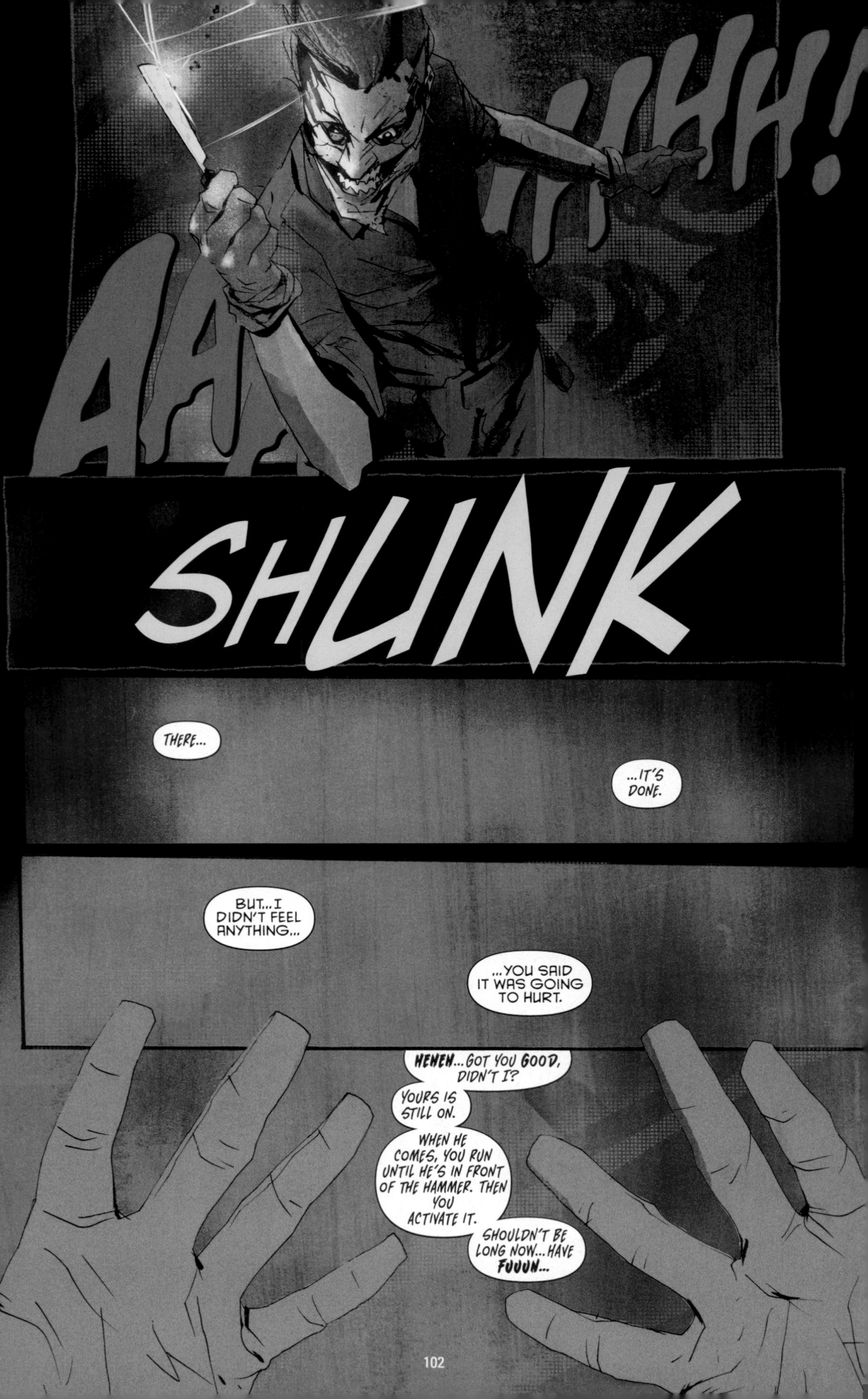
AAHHH!
SHUNK
THERE...
...IT'S DONE.
BUT...I DIDN'T FEEL ANYTHING...
...YOU SAID IT WAS GOING TO HURT.
HEHEH...GOT YOU GOOD, DIDN'T I?
YOURS IS STILL ON.
WHEN HE COMES, YOU RUN UNTIL HE'S IN FRONT OF THE HAMMER. THEN YOU ACTIVATE IT.
SHOULDN'T BE LONG NOW...HAVE FUUUN...

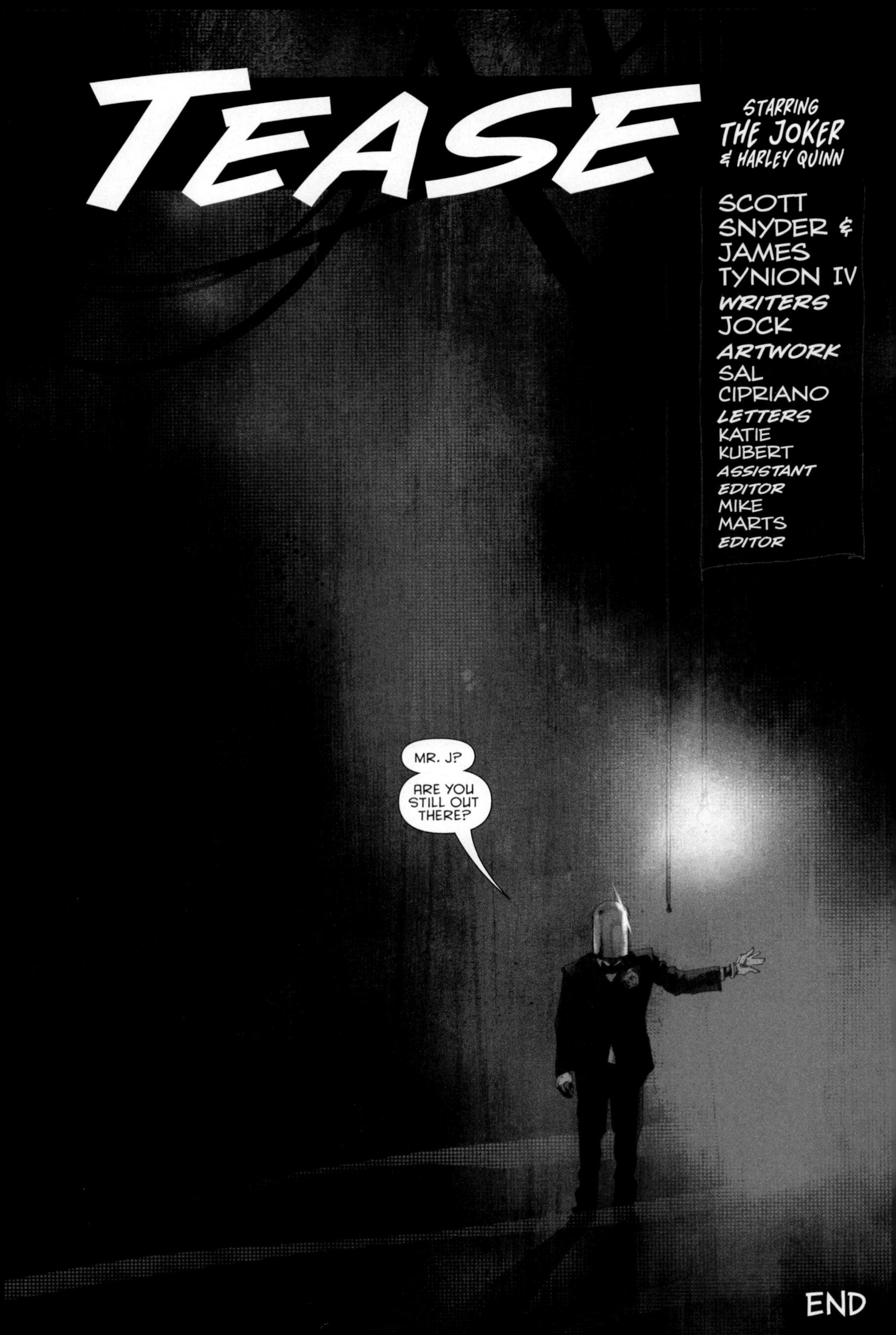
TEASE
STARRING
THE JOKER
& HARLEY QUINN
SCOTT SNYDER & JAMES TYNION IV WRITERS
JOCK ARTWORK
SAL CIPRIANO LETTERS
KATIE KUBERT ASSISTANT EDITOR
MIKE MARTS EDITOR
MR. J?
ARE YOU STILL OUT THERE?
END

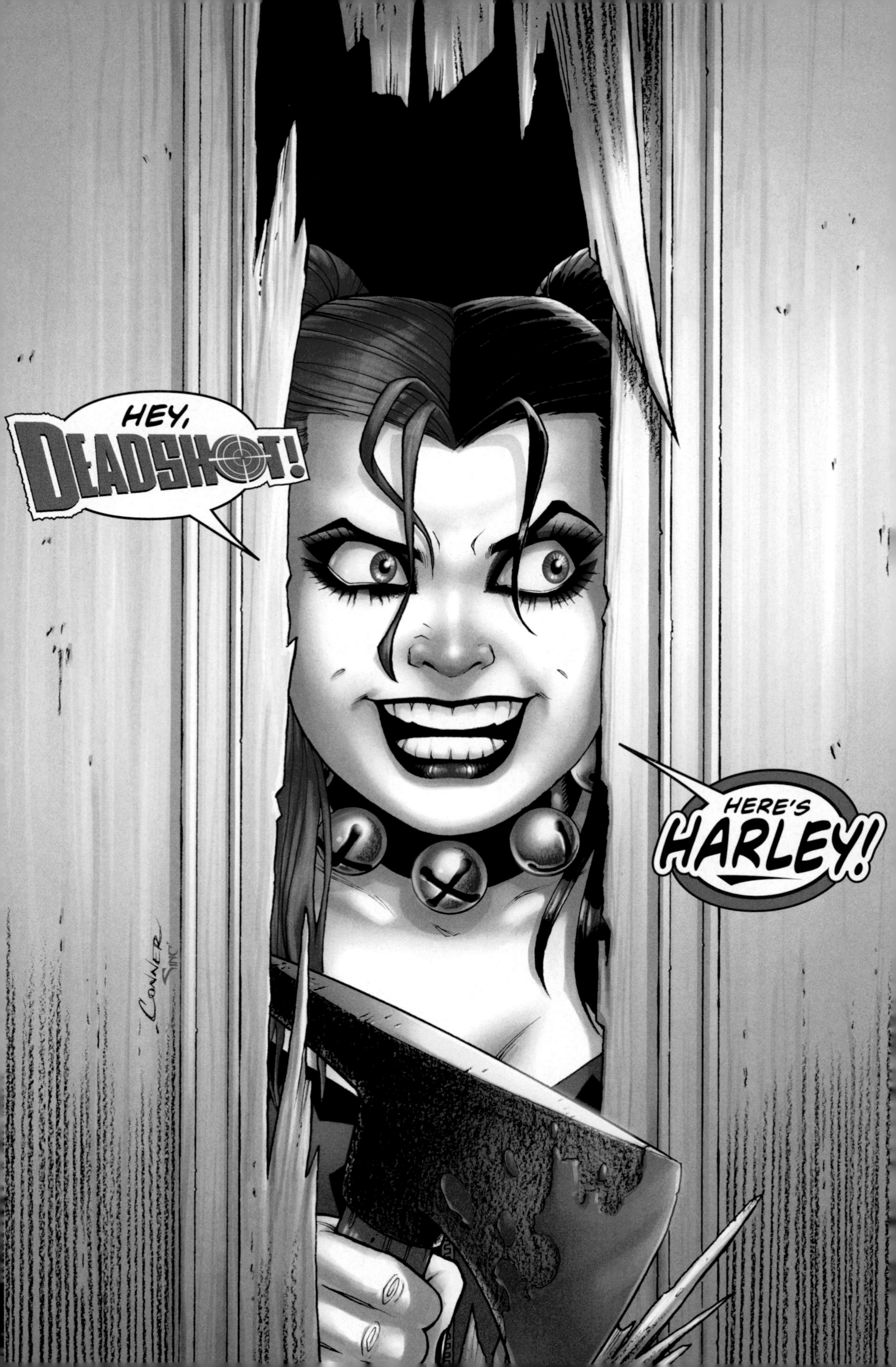
HEY, DEADSHOT!
HERE'S HARLEY!

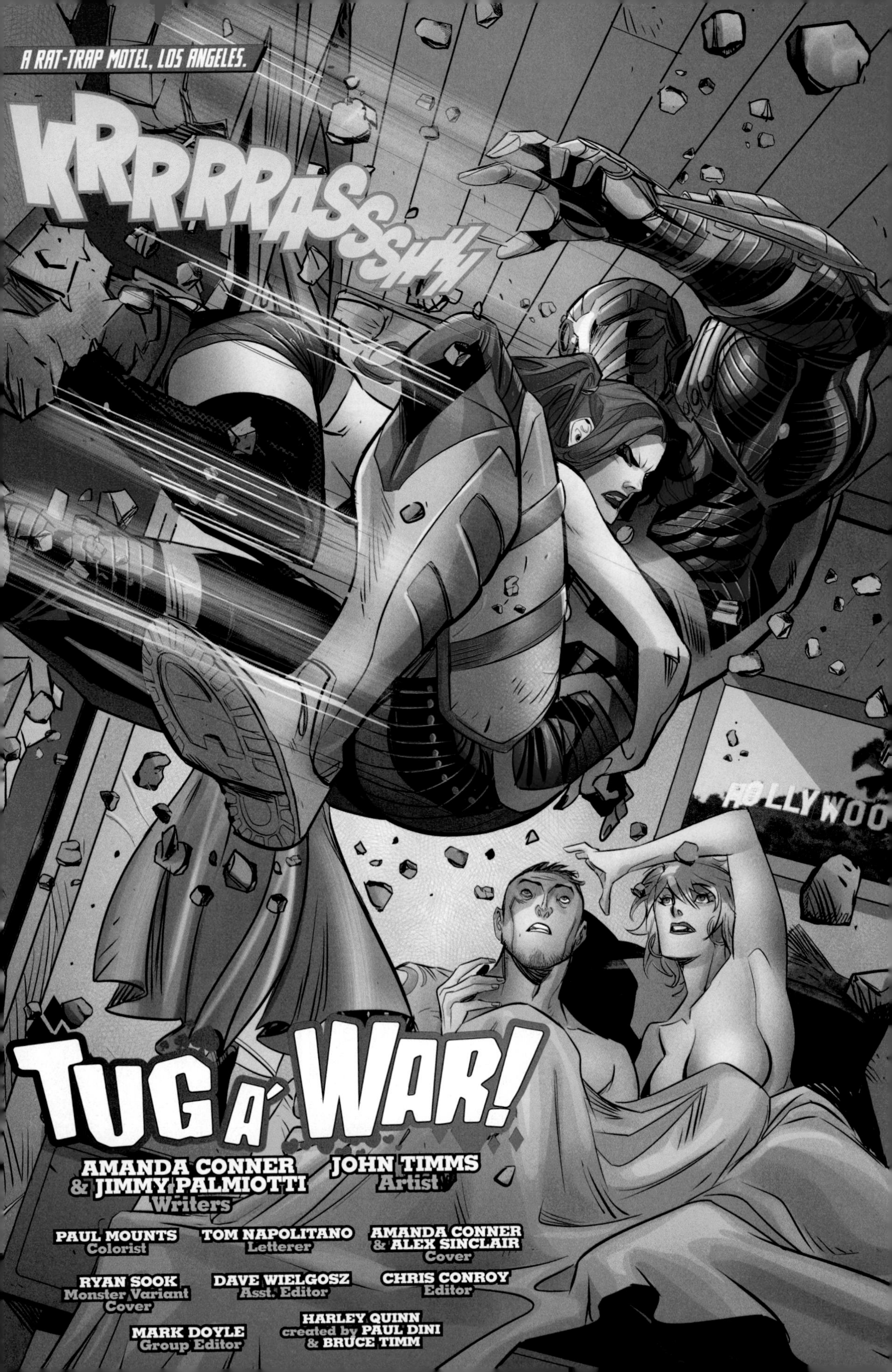
A RAT-TRAP MOTEL, LOS ANGELES.
KRRRRRASSSHH
HOLLYWOO
TUG A' WAR!
AMANDA CONNER & JIMMY PALMIOTTI Writers
JOHN TIMMS Artist
PAUL MOUNTS Colorist
TOM NAPOLITANO Letterer
AMANDA CONNER & ALEX SINCLAIR Cover
RYAN SOOK Monster Variant Cover
DAVE WIELGOSZ Asst. Editor
CHRIS CONROY Editor
MARK DOYLE Group Editor
HARLEY QUINN created by PAUL DINI & BRUCE TIMM

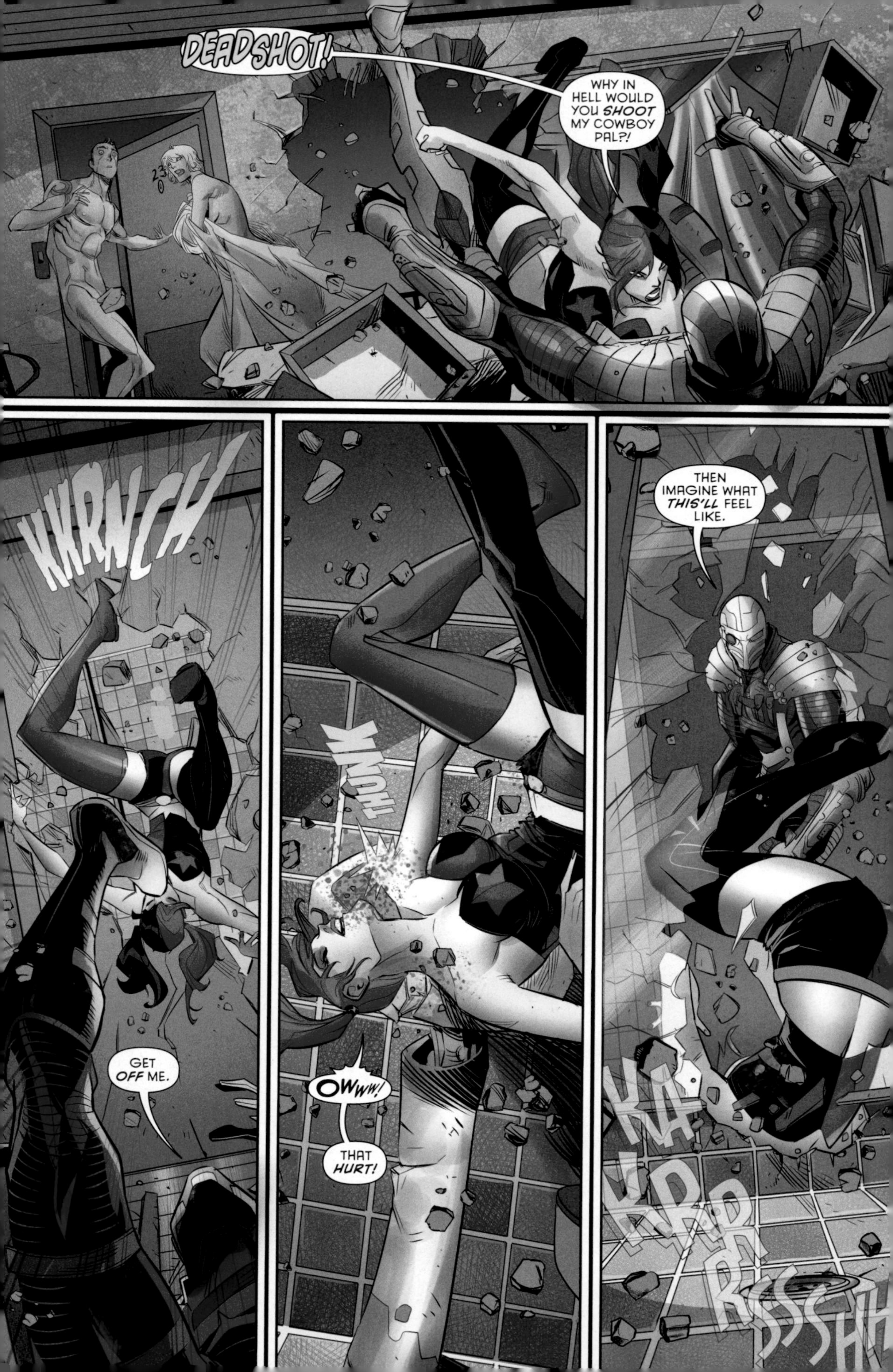
DEADSHOT!
WHY IN HELL WOULD YOU SHOOT MY COWBOY PAL?!
KKRNCH
GET OFF ME.
KRNCH!
OWWW!
THAT HURT!
THEN IMAGINE WHAT THIS'LL FEEL LIKE.
KA-KRR
RISSSHH

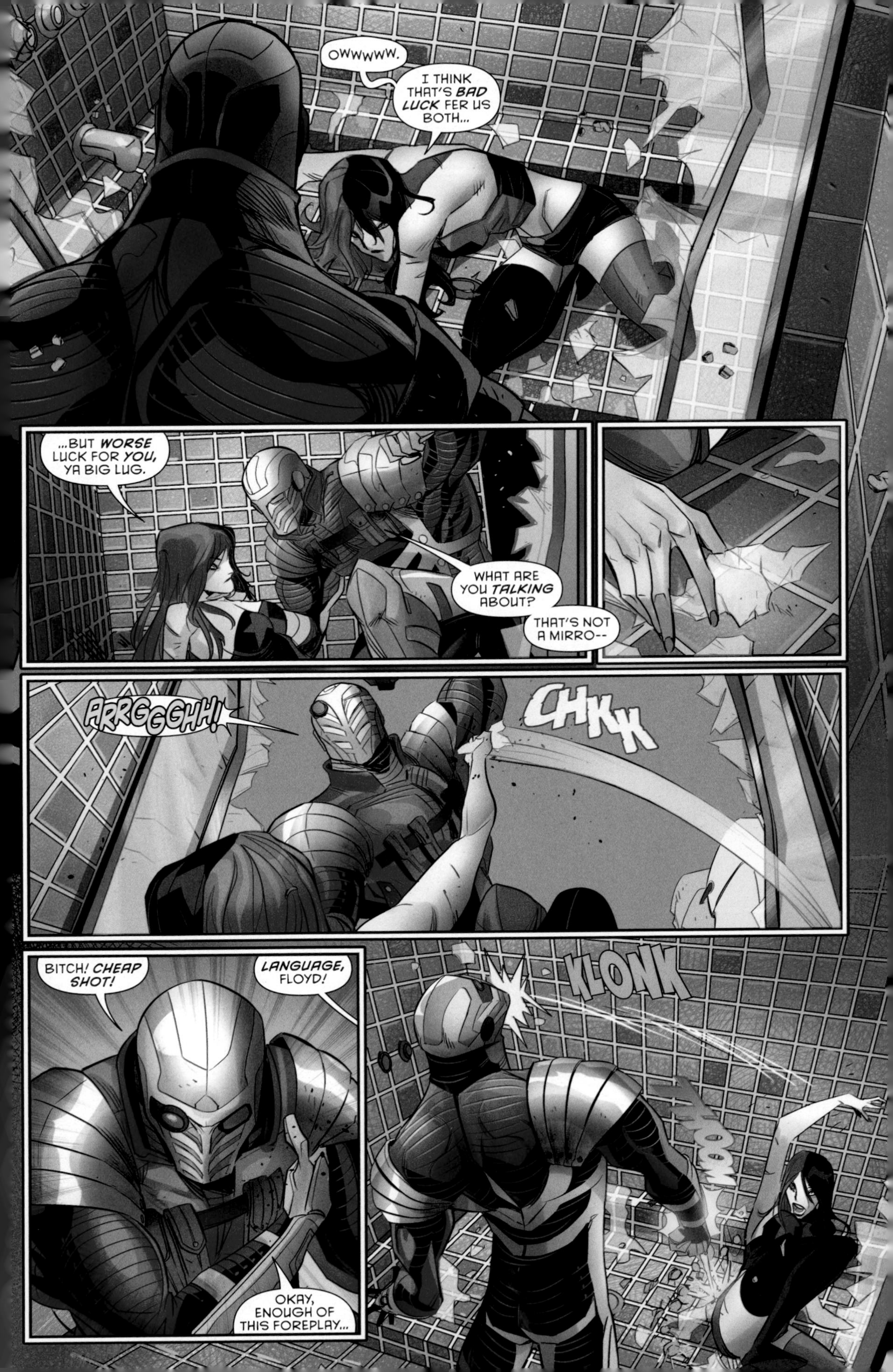
OWWWWW.
I THINK THAT'S BAD LUCK FER US BOTH...
...BUT WORSE LUCK FOR YOU, YA BIG LUG.
WHAT ARE YOU TALKING ABOUT?
THAT'S NOT A MIRRO--
ARRGGGHH!
CHKKK
BITCH! CHEAP SHOT!
LANGUAGE, FLOYD!
KLONK
THOOM
OKAY, ENOUGH OF THIS FOREPLAY...

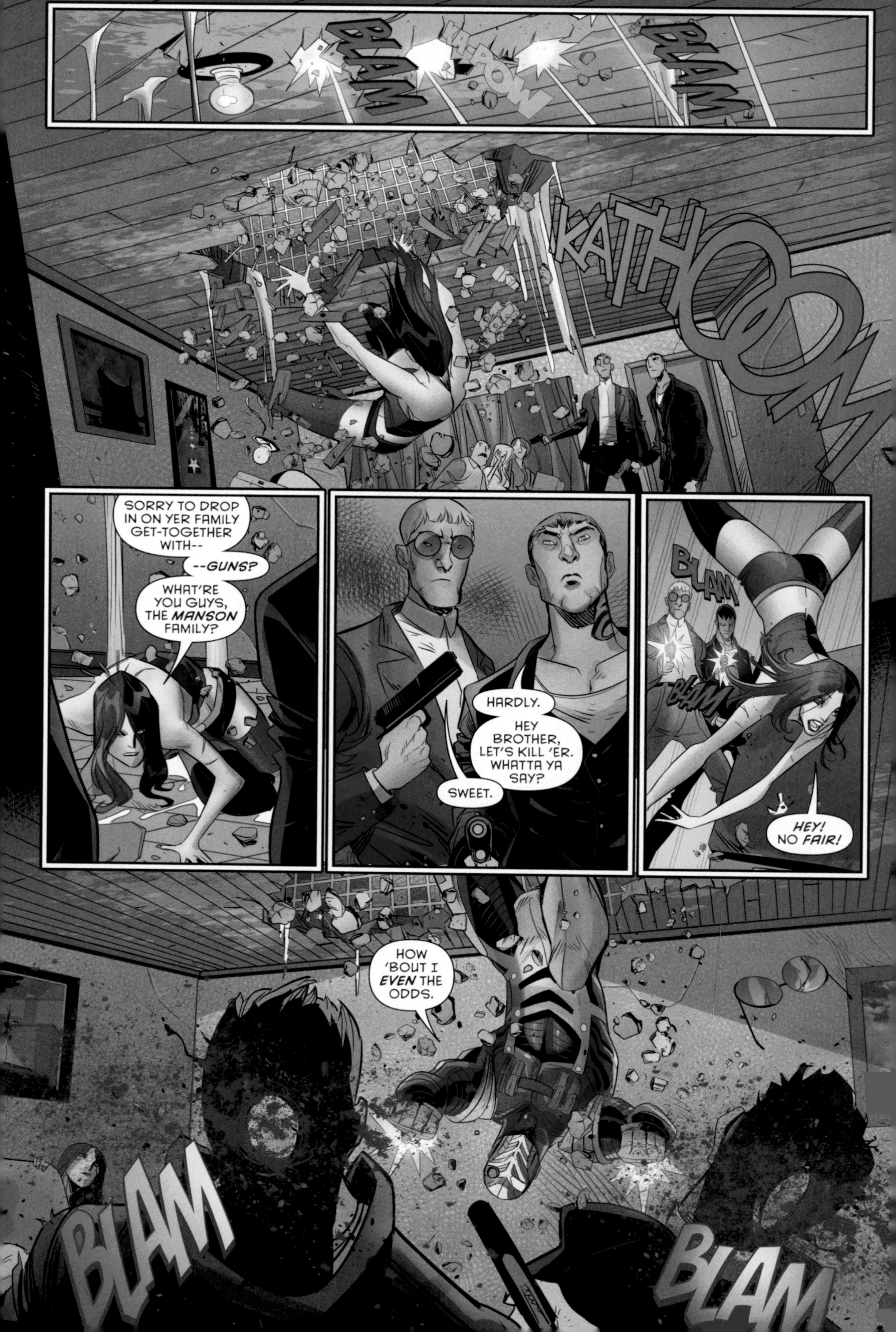
BLAM
KA-POW
BLAM
BLAM
KATHOOOM
SORRY TO DROP IN ON YER FAMILY GET-TOGETHER WITH--
--GUNS?
WHAT'RE YOU GUYS, THE MANSON FAMILY?
HARDLY.
HEY BROTHER, LET'S KILL 'ER. WHATTA YA SAY?
SWEET.
BLAM
BLAM
HEY! NO FAIR!
HOW 'BOUT I EVEN THE ODDS.
BLAM
BLAM

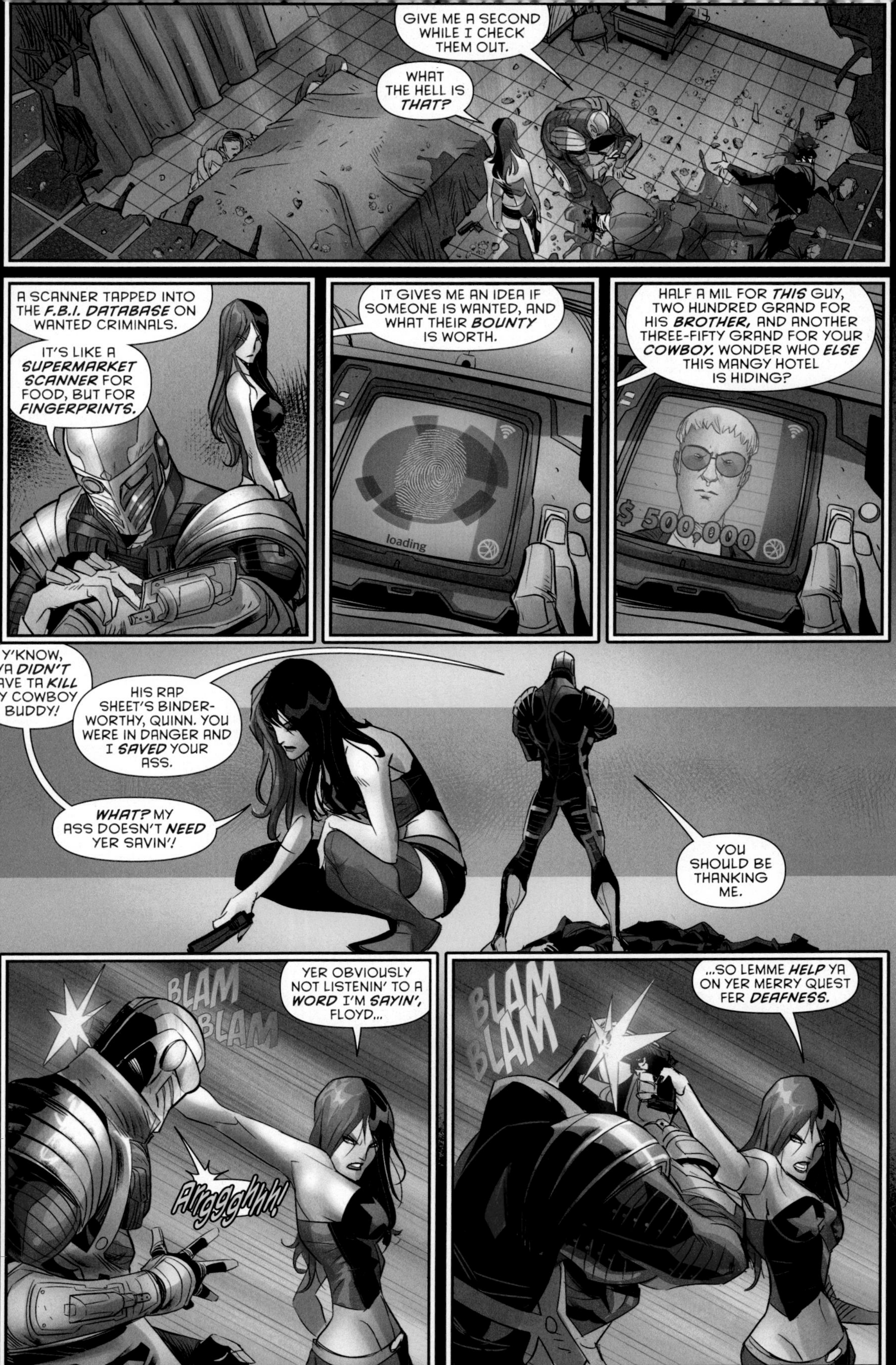
GIVE ME A SECOND WHILE I CHECK THEM OUT.
WHAT THE HELL IS *THAT?*
A SCANNER TAPPED INTO THE *F.B.I. DATABASE* ON WANTED CRIMINALS.
IT'S LIKE A *SUPERMARKET SCANNER* FOR FOOD, BUT FOR *FINGERPRINTS.*
IT GIVES ME AN IDEA IF SOMEONE IS WANTED, AND WHAT THEIR *BOUNTY* IS WORTH.
loading
HALF A MIL FOR *THIS* GUY, TWO HUNDRED GRAND FOR HIS *BROTHER,* AND ANOTHER THREE-FIFTY GRAND FOR YOUR *COWBOY.* WONDER WHO *ELSE* THIS MANGY HOTEL IS HIDING?
$ 500,000
Y'KNOW, YA *DIDN'T* HAVE TA *KILL* MY COWBOY BUDDY!
HIS RAP SHEET'S BINDER-WORTHY, QUINN. YOU WERE IN DANGER AND I *SAVED* YOUR ASS.
WHAT? MY ASS DOESN'T *NEED* YER SAVIN'!
YOU SHOULD BE THANKING ME.
BLAM BLAM
YER OBVIOUSLY NOT LISTENIN' TO A *WORD* I'M *SAYIN',* FLOYD...
Arrggghhh!
BLAM BLAM
...SO LEMME *HELP* YA ON YER MERRY QUEST FER *DEAFNESS.*

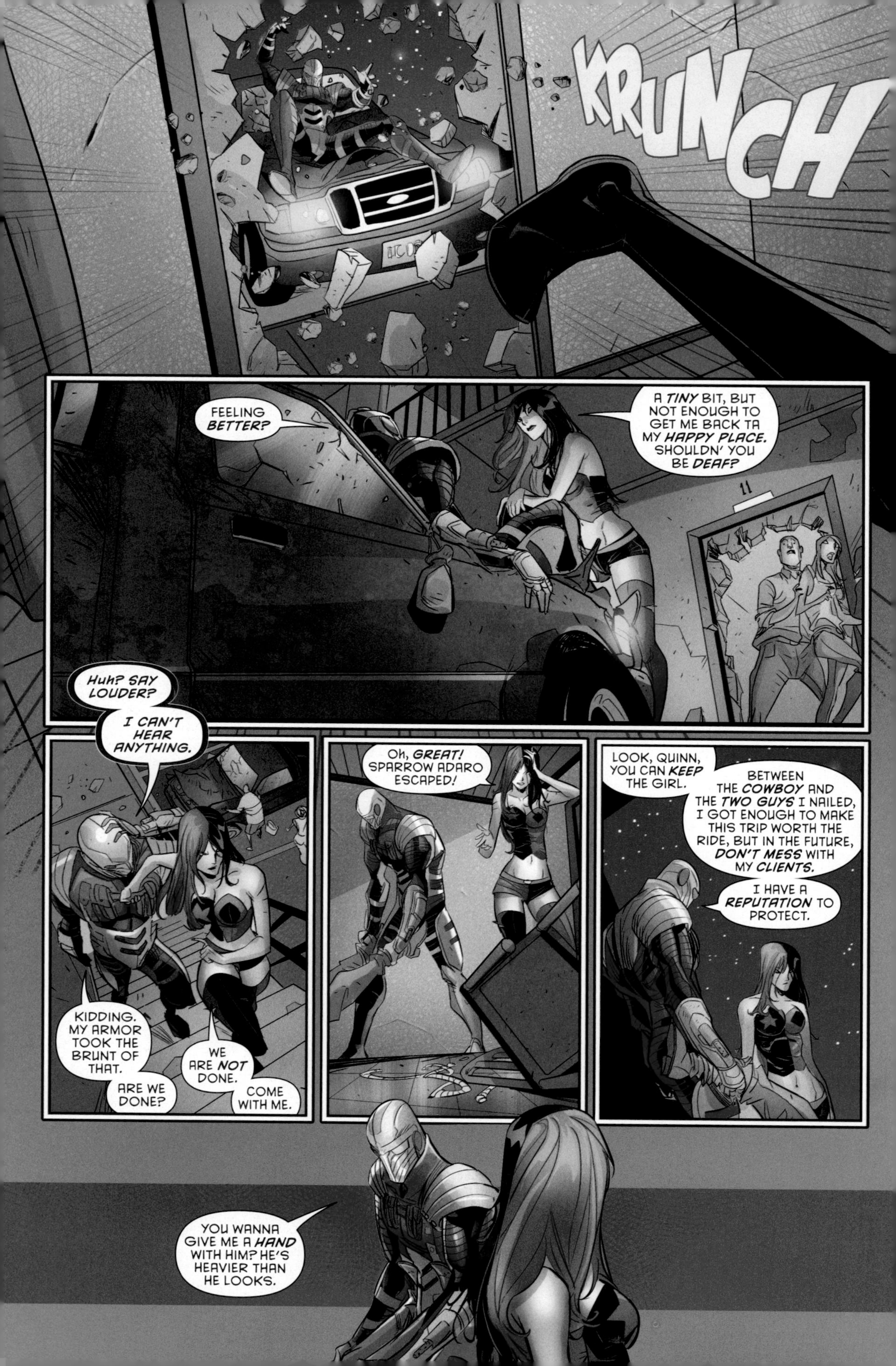
KRUNCH
FEELING BETTER?
A TINY BIT, BUT NOT ENOUGH TO GET ME BACK TA MY HAPPY PLACE. SHOULDN' YOU BE DEAF?
Huh? SAY LOUDER?
I CAN'T HEAR ANYTHING.
KIDDING. MY ARMOR TOOK THE BRUNT OF THAT.
ARE WE DONE?
WE ARE NOT DONE.
COME WITH ME.
Oh, GREAT! SPARROW ADARO ESCAPED!
LOOK, QUINN, YOU CAN KEEP THE GIRL.
BETWEEN THE COWBOY AND THE TWO GUYS I NAILED, I GOT ENOUGH TO MAKE THIS TRIP WORTH THE RIDE, BUT IN THE FUTURE, DON'T MESS WITH MY CLIENTS.
I HAVE A REPUTATION TO PROTECT.
YOU WANNA GIVE ME A HAND WITH HIM? HE'S HEAVIER THAN HE LOOKS.

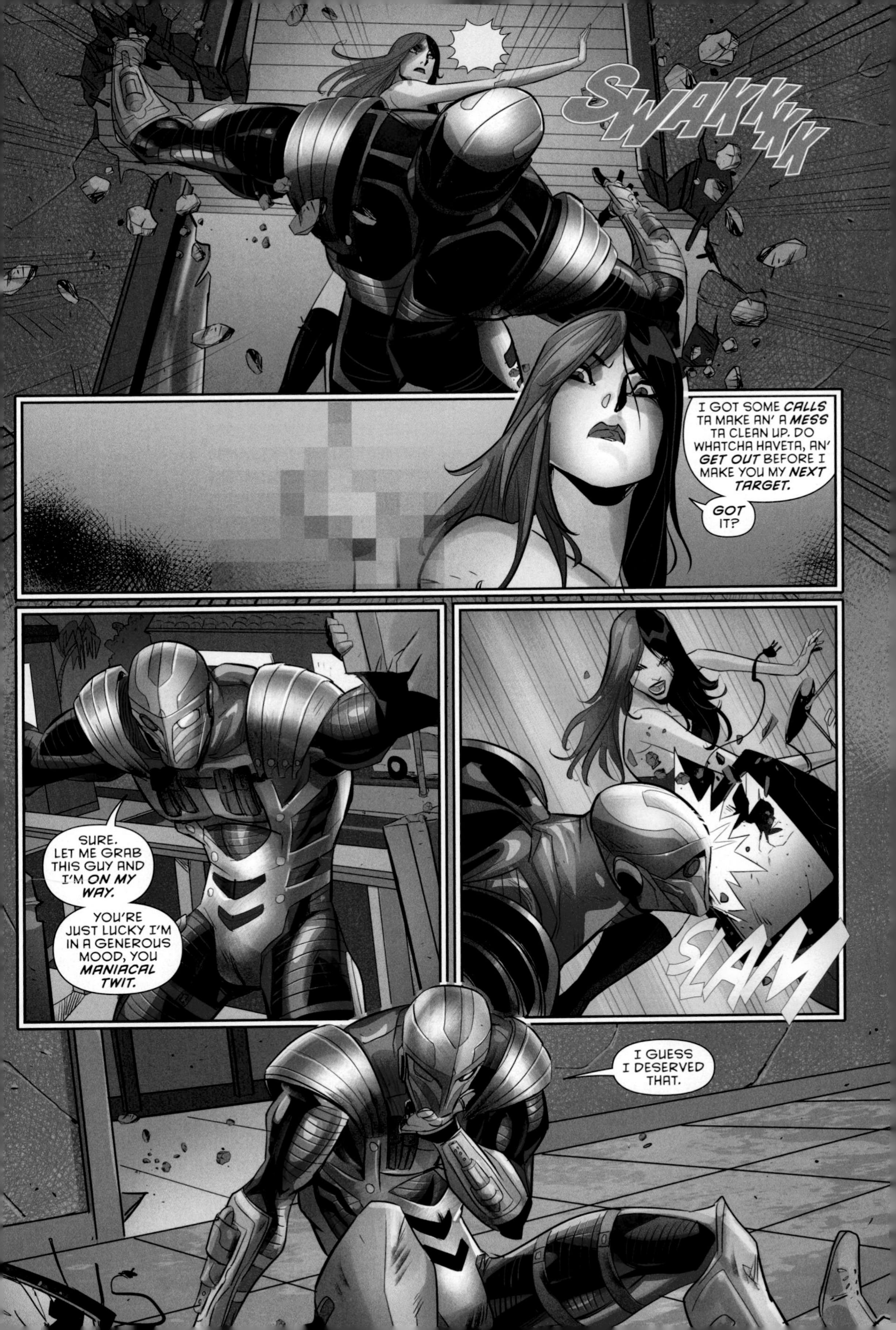
SWAKKKK
I GOT SOME CALLS TA MAKE AN' A MESS TA CLEAN UP. DO WHATCHA HAVETA, AN' GET OUT BEFORE I MAKE YOU MY NEXT TARGET.
GOT IT?
SURE. LET ME GRAB THIS GUY AND I'M ON MY WAY.
YOU'RE JUST LUCKY I'M IN A GENEROUS MOOD, YOU MANIACAL TWIT.
SLAM
I GUESS I DESERVED THAT.

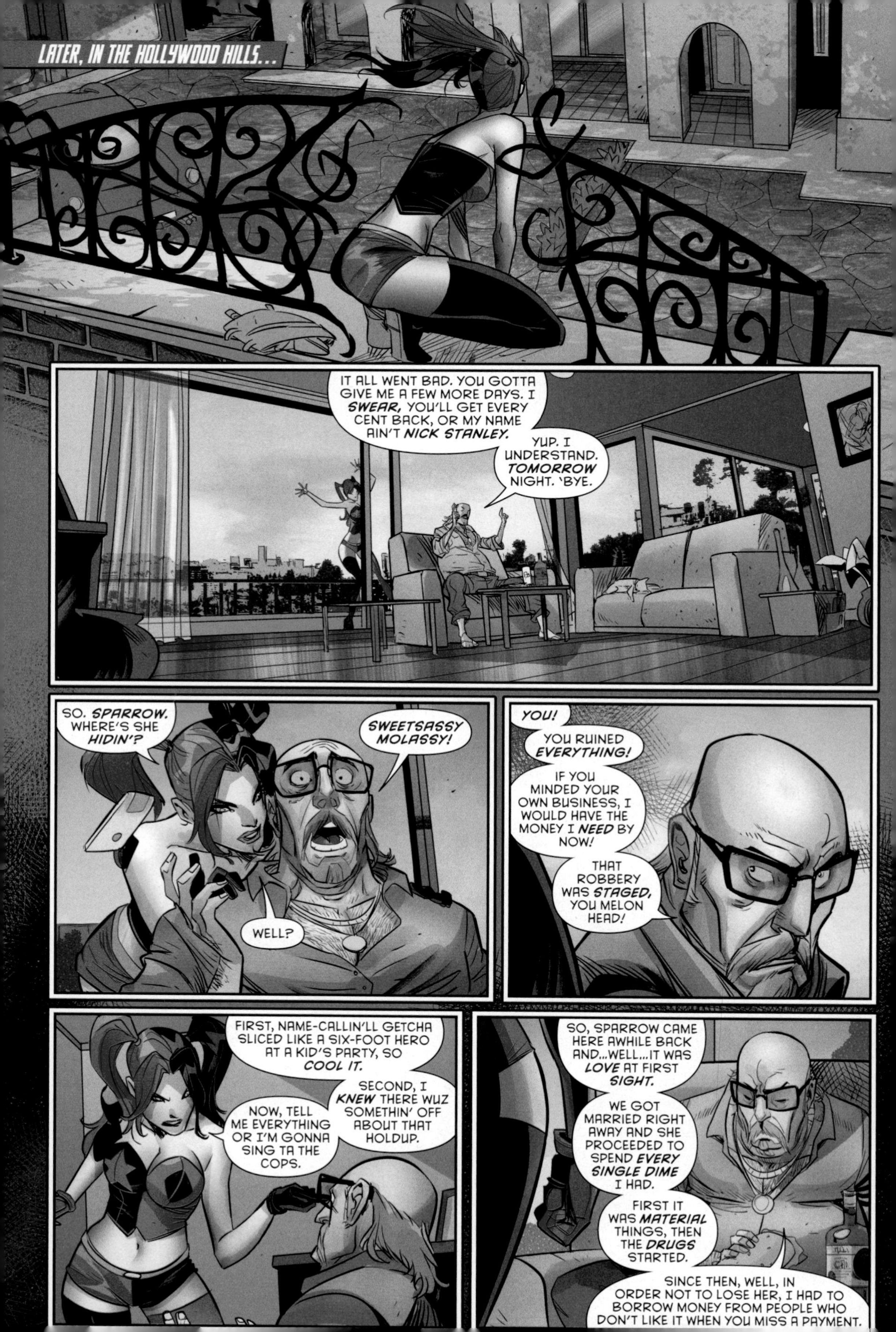
LATER, IN THE HOLLYWOOD HILLS...
IT ALL WENT BAD. YOU GOTTA GIVE ME A FEW MORE DAYS. I SWEAR, YOU'LL GET EVERY CENT BACK, OR MY NAME AIN'T NICK STANLEY.
YUP. I UNDERSTAND. TOMORROW NIGHT. 'BYE.
SO. SPARROW. WHERE'S SHE HIDIN'?
SWEETSASSY MOLASSY!
WELL?
YOU!
YOU RUINED EVERYTHING!
IF YOU MINDED YOUR OWN BUSINESS, I WOULD HAVE THE MONEY I NEED BY NOW!
THAT ROBBERY WAS STAGED, YOU MELON HEAD!
FIRST, NAME-CALLIN'LL GETCHA SLICED LIKE A SIX-FOOT HERO AT A KID'S PARTY, SO COOL IT.
SECOND, I KNEW THERE WUZ SOMETHIN' OFF ABOUT THAT HOLDUP.
NOW, TELL ME EVERYTHING OR I'M GONNA SING TA THE COPS.
SO, SPARROW CAME HERE AWHILE BACK AND...WELL...IT WAS LOVE AT FIRST SIGHT.
WE GOT MARRIED RIGHT AWAY AND SHE PROCEEDED TO SPEND EVERY SINGLE DIME I HAD.
FIRST IT WAS MATERIAL THINGS, THEN THE DRUGS STARTED.
SINCE THEN, WELL, IN ORDER NOT TO LOSE HER, I HAD TO BORROW MONEY FROM PEOPLE WHO DON'T LIKE IT WHEN YOU MISS A PAYMENT.

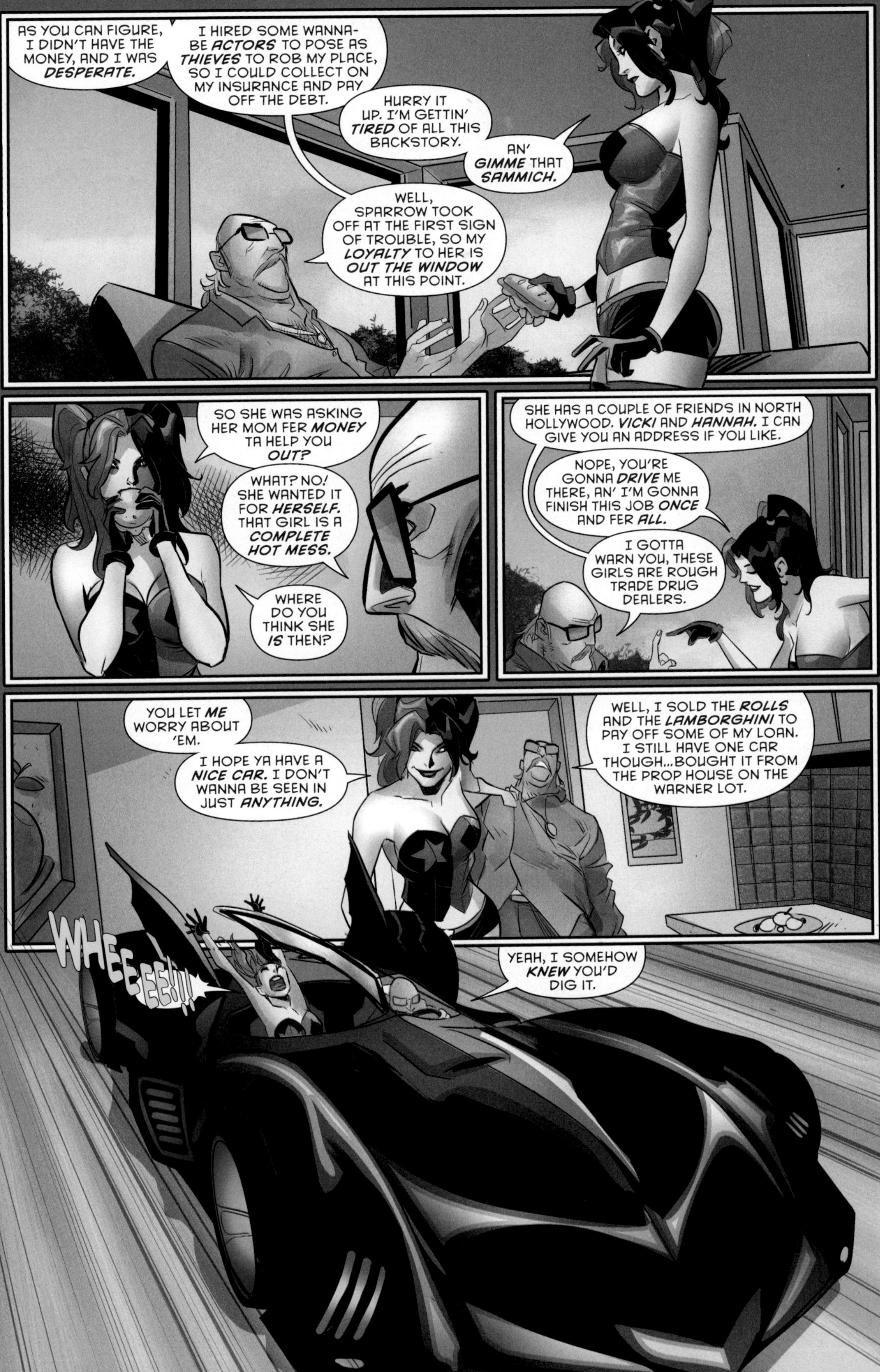

AS YOU CAN FIGURE, I DIDN'T HAVE THE MONEY, AND I WAS DESPERATE.
I HIRED SOME WANNA-BE ACTORS TO POSE AS THIEVES TO ROB MY PLACE, SO I COULD COLLECT ON MY INSURANCE AND PAY OFF THE DEBT.
HURRY IT UP. I'M GETTIN' TIRED OF ALL THIS BACKSTORY.
AN' GIMME THAT SAMMICH.
WELL, SPARROW TOOK OFF AT THE FIRST SIGN OF TROUBLE, SO MY LOYALTY TO HER IS OUT THE WINDOW AT THIS POINT.
SO SHE WAS ASKING HER MOM FER MONEY TA HELP YOU OUT?
WHAT? NO! SHE WANTED IT FOR HERSELF. THAT GIRL IS A COMPLETE HOT MESS.
WHERE DO YOU THINK SHE IS THEN?
SHE HAS A COUPLE OF FRIENDS IN NORTH HOLLYWOOD. VICKI AND HANNAH. I CAN GIVE YOU AN ADDRESS IF YOU LIKE.
NOPE, YOU'RE GONNA DRIVE ME THERE, AN' I'M GONNA FINISH THIS JOB ONCE AND FER ALL.
I GOTTA WARN YOU, THESE GIRLS ARE ROUGH TRADE DRUG DEALERS.
YOU LET ME WORRY ABOUT 'EM.
I HOPE YA HAVE A NICE CAR. I DON'T WANNA BE SEEN IN JUST ANYTHING.
WELL, I SOLD THE ROLLS AND THE LAMBORGHINI TO PAY OFF SOME OF MY LOAN. I STILL HAVE ONE CAR THOUGH...BOUGHT IT FROM THE PROP HOUSE ON THE WARNER LOT.
WHEEEEE!!!
YEAH, I SOMEHOW KNEW YOU'D DIG IT.

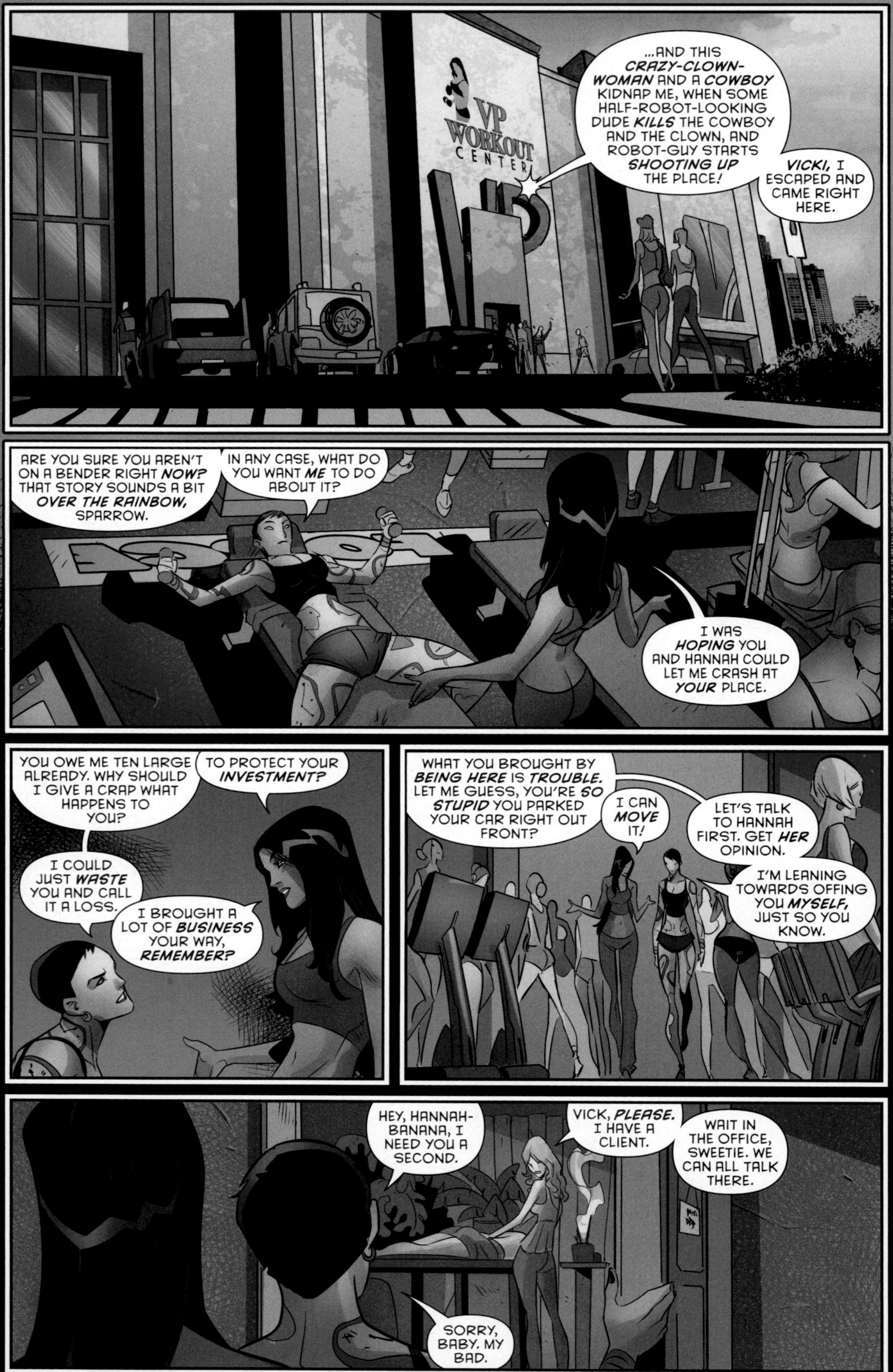
VP WORKOUT CENTER
...AND THIS CRAZY-CLOWN-WOMAN AND A COWBOY KIDNAP ME, WHEN SOME HALF-ROBOT-LOOKING DUDE KILLS THE COWBOY AND THE CLOWN, AND ROBOT-GUY STARTS SHOOTING UP THE PLACE!
VICKI, I ESCAPED AND CAME RIGHT HERE.
ARE YOU SURE YOU AREN'T ON A BENDER RIGHT NOW? THAT STORY SOUNDS A BIT OVER THE RAINBOW, SPARROW.
IN ANY CASE, WHAT DO YOU WANT ME TO DO ABOUT IT?
I WAS HOPING YOU AND HANNAH COULD LET ME CRASH AT YOUR PLACE.
YOU OWE ME TEN LARGE ALREADY. WHY SHOULD I GIVE A CRAP WHAT HAPPENS TO YOU?
TO PROTECT YOUR INVESTMENT?
I COULD JUST WASTE YOU AND CALL IT A LOSS.
I BROUGHT A LOT OF BUSINESS YOUR WAY, REMEMBER?
WHAT YOU BROUGHT BY BEING HERE IS TROUBLE. LET ME GUESS, YOU'RE SO STUPID YOU PARKED YOUR CAR RIGHT OUT FRONT?
I CAN MOVE IT!
LET'S TALK TO HANNAH FIRST. GET HER OPINION.
I'M LEANING TOWARDS OFFING YOU MYSELF, JUST SO YOU KNOW.
HEY, HANNAH-BANANA, I NEED YOU A SECOND.
VICK, PLEASE. I HAVE A CLIENT.
WAIT IN THE OFFICE, SWEETIE. WE CAN ALL TALK THERE.
SORRY, BABY. MY BAD.

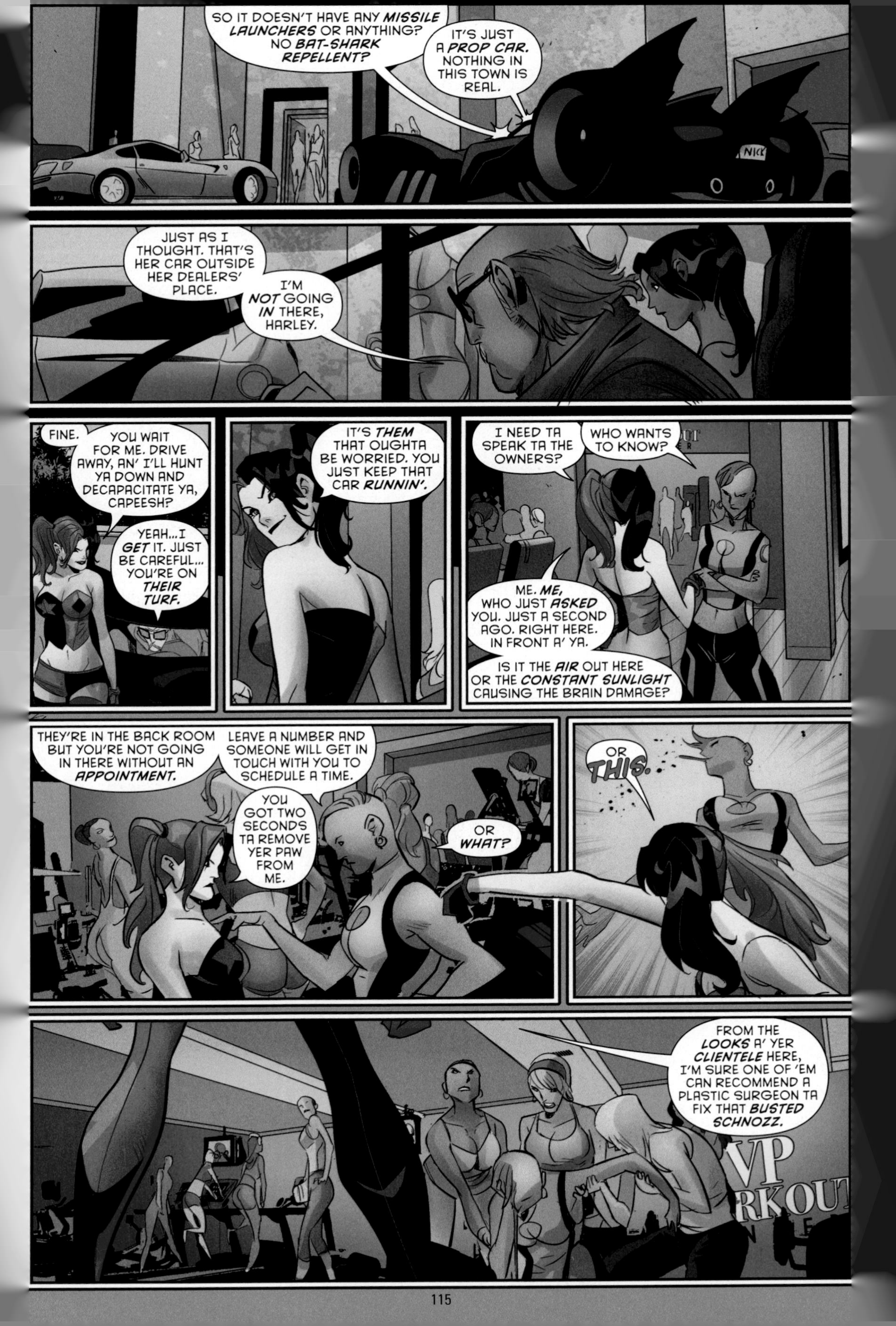
SO IT DOESN'T HAVE ANY MISSILE LAUNCHERS OR ANYTHING? NO BAT-SHARK REPELLENT?
IT'S JUST A PROP CAR. NOTHING IN THIS TOWN IS REAL.
NICK
JUST AS I THOUGHT. THAT'S HER CAR OUTSIDE HER DEALERS' PLACE.
I'M NOT GOING IN THERE, HARLEY.
FINE.
YOU WAIT FOR ME. DRIVE AWAY, AN' I'LL HUNT YA DOWN AND DECAPACITATE YA, CAPEESH?
YEAH...I GET IT. JUST BE CAREFUL... YOU'RE ON THEIR TURF.
IT'S THEM THAT OUGHTA BE WORRIED. YOU JUST KEEP THAT CAR RUNNIN'.
I NEED TA SPEAK TA THE OWNERS?
WHO WANTS TO KNOW?
ME. ME, WHO JUST ASKED YOU. JUST A SECOND AGO. RIGHT HERE. IN FRONT A' YA.
IS IT THE AIR OUT HERE OR THE CONSTANT SUNLIGHT CAUSING THE BRAIN DAMAGE?
THEY'RE IN THE BACK ROOM BUT YOU'RE NOT GOING IN THERE WITHOUT AN APPOINTMENT.
LEAVE A NUMBER AND SOMEONE WILL GET IN TOUCH WITH YOU TO SCHEDULE A TIME.
YOU GOT TWO SECONDS TA REMOVE YER PAW FROM ME.
OR WHAT?
OR THIS.
FROM THE LOOKS A' YER CLIENTELE HERE, I'M SURE ONE OF 'EM CAN RECOMMEND A PLASTIC SURGEON TA FIX THAT BUSTED SCHNOZZ.
VP
RKOUT

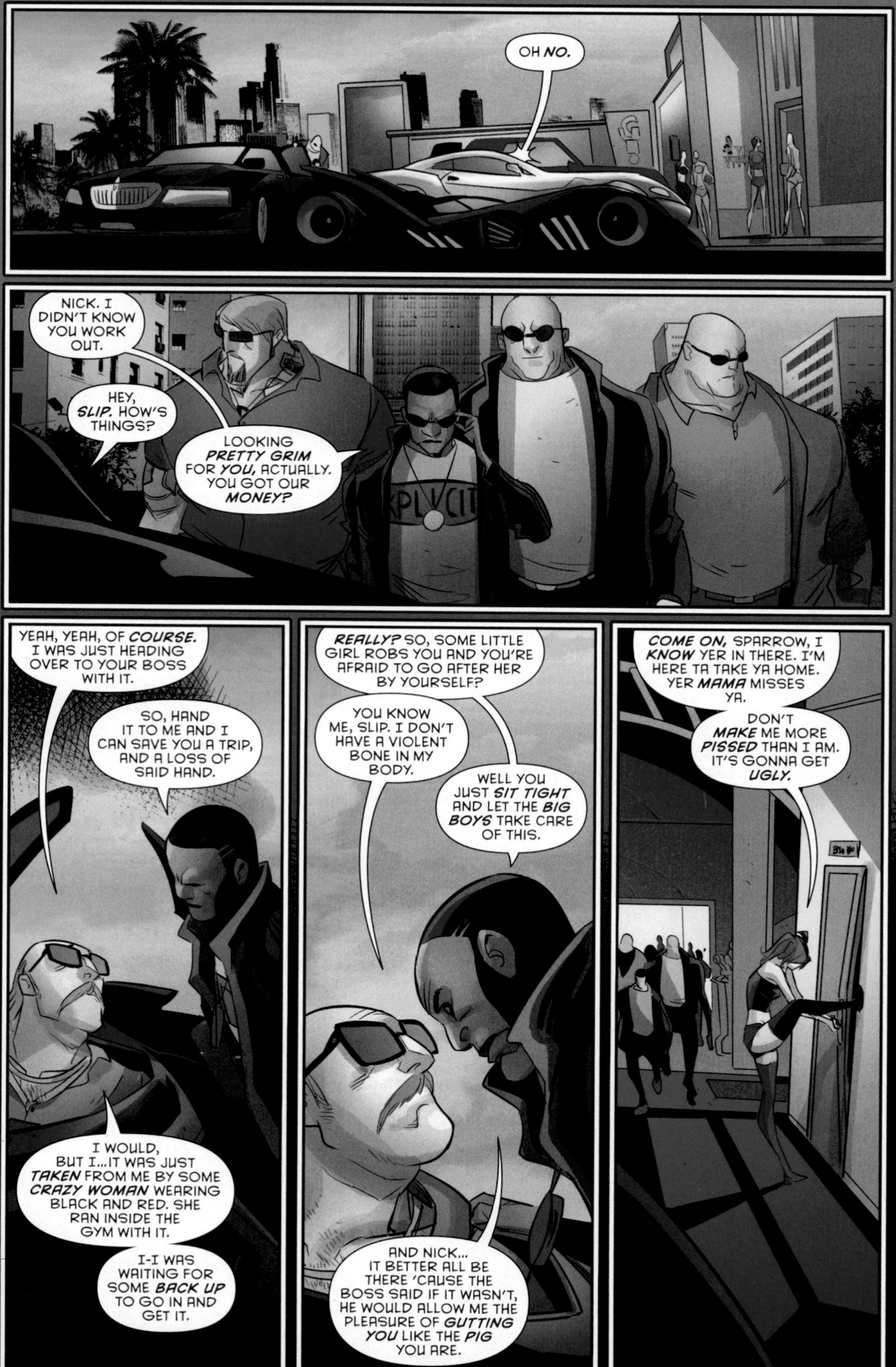
OH NO.
NICK. I DIDN'T KNOW YOU WORK OUT.
HEY, SLIP. HOW'S THINGS?
LOOKING PRETTY GRIM FOR YOU, ACTUALLY. YOU GOT OUR MONEY?
YEAH, YEAH, OF COURSE. I WAS JUST HEADING OVER TO YOUR BOSS WITH IT.
SO, HAND IT TO ME AND I CAN SAVE YOU A TRIP, AND A LOSS OF SAID HAND.
I WOULD, BUT I...IT WAS JUST TAKEN FROM ME BY SOME CRAZY WOMAN WEARING BLACK AND RED. SHE RAN INSIDE THE GYM WITH IT.
I-I WAS WAITING FOR SOME BACK UP TO GO IN AND GET IT.
REALLY? SO, SOME LITTLE GIRL ROBS YOU AND YOU'RE AFRAID TO GO AFTER HER BY YOURSELF?
YOU KNOW ME, SLIP. I DON'T HAVE A VIOLENT BONE IN MY BODY.
WELL YOU JUST SIT TIGHT AND LET THE BIG BOYS TAKE CARE OF THIS.
AND NICK... IT BETTER ALL BE THERE 'CAUSE THE BOSS SAID IF IT WASN'T, HE WOULD ALLOW ME THE PLEASURE OF GUTTING YOU LIKE THE PIG YOU ARE.
COME ON, SPARROW, I KNOW YER IN THERE. I'M HERE TA TAKE YA HOME. YER MAMA MISSES YA.
DON'T MAKE ME MORE PISSED THAN I AM. IT'S GONNA GET UGLY.

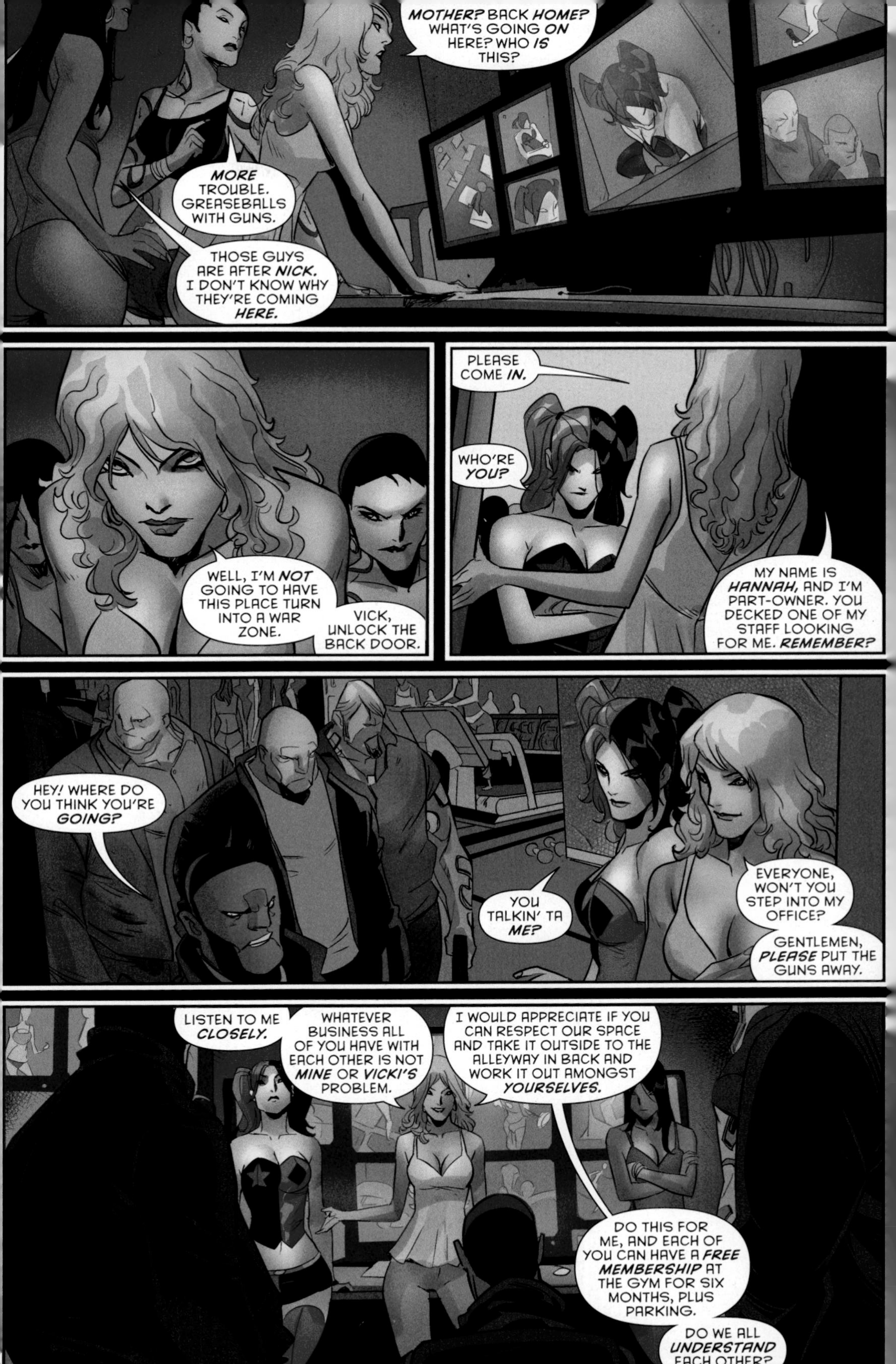
MOTHER? BACK HOME? WHAT'S GOING ON HERE? WHO IS THIS?
MORE TROUBLE. GREASEBALLS WITH GUNS.
THOSE GUYS ARE AFTER NICK. I DON'T KNOW WHY THEY'RE COMING HERE.
WELL, I'M NOT GOING TO HAVE THIS PLACE TURN INTO A WAR ZONE.
VICK, UNLOCK THE BACK DOOR.
PLEASE COME IN.
WHO'RE YOU?
MY NAME IS HANNAH, AND I'M PART-OWNER. YOU DECKED ONE OF MY STAFF LOOKING FOR ME. REMEMBER?
HEY! WHERE DO YOU THINK YOU'RE GOING?
YOU TALKIN' TA ME?
EVERYONE, WON'T YOU STEP INTO MY OFFICE?
GENTLEMEN, PLEASE PUT THE GUNS AWAY.
LISTEN TO ME CLOSELY.
WHATEVER BUSINESS ALL OF YOU HAVE WITH EACH OTHER IS NOT MINE OR VICKI'S PROBLEM.
I WOULD APPRECIATE IF YOU CAN RESPECT OUR SPACE AND TAKE IT OUTSIDE TO THE ALLEYWAY IN BACK AND WORK IT OUT AMONGST YOURSELVES.
DO THIS FOR ME, AND EACH OF YOU CAN HAVE A FREE MEMBERSHIP AT THE GYM FOR SIX MONTHS, PLUS PARKING.
DO WE ALL UNDERSTAND EACH OTHER?

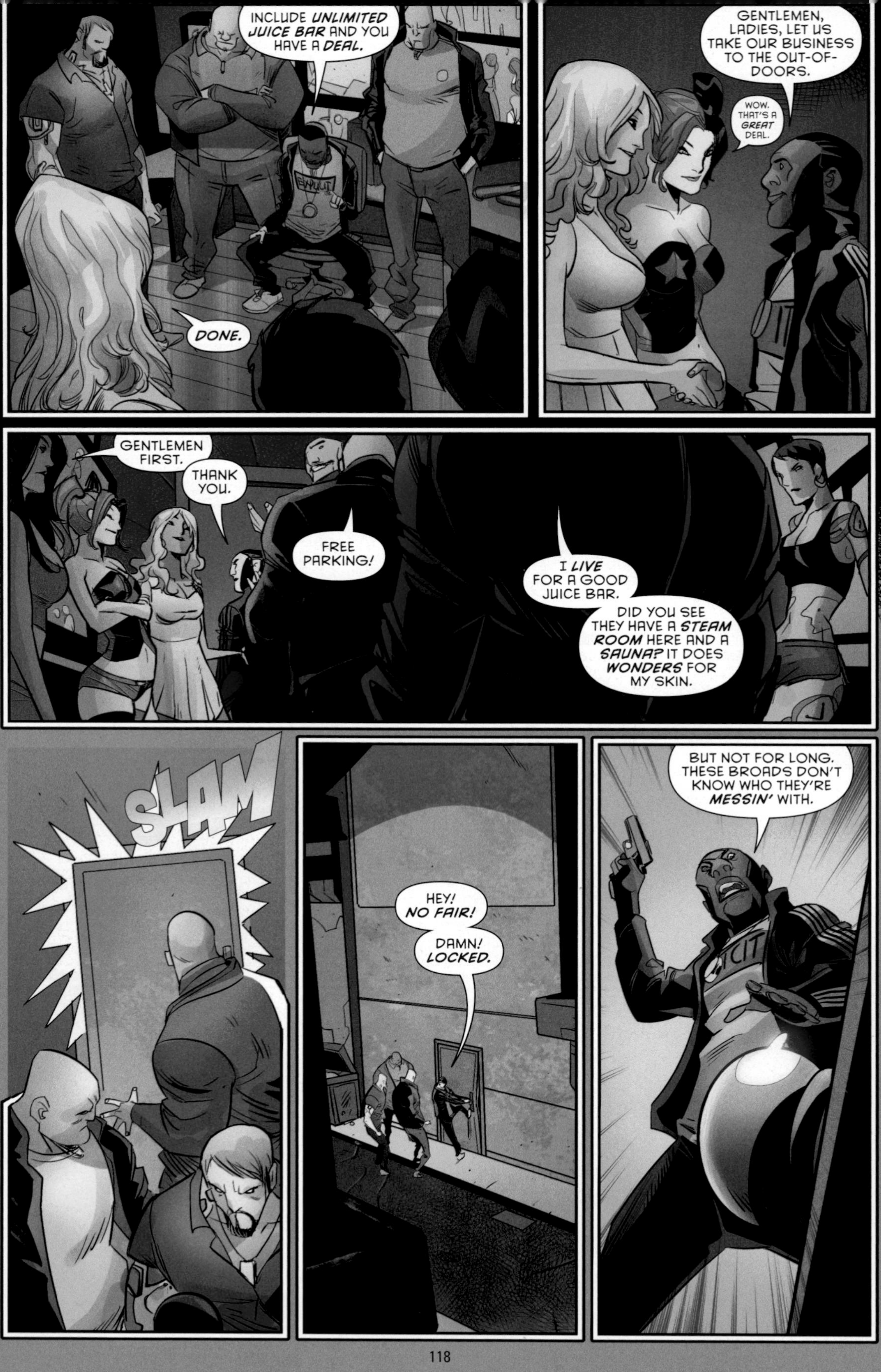

INCLUDE UNLIMITED JUICE BAR AND YOU HAVE A DEAL.
DONE.
GENTLEMEN, LADIES, LET US TAKE OUR BUSINESS TO THE OUT-OF-DOORS.
WOW. THAT'S A GREAT DEAL.
GENTLEMEN FIRST.
THANK YOU.
FREE PARKING!
I LIVE FOR A GOOD JUICE BAR.
DID YOU SEE THEY HAVE A STEAM ROOM HERE AND A SAUNA? IT DOES WONDERS FOR MY SKIN.
SLAM
HEY! NO FAIR!
DAMN! LOCKED.
BUT NOT FOR LONG. THESE BROADS DON'T KNOW WHO THEY'RE MESSIN' WITH.

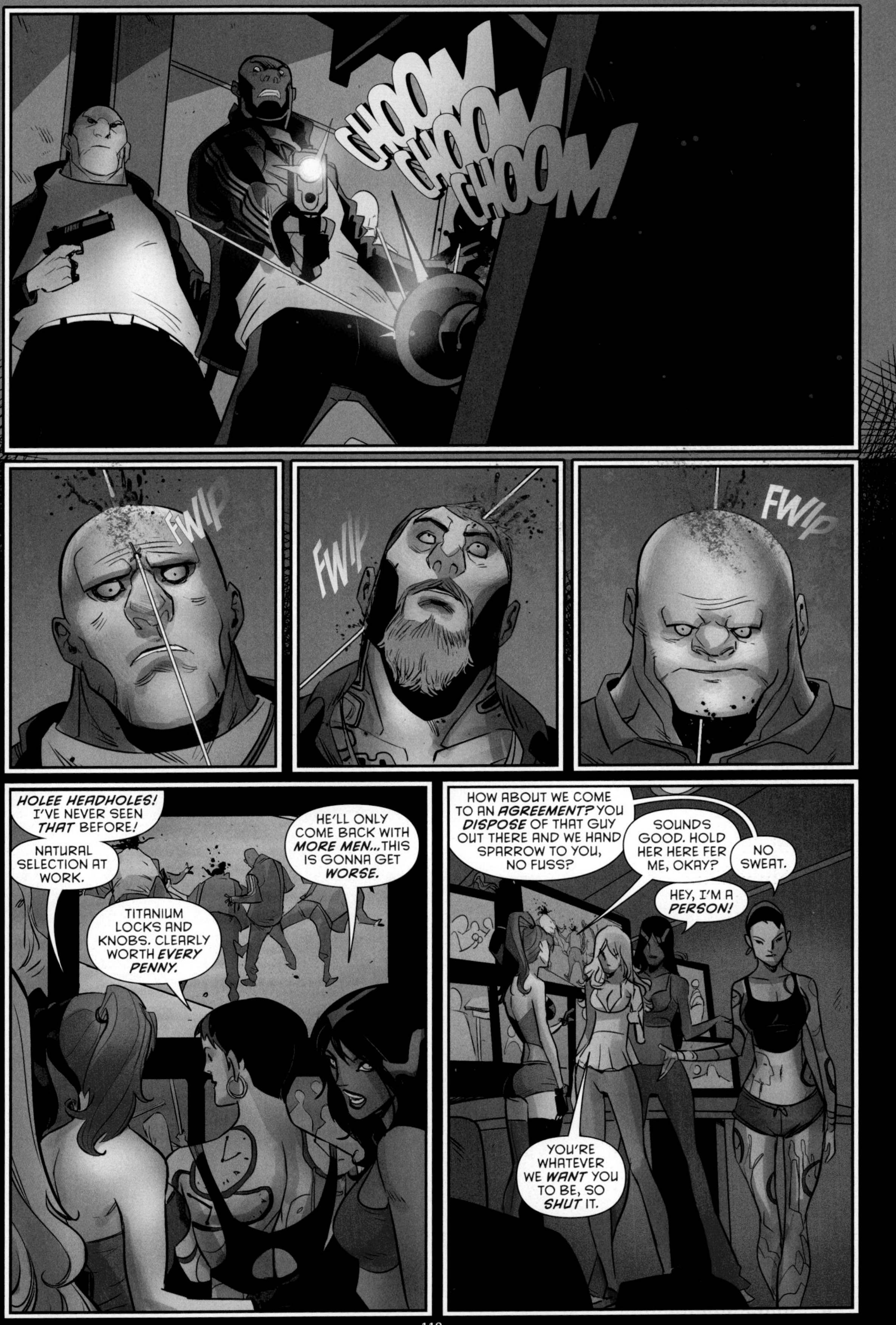
CHOOM
CHOOM
CHOOM
FWIP
FWIP
FWIP
HOLEE HEADHOLES! I'VE NEVER SEEN THAT BEFORE!
NATURAL SELECTION AT WORK.
HE'LL ONLY COME BACK WITH MORE MEN... THIS IS GONNA GET WORSE.
TITANIUM LOCKS AND KNOBS. CLEARLY WORTH EVERY PENNY.
HOW ABOUT WE COME TO AN AGREEMENT? YOU DISPOSE OF THAT GUY OUT THERE AND WE HAND SPARROW TO YOU, NO FUSS?
SOUNDS GOOD. HOLD HER HERE FER ME, OKAY?
NO SWEAT.
HEY, I'M A PERSON!
YOU'RE WHATEVER WE WANT YOU TO BE, SO SHUT IT.

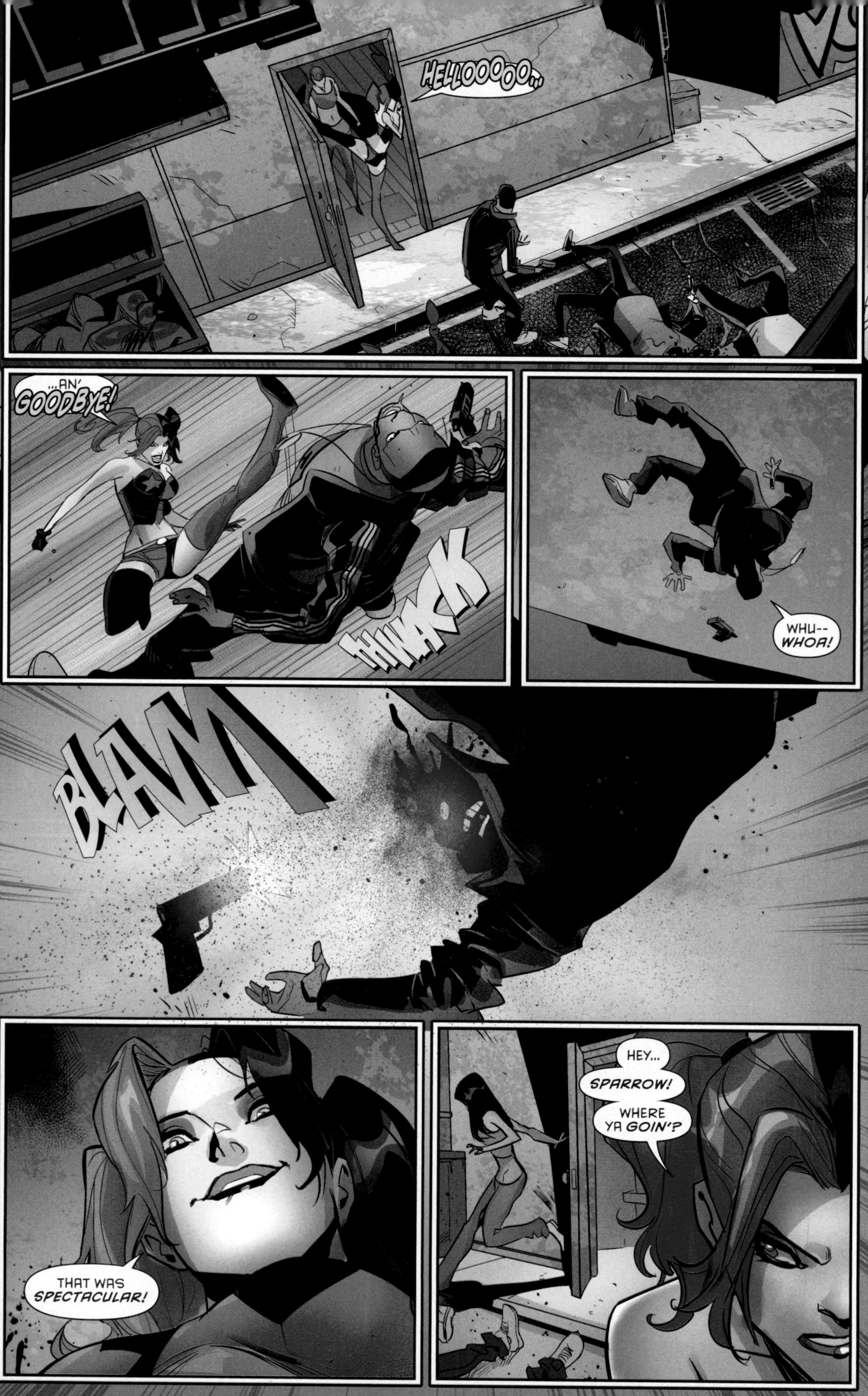
HELLOOOOO...
...AN' GOODBYE!
THWACK
WHU-- WHOA!
BLAM
THAT WAS SPECTACULAR!
HEY... SPARROW! WHERE YA GOIN'?

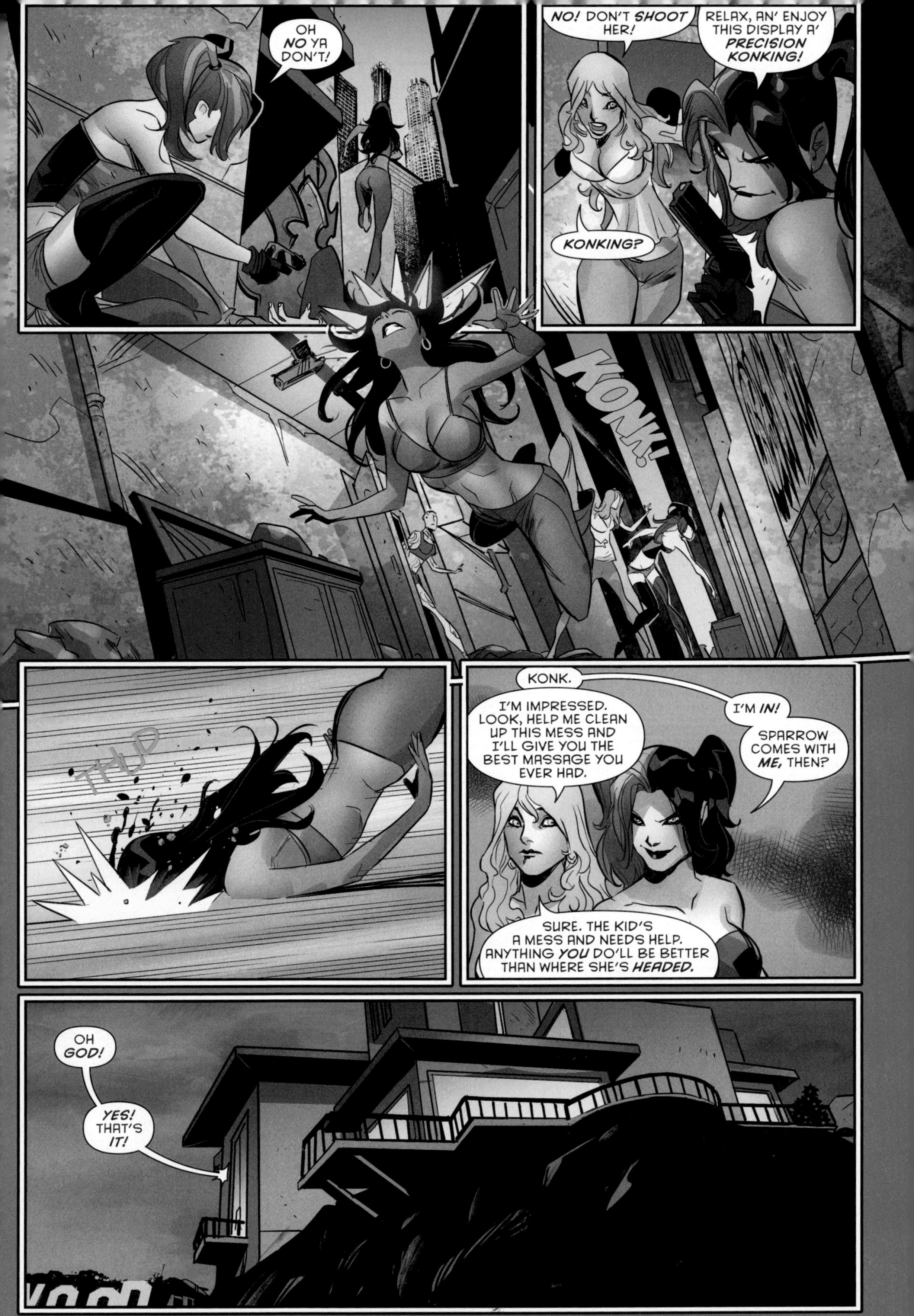

OH NO YA DON'T!
NO! DON'T SHOOT HER!
RELAX, AN' ENJOY THIS DISPLAY A' PRECISION KONKING!
KONKING?
KONK!
THUD
KONK.
I'M IMPRESSED. LOOK, HELP ME CLEAN UP THIS MESS AND I'LL GIVE YOU THE BEST MASSAGE YOU EVER HAD.
I'M IN!
SPARROW COMES WITH ME, THEN?
SURE. THE KID'S A MESS AND NEEDS HELP. ANYTHING YOU DO'LL BE BETTER THAN WHERE SHE'S HEADED.
OH GOD!
YES! THAT'S IT!

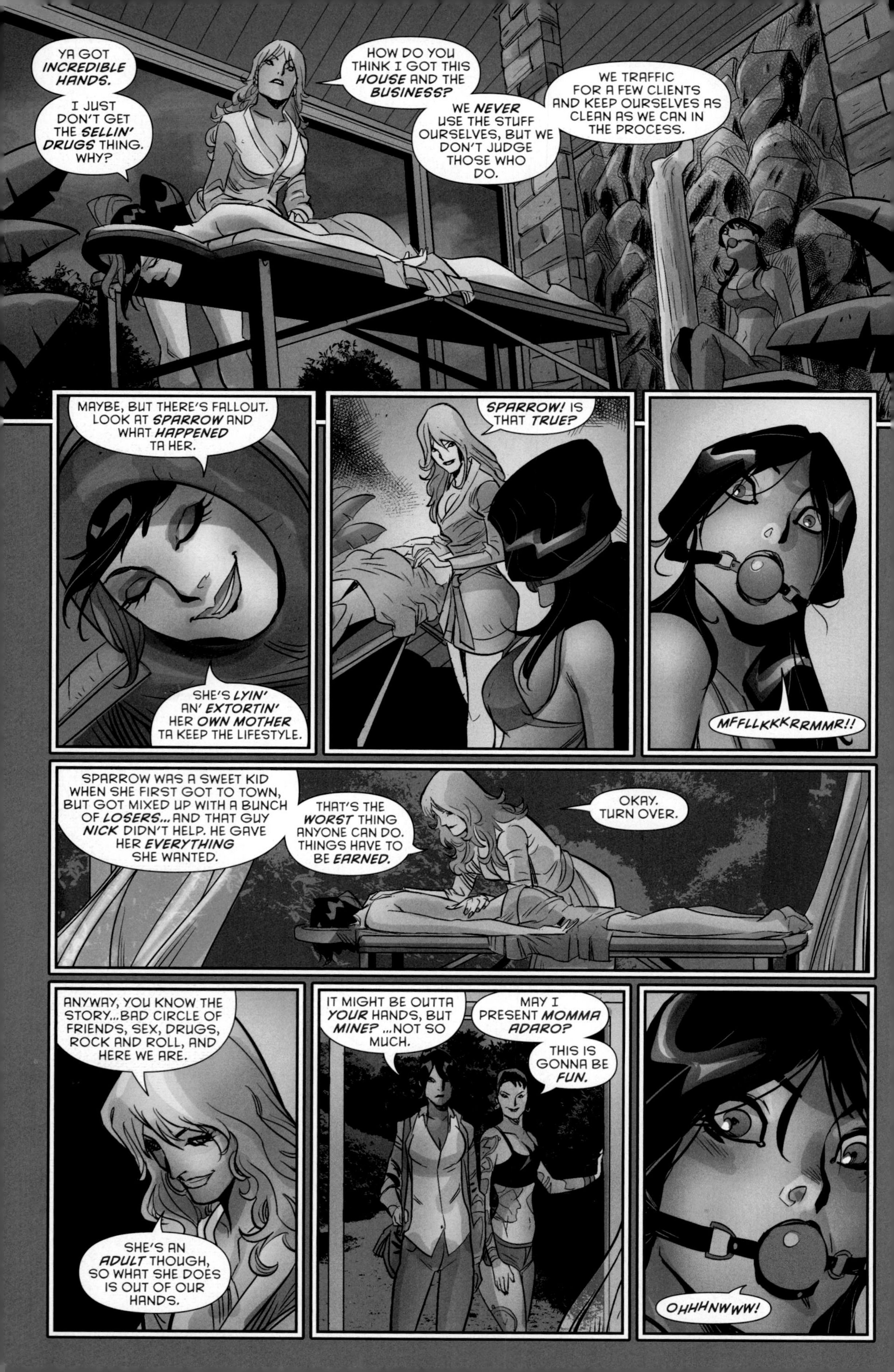
YA GOT INCREDIBLE HANDS.
I JUST DON'T GET THE SELLIN' DRUGS THING. WHY?
HOW DO YOU THINK I GOT THIS HOUSE AND THE BUSINESS?
WE NEVER USE THE STUFF OURSELVES, BUT WE DON'T JUDGE THOSE WHO DO.
WE TRAFFIC FOR A FEW CLIENTS AND KEEP OURSELVES AS CLEAN AS WE CAN IN THE PROCESS.
MAYBE, BUT THERE'S FALLOUT. LOOK AT SPARROW AND WHAT HAPPENED TA HER.
SHE'S LYIN' AN' EXTORTIN' HER OWN MOTHER TA KEEP THE LIFESTYLE.
SPARROW! IS THAT TRUE?
MFFLLKKKRRMMR!!
SPARROW WAS A SWEET KID WHEN SHE FIRST GOT TO TOWN, BUT GOT MIXED UP WITH A BUNCH OF LOSERS... AND THAT GUY NICK DIDN'T HELP. HE GAVE HER EVERYTHING SHE WANTED.
THAT'S THE WORST THING ANYONE CAN DO. THINGS HAVE TO BE EARNED.
OKAY. TURN OVER.
ANYWAY, YOU KNOW THE STORY...BAD CIRCLE OF FRIENDS, SEX, DRUGS, ROCK AND ROLL, AND HERE WE ARE.
SHE'S AN ADULT THOUGH, SO WHAT SHE DOES IS OUT OF OUR HANDS.
IT MIGHT BE OUTTA YOUR HANDS, BUT MINE? ...NOT SO MUCH.
MAY I PRESENT MOMMA ADARO?
THIS IS GONNA BE FUN.
OHHHNWWW!

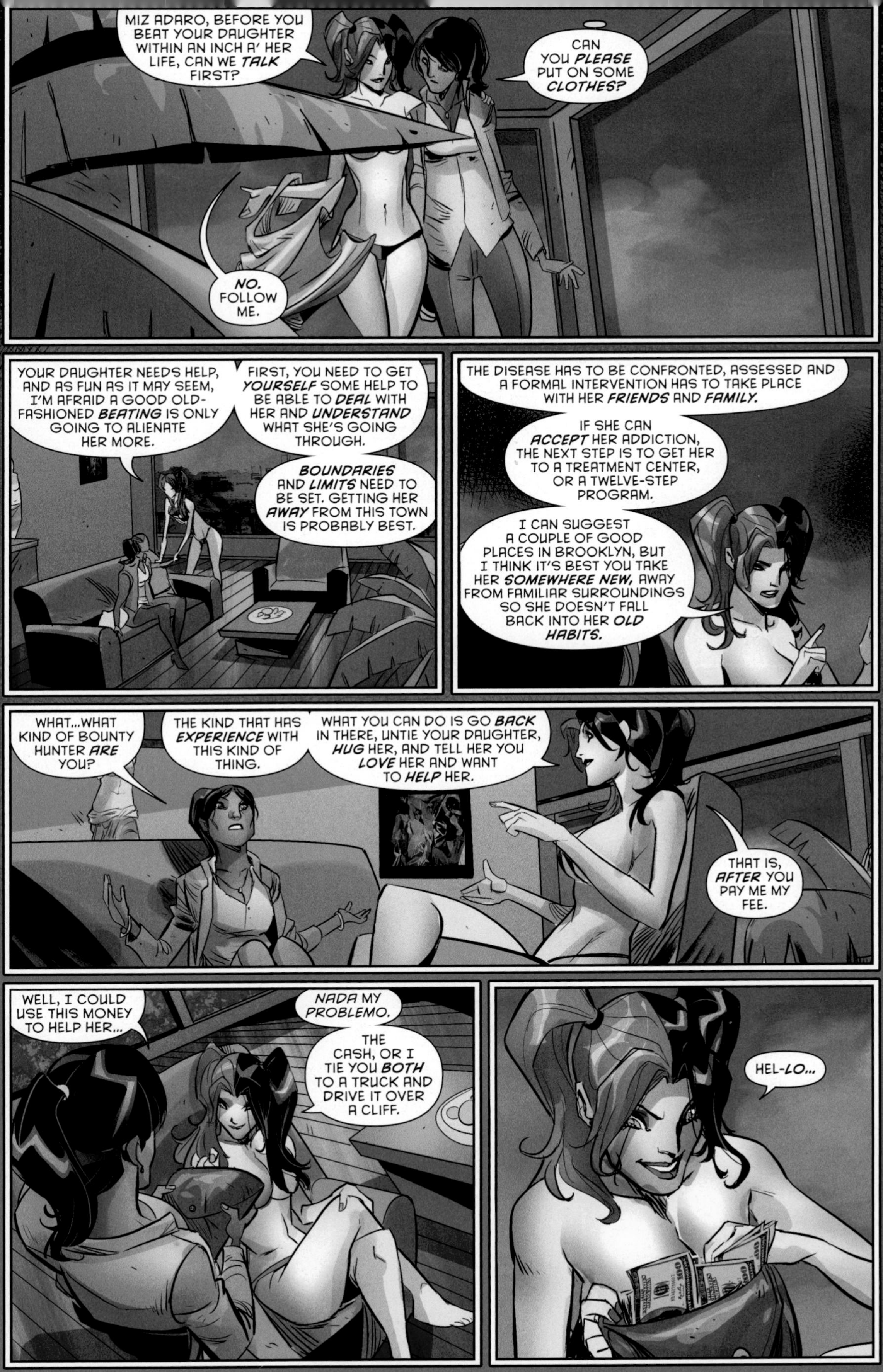
MIZ ADARO, BEFORE YOU BEAT YOUR DAUGHTER WITHIN AN INCH A' HER LIFE, CAN WE *TALK* FIRST?
CAN YOU *PLEASE* PUT ON SOME *CLOTHES?*
NO. FOLLOW ME.
YOUR DAUGHTER NEEDS HELP, AND AS FUN AS IT MAY SEEM, I'M AFRAID A GOOD OLD-FASHIONED *BEATING* IS ONLY GOING TO ALIENATE HER MORE.
FIRST, YOU NEED TO GET *YOURSELF* SOME HELP TO BE ABLE TO *DEAL* WITH HER AND *UNDERSTAND* WHAT SHE'S GOING THROUGH.
BOUNDARIES AND *LIMITS* NEED TO BE SET. GETTING HER *AWAY* FROM THIS TOWN IS PROBABLY BEST.
THE DISEASE HAS TO BE CONFRONTED, ASSESSED AND A FORMAL INTERVENTION HAS TO TAKE PLACE WITH HER *FRIENDS* AND *FAMILY.*
IF SHE CAN *ACCEPT* HER ADDICTION, THE NEXT STEP IS TO GET HER TO A TREATMENT CENTER, OR A TWELVE-STEP PROGRAM.
I CAN SUGGEST A COUPLE OF GOOD PLACES IN BROOKLYN, BUT I THINK IT'S BEST YOU TAKE HER *SOMEWHERE NEW,* AWAY FROM FAMILIAR SURROUNDINGS SO SHE DOESN'T FALL BACK INTO HER *OLD HABITS.*
WHAT...WHAT KIND OF BOUNTY HUNTER *ARE* YOU?
THE KIND THAT HAS *EXPERIENCE* WITH THIS KIND OF THING.
WHAT YOU CAN DO IS GO *BACK* IN THERE, UNTIE YOUR DAUGHTER, *HUG* HER, AND TELL HER YOU *LOVE* HER AND WANT TO *HELP* HER.
THAT IS, *AFTER* YOU PAY ME MY FEE.
WELL, I COULD USE THIS MONEY TO HELP HER...
NADA MY *PROBLEMO.*
THE CASH, OR I TIE YOU *BOTH* TO A TRUCK AND DRIVE IT OVER A CLIFF.
HEL-*LO*...

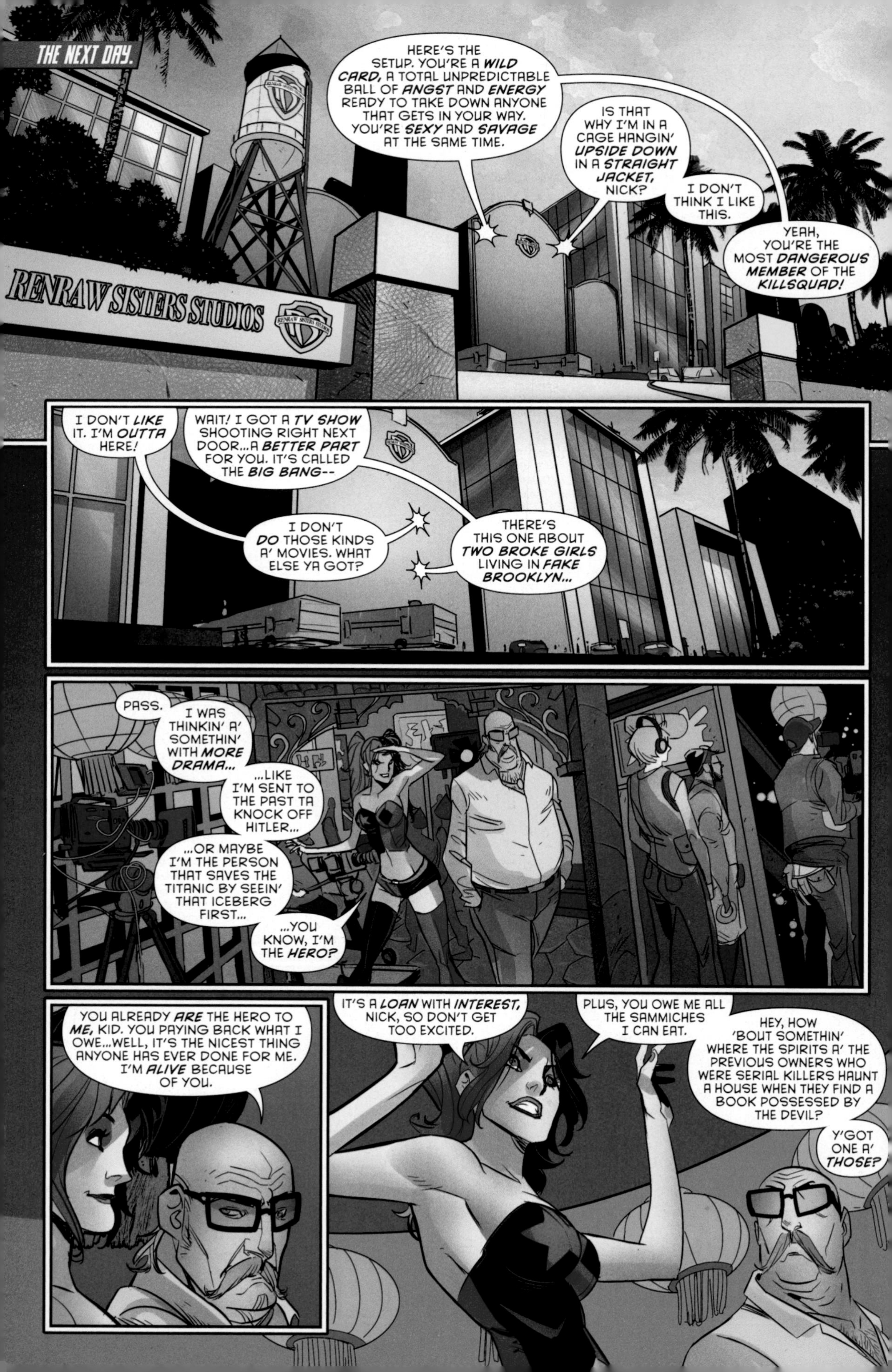
THE NEXT DAY.
HERE'S THE SETUP. YOU'RE A WILD CARD, A TOTAL UNPREDICTABLE BALL OF ANGST AND ENERGY READY TO TAKE DOWN ANYONE THAT GETS IN YOUR WAY. YOU'RE SEXY AND SAVAGE AT THE SAME TIME.
IS THAT WHY I'M IN A CAGE HANGIN' UPSIDE DOWN IN A STRAIGHT JACKET, NICK?
I DON'T THINK I LIKE THIS.
YEAH, YOU'RE THE MOST DANGEROUS MEMBER OF THE KILLSQUAD!
RENRAW SISTERS STUDIOS
I DON'T LIKE IT. I'M OUTTA HERE!
WAIT! I GOT A TV SHOW SHOOTING RIGHT NEXT DOOR...A BETTER PART FOR YOU. IT'S CALLED THE BIG BANG--
I DON'T DO THOSE KINDS A' MOVIES. WHAT ELSE YA GOT?
THERE'S THIS ONE ABOUT TWO BROKE GIRLS LIVING IN FAKE BROOKLYN...
PASS.
I WAS THINKIN' A' SOMETHIN' WITH MORE DRAMA...
...LIKE I'M SENT TO THE PAST TA KNOCK OFF HITLER...
...OR MAYBE I'M THE PERSON THAT SAVES THE TITANIC BY SEEIN' THAT ICEBERG FIRST...
...YOU KNOW, I'M THE HERO?
YOU ALREADY ARE THE HERO TO ME, KID. YOU PAYING BACK WHAT I OWE...WELL, IT'S THE NICEST THING ANYONE HAS EVER DONE FOR ME. I'M ALIVE BECAUSE OF YOU.
IT'S A LOAN WITH INTEREST, NICK, SO DON'T GET TOO EXCITED.
PLUS, YOU OWE ME ALL THE SAMMICHES I CAN EAT.
HEY, HOW 'BOUT SOMETHIN' WHERE THE SPIRITS A' THE PREVIOUS OWNERS WHO WERE SERIAL KILLERS HAUNT A HOUSE WHEN THEY FIND A BOOK POSSESSED BY THE DEVIL?
Y'GOT ONE A' THOSE?

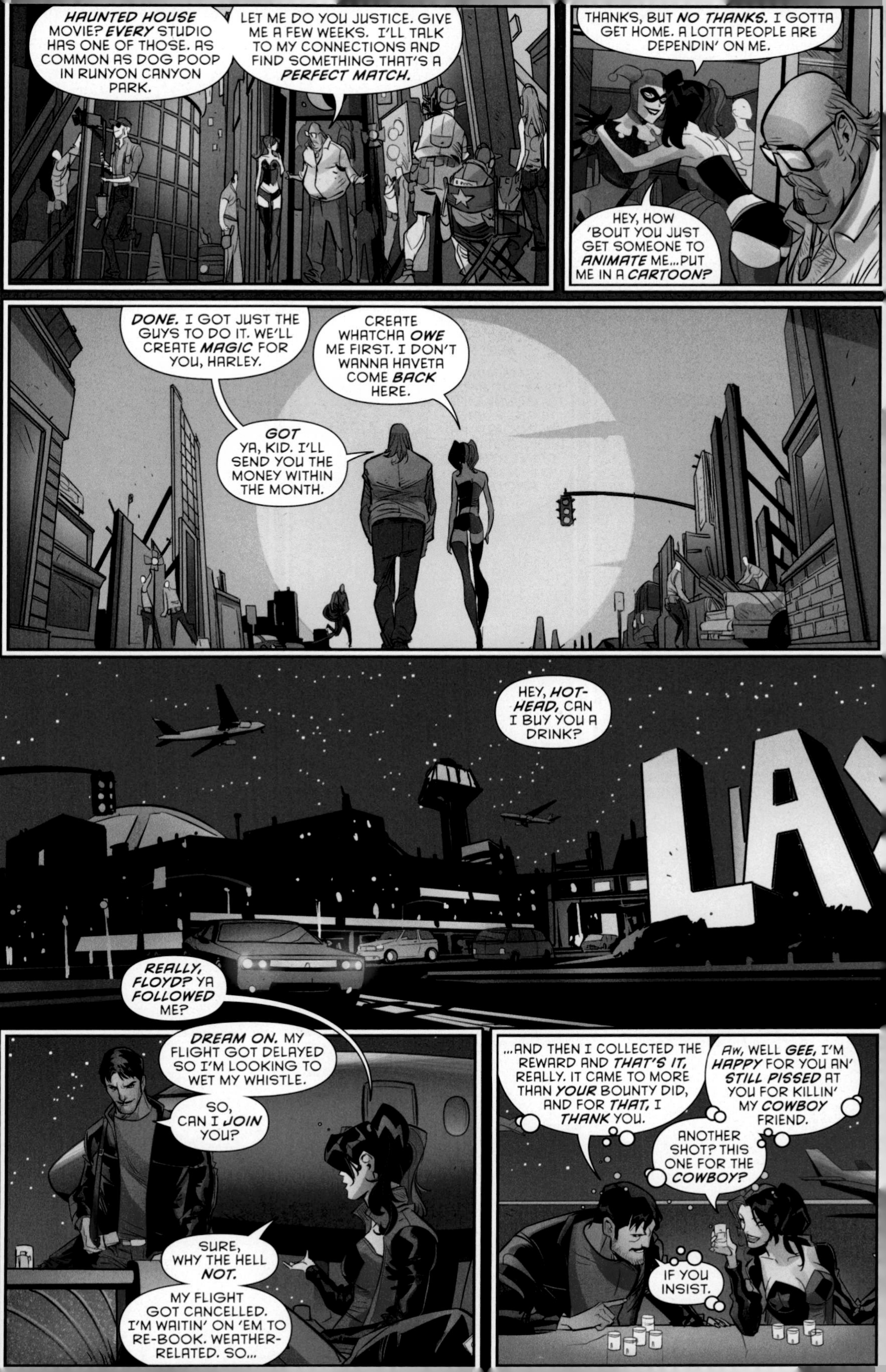
HAUNTED HOUSE MOVIE? EVERY STUDIO HAS ONE OF THOSE. AS COMMON AS DOG POOP IN RUNYON CANYON PARK.
LET ME DO YOU JUSTICE. GIVE ME A FEW WEEKS. I'LL TALK TO MY CONNECTIONS AND FIND SOMETHING THAT'S A PERFECT MATCH.
THANKS, BUT NO THANKS. I GOTTA GET HOME. A LOTTA PEOPLE ARE DEPENDIN' ON ME.
HEY, HOW 'BOUT YOU JUST GET SOMEONE TO ANIMATE ME...PUT ME IN A CARTOON?
DONE. I GOT JUST THE GUYS TO DO IT. WE'LL CREATE MAGIC FOR YOU, HARLEY.
CREATE WHATCHA OWE ME FIRST. I DON'T WANNA HAVETA COME BACK HERE.
GOT YA, KID. I'LL SEND YOU THE MONEY WITHIN THE MONTH.
HEY, HOT-HEAD, CAN I BUY YOU A DRINK?
LA
REALLY, FLOYD? YA FOLLOWED ME?
DREAM ON. MY FLIGHT GOT DELAYED SO I'M LOOKING TO WET MY WHISTLE.
SO, CAN I JOIN YOU?
SURE, WHY THE HELL NOT.
MY FLIGHT GOT CANCELLED. I'M WAITIN' ON 'EM TO RE-BOOK. WEATHER-RELATED. SO...
...AND THEN I COLLECTED THE REWARD AND THAT'S IT, REALLY. IT CAME TO MORE THAN YOUR BOUNTY DID, AND FOR THAT, I THANK YOU.
AW, WELL GEE, I'M HAPPY FOR YOU AN' STILL PISSED AT YOU FOR KILLIN' MY COWBOY FRIEND.
ANOTHER SHOT? THIS ONE FOR THE COWBOY?
IF YOU INSIST.

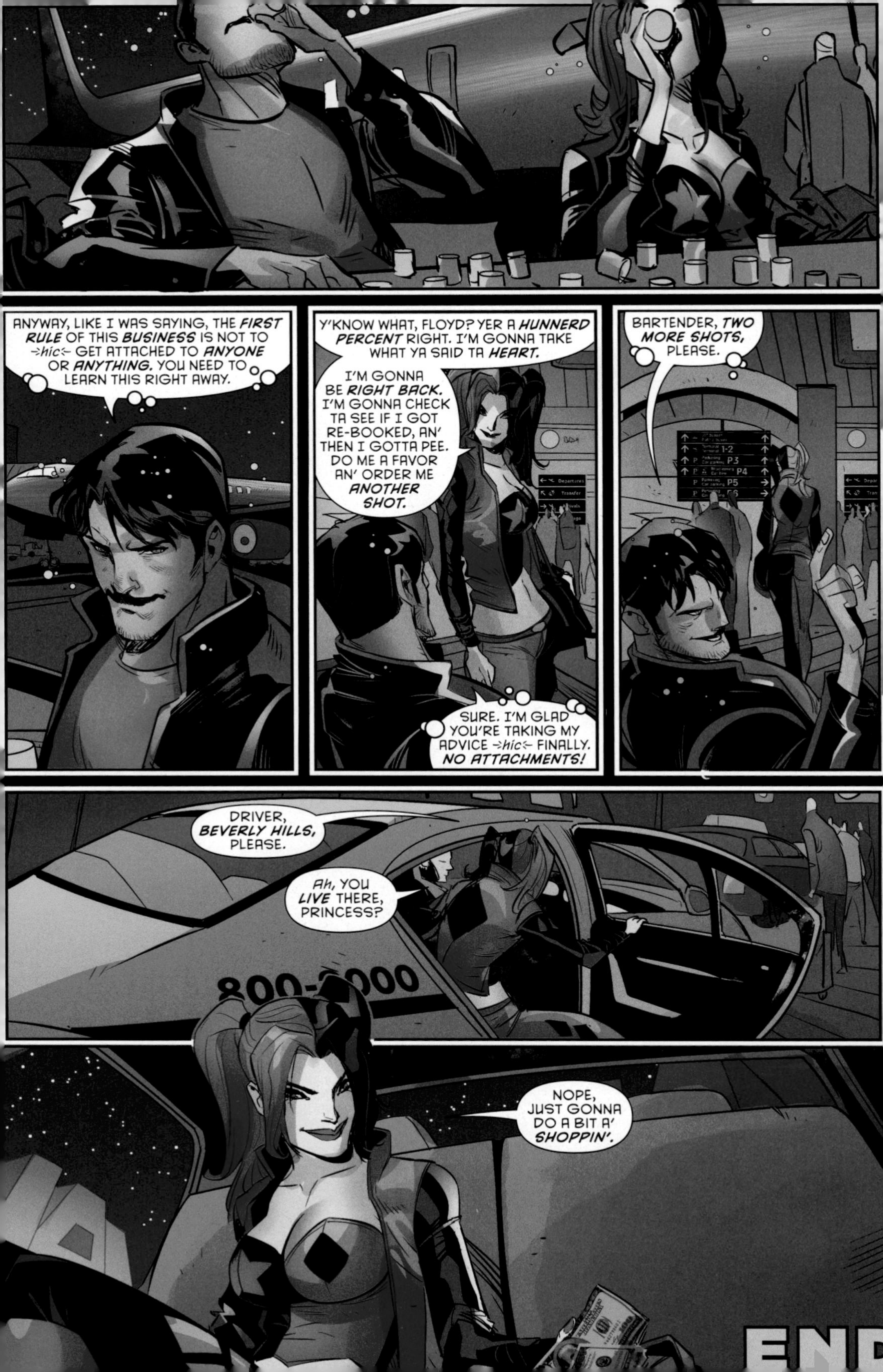
ANYWAY, LIKE I WAS SAYING, THE *FIRST RULE* OF THIS *BUSINESS* IS NOT TO ⇒*hic*⇐ GET ATTACHED TO *ANYONE* OR *ANYTHING.* YOU NEED TO LEARN THIS RIGHT AWAY.
Y'KNOW WHAT, FLOYD? YER A *HUNNERD PERCENT* RIGHT. I'M GONNA TAKE WHAT YA SAID TA *HEART.*
I'M GONNA BE *RIGHT BACK.* I'M GONNA CHECK TA SEE IF I GOT RE-BOOKED, AN' THEN I GOTTA PEE. DO ME A FAVOR AN' ORDER ME *ANOTHER SHOT.*
SURE. I'M GLAD YOU'RE TAKING MY ADVICE ⇒*hic*⇐ FINALLY. *NO ATTACHMENTS!*
BARTENDER, *TWO MORE SHOTS,* PLEASE.
DRIVER, *BEVERLY HILLS,* PLEASE.
Ah, YOU *LIVE* THERE, PRINCESS?
NOPE, JUST GONNA DO A BIT A' *SHOPPIN'.*
END

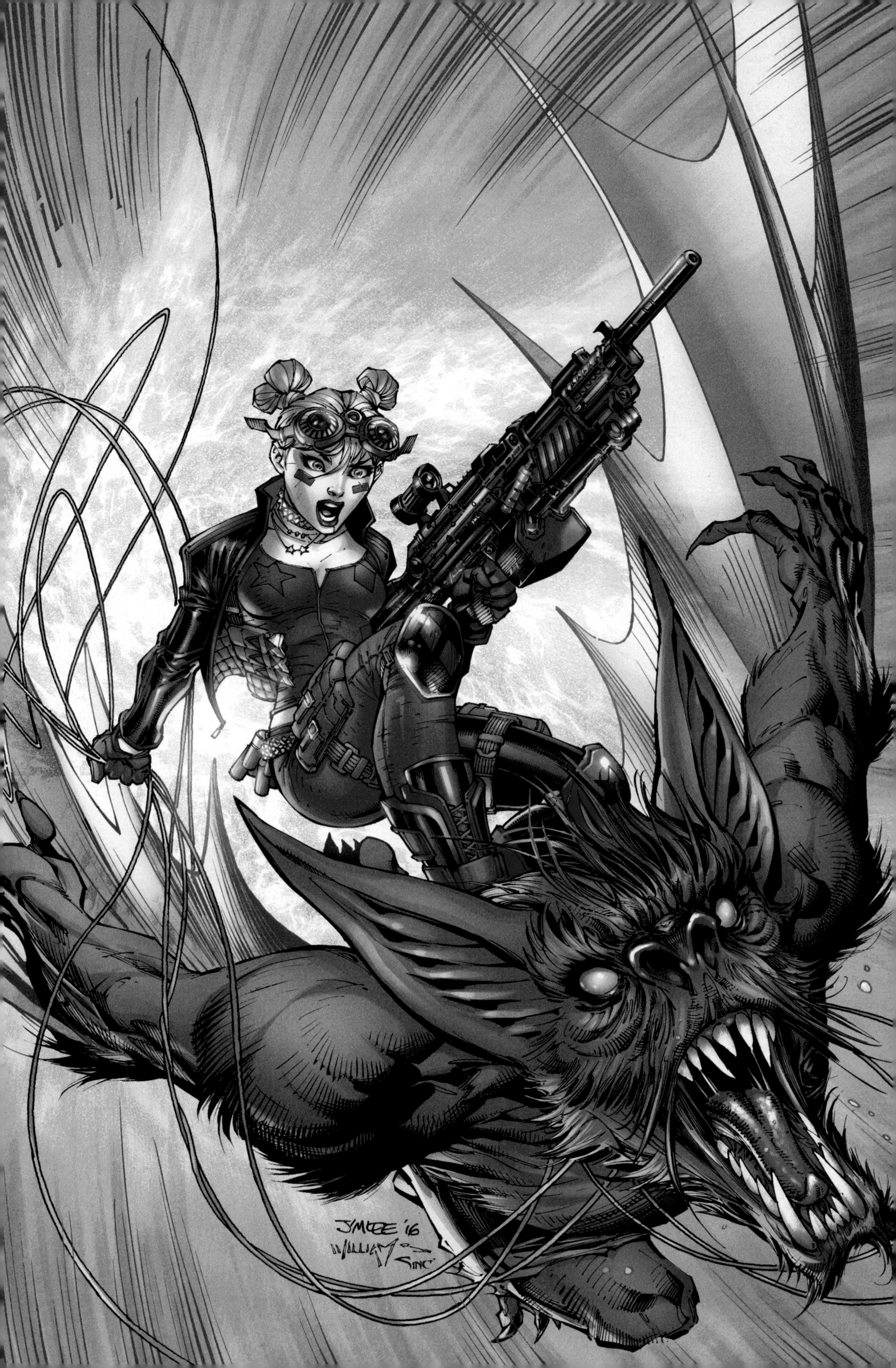

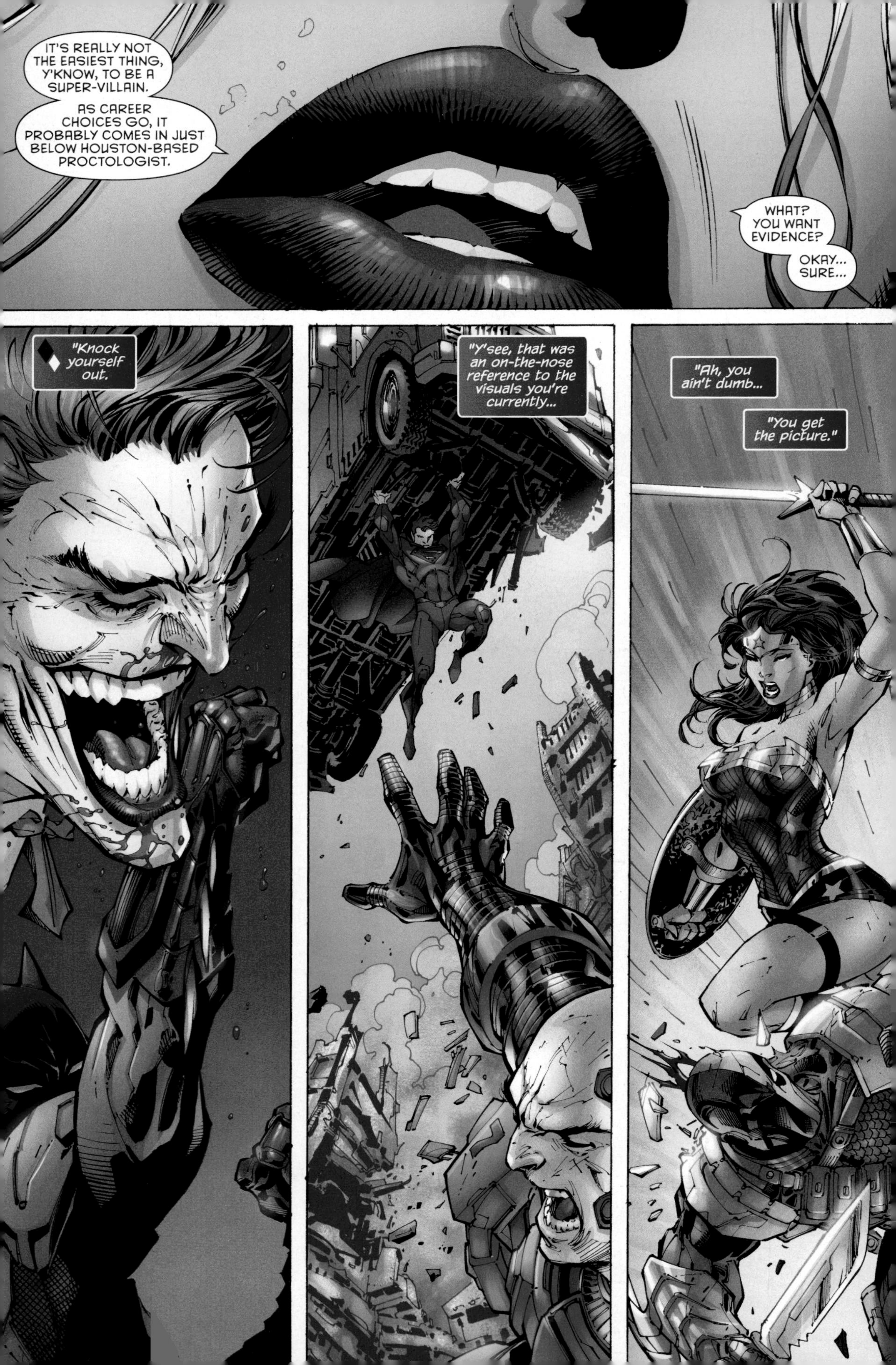

IT'S REALLY NOT THE EASIEST THING, Y'KNOW, TO BE A SUPER-VILLAIN.
AS CAREER CHOICES GO, IT PROBABLY COMES IN JUST BELOW HOUSTON-BASED PROCTOLOGIST.
WHAT? YOU WANT EVIDENCE?
OKAY... SURE...
"Knock yourself out.
"Y'see, that was an on-the-nose reference to the visuals you're currently...
"Ah, you ain't dumb...
"You get the picture."

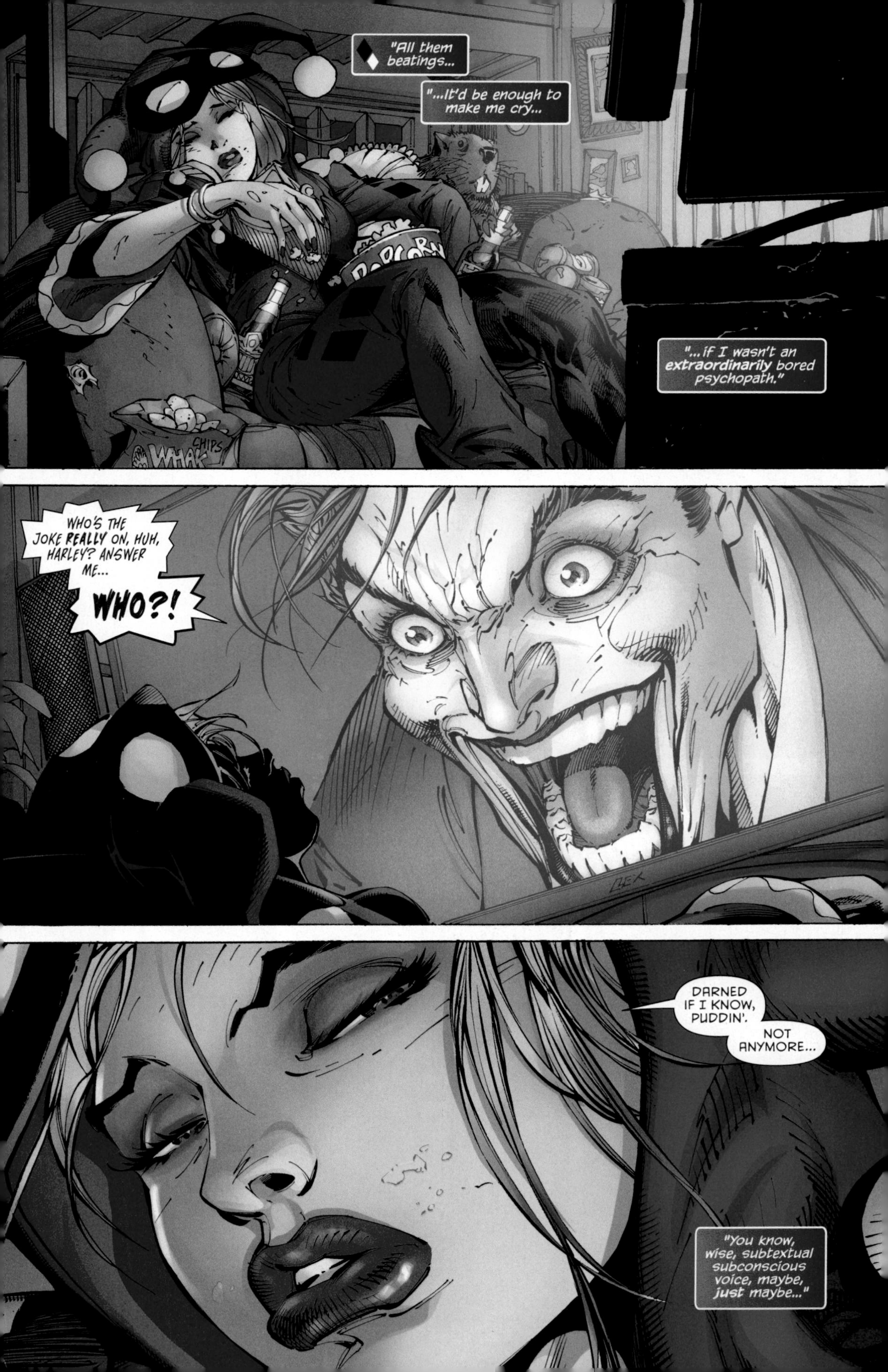
"All them beatings...
"...It'd be enough to make me cry...
"...if I wasn't an **extraordinarily** bored psychopath."
POPCORN
CHIPS WHAK
WHO'S THE JOKE **REALLY** ON, HUH, HARLEY? ANSWER ME...
WHO?!
DARNED IF I KNOW, PUDDIN'.
NOT ANYMORE...
"You know, wise, subtextual subconscious voice, maybe, **just** maybe..."

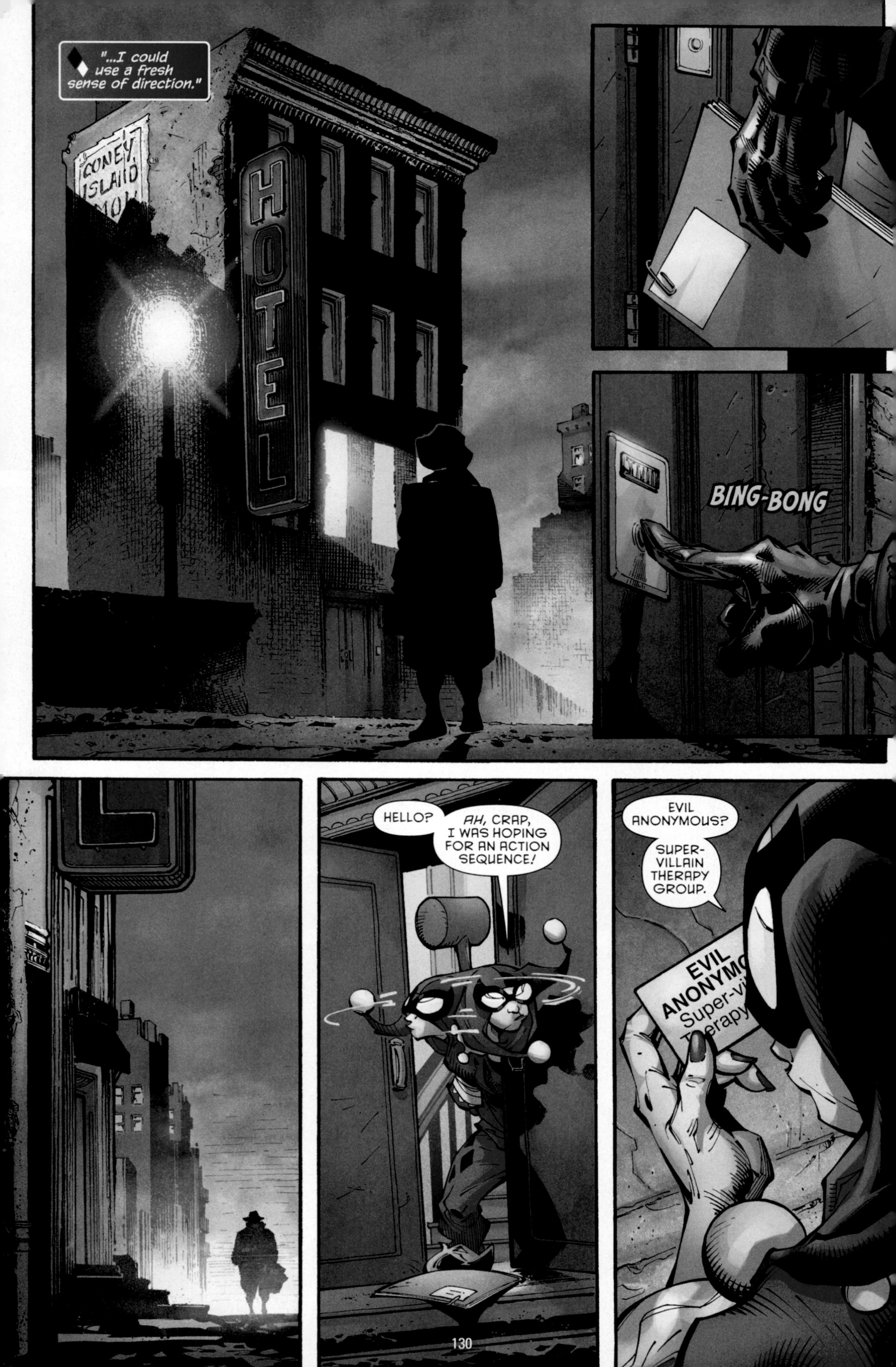
"...I could use a fresh sense of direction."
CONEY ISLAND
HOTEL
BING-BONG
HELLO?
AH, CRAP, I WAS HOPING FOR AN ACTION SEQUENCE!
EVIL ANONYMOUS?
SUPER-VILLAIN THERAPY GROUP.
EVIL ANONYMO
Super-vi
Therapy

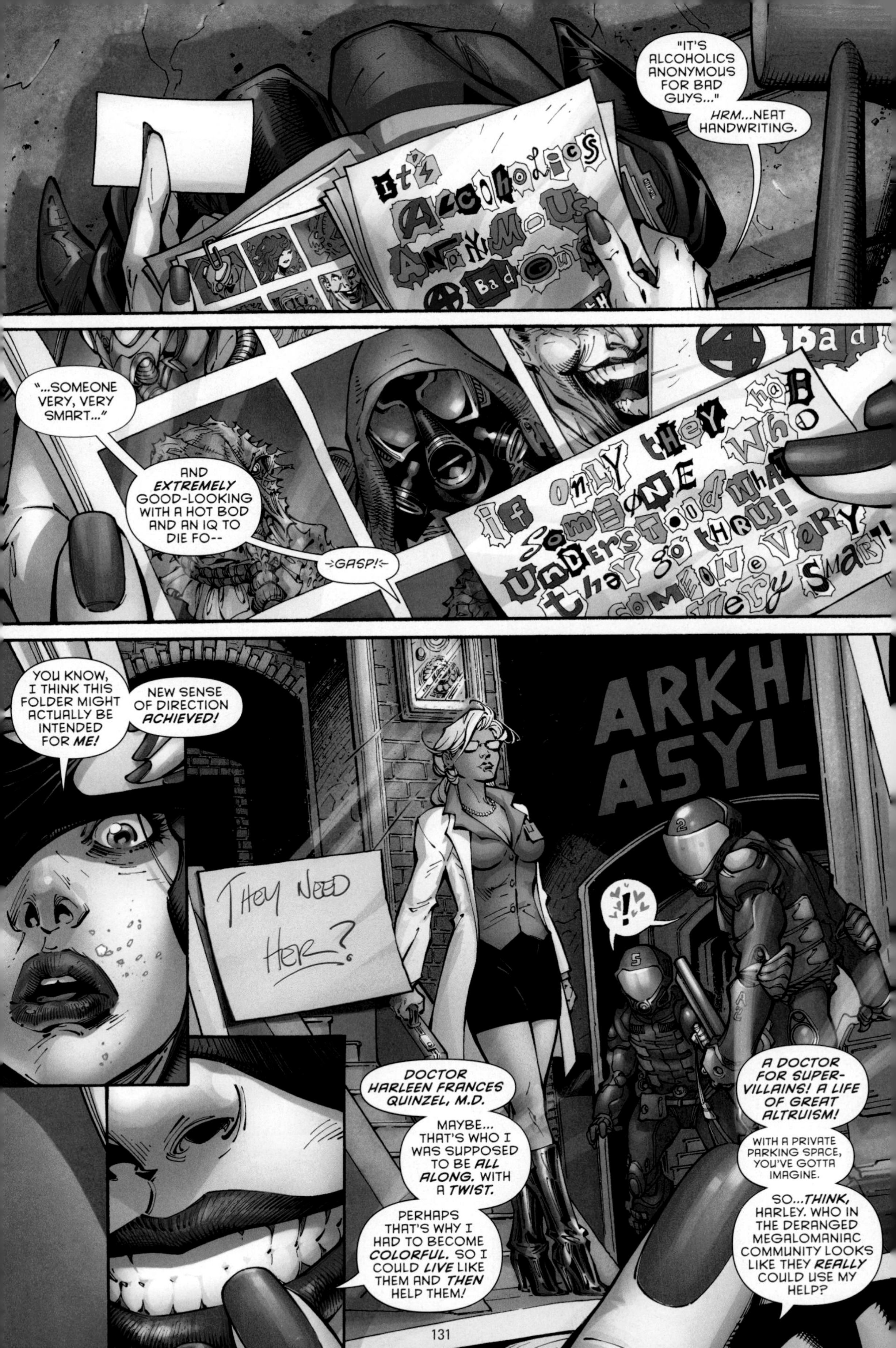
It's Alcoholics Anonymous 4 Bad Guys
"IT'S ALCOHOLICS ANONYMOUS FOR BAD GUYS..."
HRM...NEAT HANDWRITING.
"...SOMEONE VERY, VERY SMART..."
AND *EXTREMELY* GOOD-LOOKING WITH A HOT BOD AND AN IQ TO DIE FO--
If only they haD someone who understood what they go thru! someone very very smart!
GASP!
YOU KNOW, I THINK THIS FOLDER MIGHT ACTUALLY BE INTENDED FOR *ME!*
NEW SENSE OF DIRECTION *ACHIEVED!*
THEY NEED HER?
!
DOCTOR HARLEEN FRANCES QUINZEL, M.D.
MAYBE... THAT'S WHO I WAS SUPPOSED TO BE *ALL ALONG.* WITH A *TWIST.*
PERHAPS THAT'S WHY I HAD TO BECOME *COLORFUL.* SO I COULD *LIVE* LIKE THEM AND *THEN* HELP THEM!
A DOCTOR FOR SUPER-VILLAINS! A LIFE OF GREAT ALTRUISM!
WITH A PRIVATE PARKING SPACE, YOU'VE GOTTA IMAGINE.
SO...*THINK,* HARLEY. WHO IN THE DERANGED MEGALOMANIAC COMMUNITY LOOKS LIKE THEY *REALLY* COULD USE MY HELP?

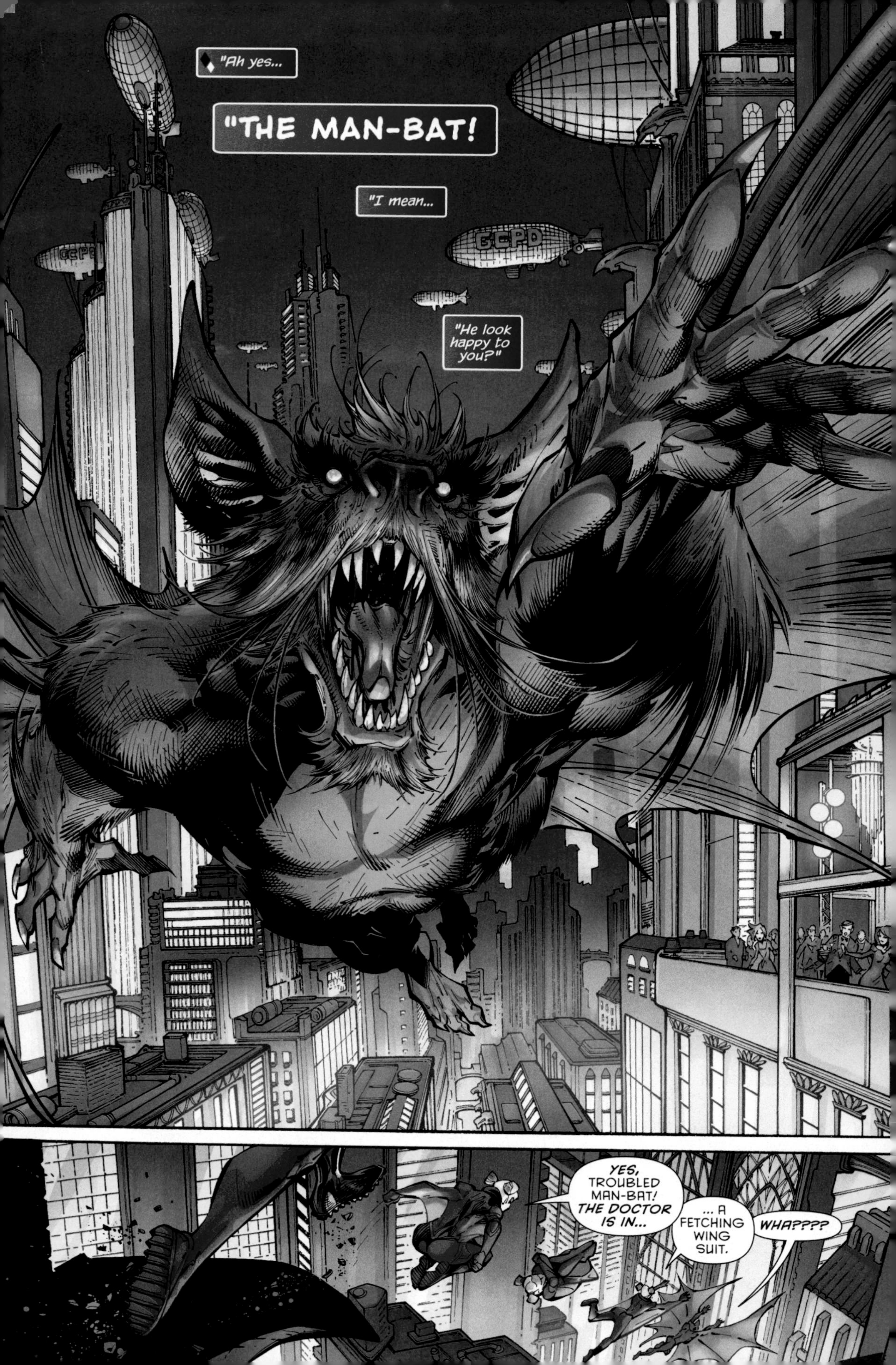
"Ah yes...
"THE MAN-BAT!
"I mean...
"He look happy to you?"
GCPD
YES, TROUBLED MAN-BAT! THE DOCTOR IS IN...
... A FETCHING WING SUIT.
WHA????

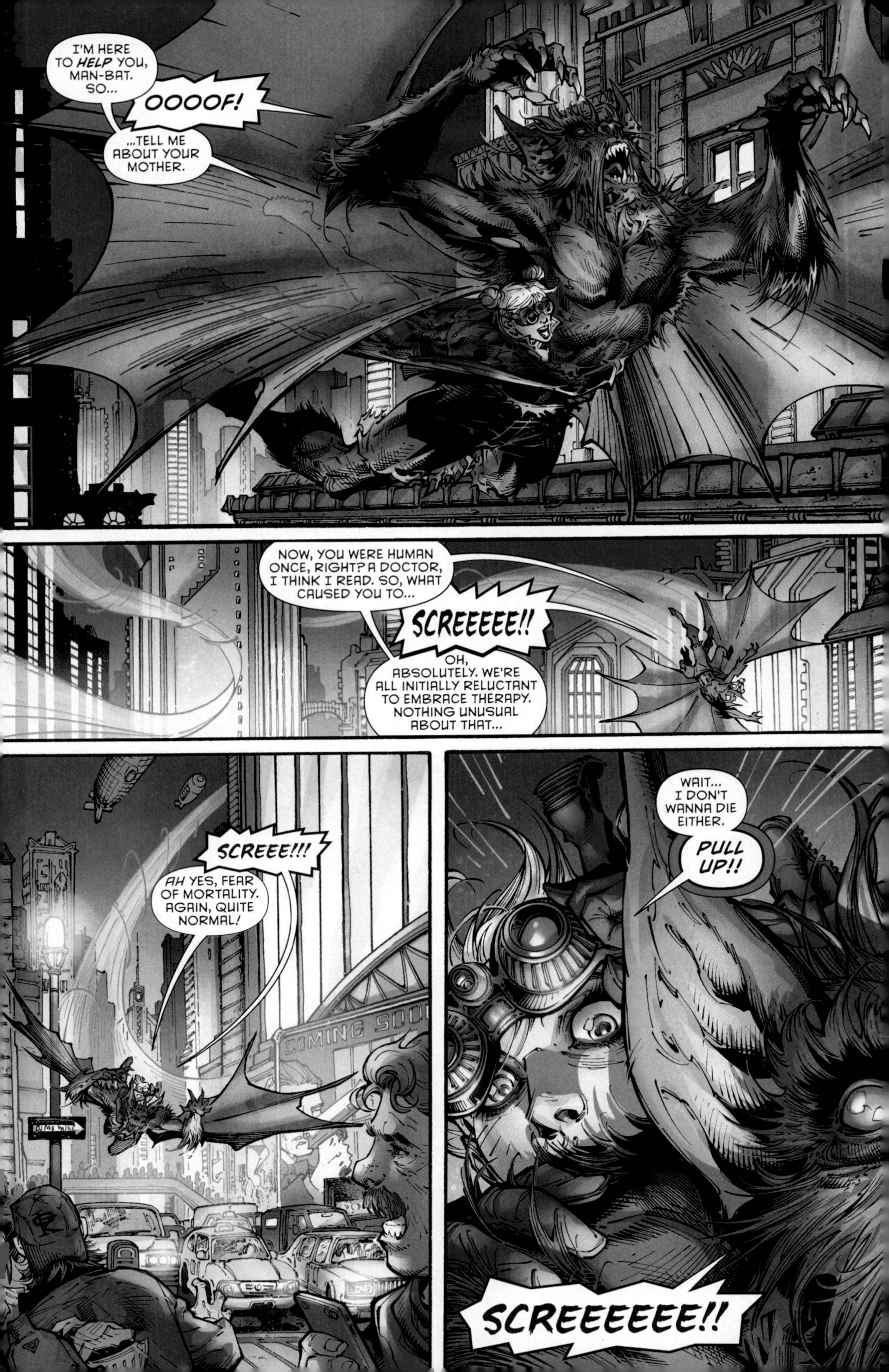
I'M HERE TO HELP YOU, MAN-BAT. SO...
OOOOF!
...TELL ME ABOUT YOUR MOTHER.
NOW, YOU WERE HUMAN ONCE, RIGHT? A DOCTOR, I THINK I READ. SO, WHAT CAUSED YOU TO...
SCREEEEE!!
OH, ABSOLUTELY. WE'RE ALL INITIALLY RELUCTANT TO EMBRACE THERAPY. NOTHING UNUSUAL ABOUT THAT...
SCREEE!!!
AH YES, FEAR OF MORTALITY. AGAIN, QUITE NORMAL!
COMING SOO
WAIT... I DON'T WANNA DIE EITHER.
PULL UP!!
SCREEEEEEE!!

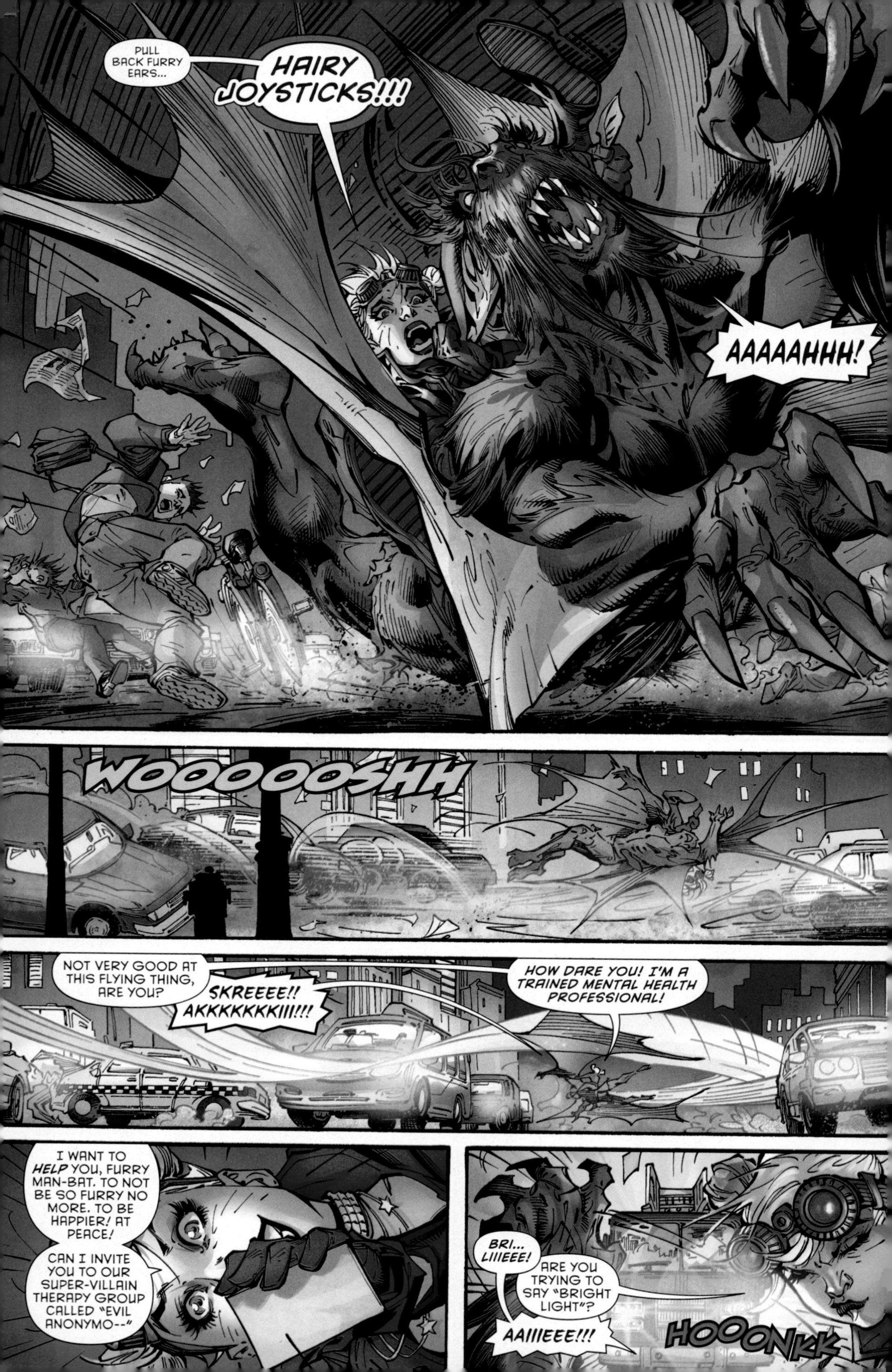
PULL BACK FURRY EARS...
HAIRY JOYSTICKS!!!
AAAAAHHH!
WOOOOOSHH
NOT VERY GOOD AT THIS FLYING THING, ARE YOU?
SKREEEE!! AKKKKKKIII!!!
HOW DARE YOU! I'M A TRAINED MENTAL HEALTH PROFESSIONAL!
I WANT TO HELP YOU, FURRY MAN-BAT. TO NOT BE SO FURRY NO MORE. TO BE HAPPIER! AT PEACE!
CAN I INVITE YOU TO OUR SUPER-VILLAIN THERAPY GROUP CALLED "EVIL ANONYMO--"
BRI... LIIIEEE!
ARE YOU TRYING TO SAY "BRIGHT LIGHT"?
AAIIIEEE!!!
HOOONKK

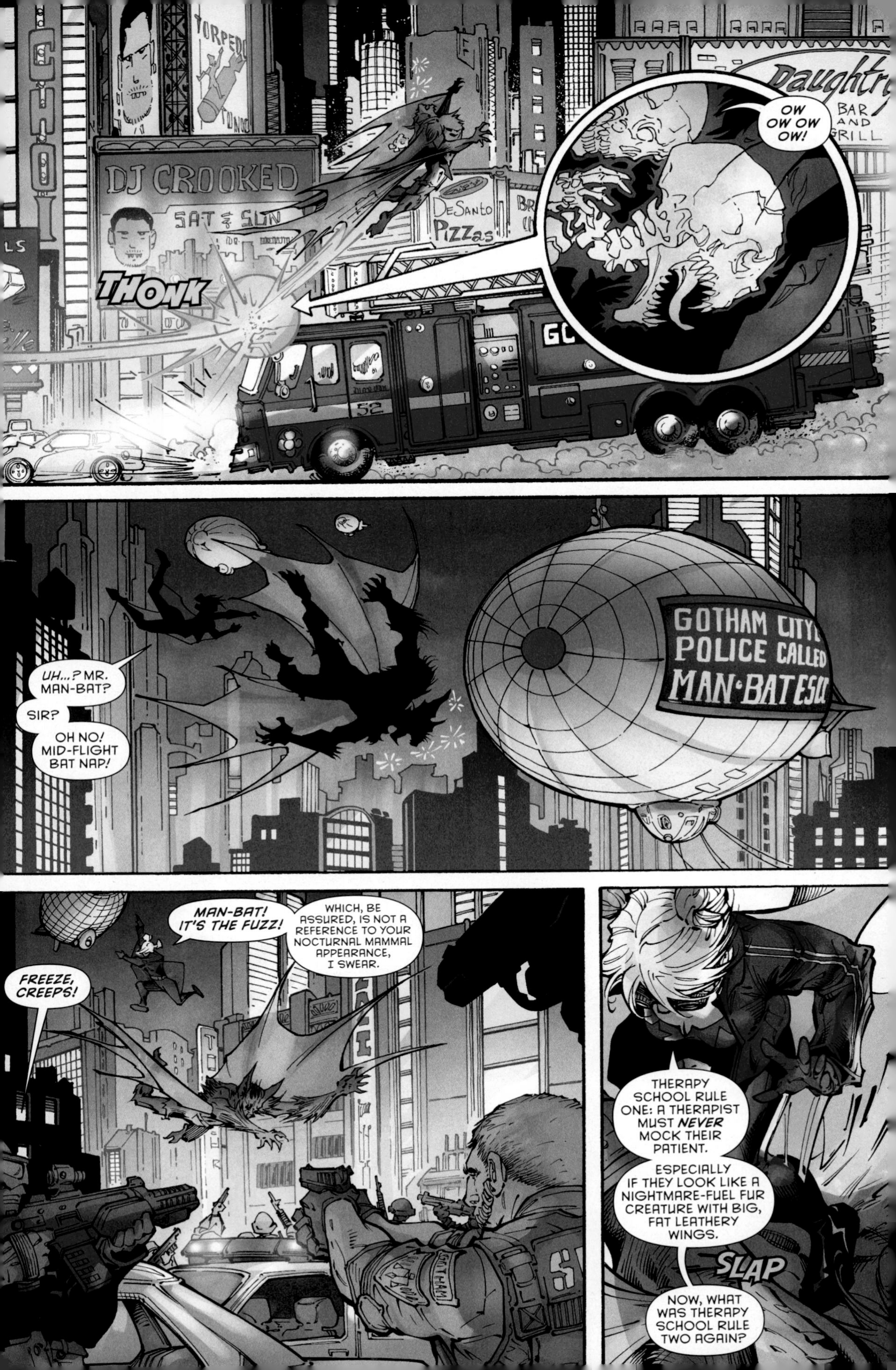
CHO
TORPEDO
DJ CROOKED
SAT & SUN
DeSanto Pizzas
Daughtry
BAR AND GRILL
OW OW OW OW!
THONK
52
GOTHAM CITY POLICE CALLED MAN-BAT ESC
UH...? MR. MAN-BAT?
SIR?
OH NO! MID-FLIGHT BAT NAP!
FREEZE, CREEPS!
MAN-BAT! IT'S THE FUZZ!
WHICH, BE ASSURED, IS NOT A REFERENCE TO YOUR NOCTURNAL MAMMAL APPEARANCE, I SWEAR.
GOTHAM
THERAPY SCHOOL RULE ONE: A THERAPIST MUST NEVER MOCK THEIR PATIENT.
ESPECIALLY IF THEY LOOK LIKE A NIGHTMARE-FUEL FUR CREATURE WITH BIG, FAT LEATHERY WINGS.
SLAP
NOW, WHAT WAS THERAPY SCHOOL RULE TWO AGAIN?

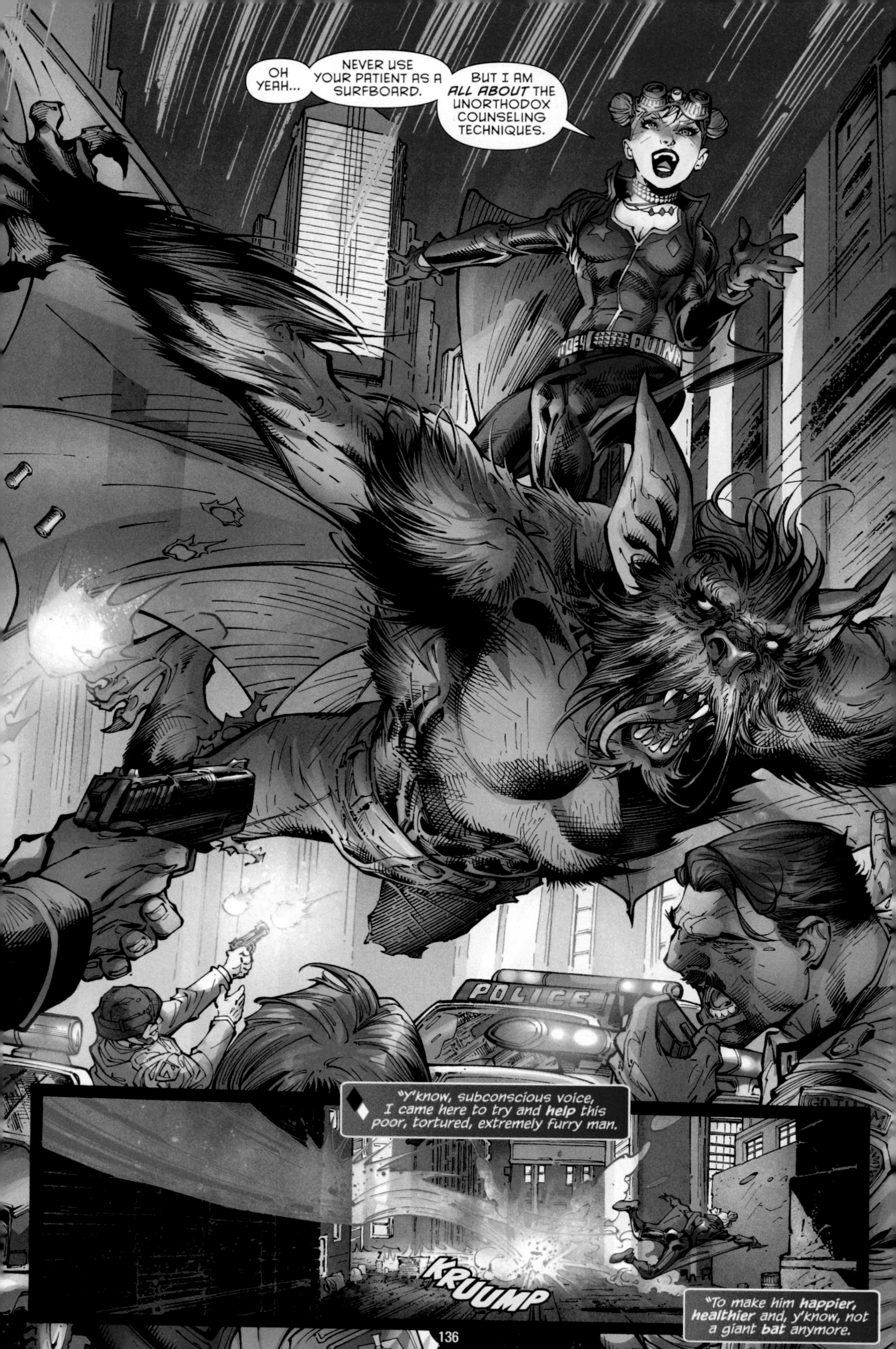

OH YEAH...
NEVER USE YOUR PATIENT AS A SURFBOARD.
BUT I AM ALL ABOUT THE UNORTHODOX COUNSELING TECHNIQUES.
POLICE
"Y'know, subconscious voice, I came here to try and help this poor, tortured, extremely furry man.
KRUUMP
"To make him happier, healthier and, y'know, not a giant bat anymore.

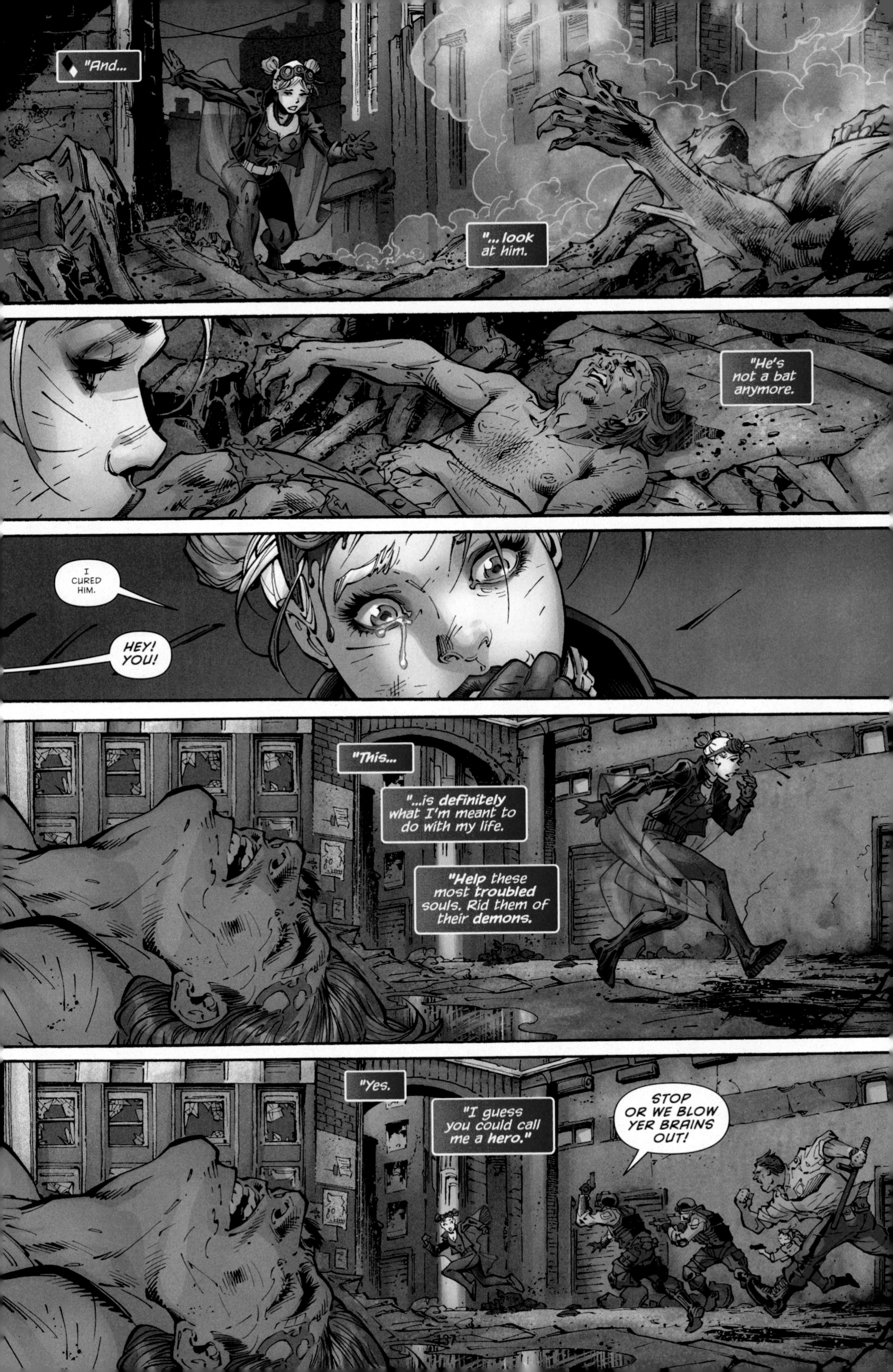
"And...
"...look at him.
"He's not a bat anymore.
I CURED HIM.
HEY! YOU!
"This...
"...is definitely what I'm meant to do with my life.
"Help these most troubled souls. Rid them of their demons.
"Yes.
"I guess you could call me a hero."
STOP OR WE BLOW YER BRAINS OUT!

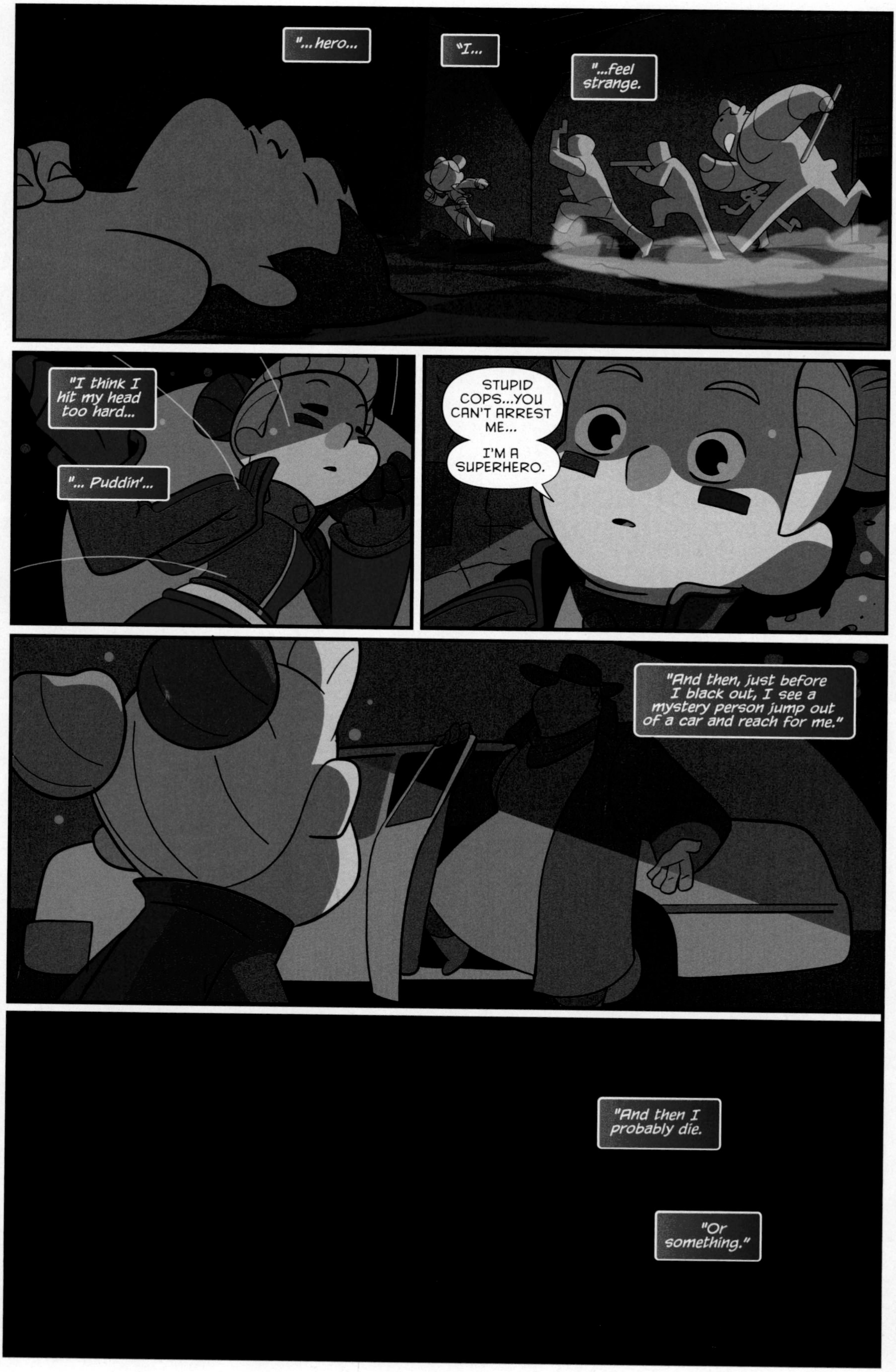
"...hero...
"I...
"...feel strange.
"I think I hit my head too hard...
"... Puddin'...
STUPID COPS...YOU CAN'T ARREST ME...
I'M A SUPERHERO.
"And then, just before I black out, I see a mystery person jump out of a car and reach for me."
"And then I probably die.
"Or something."

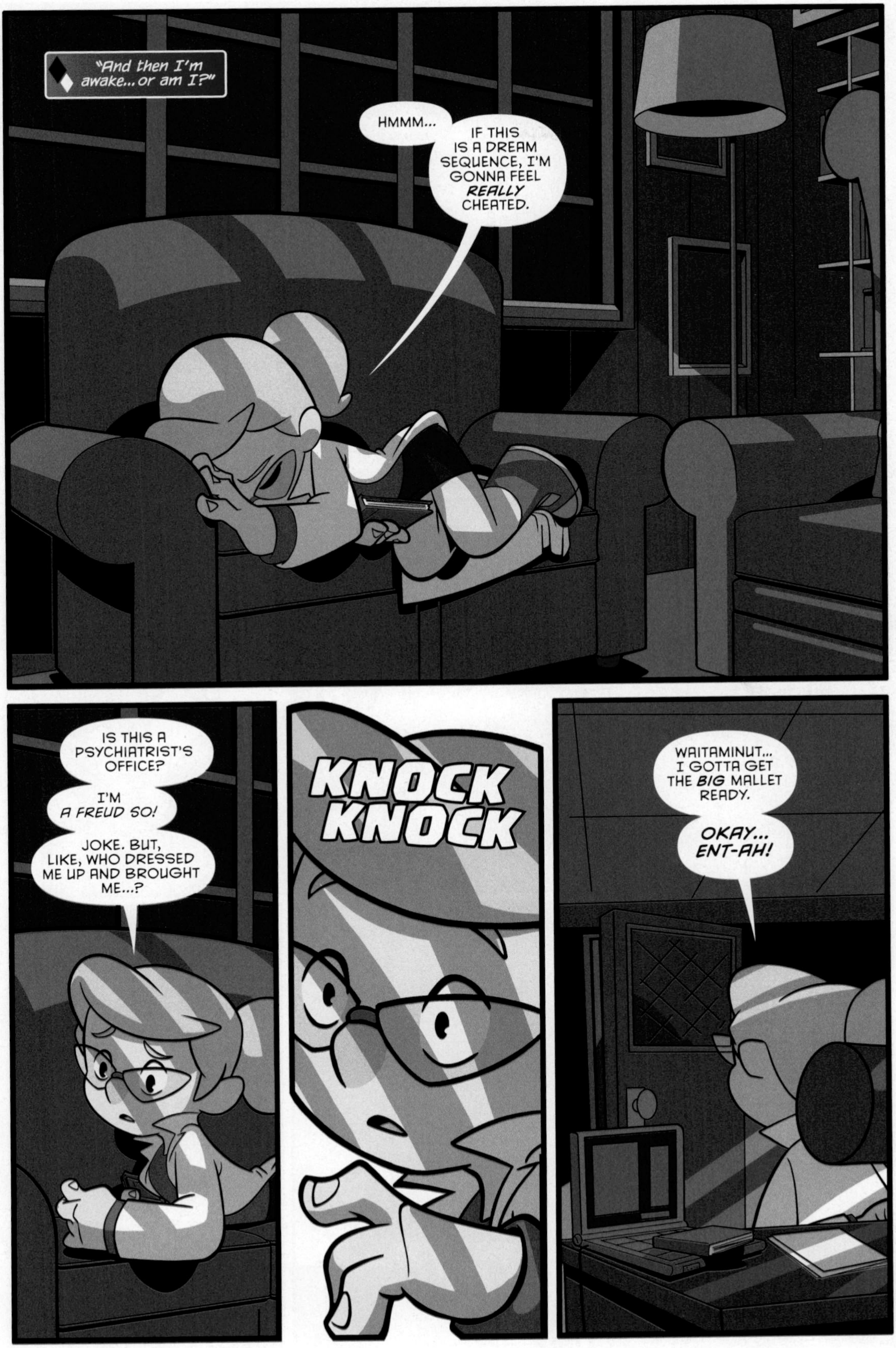
"And then I'm awake... or am I?"
HMMM...
IF THIS IS A DREAM SEQUENCE, I'M GONNA FEEL *REALLY* CHEATED.
IS THIS A PSYCHIATRIST'S OFFICE?
I'M *A FREUD SO!*
JOKE. BUT, LIKE, WHO DRESSED ME UP AND BROUGHT ME...?
KNOCK KNOCK
WAITAMINUT... I GOTTA GET THE *BIG* MALLET READY.
OKAY... ENT-AH!

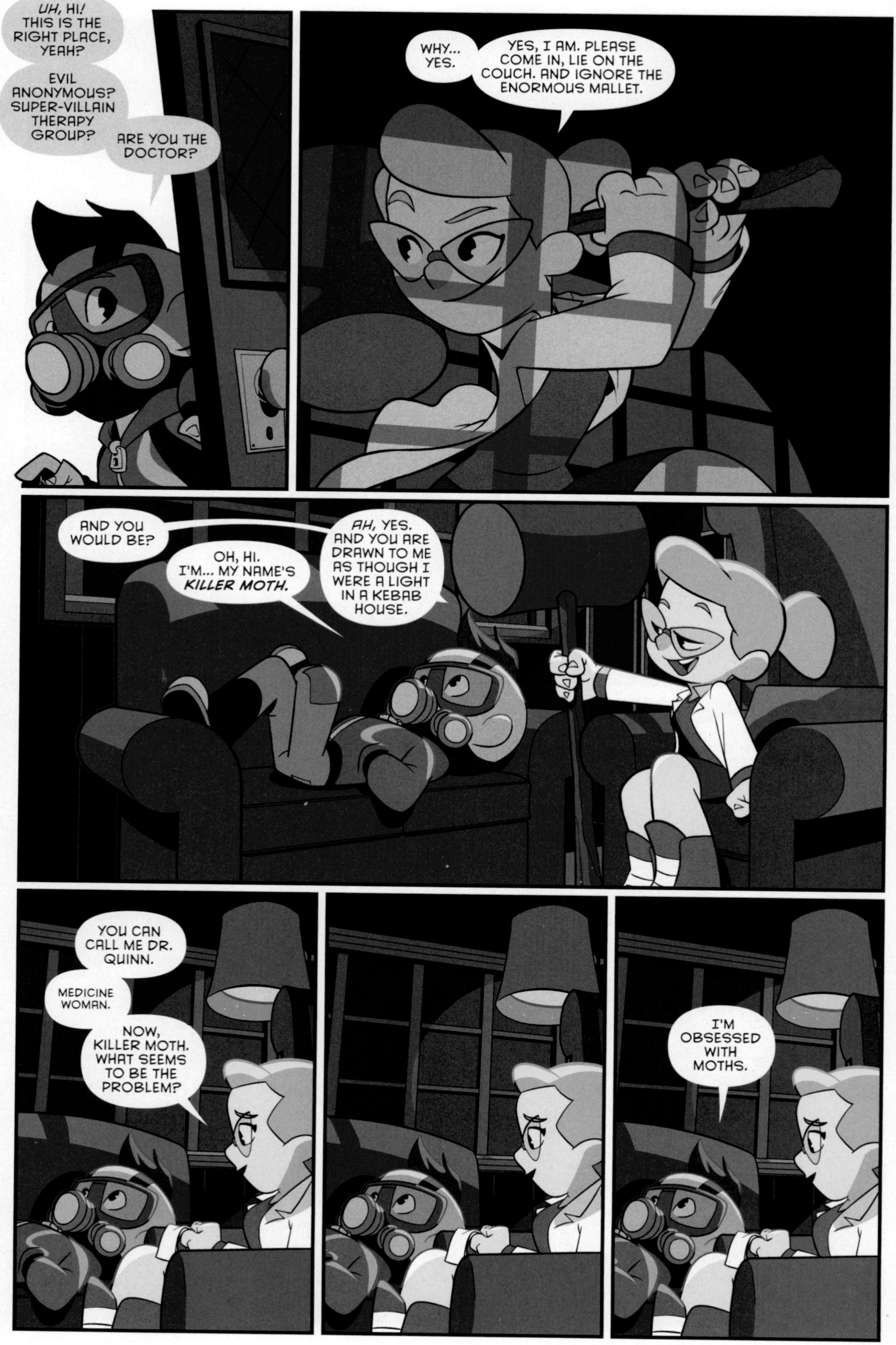
UH, HI! THIS IS THE RIGHT PLACE, YEAH?
EVIL ANONYMOUS? SUPER-VILLAIN THERAPY GROUP?
ARE YOU THE DOCTOR?
WHY... YES.
YES, I AM. PLEASE COME IN, LIE ON THE COUCH. AND IGNORE THE ENORMOUS MALLET.
AND YOU WOULD BE?
OH, HI. I'M... MY NAME'S KILLER MOTH.
AH, YES. AND YOU ARE DRAWN TO ME AS THOUGH I WERE A LIGHT IN A KEBAB HOUSE.
YOU CAN CALL ME DR. QUINN.
MEDICINE WOMAN.
NOW, KILLER MOTH. WHAT SEEMS TO BE THE PROBLEM?
I'M OBSESSED WITH MOTHS.

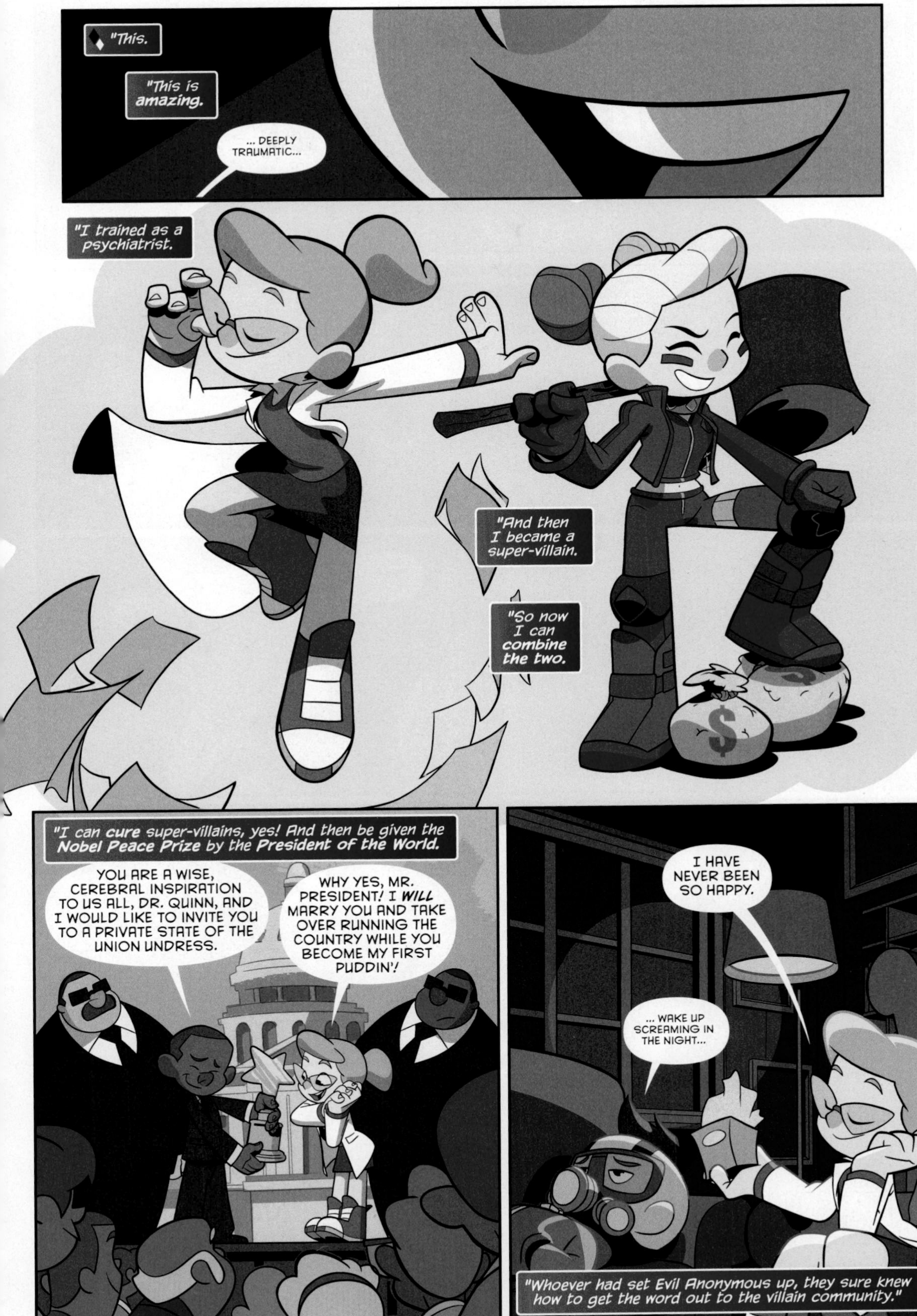
"This.
"This is amazing.
... DEEPLY TRAUMATIC...
"I trained as a psychiatrist.
"And then I became a super-villain.
"So now I can combine the two.
"I can cure super-villains, yes! And then be given the Nobel Peace Prize by the President of the World.
YOU ARE A WISE, CEREBRAL INSPIRATION TO US ALL, DR. QUINN, AND I WOULD LIKE TO INVITE YOU TO A PRIVATE STATE OF THE UNION UNDRESS.
WHY YES, MR. PRESIDENT! I WILL MARRY YOU AND TAKE OVER RUNNING THE COUNTRY WHILE YOU BECOME MY FIRST PUDDIN'!
I HAVE NEVER BEEN SO HAPPY.
... WAKE UP SCREAMING IN THE NIGHT...
"Whoever had set Evil Anonymous up, they sure knew how to get the word out to the villain community."

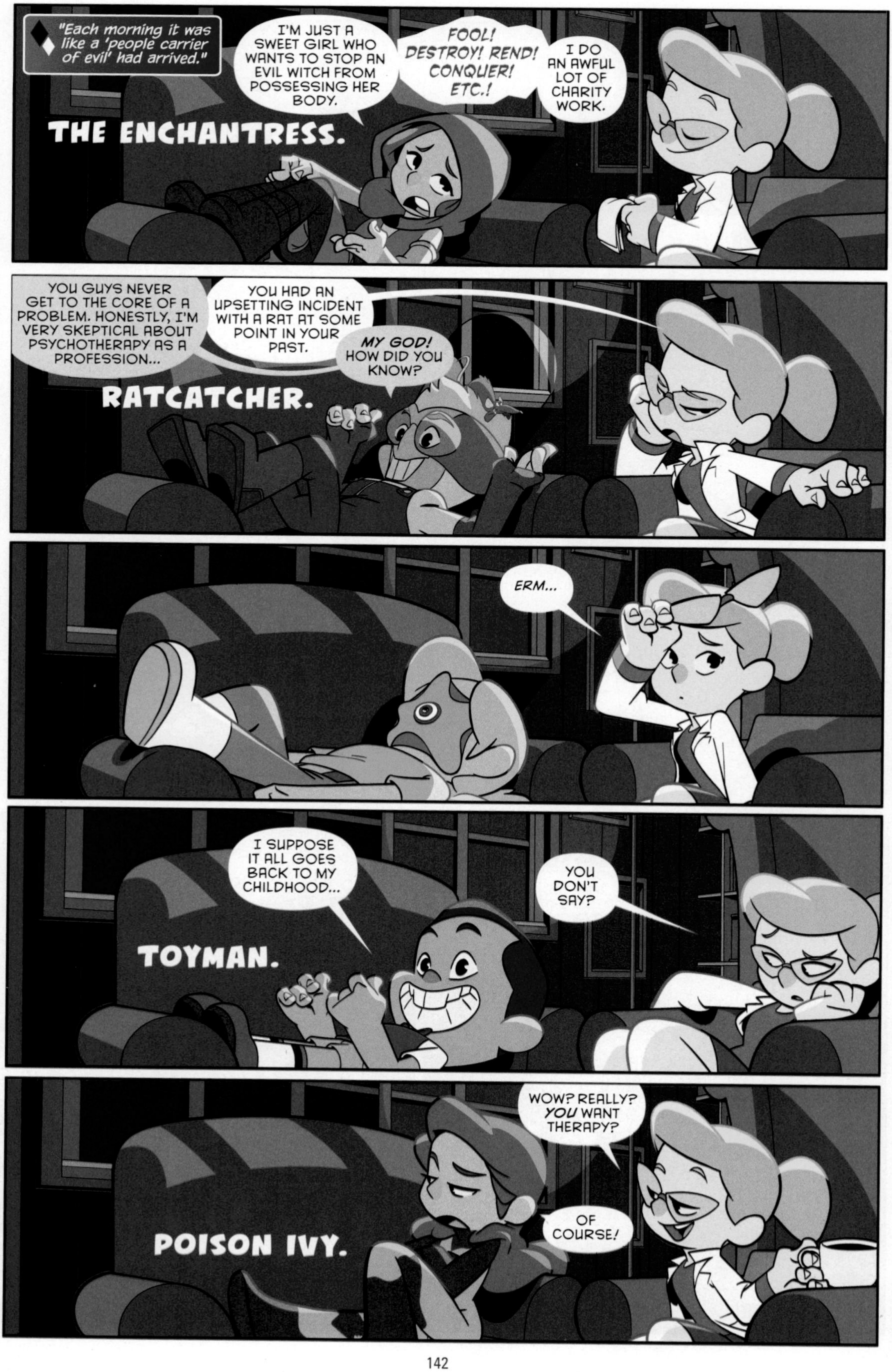
"Each morning it was like a 'people carrier of evil' had arrived."
I'M JUST A SWEET GIRL WHO WANTS TO STOP AN EVIL WITCH FROM POSSESSING HER BODY.
FOOL! DESTROY! REND! CONQUER! ETC.!
I DO AN AWFUL LOT OF CHARITY WORK.
THE ENCHANTRESS.
YOU GUYS NEVER GET TO THE CORE OF A PROBLEM. HONESTLY, I'M VERY SKEPTICAL ABOUT PSYCHOTHERAPY AS A PROFESSION...
YOU HAD AN UPSETTING INCIDENT WITH A RAT AT SOME POINT IN YOUR PAST.
MY GOD! HOW DID YOU KNOW?
RATCATCHER.
ERM...
I SUPPOSE IT ALL GOES BACK TO MY CHILDHOOD...
YOU DON'T SAY?
TOYMAN.
WOW? REALLY? YOU WANT THERAPY?
OF COURSE!
POISON IVY.

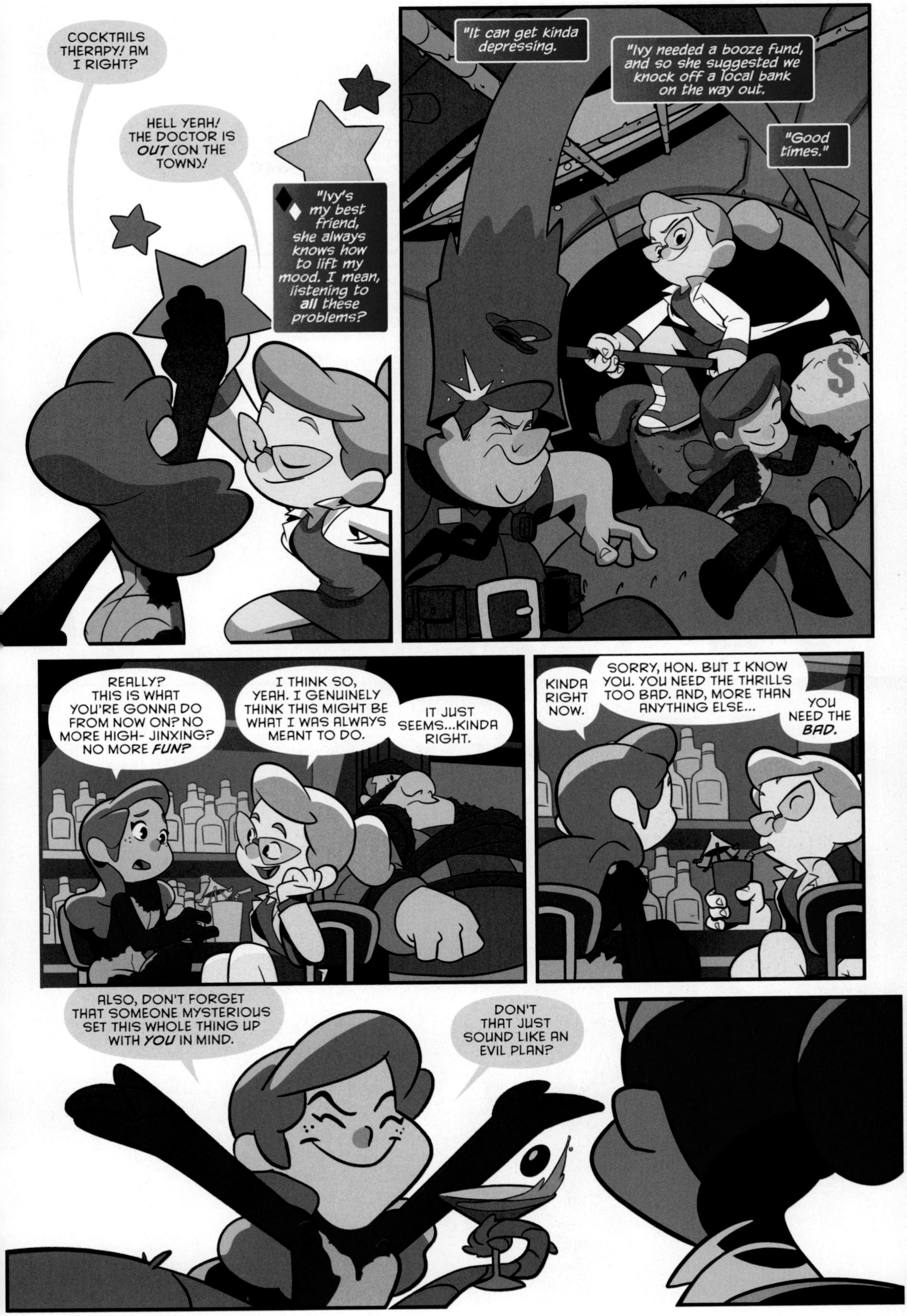

COCKTAILS THERAPY! AM I RIGHT?
HELL YEAH! THE DOCTOR IS *OUT* (ON THE TOWN)!
"Ivy's my best friend, she always knows how to lift my mood. I mean, listening to **all** these problems?
"It can get kinda depressing.
"Ivy needed a booze fund, and so she suggested we knock off a local bank on the way out.
"Good times."
REALLY? THIS IS WHAT YOU'RE GONNA DO FROM NOW ON? NO MORE HIGH- JINXING? NO MORE *FUN?*
I THINK SO, YEAH. I GENUINELY THINK THIS MIGHT BE WHAT I WAS ALWAYS MEANT TO DO.
IT JUST SEEMS...KINDA RIGHT.
KINDA RIGHT NOW.
SORRY, HON. BUT I KNOW YOU. YOU NEED THE THRILLS TOO BAD. AND, MORE THAN ANYTHING ELSE...
YOU NEED THE *BAD.*
ALSO, DON'T FORGET THAT SOMEONE MYSTERIOUS SET THIS WHOLE THING UP WITH *YOU* IN MIND.
DON'T THAT JUST SOUND LIKE AN EVIL PLAN?

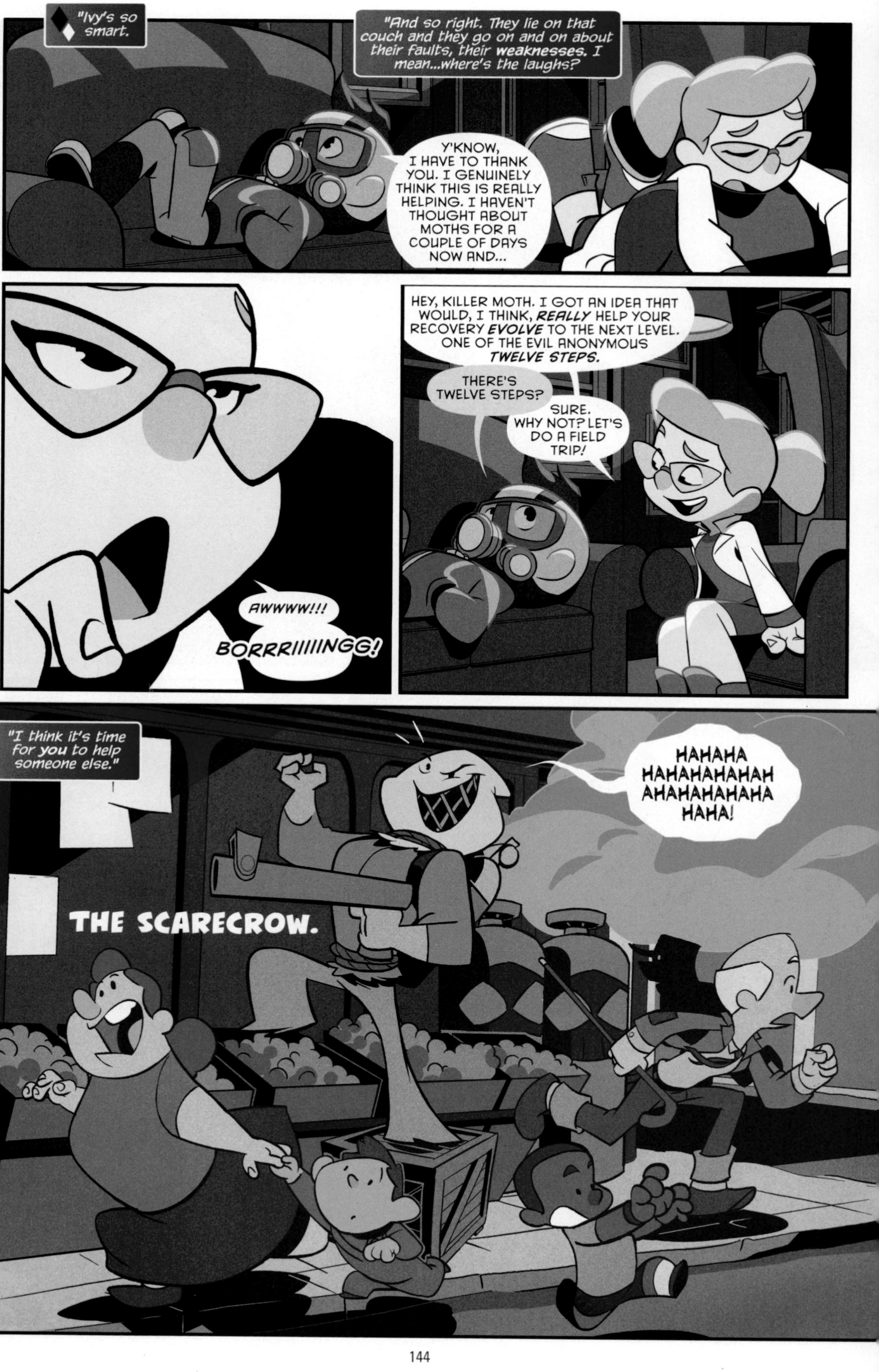
"Ivy's so smart.
"And so right. They lie on that couch and they go on and on about their faults, their weaknesses. I mean...where's the laughs?
Y'KNOW, I HAVE TO THANK YOU. I GENUINELY THINK THIS IS REALLY HELPING. I HAVEN'T THOUGHT ABOUT MOTHS FOR A COUPLE OF DAYS NOW AND...
AWWWW!!!
BORRRIIIIINGG!
HEY, KILLER MOTH. I GOT AN IDEA THAT WOULD, I THINK, REALLY HELP YOUR RECOVERY EVOLVE TO THE NEXT LEVEL. ONE OF THE EVIL ANONYMOUS TWELVE STEPS.
THERE'S TWELVE STEPS?
SURE. WHY NOT? LET'S DO A FIELD TRIP!
"I think it's time for you to help someone else."
HAHAHA HAHAHAHAHAH AHAHAHAHAHA HAHA!
THE SCARECROW.

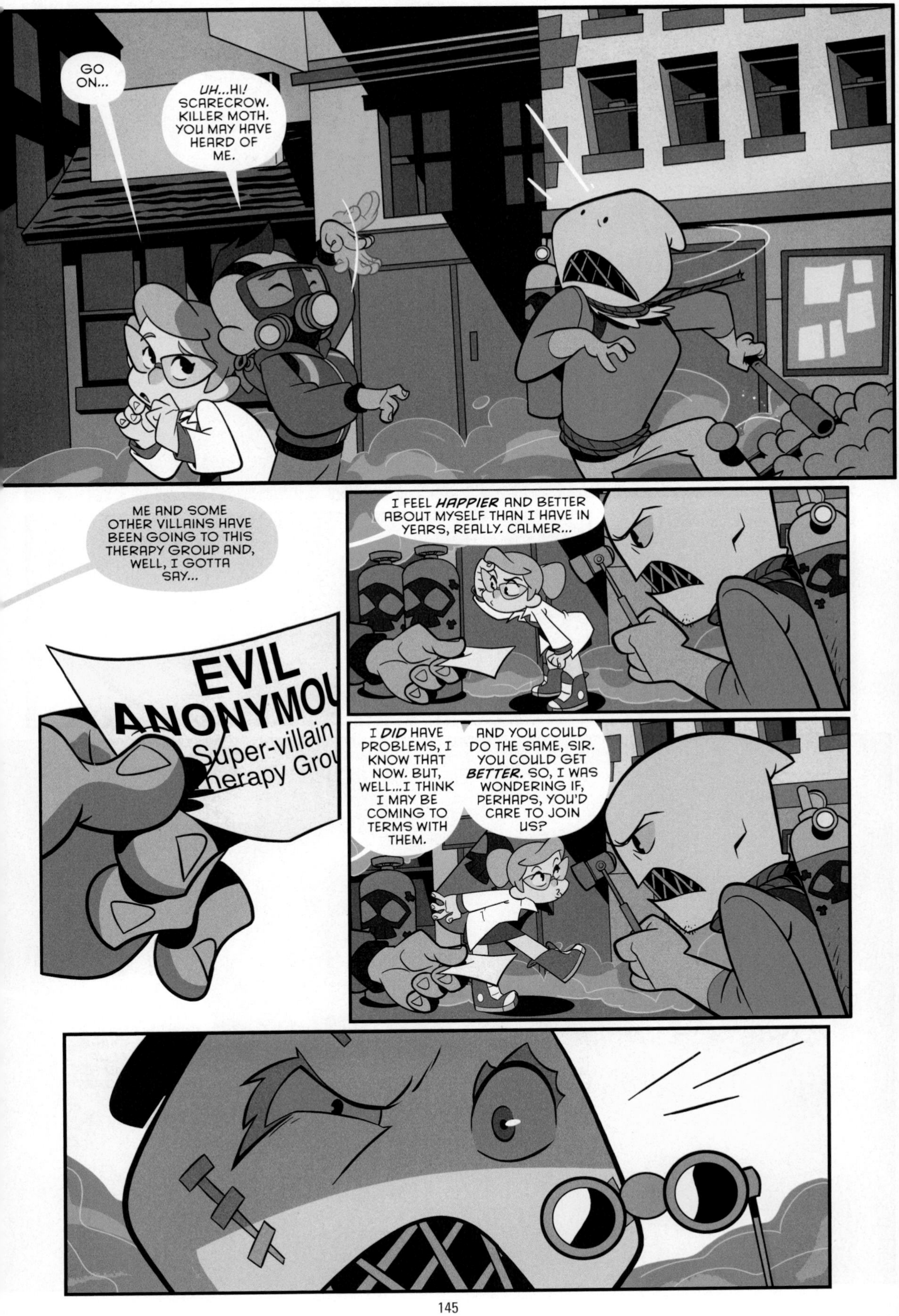
GO ON...
UH...HI! SCARECROW. KILLER MOTH. YOU MAY HAVE HEARD OF ME.
ME AND SOME OTHER VILLAINS HAVE BEEN GOING TO THIS THERAPY GROUP AND, WELL, I GOTTA SAY...
I FEEL HAPPIER AND BETTER ABOUT MYSELF THAN I HAVE IN YEARS, REALLY. CALMER...
EVIL ANONYMOU
Super-villain
herapy Grou
I DID HAVE PROBLEMS, I KNOW THAT NOW. BUT, WELL...I THINK I MAY BE COMING TO TERMS WITH THEM.
AND YOU COULD DO THE SAME, SIR. YOU COULD GET BETTER. SO, I WAS WONDERING IF, PERHAPS, YOU'D CARE TO JOIN US?

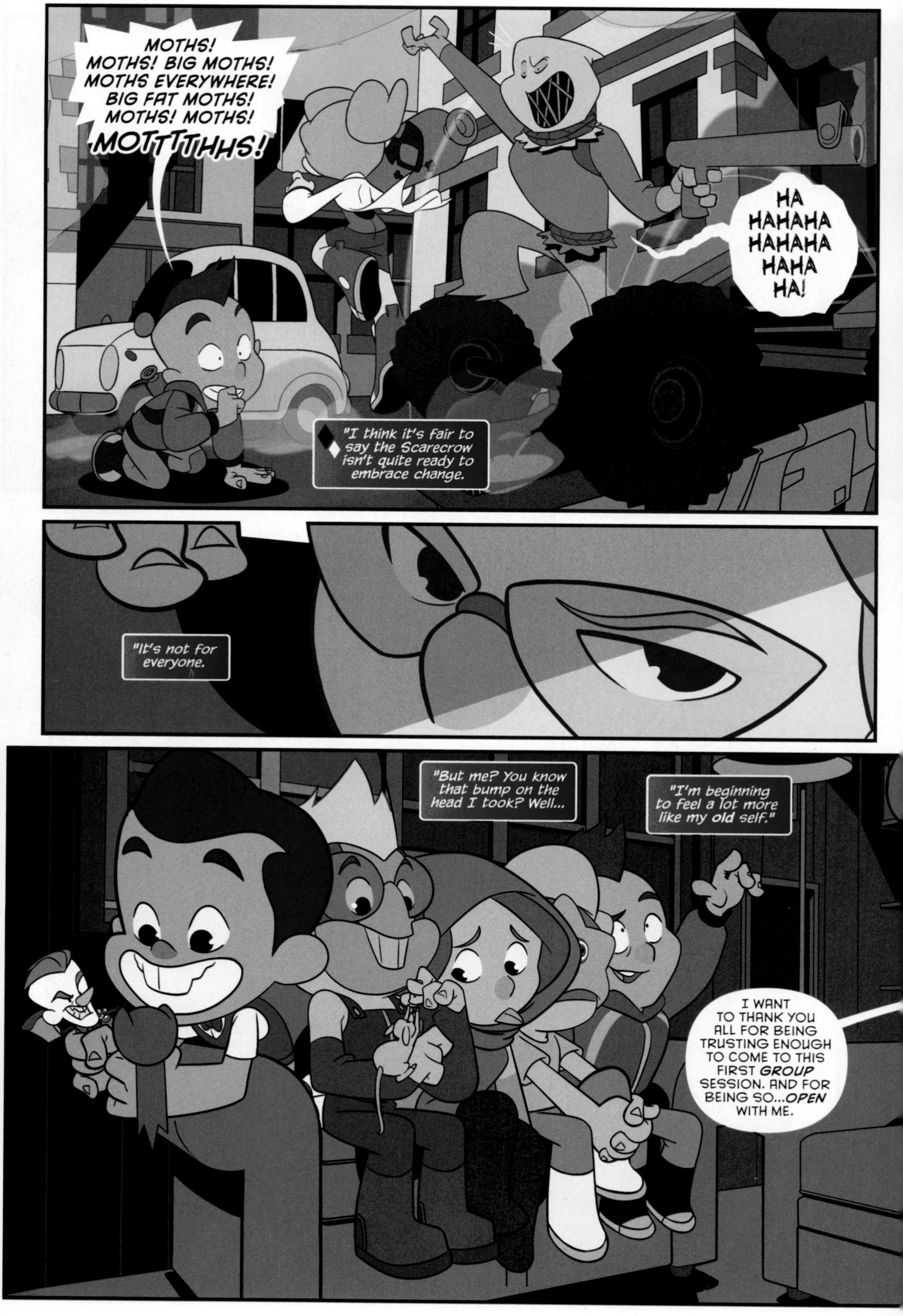
MOTHS! MOTHS! BIG MOTHS! MOTHS EVERYWHERE! BIG FAT MOTHS! MOTHS! MOTHS! MOTTTTHHS!
HA HAHAHA HAHAHA HAHA HA!
"I think it's fair to say the Scarecrow isn't quite ready to embrace change.
"It's not for everyone.
"But me? You know that bump on the head I took? Well...
"I'm beginning to feel a lot more like my old self."
I WANT TO THANK YOU ALL FOR BEING TRUSTING ENOUGH TO COME TO THIS FIRST GROUP SESSION, AND FOR BEING SO...OPEN WITH ME.

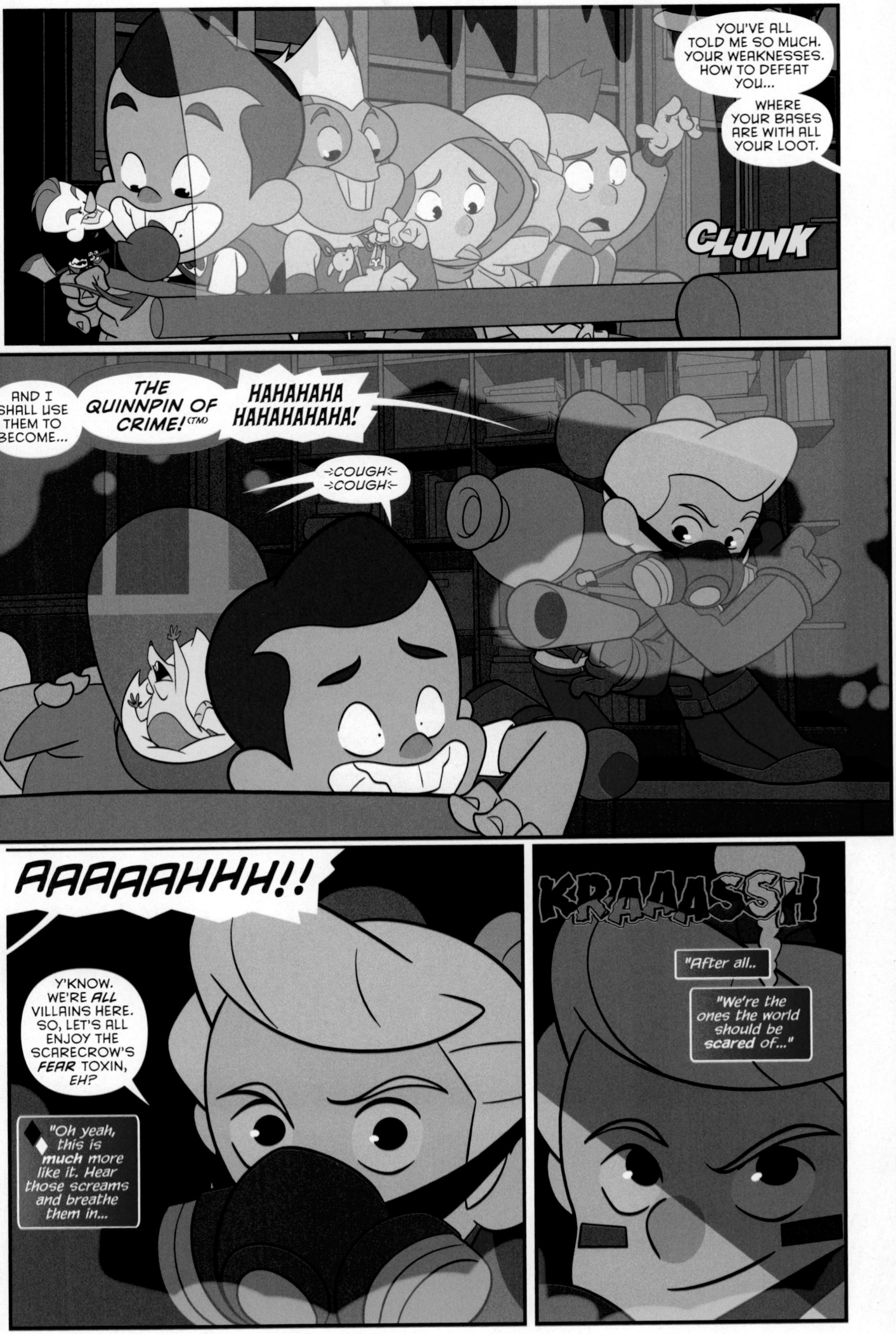
YOU'VE ALL TOLD ME SO MUCH. YOUR WEAKNESSES. HOW TO DEFEAT YOU...
WHERE YOUR BASES ARE WITH ALL YOUR LOOT.
CLUNK
AND I SHALL USE THEM TO BECOME...
THE QUINNPIN OF CRIME!(TM)
HAHAHAHA HAHAHAHAHA!
COUGH COUGH
AAAAAHHH!!
Y'KNOW. WE'RE ALL VILLAINS HERE. SO, LET'S ALL ENJOY THE SCARECROW'S FEAR TOXIN, EH?
"Oh yeah, this is much more like it. Hear those screams and breathe them in...
KRAAASSH
"After all..
"We're the ones the world should be scared of..."

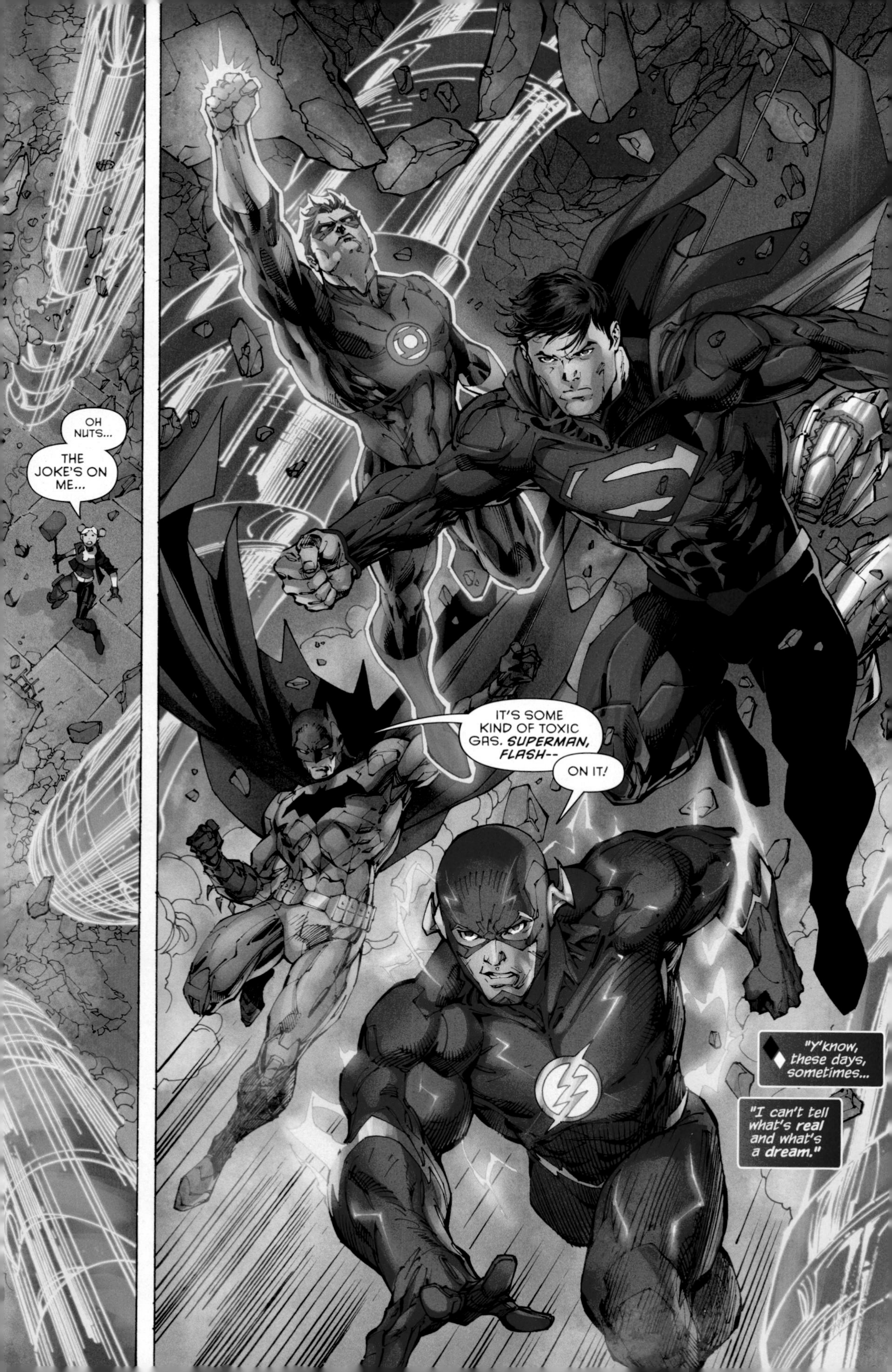
OH NUTS...
THE JOKE'S ON ME...
IT'S SOME KIND OF TOXIC GAS. *SUPERMAN*, *FLASH*--
ON IT!
"Y'know, these days, sometimes...
"I can't tell what's *real* and what's a *dream*."

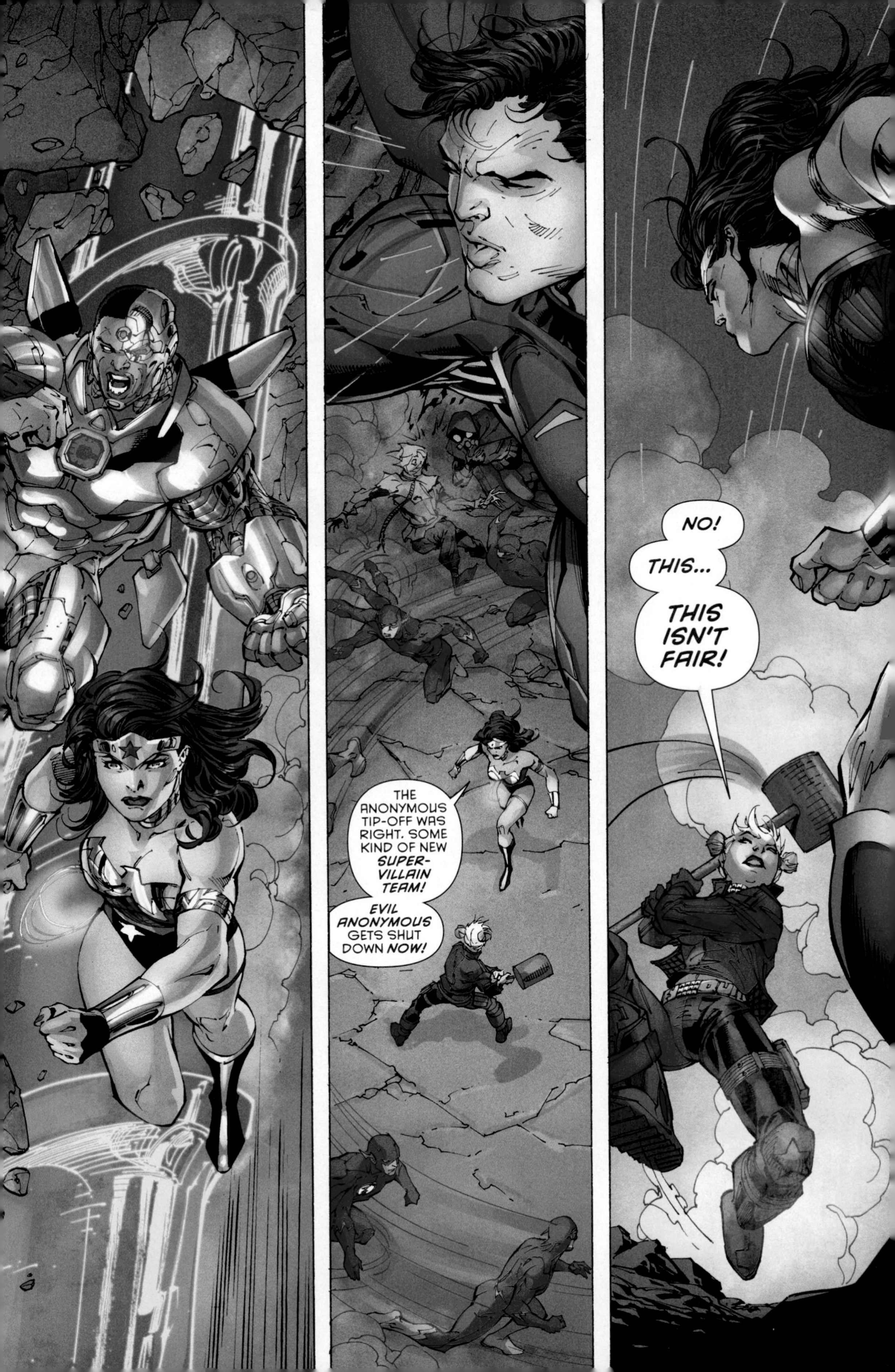
THE ANONYMOUS TIP-OFF WAS RIGHT. SOME KIND OF NEW SUPER-VILLAIN TEAM!
EVIL ANONYMOUS GETS SHUT DOWN NOW!
NO!
THIS...
THIS ISN'T FAIR!

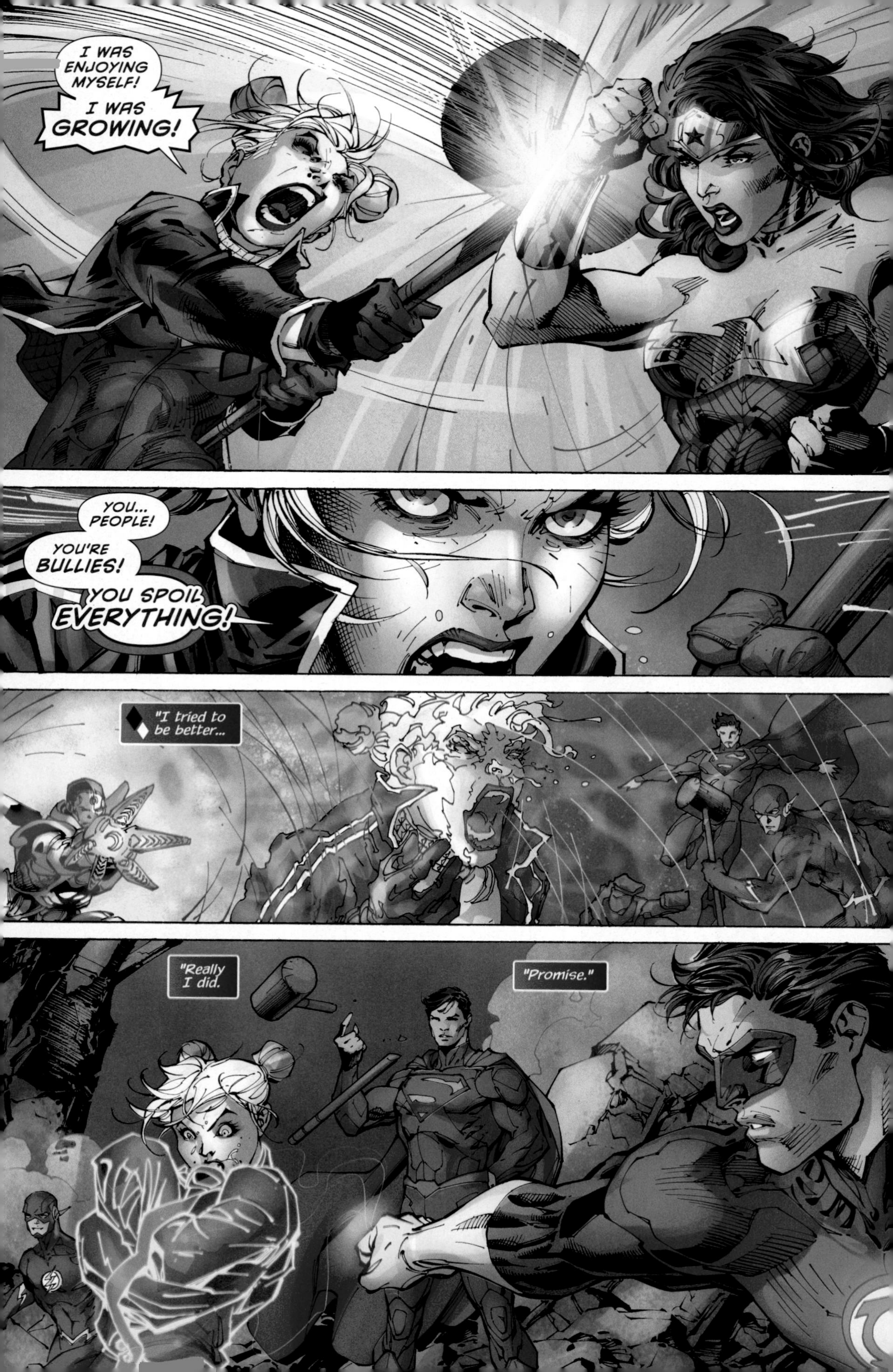
I WAS ENJOYING MYSELF!
I WAS GROWING!
YOU... PEOPLE!
YOU'RE BULLIES!
YOU SPOIL EVERYTHING!
"I tried to be better...
"Really I did.
"Promise."

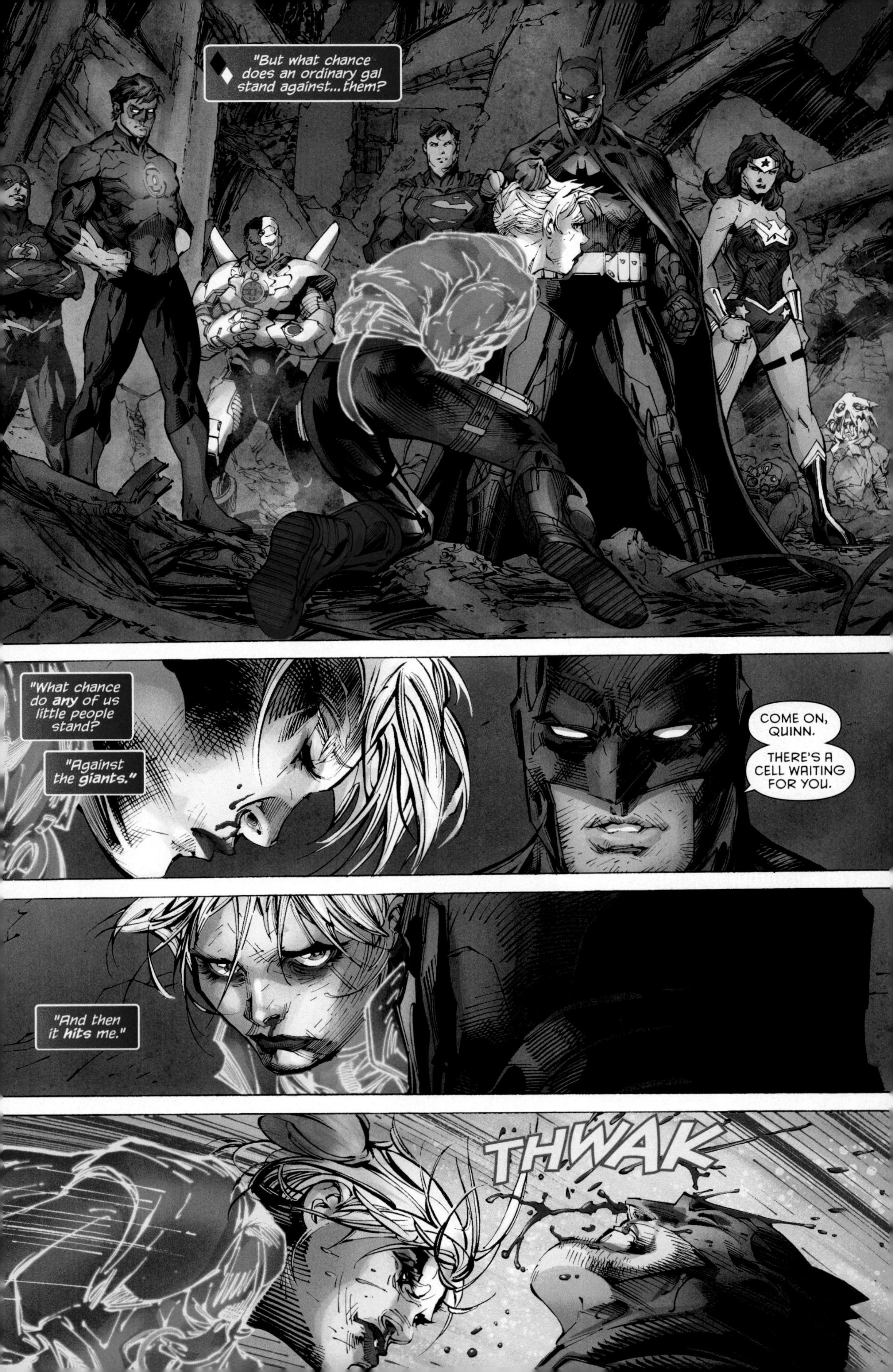
"But what chance does an ordinary gal stand against...them?
"What chance do any of us little people stand?
"Against the giants."
COME ON, QUINN.
THERE'S A CELL WAITING FOR YOU.
"And then it hits me."
THWAK

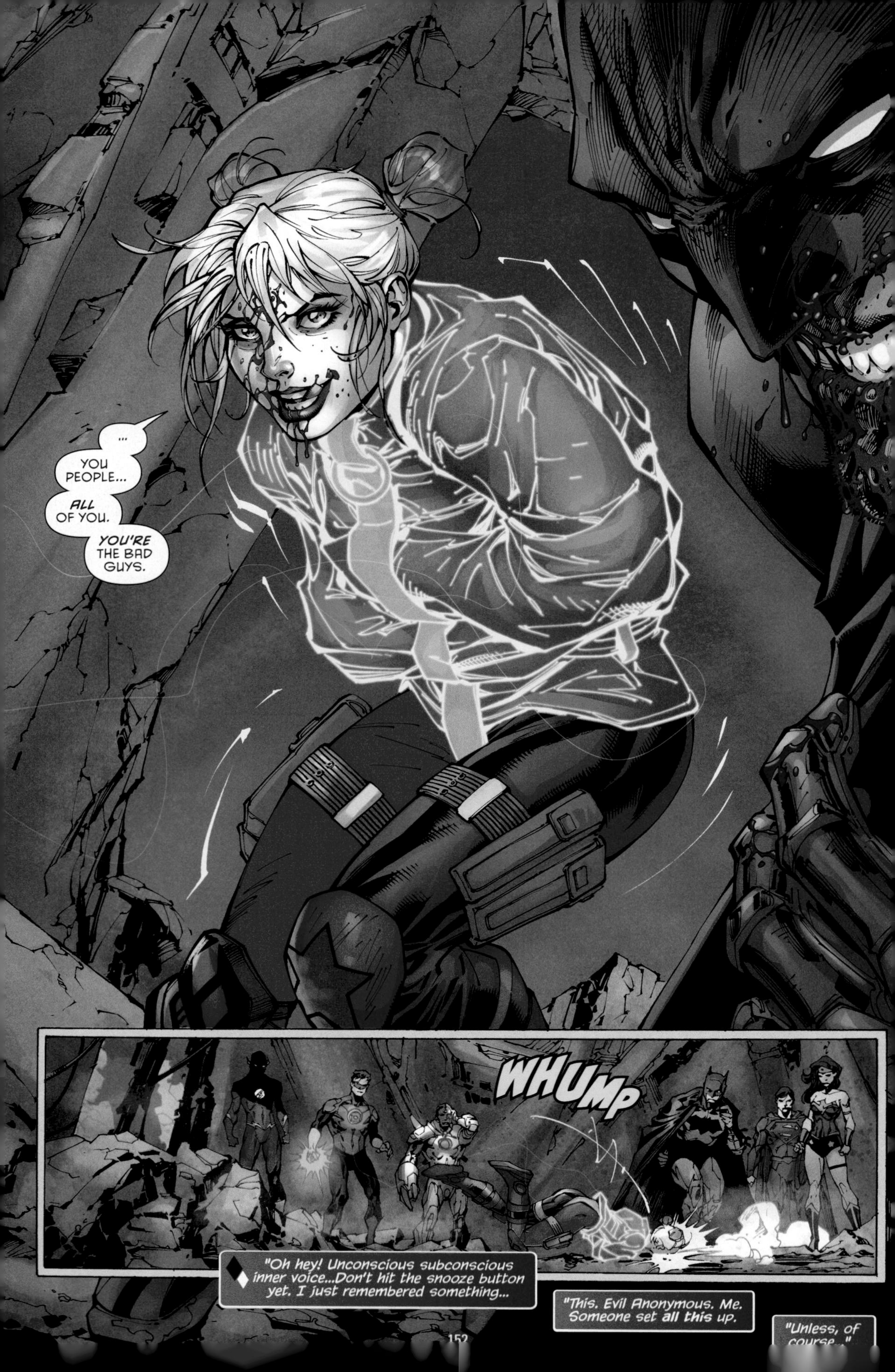
...
YOU PEOPLE...
ALL OF YOU.
YOU'RE THE BAD GUYS.
WHUMP
"Oh hey! Unconscious subconscious inner voice...Don't hit the snooze button yet. I just remembered something...
"This. Evil Anonymous. Me. Someone set all this up.
"Unless, of course..."

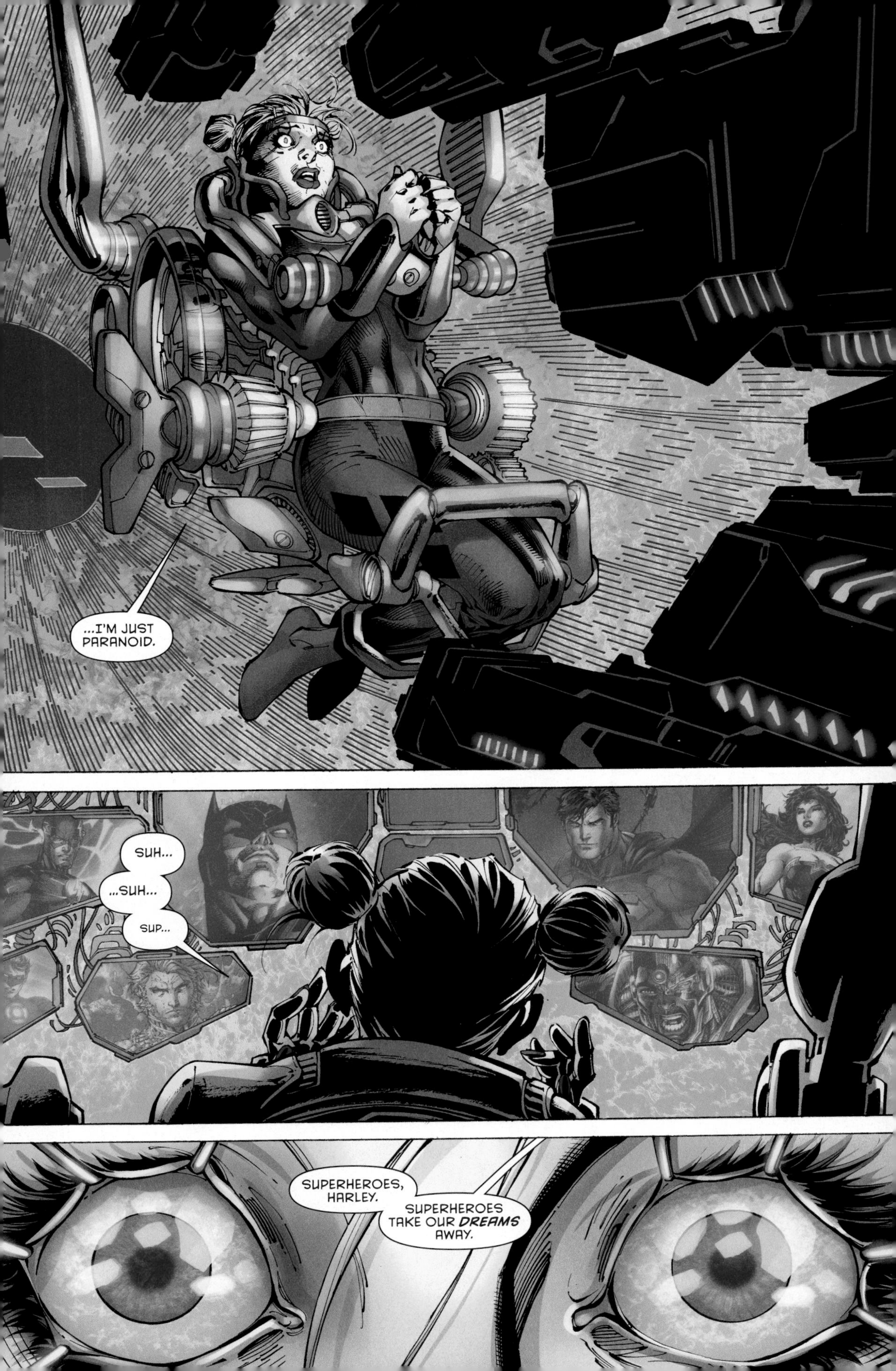
...I'M JUST PARANOID.
SUH...
...SUH...
SUP...
SUPERHEROES, HARLEY.
SUPERHEROES TAKE OUR *DREAMS* AWAY.

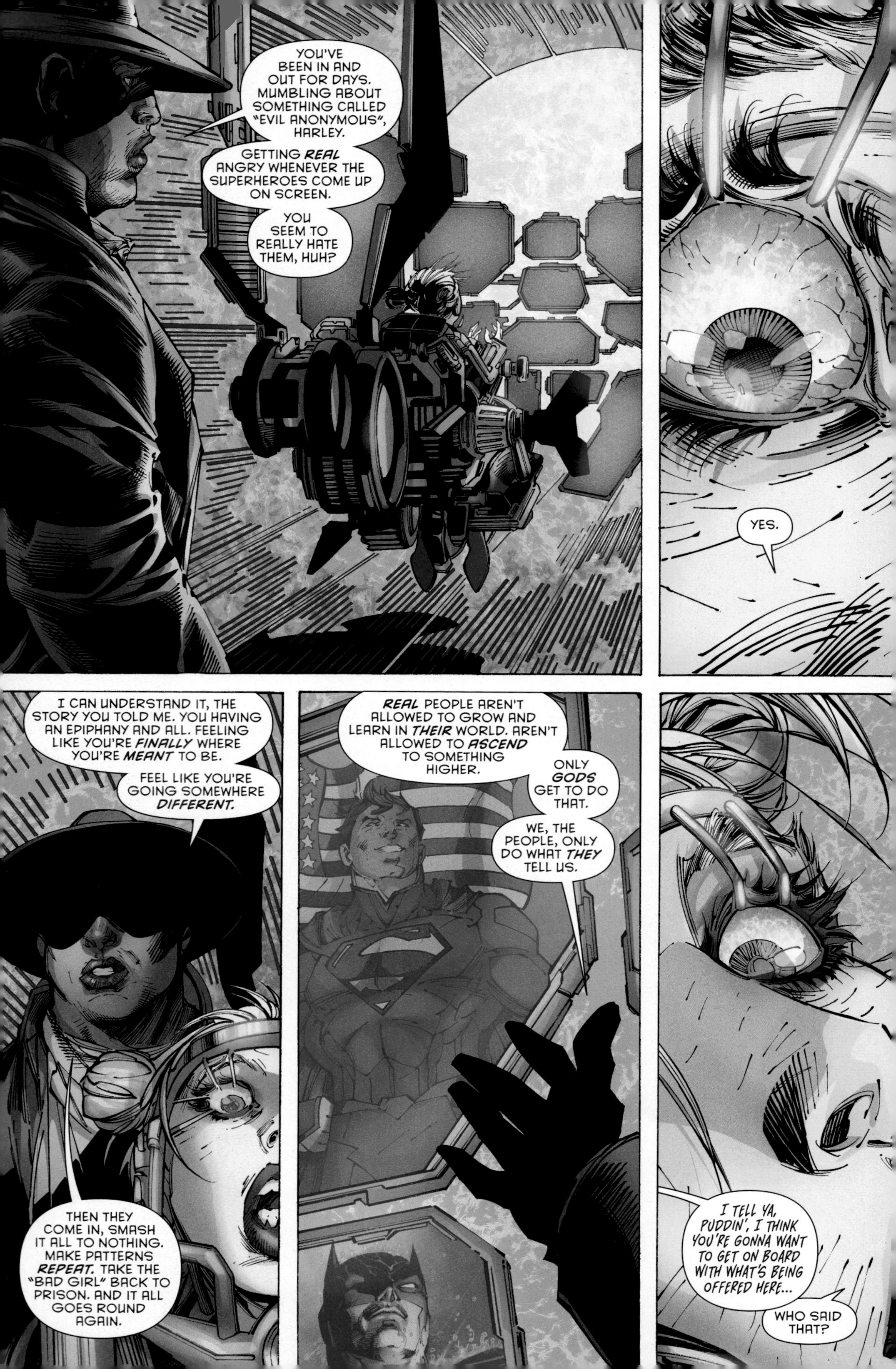
YOU'VE BEEN IN AND OUT FOR DAYS. MUMBLING ABOUT SOMETHING CALLED "EVIL ANONYMOUS", HARLEY.
GETTING REAL ANGRY WHENEVER THE SUPERHEROES COME UP ON SCREEN.
YOU SEEM TO REALLY HATE THEM, HUH?
YES.
I CAN UNDERSTAND IT, THE STORY YOU TOLD ME. YOU HAVING AN EPIPHANY AND ALL. FEELING LIKE YOU'RE FINALLY WHERE YOU'RE MEANT TO BE.
FEEL LIKE YOU'RE GOING SOMEWHERE DIFFERENT.
THEN THEY COME IN, SMASH IT ALL TO NOTHING. MAKE PATTERNS REPEAT. TAKE THE "BAD GIRL" BACK TO PRISON. AND IT ALL GOES ROUND AGAIN.
REAL PEOPLE AREN'T ALLOWED TO GROW AND LEARN IN THEIR WORLD. AREN'T ALLOWED TO ASCEND TO SOMETHING HIGHER.
ONLY GODS GET TO DO THAT.
WE, THE PEOPLE, ONLY DO WHAT THEY TELL US.
I TELL YA, PUDDIN', I THINK YOU'RE GONNA WANT TO GET ON BOARD WITH WHAT'S BEING OFFERED HERE...
WHO SAID THAT?

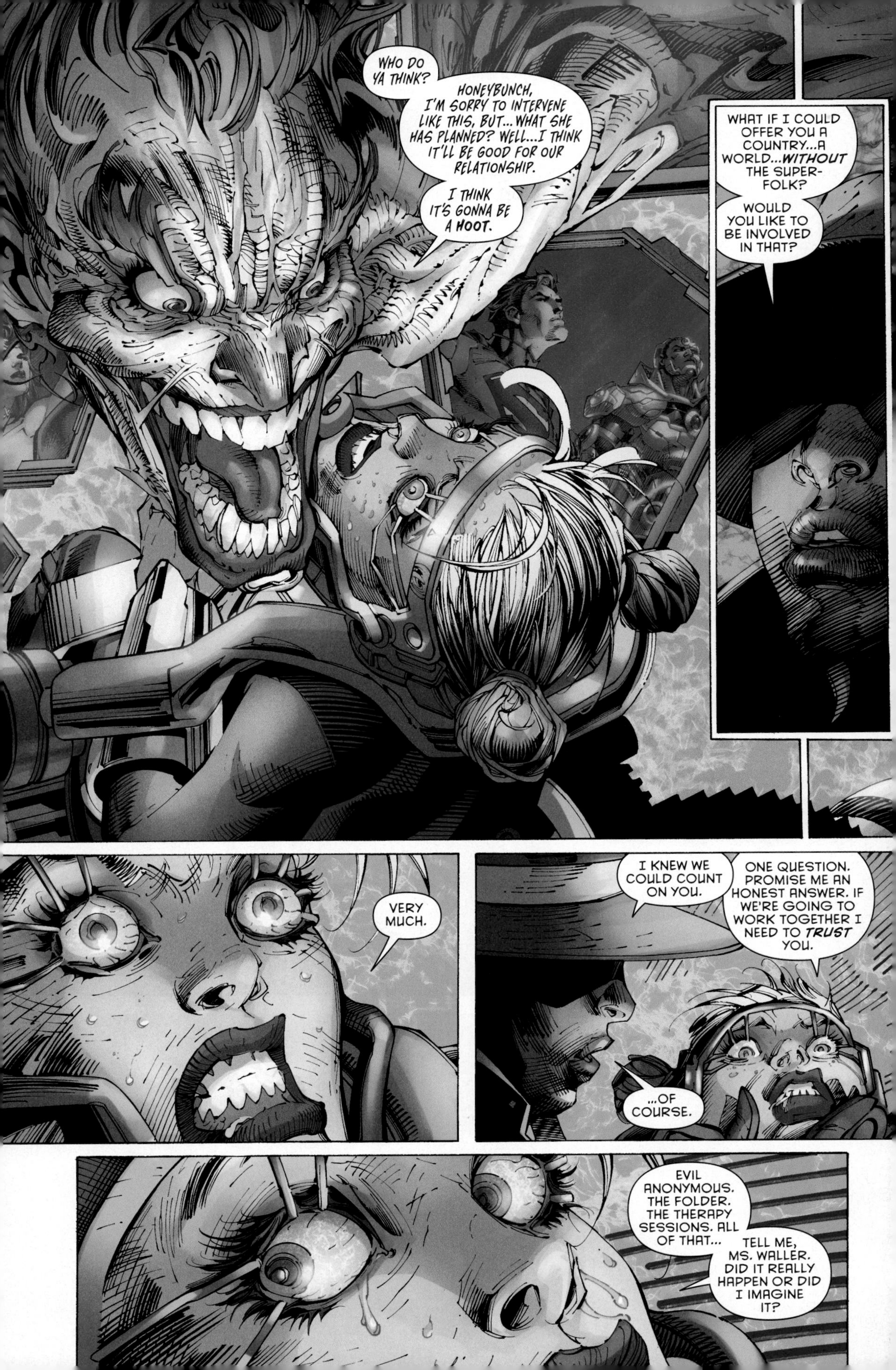
WHO DO YA THINK?
HONEYBUNCH, I'M SORRY TO INTERVENE LIKE THIS, BUT...WHAT SHE HAS PLANNED? WELL...I THINK IT'LL BE GOOD FOR OUR RELATIONSHIP.
I THINK IT'S GONNA BE A HOOT.
WHAT IF I COULD OFFER YOU A COUNTRY...A WORLD...WITHOUT THE SUPER-FOLK?
WOULD YOU LIKE TO BE INVOLVED IN THAT?
VERY MUCH.
I KNEW WE COULD COUNT ON YOU.
ONE QUESTION. PROMISE ME AN HONEST ANSWER. IF WE'RE GOING TO WORK TOGETHER I NEED TO TRUST YOU.
...OF COURSE.
EVIL ANONYMOUS. THE FOLDER. THE THERAPY SESSIONS. ALL OF THAT...
TELL ME, MS. WALLER. DID IT REALLY HAPPEN OR DID I IMAGINE IT?

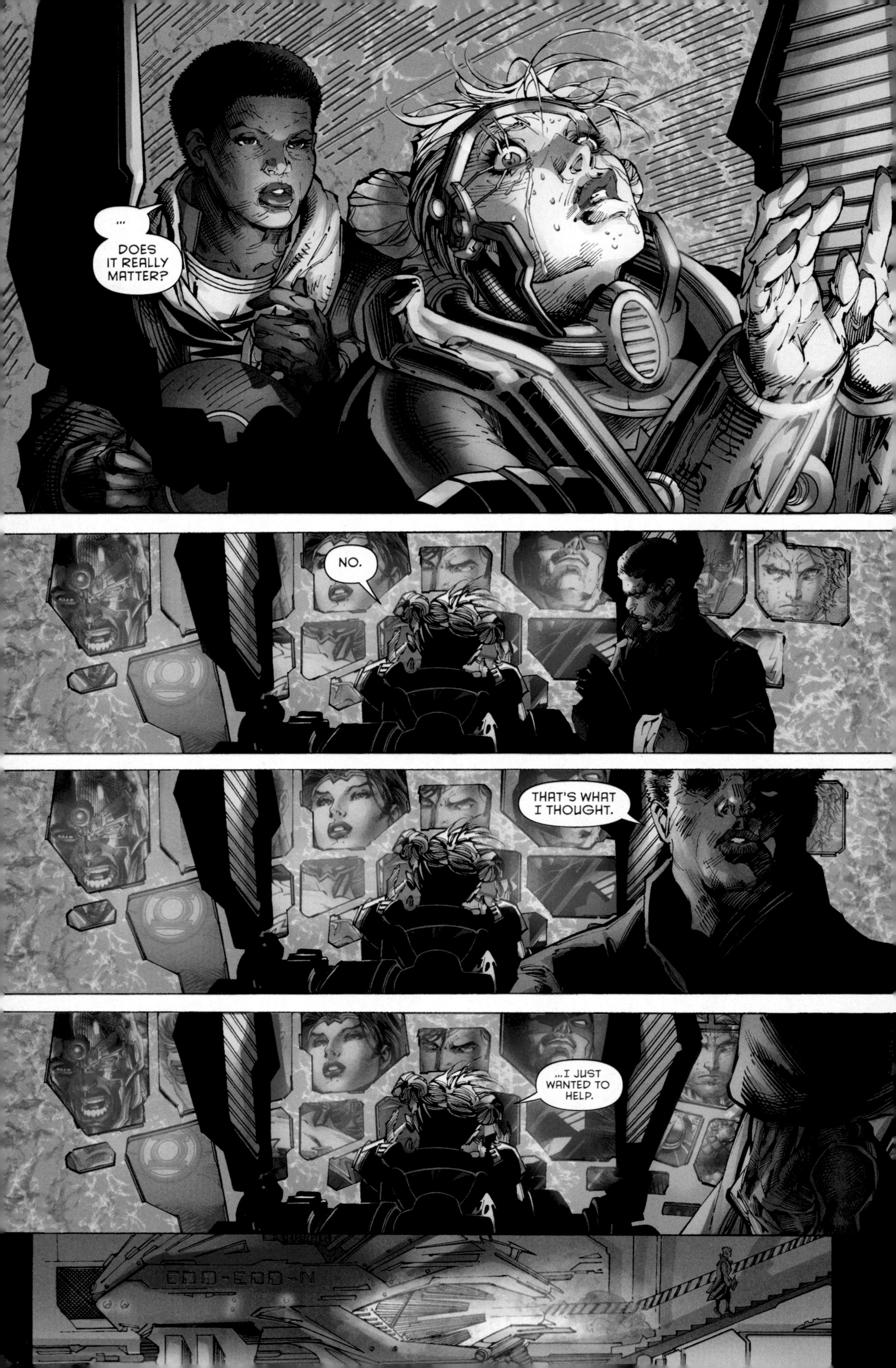
...
DOES IT REALLY MATTER?
NO.
THAT'S WHAT I THOUGHT.
...I JUST WANTED TO HELP.

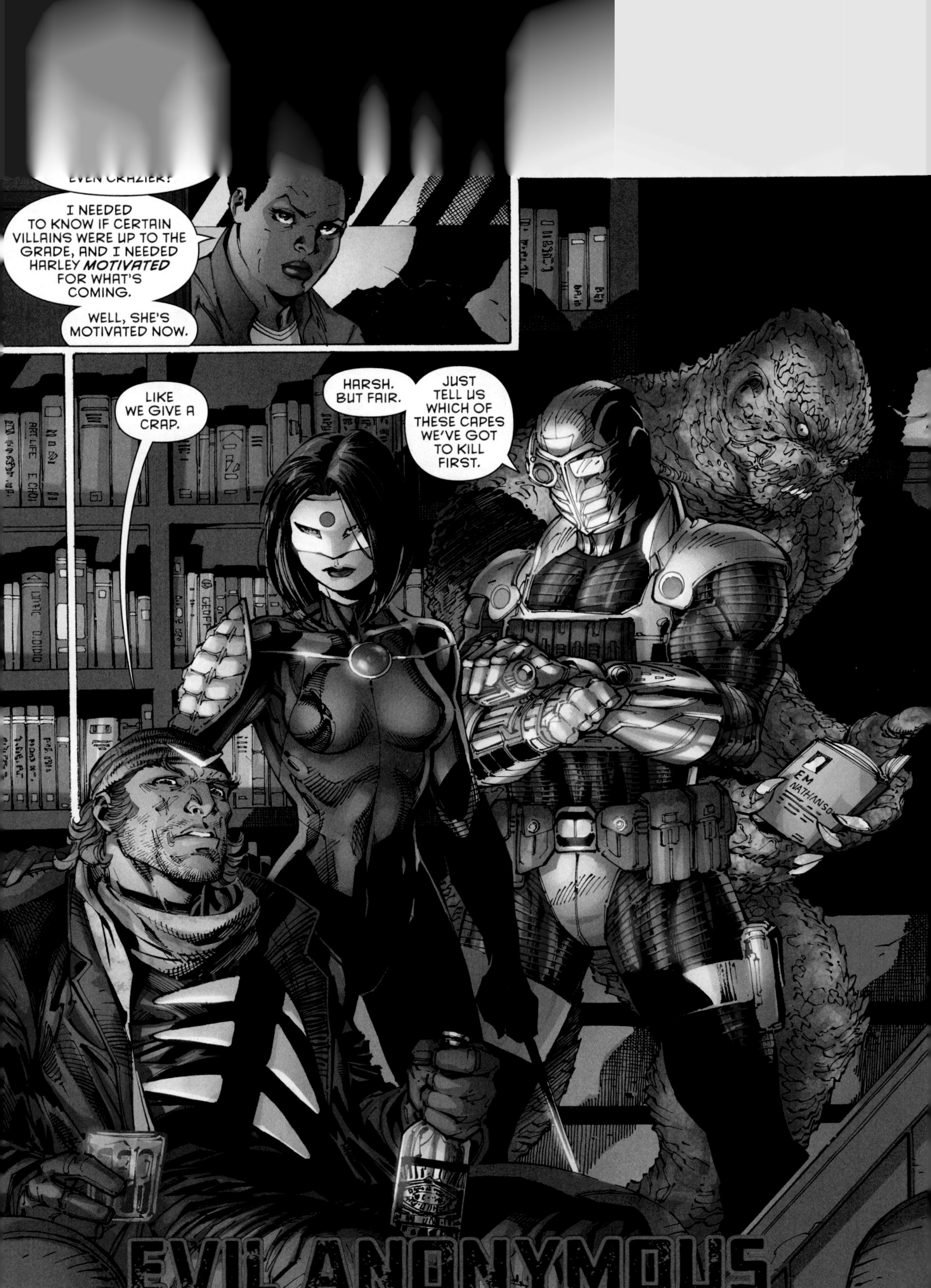

EVEN CRAZIER?
I NEEDED TO KNOW IF CERTAIN VILLAINS WERE UP TO THE GRADE, AND I NEEDED HARLEY *MOTIVATED* FOR WHAT'S COMING.
WELL, SHE'S MOTIVATED NOW.
LIKE WE GIVE A CRAP.
HARSH. BUT FAIR.
JUST TELL US WHICH OF THESE CAPES WE'VE GOT TO KILL FIRST.

EVIL ANONYMOUS

ROB WILLIAMS: writer JIM LEE: artist [1-10, 21-30] SEAN "CHEEKS" GALLOWAY: art and color [11-20]
SCOTT WILLIAMS, SANDRA HOPE, RICHARD FRIEND: inkers [1-10, 21-30]
ALEX SINCLAIR: colorist [1-10, 21-30] TRAVIS LANHAM: letterer LEE, WILLIAMS AND SINCLAIR: Cover
SEAN "CHEEKS" GALLOWAY: Variant Cover BRIAN CUNNINGHAM: Group Editor HARVEY RICHARDS: Associate Editor ANDY KHOURI: Editor
SUPERMAN created by JERRY SIEGEL and JOE SHUSTER. By special arrangement with the JERRY SIEGEL FAMILY.

DC COMICS™

HARLEY QUINN
VOLUME 1: HOT IN THE CITY

**SUICIDE SQUAD VOL. 1:
KICKED IN THE TEETH**

**with ADAM GLASS and
FEDERICO DALLOCCHIO**

**HARLEY QUINN:
PRELUDES AND
KNOCK-KNOCK JOKES**

**with KARL KESEL and
TERRY DODSON**

**BATMAN: MAD LOVE
AND OTHER STORIES**

**with PAUL DINI
and BRUCE TIMM**

THE NEW 52!

DC COMICS™

VOLUME 1
HOT IN THE CITY

"CHAOTIC AND UNABASHEDLY
FUN AS ONE WOULD EXPECT."
— IGN

AMANDA **CONNER**   JIMMY **PALMIOTTI**   CHAD **HARDIN**
STEPHANE **ROUX**   ALEX **SINCLAIR**   PAUL **MOUNTS**

HARLEY QUINN
VOLUME 1: PRELUDES AND KNOCK-KNOCK JOKES

HARLEY QUINN VOL. 2: NIGHT AND DAY

with KARL KESEL,
TERRY DODSON,
and PETE WOODS

HARLEY QUINN VOL. 3: WELCOME TO METROPOLIS

with KARL KESEL,
TERRY DODSON and
CRAIG ROUSSEAU

HARLEY QUINN VOL. 4: VENGEANCE UNLIMITED

with A.J. LIEBERMAN
and MIKE HUDDLESTON

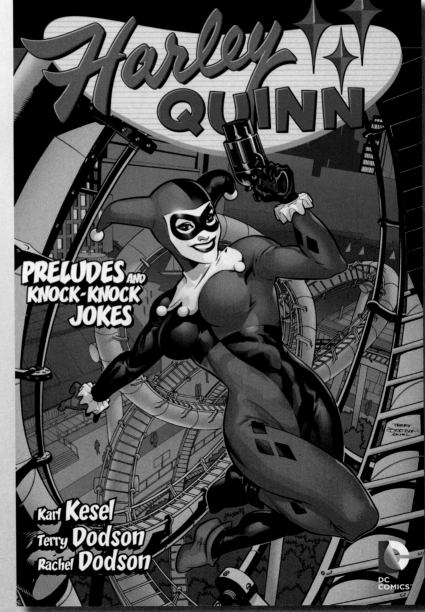

DC COMICS™

"A pretty irresistible hook. What if the good guys assembled a bunch of bad guys to work as a Dirty Dozen-like superteam and do the dirty work traditional heroes would never touch (or want to know about)?"—THE ONION/AV CLUB

START AT THE BEGINNING!

SUICIDE SQUAD

VOLUME 1: KICKED IN THE TEETH

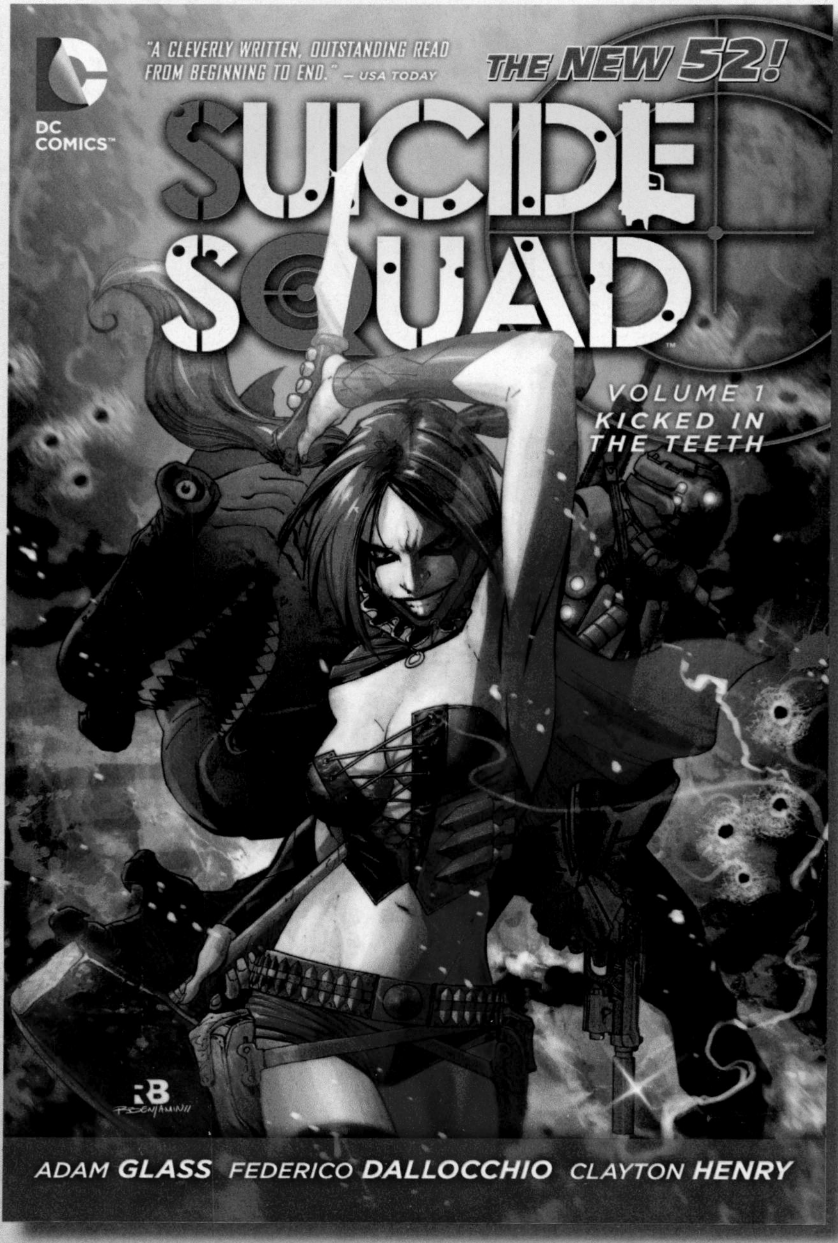
DC COMICS™
"A CLEVERLY WRITTEN, OUTSTANDING READ FROM BEGINNING TO END." – USA TODAY
THE NEW 52!
SUICIDE SQUAD
VOLUME 1
KICKED IN THE TEETH
ADAM GLASS FEDERICO DALLOCCHIO CLAYTON HENRY

SUICIDE SQUAD VOL. 2: BASILISK RISING

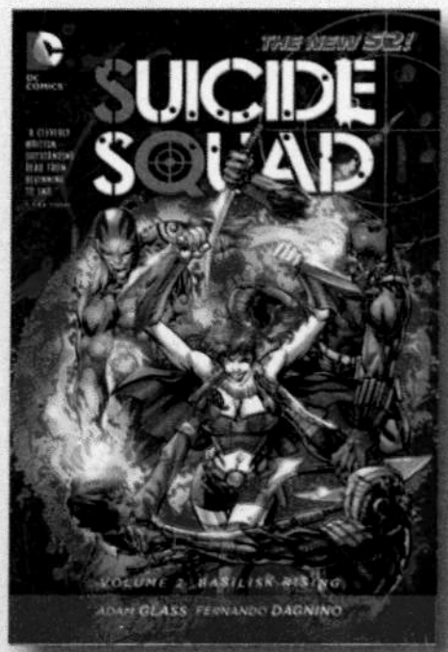
THE NEW 52!
SUICIDE SQUAD
VOLUME 2 BASILISK RISING
ADAM GLASS FERNANDO DAGNINO

SUICIDE SQUAD VOL. 3: DEATH IS FOR SUCKERS

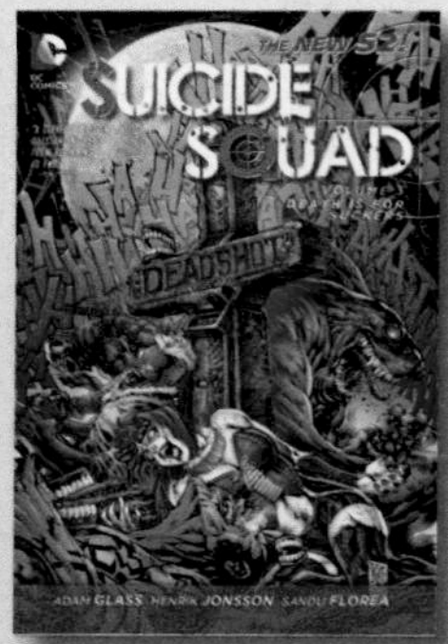
SUICIDE SQUAD
DEADSHOT
ADAM GLASS HENRIK JONSSON SANDU FLOREA

DEATHSTROKE VOL. 1: LEGACY

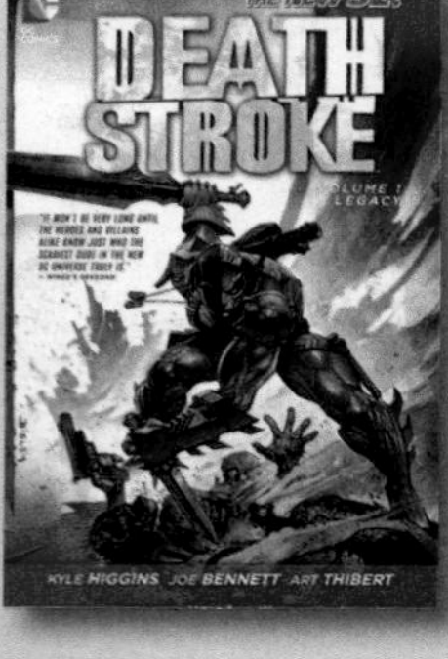
THE NEW 52!
DEATH STROKE
KYLE HIGGINS JOE BENNETT ART THIBERT